Models in the Mind

MODELS IN THE MIND
Theory, Perspective and Application

edited by

Yvonne Rogers
School of Cognitive and Computing Sciences
University of Sussex
Brighton

Andrew Rutherford
Department of Psychology
University of Keele
Keele
Staffordshire

Peter A. Bibby
Department of Psychology
University of Nottingham
Nottingham

ACADEMIC PRESS

Harcourt Brace Jovanovich
London   San Diego   New York
Boston   Sydney   Tokyo   Toronto

ACADEMIC PRESS LIMITED
24-28 Oval Road
London NW1 7DX

United States Edition published by
ACADEMIC PRESS INC.
San Diego, CA 92101

A catalogue record for this book is available from the British Library
ISBN 0-12-592970-6

Printed in Great Britain by T.J. Press (Padstow) Ltd. Padstow, Cornwall

Contents

Contributors

Anderson, T. Department of Psychology, University of Strathclyde, Turnbull Building, 155 George Street, Glasgow, G1 1RD.

Bainbridge, L. Department of Psychology, University College London, Gower Street, London, WC1E 6BT.

Bibby, P.A. Department of Psychology, University of Nottingham, Nottingham, NG7 2RD.

Byrne, R.M.J. Department of Psychology, Trinity College, University College Dublin, 24–28 Westland Row, Dublin 2.

Draper, S. Department of Psychology, University of Glasgow, Hillhead Street, Gilmore Hill, Glasgow, G12 8QT.

Duff, S. MRC Applied Psychology Unit, 15 Chaucer Road, Cambridge, CB2 2EF.

Howe, C. Department of Psychology, University of Strathclyde, Turnbull Building, 155 George Street, Glasgow, G1 1RD.

Leiser, R. BAe SEMA, 1 Atlantic Quay, Broomielaw, Glasgow, G2 8JE.

Mackenzie, M. Department of Psychology, University of Strathclyde, Turnbull Building, 155 George Street, Glasgow, G1 1RD.

Manktelow, K.I. Faculty of Arts and Social Studies, Sunderland Polytechnic, Douro House, Douro Terrace, Sunderland, SR2 7DX.

Mayes, T. Department of Psychology, University of Strathclyde, Turnbull, Building, 155 George Street, Glasgow, G1 1RD.

O'Malley, C. Department of Psychology, University of Nottingham, Nottingham, NG7 2RD.

Over, D.E. Faculty of Arts and Social Studies, Sunderland Polytechnic, Douro House, Douro Terrace,Sunderland, SR2 7DX.

Payne, S.J. School of Psychology, University of Wales College of Cardiff, Tower Building, Park Place, P.O. Box 901, Cardiff, CF1 3YG.

Rogers, Y. School of Cognitive and Computing Sciences, University of Sussex, Brighton, BN1 9QN.

Rutherford, A. Department of Psychology, University of Keele, Keele, Staffordshire, ST5 5BG.

Sasse, M. Department of Computer Science, University College London, Gower Street, London, WC1E 6PB.

Stenning, K. Human Communication Research Centre, Edinburgh University, 2 Buccleuch Place, Edinburgh, EH8 9LW.

Tolmie, A. Department of Psychology, University of Strathclyde, Turnbull Building, 155 George Street, Glasgow, G1 1RD.

Wilson, J.R. Department of Manufacturing Engineering and Operations Management, University of Nottingham, Nottingham, NG7 2RD.

Chapter 1

Introduction

Yvonne Rogers

Models *of* the mind are the bread and butter of cognitive psychology. Attempts to understand the way the mind works has led to a proliferation of models, each representing some aspect of cognition. Models *in* the mind, on the other hand, refers to models created as part of the mind, which underpin many complex and dynamic aspects of mental life. Since it's inception in the early 1940s, when Kenneth Craik described the brain's internal activity as that in which, "thought models, or parallels reality" (p. 57), the concept of mental models has manifest itself in psychological theorizing and practice in a multitude of ways and to such an extent that it is at the forefront of contemporary psychological research. From basic theoretical cognitive psychology to applied problems of human–computer interaction (HCI) and human–machine systems (HMS) mental models are being utilized now to explain a range of psychological phenomena. As a consequence, the term can no longer be regarded as a unitary concept, but takes on different assumptions and constraints for the various domains to which it has been applied. The positive side of all this sharing of the term has been to create a truly interdisciplinary debate with a raw edge of controversy. The negative side is that the term has become rather confused and in some cases even has been hijacked to elevate falsely the status of certain pieces of research that say very little about human cognitive processes.

The purpose of this book is not to give a definitive explanation as to what is a mental model, but to provide a forum in which the various perspectives that currently exist on mental models and their criticisms can be presented together as a state-of-the-art collection. The contributions are structured in six sections which relate to the prevalent and interesting themes that have emerged in the domains to which the term has been applied. A short chapter follows each part in which the editors discuss the disparate views.

MODELS IN THE MIND:
Theory, perspective and applications. ISBN 0–12–592970–6

Craik's (1943) original thesis advocated that we construct internal models of the environment around us that form the basis from which we reason and predict the outcome of events Just as an engineer may build a scale-model of a building so as to see the effects of applying various stresses prior to building the real thing, we too build models which enable us to make predictions about an external event before carrying out an action. Likewise, just as an engineer's model is a simplified version of the real object, mental models need only have a similar "relation-structure to that of the process it imitates". Therefore within this framework, mental models are considered essentially as internal constructions of some aspect of the external world that can be manipulated enabling predictions and inferences to be made.

While Craik provided the impetus, Johnson-Laird (1983) did much in the way of elucidating and distinguishing the various semantic characteristics of mental models. In his seminal work he describes both the structural and functional aspects of mental models with particular reference to how they are constructed during language understanding and reasoning. Much of the empirical research upon which Johnson-Laird has built his theory is based on experiments involving formal types of deductive reasoning where subjects are required to deduce the conclusion given a set of premises. The impact of this work has caused quite a stir within the academic community. His most controversial claim has been to advocate that a theory of thinking needs to provide an account of *semantics*. It is this notion which contrasts sharply with the conventional *syntactic* approaches that have dominated cognitive psychological theories in which it is assumed that people solve problems by using mental rules comparable to the rules of formal logic.

Johnson-Laird's perspective has been taken and extended by Ruth Byrne. In Chapter 2, she provides an account of human deduction by explaining *what* takes place in the domains of propositional, relational and quantificational inferencing. Namely, people construct mental models of the state of affairs given in the problem and establish conclusions from them. To make an inference they search for alternative models which negate their putative conclusion. If there are none, then their conclusion is valid. If there are alternative models, then they will attempt to find a conclusion which is true for all of the models. Hence constructing mental models provides the person with a means to evaluate alternative solutions to the problem. Empirical evidence is presented to support the mental model theory at the expense of syntactic rule theories.

In the third chapter, Keith Stenning argues that the debate over whether mental models or mental rules of logic are used during reasoning is misguided. He shows how the distinction between syntax and semantics given in this context becomes very unclear in so far as it is possible to interpret syntactical methods as semantic methods and vice versa. Alternatively, he states that the real issue is not what a person does when solving a problem but *how* this is implemented as a cognitive process. This means specifying what representational structures and processes are involved. Stenning describes how he and his colleagues have attempted tto address this issue by constructing a PDP model to simulate parts of the cognitive processes used in the implementation of logic in working memory. This alternative perspective is considered together with Byrne's theory of mental models in Chapter 4.

In the same year in which Johnson-Laird's book was published, another highly influential collection of papers on mental models edited by Dedre Gentner and Albert Stevens was published. The central focus of this collection was concerned with people's common-sense understanding of physical phenomena in domains like mechanics, liquids, electricity and various artificial devices. The term mental models is used in this sense to refer to the domain-knowledge that provides the basis from which inferences are made about the domain. A theme running throughout the Gentner and Stevens book is concerned with the types of knowledge people develop from their experience with the physical world. Specifically, there is one school of thought which believes that people develop coherent,but erroneous theories of physical phenomena, while another advocates that people possess only fragmented knowledge which essentially is a set of loosely connected ideas.

This controversy is taken on board by Tony Anderson, Andrew Tolmie, Christine Howe, Terry Mayes and Mhairi Mackenzie in Chapter 5, where they test the two opposing theories. They describe an experiment in which they asked subjects to make predictions and explain how they solved a set of paper and pencil problems concerned with motion. Based on their findings they adopt the eclectic stance that both types of knowledge are implicated. Also, they point out that mental models play a much larger role in the generation of predictions for experts than for novices. Furthermore, the results show evidence of a dissociation between the knowledge used to make predictions and that used subsequently to explain: where subjects found it easy to predict the outcome they found it difficult to explain their underlying reasoning, while conversely, subjects who gave good explanations gave totally incorrect predictions.

The view that mental models are internal representations serving the purpose of guiding inferences and making predictions is turned on its head by Claire O'Malley and Steve Draper in Chapter 6. They argue that mental models should be reconceptualized as distributed representations. In this sense, knowledge is viewed as being distributed across a number of internal knowledge structures and across external representations manifesting themselves in the environment. An example of the latter is the use of external memory aids as a way of helping the person carry out their activities. The domain in which the authors explicate this notion is user interaction with display-based computers. They describe a number of experiments that examine what people know about a menu-based interface and how much information they internalize from the display. In contrast with previous studies which have shown users to have relatively poor memories of the display-based information, their results show that users are quite good at predicting the spatial location of menu items. From these findings they propose that users need to internalize information that is not displayed explicitly and knowledge about interacting with the display. Thus it is assumed that users' knowledge is distributed rather than coherent or structured.

The conceptualization of mental models in relation to a person's interaction with computer systems is the focus of Part 3 also. In Chapter 8, Steve Payne explores the notion of mental models as it has been utilized in human–computer interaction research. He argues that this area of research offers great potential for cross-fertilization of cognitive science and human-computer interaction (HCI). In particular, he suggests that while the tradition has been for HCI researchers to draw from cognitive science theory as a way of conceptualizing human–computer interaction, the study of people interacting with computers provides cognitive science with a testbed in which to further its theoretical development and understanding of complex human activity. To show how this might be achieved, Payne discusses the relationship between mental models and "cognitive artefacts", which he defines as tools that support cognition. To elucidate the nature of this relationship, first he discusses the way in which such artefacts can be classified in terms of the different representational properties that each possesses and then, the different levels of theoretical commitment that are associated with mental models research. He argues that the key issue in understanding the role of mental models when interacting with cognitive artefacts is to identify the different demands made by the various types of representation that the system possesses (i.e. surface or internal) on the users' conceptualizations of the artefact. When the internal representation of the artefact is simple, it follows that the demands on the user to make sense and use the artefact should be relatively easy. When the internal representation is more complex, as is frequently the case with computer applications, the demands on the users' mental models will be much greater.

In Chapter 9, Lisanne Bainbridge explores how the concept of mental models has been applied to complex tasks, as they arise in HMS contexts. Specifically, she describes the various types of knowledge structure and cognitive mechanism utilized during industrial process operation. The purpose of studying mental models in this context is that the resulting researcher's model description should have both theoretical and practical implications. Compared with the limited and highly constrained types of task which are investigated in the laboratory, she points out that the operation of industrial processes is highly complex, consisting of a large number of tasks entailing a myriad of variables. Therefore, the adoption of concept-ualizations of knowledge structures and cognitive mechanisms developed solely in *basic* psychological research is considered to be insufficient. In addition, it is necessary to develop further characterizations to model adequately the type of mental activities that occur during process operation. Bainbridge maps out what these are and, where appropriate, draws from existing theoretical concepts of knowledge. She distinguishes between knowledge that underlies cognitive skills and knowledge that provides the basis for understanding the skills. From this perspective, mental models are seen as the implementation of the differing knowledge bases enabling the operator actively to gather information, make inferences, anticipate outcomes and make plans for future decision-making.

The central concern of Part 4 is the acquisition of mental models in HCI. In particular, the two chapters explore representational issues surrounding instruction use and the implications for user performance with interactive artefacts. In Chapter 11, Bibby proposes that mental models should be viewed in terms of the interplay between multiple mental representations. His claim is supported by empirical studies which demonstrate how performance varies in relation to the content of the instructions a user is given. Specifically, he found that users receiving operational information found it easier to perform tasks that involve changing switches, whereas users receiving instructions consisting of a look-up table of the inter-relationships between components were better at tasks that required fault-finding. Bibby explains this phenomenon in terms of internalization: the process whereby the computational properties of the external representation of the instructions is preserved when represented mentally. In an attempt to define more rigourously the nature of instruction use, Bibby ends his chapter with a discussion of his attempts to model computationally the knowledge representations underlying the construction and manipulation of multiple mental representations.

In Chapter 12, Duff also describes a set of experiments in which subjects were either given various combinations of instructions or simply left to use their own initiative The type of instructions either described "how-a-system-works" or "how-to-carry-out-a-task". Systematic effects on performance in relation to the types of information presented were found. From the findings, Duff infers that the different experimental conditions caused different forms of knowledge to be developed, which in turn facilitated or hindered the subject's task performance. As a way of characterizing the different knowledge structures, Duff uses the Interacting Cognitive Subsystems modular computational architecture. From this, Duff suggests that a person's understanding of a complex task is based on interacting representations.

In Part 5, the authors discuss the scientific status of mental models and methodological issues involved in the attempt to capture the mental models people use when interacting with systems. In Chapter 14, Andrew Rutherford and John Wilson discuss the scientific status of the mental model concept and the techniques that have been used to identify mental models. Importantly, they stress that the way in which mental models are conceived can dictate which type of data is collected and in turn, this may constrain the nature of the description of the mental model. They advocate that the most appropriate strategy to identify accurately mental models consists of two stages as prescribed by the standard scientific method. The first stage involves characterizing a mental model inductively on the basis of the collected data. The second stage should involve deductive methods, which allow the initial model of the mental model to be tested and validated empirically.

In Chapter 15, Sasse discusses some studies which have been carried out to capture users' mental models of computer systems. She provides a critique of the various types of method that were employed. She goes on to describe a study that attempted to elicit mental models of users. The approach she adopted was to use a battery of methods where users were observed learning and using a number of different computer systems. The users also were asked to predict and explain the behaviour of the system. In her analysis she discusses the merits and problems of the techniques and suggests whether each method is better for eliciting general knowledge about mental models or for testing more specific hypotheses about a mental model.

The last part considers the social and pragmatic factors surrounding the use of mental models. The approach differs from all the other sections in that it takes into account the effects of social context on a person's behaviour, be it general reasoning or using a computer. In Chapter 17, Ken Manktelow and David Over discuss the reasoning that occurs when people are asked to work out the truth of various statements involving permission and obligation. The problems considered are emotive and require moral and social considerations. They argue that when confronted with such dilemmas people will interpret the problem in terms of the expected utility of conforming or not conforming. In support of Byrne and Johnson-Laird, they propose that in deciding between alternative choices, initially people will construct mental models representing the possible consequences of actions before selecting the preferred one. Also, they discuss why their empirical data are better accommodated by a mental models account than the schema-based accounts presented.

In Chapter 18, Bob Leiser discusses the requirements of the mental model construct for it to be a viable applied tool and the importance of social factors in affecting a person's mental model of a situation. He describes the role played by the "presence" of the computer in human–computer interaction: the presence phenomenon refers to the way computers can elicit "social" reactions from users, which are derived from normal human–human interactions. To illustrate his view, he cites a number of examples where people have implicitly adopted certain conceptions about computer systems, resulting in unwitting and unusual reactions. He argues that for the concept of mental models to be applicable at the user–interface, it is necessary to take into account social factors of this nature.

The final chapter discusses the main issues which the editors consider are important in current and future theorizing on mental models and their potential application. The aim is to characterize and bring together the many threads which now exist in the mental models literature and, in doing so, to identify any underlying links. This includes a discussion of how mental models compare with other types of mental representation that have been proposed and the level at which theoretical treatments should be pitched. The implicit assumption of mental model's "runnability" and their phenomenological nature is discussed with respect to these issues. The relationship between socio-cultural and individualistic accounts of meaning is considered, with the view to developing a framework that would accommodate both perspectives.

There is a lack of applied papers in the collection. However, rather than see this as a shortcoming, it is true to say that this is a reflection of the actual state of affairs. In reality, the focus of research employing the mental model notion has been one-sided: geared towards theoretical development rather than practical use. The last section of the final chapter discusses why this is the case and how the mismatch between basic and applied research may be resolved.

Acknowledgements

The contributions to this book are extensively revised versions of a representative selection of papers presented at an interdisciplinary workshop entitled "How Mental are Mental Models?" held at Nottingham University in March 1990. The event was sponsored by the British Computer Society Human–Computer Interaction Specialist Group and the British Psychological Society Cognitive Psychology Section. The editors would like to thank everyone who presented papers and all the other attendees for making the event a great success. Special thanks to Angela Sasse who was one of the original instigators and organizers of the workshop.

References

Craik, K.J.W. (1943). *The Nature of Explanation*. Cambridge: CUP.

Gentner, D. and Gentner, D.R. (1983). Flowing waters or teeming crowds: mental models of electricity. In Gentner, D. and Stevens, A.L. (eds), *Mental Models*. Hillsdale, NJ: LEA.

Johnson-Laird, P.N. (1983). *Mental Models*. Cambridge: CUP.

Part 1

**Mental Models
and Reasoning**

Chapter 2

The Model Theory of Deduction

Ruth M. J. Byrne

2.1 Human reasoning

Our reasoning abilities are the foundation for many of our cognitive skills: they guide us when we make plans, reach decisions or solve problems. Deduction has long attracted the attention of philosophers, cognitive psychologists, linguists and artificial intelligence workers. Their studies have resulted in contrasting views of the cognitive processes that underlie deduction. My aim is to show that the experimental evidence favours the idea that human reasoning is based on mental models. I will outline recent empirical work which suggests that people make deductions by manipulating models.

Cognitive psychologists have traditionally argued that the mechanisms underlying reasoning depend on formal rules of inference (e.g. Braine, 1978; Braine et al, 1984; Rips, 1983; 1989). They propose that the mind is equipped with inference rules, such as:

If A then B
A
Therefore B.

Such an inference rule is syntactic in that it applies to premises by virtue of their syntax alone. People make inferences by first recovering the logical form of the premises, and then they construct a mental derivation of the conclusion, using their mental inference rules. Logicians are familiar with a similar "proof-theoretic" means of deriving conclusions. The psychological theory proposes that people make a valid deduction if they can construct a derivation for a conclusion. They make errors if they fail to recover the correct logical form of the premises, or if they

MODELS IN THE MIND:
Theory, perspective and applications. ISBN 0-12-592970-6

fail to construct a derivation where there is one. A problem for the theory is that human reasoning is influenced by the meaning of the premises. Formal rules are blind to meaning, and so rule theorists must invoke some other mechanism to account for the effects of meaning. They suggest that meaning exerts its influence on the interpretation of the premises, before reasoning occurs.

A more radical view is that the rules of inference are content-sensitive (e.g. Anderson, 1983; Cheng and Holyoak, 1985). Cheng and Holyoak have proposed that people make inferences by accessing "pragmatic reasoning schemas". For example, reasoners are equipped with a schema to deal with permission situations. Such a scheme governs actions that occur within the context of moral conventions and contains rules like:

If action A is to be taken then precondition B must be satisfied.

Artificial intelligence workers are familiar with a similar method in production systems that contain condition-action rules specific to the content of particular domains. The psychological theory proposes that people make a valid deduction when the schema's rules happen to correspond to logical strictures. They make errors if they fail to access the appropriate schema, or if the schema's rules are logically incorrect. A problem for the theory is that people can make deductions about unfamiliar situations. Content-sensitive rules do not capture this deductive competence. Even though general knowledge undoubtedly enters into everyday deductions, it remains an open question whether it is represented by schemas.

The third alternative is a theory of reasoning that purports to account for both the effects of meaning and the ability of reasoners to make inferences based on unfamiliar premises. The theory proposes that people rely on mental models to make deductions (e.g. Johnson-Laird, 1983; Johnson-Laird and Byrne, 1991). A mental model is a representation of the way the world would be if the premises were true. People make inferences by a semantic procedure that constructs and interrogates models – logicians are familiar with a similar "model-theoretic" means of making inferences. The psychological theory proposes that people understand the premises by constructing an internal model of the situation that the premises describe. The procedures that construct models rely on the meanings of words such as "if" and so they can construct models of premises with unfamiliar content. When the content is familiar, the models can be "fleshed out" to incorporate any extra information suggested by world knowledge. People formulate a description of the models they have constructed, and they can make a valid inference if they establish that their conclusion is true in every model that can be constructed of the premises.

If there is no alternative model in which their putative conclusion is false, then the conclusion is valid; if there is an alternative, they try to formulate a conclusion that is true in all the models. Where there is no such conclusion, they respond that nothing follows from the premises. They make errors if they fail to consider all the possible models of the premises, perhaps because of their limited processing capacity.

Which of the three theories – the formal rule theory, the content-specific rule theory, or the model theory – is closest to the truth? Johnson-Laird and Byrne have pitted them against each other in experiments in each of the three main domains of deduction: propositional inference, relational inference and quantificational inference (e.g.Johnson-Laird and Byrne, 1991). The results of the experiments corroborate the model theory and go against rule theories, as will be shown.

2.2 Propositional inference

Consider the following deduction:

> If there is a circle then there is a triangle.
> There is a circle.
> What follows?

Most people make the valid inference:

> Therefore, there is a triangle.

(See Evans, 1982, for a review.) According to formal rule theorists, the mind contains rules that capture the deductions we can make from conditionals, and so it contains a rule for modus ponens:

> If p then q
> p
> ———
> q

which matches the form of the premises above, and the inference can be made readily. Consider the following deduction:

> If there is a triangle then there is a circle.

There is not a circle.
What follows?

Most people find it more difficult to infer:

Therefore, there is not a triangle.

Rule theorists propose that there is no rule corresponding to this modus tollens inference and it must be made by constructing a mental proof, e.g. :

1. If p then q	[logical form of premiss 1]
2. not q	[logical form of premiss 2]
3. p	[by hypothesis]
4. q	[modus ponens rule applied to steps 1 and 3]
5. q and not q	[conjunction rule applied to steps 2 and 4]
6. not p	[reductio ad absurdum rule from contradiction in 5]

The inference is more difficult because it requires more steps. Rule theories explain the difference in difficulty between the two inferences in terms of the number of steps in their mental derivations. An alternative account of propositional inferences is given by the model theory. (The content-specific rule theory does not apply to deductions based on unfamiliar content such as those above.) The model theory proposes that people make these inferences by constructing mental models (Johnson-Laird, Byrne and Schaeken, in press). Consider the premises of the modus ponens inference:

If there is a triangle then there is a circle.
There is a triangle.

The meaning of the conditional premiss is represented by a set of models of the following sort:

[Δ]   o
...

where we have adopted the convention of representing separate models on separate lines. The first model contains shapes corresponding to the triangle and the circle, and they both occur in the same model. The second model – the three dots – represents the idea that there may be alternatives to the first model. The information in this implicit model can be "fleshed out" to make the alternatives explicit. The theory assumes that because of limitations of processing, people try to represent the minimum amount of information. But they can make their models more explicit if need be – when an inference demands it, as we will see below, or when their world knowledge suggests that they do so. In the models above, the square brackets around the triangle indicate that it is exhaustively represented in the first model – it cannot appear in an alternative model. As we will see shortly, this exhaustive representation of the triangle constrains the nature of the fully "fleshed out " models. The second premiss:

There is a triangle.

is represented by a model of the following sort:

Δ

The information in this model can be added to the models for the conditional by eliminating the three dots, to leave the model:

Δ   o

This model supports the conclusion:

There is a circle.

Now consider the modus tollens inference:

If there is a triangle then there is a circle.
There is not a circle.
Therefore, there is not a triangle.

The conditional premiss is represented as before:

[Δ]   o
...

The second premiss:

There is not a circle

is represented by a model of the following sort:

¬ o

where "¬" is a propositional-like tag representing negation (see Johnson-Laird and Byrne, 1989, for a defence of annotated models). The meaning of the second premiss thus eliminates from consideration the first model, in which there is a triangle, and so it seems that nothing follows: this response is the most common error that people make. To make the correct inference the models must be "fleshed out" to make explicit the alternative states of affairs. The fully fleshed-out models for the conditional are the following:

Δ   o
¬Δ   o
¬Δ   ¬o

A conditional assertion can be true in three different situations, and to understand fully a conditional, these three situations must be kept in mind. When the information from the second premiss is added to this set of models, it eliminates the models in which there is a circle, and just the third model is left:

¬Δ   ¬o

This model supports the conclusion:

There is not a triangle.

The model theory explains the difference in difficulty between the two inferences because the harder inference calls for the models to be fleshed out and for more models to be kept in mind. The theory predicts that the greater the number of explicit models that a reasoner has to keep in mind the harder the task will be.

Both theories can account for the difference in difficulty between the easy and the hard inferences based on conditionals. In addition, both theories predict a difference in difficulty between the analogous inferences based on bi-conditionals, that is, on premises of the following sort:

If and only if there is a triangle then there is a circle.

The modus ponens inference based on the bi-conditional should be easier than the modus tollens inference, according to both theories. The model theory makes one further novel prediction. It predicts that the difference between the two inferences based on conditionals should be greater than the difference between the two inferences based on bi-conditionals. The reason for this prediction is simple. The initial models for the bi-conditional are similar to those for the conditional. But, the bi-conditional premiss is consistent with fewer alternative states of affairs than the conditional. The fully fleshed-out set of models for the bi-conditional contains fewer models than those for the conditional:

Conditional		Bi-conditional	
Δ	o	Δ	o
$\neg\,\Delta$	o	$\neg\,\Delta$	$\neg\,$o
$\neg\,\Delta$	$\neg\,$o		

Hence, the model theory predicts that the modus tollens inference, which requires the models to be fleshed out, will be easier from the bi-conditional than from the conditional, because there are fewer models to keep in mind for the bi-conditional. The rule theory makes no such prediction.

This prediction was tested in an experiment carried out by Byrne in collaboration with Johnson-Laird and Schaeken (see Johnson-Laird, Byrne and Schaeken, in press). Sixteen subjects drew their own conclusions for two problems of each sort. For the conditional, the difference in difficulty between the easy inference (97% correct) and the hard inference (38% correct) was reliably greater than the difference in difficulty between the easy inference (97% correct) and the hard inference (59% correct) based on the bi-conditional. These and related data suggest that the model theory provides a good account of the mechanisms underlying propositional deductions (Byrne, 1989a; 1989b; Johnson-Laird, Byrne and Schaeken, in press). In addition, the theory has been developed to account for deductions that depend on relations internal to propositions.

2.3 Relational inference

Many deductions depend not on the connections between propositions but on relations that are internal to propositions, such as:

> The circle is on the right of the cross.
> The triangle is on the left of the cross.
> Therefore, the circle is on the right of the triangle.

No formal rule theory has been proposed for these linear syllogisms, and so the main contending explanations are content-specific rule theories (e.g. Clark, 1969), model theories (e.g. Huttenlocher, 1968), or some mixture of the two (Sternberg, 1981). It has been difficult to distinguish empirically between the theories for these simple problems. But they do make divergent predictions for more complex relational deductions. Consider the following problem:

> A.   The circle is on the right of the cross.
> The triangle is on the left of the circle.
> The bar is in front of the triangle.
> The line is in front of the circle.
> What is the relation between the bar and the line?

The valid conclusion is:

> The bar is on the left of the line.

or equivalently:

> The line is on the right of the bar.

Rule theories for such problems propose that people rely on content-specific rules, such as:

> Left (x, y) and Front (z, x) -> Left (front (z, x) y).
> (where the right-hand side means that z is in front of x, which is all on the left of y)

(e.g. Hagert, 1983;1984). The content-specific rules are applied to the premises of the problem to construct a proof of the conclusion. In problem A, the second premiss asserts the relation between the triangle and the circle. Because the bar and the line are related to the triangle and the circle, the relation between the bar and the line can be inferred directly. Hence, the first premiss is irrelevant and only the remaining three need to be used in the proof. The solution to other problems is not so straightforward. Consider the following premises:

B.   The cross is on the right of the circle.
      The triangle is on the left of the circle.
      The bar is in front of the triangle.
      The line is in front of the cross.
      What is the relation between the bar and the line?

Once again the valid conclusion is:

      The bar is on the left of the line.

But, the problem does not contain any premiss that directly asserts the relation between the triangle and the cross, to which the bar and the line are related. The relation between the triangle and the cross has to be inferred from the first two premises:

      The triangle is on the left of the cross.

Once this inference has been made, the relation between the bar and the line can then be inferred using the same steps as in problem A. Hence, Problem B requires more steps in its derivation than Problem A. The content-specific rule theory thus predicts that Problem B will be harder than Problem A.

We compared this theory to one based on the model theory (Byrne and Johnson-Laird, 1989). The first premiss in Problem A above:

      The circle is on the right of the cross.

leads to the construction of a minimal spatial array:

      +   o

Models cannot be understood in isolation from the processes that construct them, and in this case, the processes for constructing models of relations such as "on the right of" ensure that the models represent the relative positions of the items. The information in each subsequent premiss can be added to the model, inserting tokens in the appropriate place in the array to satisfy the meaning of the premises:

Δ   +   o

− |

But, notice that the premises of Problem A are equally consistent with a different layout:

+   Δ   o

− |

Each model supports the conclusion:

The bar is on the left of the line.

and as there are no alternative models in which the conclusion is false, it is a valid one. But, to make the right answer for the right reasons, people have to bear more than one model in mind. Unlike Problem A, Problem B requires just a single model:

Δ   o   +

− |

The model supports the conclusion:

The bar is on the left of the line.

The model theory predicts that Problem B should be easier than Problem A because Problem B requires just one model.

Thus, the two theories make directly opposing predictions for problems of this sort. If people are using content-specific rules they should find B harder than A; if they are using models they should find A harder than B. Byrne and Johnson-Laird carried out an experiment to pit the two theories against each other using such problems (Byrne and Johnson-Laird, 1989). Eighteen subjects carried out six inferences of each of the two sorts. The percentages of correct conclusions to Problem B was 70% and to Problem A was 46%. Hence, the results indicate that people use models to make relational inferences.

2.4 Quantificational inference

When people make relational inferences they are sometimes concerned not just with the relations between single entities, such as "the cross is behind the circle" but also with relations between groups of entities, such as "all of the crosses are behind some of the circles". These inferences depend on the meaning of quantifiers, such as "all" and "some". Quantifiers have long been studied by philosophers, psychologists, and linguists, primarily in the guise of "syllogisms", such as:

> All of the children are boys.
> All of the boys are scouts.
> Therefore, all of the children are scouts.

(See Johnson-Laird, 1983, for a review.) Complex quantified deductions depend on premises that contain more than one quantifier, such as:

> None of the children is in the same place as any of the adults.
> All of the adults are in the same place as all of the teachers.

from which it follows:

> Therefore, none of the children is in the same place as any of the teachers.

Experiments carried out by Byrne in collaboration with Johnson-Laird and Tabossi have shown that people can readily make multiply quantified deductions of this sort (Johnson-Laird, Byrne and Tabossi, 1989). In fact, 78% of subjects in one experiment spontaneously constructed a valid conclusion to the premises above. But, we also established that they found some multiply-quantified inferences very difficult. The following premises:

> None of the children is in the same place as any of the adults.
> All of the adults are in the same place as some of the teachers.

support the conclusion:

Therefore, none of the children is in the same place as some of the teachers.

or equivalently:

Therefore, some of the teachers are not in the same place as any of the children.

But only 23% of the subjects produced any valid conclusion to this problem. Why is the second inference more difficult? Formal rule theories cannot account for the difference in difficulty between the two inferences. Such theories would be similar to formal proofs of multiply-quantified deductions in the predicate calculus. These proofs require three stages of reasoning – the elimination of quantifiers, the application of rules for connectives and the restoration of quantifiers. But, the formal derivations of each of the conclusions above require exactly the same number of steps, and in fact their steps are almost identical. Hence, formal rule theories would not be able to account for the difference between them. Rule theories based on content-specific rules do not apply to these inferences and so the main contending explanation is based on models.

What sorts of model do people rely on to make multiply-quantified deductions? Multiply quantified-assertions highlight an important difference between the sorts of model described and Euler circles or Venn diagrams. As logicians recognize, multiply-quantified assertions are too powerful to be represented in either Euler circles or Venn diagrams. The representational machinery of Euler circles and Venn diagrams is restricted to dealing with just singly quantified assertions, such as "All the teachers are adults". This assertion can be represented by an Euler circle where all the teachers are adults, and there may be some adults who are not teachers (figure 2.1a) or by an Euler circle where all the teachers are adults, and all the adults are teachers (figure 2.1.b).
Now try to represent a multiply-quantified assertion, such as:

All the teachers are in the same place as some of the adults.

within this representational framework. A moment's reflection will show that it would be possible to represent the fragment "all the teachers", but not to represent "some of the adults" as well. One could perhaps contrive an adaptation of Euler circles to deal with multiply quantified assertions, but this adaptation would constitute a new theory – it is not possible to represent multiply-quantified assertions directly within Euler circles.

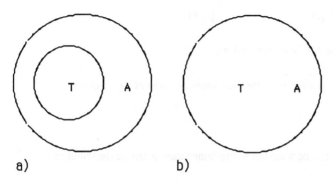

Figure 2.1 Euler circle representation.

But multiply-quantified assertions can be represented in mental models. The theory proposes that people construct the following sort of model of the premises in the first problem:

| [c] [c] [c] | [a] [a] [a] [t] [t] [t] |

The number of individuals is arbitrary, but the square brackets indicate, as we saw earlier, that an individual has been exhaustively represented – no such individuals will occur elsewhere – and the vertical lines demarcate different places. The model supports the conclusion:

None of the children is in the same place as any of the adults.

and there is no alternative model of the premises that refutes it. The first problem requires just a single model to make the valid deduction. The second problem may be represented by a model of the following sort:

| [c] [c] [c] | [a] [a] [a] t t |

This model supports the conclusion:

None of the children is in the same place as any of the teachers.

which is one of the most common errors from these premises. An alternative model refutes this erroneous conclusion:

| [c] [c] t | [a] [a] [a] t t |

and supports instead the valid conclusion:

None of the children is in the same place as some of the teachers.

or equivalently:

Some of the teachers are not in the same place as any of the children.

The second problem requires multiple models to make the valid deduction. The model theory is able to account for the difference in difficulty between the two problems because the second problem requires more models to be borne in mind than the first problem.

The research discussed suggests that the model theory provides a good account of human deduction, in the primary domains of propositional, relational and quantificational inference. The mental machinery responsible for reasoning depends on procedures that construct mental models, add further information to them and revise them.

2.5 Mental models: a critique

My aim in this chapter has been to show that the available experimental evidence corroborates the predictions of the model theory and goes against the predictions of rule theories. However, some critics have proposed that there is no difference between mental models and rules of inference. For example, Goldman writes:

Procedures are necessary to specify how the models should be used. So manipulation of mental models is not fundamentally different from manipulation of mental propositions. It seems then the rules that operate on the models must be inference rules (Goldman, 1986, p. 292).

But there is a profound difference between the two sorts of psychological theory in terms of the mental representations and processes that they propose people rely on. Rule theories rely on mental representations that are close to the structure of language, whereas mental models are close to the structure of the world as we perceive it. Rule theories depend on processes that apply formal rules of inference to representations of the logical forms of sentences. Model theories depend on processes that search for alternative models of the premises. To confuse one theory with the other is akin to confusing the semantic method of truth tables with the syntactic method of proof in the propositional calculus (e.g. Jeffrey, 1981). Likewise, the model theory is not the first-order predicate calculus. The predicate calculus applies to both infinite and finite sets, there is no decision procedure for it, and there is no way of proving theorems within it using models directly (e.g. Jeffrey, 1981). The model theory applies only to finite sets, it has a decision procedure, and it works directly with models (see Johnson-Laird and Byrne, 1991).

A related misapprehension is that mental models and formal rules both depend on syntactic procedures. It is true that the computer programs that model both sorts of theory depend on syntactic rules, but, people do have access to the meanings of expressions: their models can be real because of the causal links between models and the world (see Johnson-Laird, 1983, and for a fuller discussion of criticisms of mental models, see Johnson-Laird and Byrne, 1991, Chapter 10).

A criticism more relevant to the topic of this book is that the term "mental models" is overworked and under-specified. I have tried to show in this chapter that the sorts of mental model used for different sorts of reasoning can be specified in a uniform and precise way (see Johnson-Laird and Byrne, 1991). But, the confusion seems to arise when we consider not just the sorts of model described, but also the sorts of mental model examined in related domains. The theory of reasoning is based on the conception of mental models introduced by Phil Johnson-Laird (Johnson-Laird, 1983). They are sometimes called APU-models because they were developed in part at the MRC Applied Psychology Unit, Cambridge, England (see Keane, Byrne and Gentner, 1991). A related conception of mental models was introduced by Gentner and Stevens (Gentner and Stevens, 1983). They are sometimes called BBN-models because they were developed in part at the Bolt, Berenek and Newman Labs, Cambridge, Ma. (also see Keane et al, 1991). Are the two sorts of mental models different?

Some differences between the two conceptions are clearly discernible (for a fuller discussion see Keane, Byrne and Gentner, 1991). Perhaps the most important difference is that BBN-models and APU-models represent similar things in different ways (and accordingly, their notational conventions differ). BBN-models adopt a representation that is close to the structure of language, often relying on a notation derived from the predicate calculus. APU-models adopt a representation that is close to the structure of the world, and not to the language in which the world is described. To illustrate the difference between these two sorts of representation, consider how they represent variables. Variables correspond to the structure of language, not to anything in the world. BBN-models represent variables directly, whereas APU-models represent them by instantiating them with specific mental tokens. APU-models do not normally contain variables because the work of instantiation is a part of comprehension. Universal quantifiers such as "all", for example, are instantiated by mental tokens that exhaust the relevant set, existential quantifiers, such as "some" are instantiated by sets of mental tokens that satisfy the relevant set, and optional items that fail to satisfy it. Thus for APU-models, procedures that can revise the models are crucial in order to change specific instantiations when they are found to be wrong. The difference in the representational claims of APU and BBN models is paralleled by the difference in their relation to memory structures. BBN-models have been examined in the context of permanent knowledge structures stored in long-term memory until they are required for use. APU-models have been addressed primarily as temporary structures constructed in working memory in the process of, say, carrying out an inference.

But perhaps the most telling difference is that the two sorts of mental model were developed to explain different phenomena. APU-models have been developed to explain deductive reasoning – such as propositional inference, spatial inference, quantificational inference and meta-deduction – and language comprehension. BBN-models have been developed to explain the acquisition of technical knowledge, the solution of problems by analogy, the comprehension of complex physical mechanisms, and the interaction of people with computers. The two sorts of model may be, despite their differences, "glimpses of the same beast" (Johnson-Laird, 1989). What I have tried to show is that the model theory provides a good explanation of the glimpses we have had of human deductive reasoning.

Acknowledgements

I am grateful to Mark Keane for his helpful comments on an earlier draft.

References

Anderson, J.R. (1983). *The Architecture of Cognition.* Hillsdale, NJ: LEA.

Braine, M.D.S. (1978). On the relation between the natural logic of reasoning and standard logic. *Psychological Review 85*, 1–21.

Braine, M.D.S., Reiser, B.J. and Rumain, B. (1984). Some empirical justification for a theory of natural propositional logic. *The Psychology of Learning and Motivation, Vol. 8.* New York: Academic Press.

Byrne, R.M.J. (1989a). Suppressing valid inferences with conditionals. *Cognition 31*, 61–83.

Byrne, R.M.J. (1989b). Everyday reasoning with conditional sequences. *Quarterly Journal of Experimental Psychology 41A*, 141–166.

Byrne, R.M.J. and Johnson-Laird, P.N. (1989). Spatial reasoning. *Journal of Memory and Language 28*, 564–575.

Cheng, P.N. and Holyoak, K.J. (1985). Pragmatic reasoning schemas. *Cognitive Psychology 17*, 391–416.

Clark, H.H. (1969). Linguistic processes in deductive reasoning. *Psychological Review 76*, 387–404.

Evans, J. St.B.T. (1982). *The Psychology of Deductive Reasoning.* London: Routledge.

Gentner, D. and Stevens, A.L. (1983). (eds), *Mental Models.* Hillsdale, NJ: LEA.

Goldman, A.I. (1986). *Epistemology and Cognition.* Cambridge, Ma.: Harvard University Press.

Hagert, G. (1983). Report of the Uppsala programming methodology and artificial intelligence laboratory. Unpublished manuscript. Upsala University.

Hagert, G. (1984). Modelling mental models: experiments in cogntive modeling of spatial reasoning. In O'Shea, T. (ed.) *Advances in Artificial Intelligence.* Amsterdam: North Holland.

Huttenlocher, J. (1968). Constructing spatial images: a strategy in reasoning. *Psychological Review 75*, 286–298.

Jeffrey, R. (1981). *Formal Logic: Its Scope and Limits* (2nd edn). New York: McGraw-Hill.

Johnson-Laird, P.N. (1983). *Mental Models.* Cambridge: CUP.

Johnson-Laird, P.N. (1989). Mental models. In Posner, M. (ed.) *Foundations of Cognitive Science.* Cambridge, Ma.: MIT Press.

Johnson-Laird, P.N. and Byrne, R.M.J. (1989). *Only* reasoning. *Journal of Memory and Language 28*, 313–330.

Johnson-Laird, P.N. and Byrne, R.M.J. (1991). *Deduction*. Hove, Sussex: LEA.

Johnson-Laird, P.N., Byrne, R.M.J. and Schaeken, W. (1992). Reasoning by model: the case of propositional inference. *Psychological Review.*

Johnson-Laird, P.N. Byrne, R.M.J. and Tabossi, P. (1989). Reasoning by model: the case of multiple quantification. *Psychological Review 96*, 658–673.

Keane, M.T.G., Byrne, R.M.J. and Gentner, D. (1991). *Mental models: two views*. Unpublished manuscript. Department of Computer Science, Trinity College, Dublin.

Rips, L.J. (1983). Cognitive processes in propositional reasoning. *Psychological Review 90*, 38-71.

Rips, L.J. (1989). The psychology of knights and knaves. *Cognition 31*, 85–116.

Sternberg, R.J. (1981). Reasoning with determinate and indeterminate syllogisms. *British Journal of Psychology 72*, 407–420.

Chapter 3

Distinguishing Conceptual and Empirical Issues about Mental Models[1]

Keith Stenning

3.1 Introduction

This chapter focuses on what it claims are confusions which have arisen in the use of "model" chiefly in discussions about the relation between logic and human verbal reasoning (e.g. Braine 1978; Johnson-Laird, 1983; Byrne, Chapter 2, this volume). On the one hand, Braine has argued that a natural deduction system, a system of rewriting rules for introducing and eliminating logical vocabulary from formulae, provides a metric on the difficulty of inferences in the form of the numbers of steps in proofs. He has concluded from the observation that the data of people's reasoning corresponds with this metric, that this is their mental logic. On the other hand, Johnson-Laird has argued that there is no mental logic and that people use "mental models", a *semantic* system of reasoning which fits the data of syllogistic reasoning in a way that no syntactic system can.

This chapter will argue that both sides of this argument are misguided. Logics must be distinguished from their implementations. Braine's claim is best construed as a claim that a particular implementation of a natural deduction system is used by subjects, an implementation close to the pencil-and-paper one which we learn in logic classes. In this implementation we search a pool of premises and conclusions for matches to the lefthand side of rewrite rules and then add the right-hand sides to the pool of formulae when we find such a match, repeating until we find the target formula in our pool of statements.

Johnson-Laird's claim that the computational processes involved are semantic cannot have empirical import applied to a decidable subset such as the syllogism, nor to the decidable fragments which people can implement within undecidable systems (decidability is defined below). Johnson-Laird's claim can be made most sense of by construing it as a claim that logic is implemented in some way very different from the conventional machine or paper-and-pencil implementations. In order to illustrate the force of this reinterpretation, we here propose a particular style of implementation based on a distributed representation of attribute binding which explains the most important aspects of Johnson-Laird's data.

The logician's concept of "model" is a well defined abstract object which has been the foundation of modern formulations of logic at least since Tarski (1932). Mental models were introduced by Johnson-Laird in order to fulfil a role distinct from that of logical models in psychological theories of reasoning. Our argument here is that what is needed is a psychological theory of how models (in the logician's sense) are implemented. If we are right, the logician's concept of model will play a central role in psychological theory (Stenning, 1978). If the argument is sustained, we are left with the logical concept of model, and a psychological theory of implementation. In this context, there is no use for a distinct concept of mental model.

In the broader context of this book, this conceptual confusion is of importance because there is yet a further sense of mental model which descends to us from psychologists such as Gentner (e.g. Gentner and Stevens, 1983) and which has an honourable function in discussions of human–computer interaction (HCI). This sense of the term refers to analogies for intangible concepts, for example, hydraulics or crowd-flow, as analogies for thinking about electricity. This is the sense in which computer users might adopt typewriters or filing cabinets as analogies for word-processors.

While this latter sense of mental model is distinct from the use to which Johnson-Laird wants to put the term, it is not unrelated. In both uses, there is a mapping involved. The logical concept of model is just the concept of a mapping from vocabulary of a language onto entities in a world. In the analogical sense of mental model, there is a mapping from analogy to analogized – from water pressure or people-density to voltage, from water- or people-flow to electrical current. The latter sense's mappings are second-order versions of the former sense's mappings.

In terms of the application of these concepts in psychological theories, there is a further important difference disguised by this difference between first- and second-order mappings of vocabulary. This is the difference between episodic mappings of properties onto hypothetical individuals as opposed to general knowledge mappings of vocabulary onto categories of individual.

Although logical models are mappings of vocabulary of a language onto elements in the whole of the language's domain, their actual application to verbal reasoning problems invariably applies to a subsidiary mapping down from the "universal" domains on which languages such as English are apparently interpreted, to tiny domains within which verbal reasoning problems are couched. The operative mapping is from the predicates occurring in the problem fragment to the handful of individuals with regard to which reasoning proceeds. For example, in a syllogism about artists, beekeepers and chemists, we imagine some small domain of folk (perhaps gathered in a room) rather than all past, present and future members of these categories. We might suppose that Fred, say, is an artist and a beekeeper but not a chemist and that say Jim is not an artist but is a beekeeper and a chemist, and so map down from the universal interpretation of English (which tells us which things are artists, beekeepers and chemists in general) onto a hypothetical domain of two individuals.

The mappings involved in analogical models of concepts such as electricity are, in contrast, general knowledge mappings like those which ground the language's relation to the world in general. This difference between episodic and general applications of "model" makes a great deal of difference to the psychological applications. Most HCI applications of mental model are closer to the second analogical sense of the term and are hence involved in relatively long-term mental structures which users bring to the interpretation of their machines. The difference between episodic memory of arbitrary relations between small sets of artists, beekeepers and chemists, as opposed to general knowledge mappings from pressure onto voltage distinguish fundamentally different types of memory (e.g. Tulving, 1983). I will return to this point after presenting the arguments for the reinterpretation of the evidence used to support the first use of the term mental model.

One reason for labouring what many psychologists (and perhaps HCI researchers) may regard as terminological issues is their importance in interdisciplinary communication. This book seems a particularly appropriate place to try to clarify how to talk about each other's subject matter.

The plan of the chapter is as follows. The first section takes up the conceptual issues. What is the relevance of the distinction between proof theory and model theory to psychological claims about reasoning? And how does the distinction bear on claims about syntactic and semantic processing made by psychologists. What is the relation between a logic and its implementations, and how does this distinction relate to psychological theories of reasoning and the part played by models in such theories?

The second section focuses on empirical issues in verbal reasoning. It redefines the issues of semantic versus syntactic processing as issues about whether human reasoning strategies are what I will call "agglomerative" or "analytic". It having established that the psychological work to be done consists in giving a theory of implementation for logic, an example is then given of an implementational theory. A theory of memory representations developed elsewhere (Stenning and Levy, 1988) can form the basis of an explanation of how human working memory implements logic in a way very different from conventional machine implementations. For the purposes of this book, it is less important whether this example explanation is correct than that it illustrates a quite different relation between psychology, logic and computation than the conventionally received relation, and one that puts the term "model" to good psychological use without distorting its use in logic. We conclude with some comments on the relation between this use and the other use of mental models alluded to above.

3.2 Conceptual issues

Logic is generally divided into model theory and proof theory.[2] Model theory, which is in some sense the more basic, defines logic in terms of the relation of semantic consequence. In model theory, statements such as (1) occur:

$$P, P \supset Q \vDash Q \tag{1}$$

which is to be read as stating that all models in which P is true and $P \supset Q$ is true, are also models in which Q is true. Here models are a subset of interpretations which make the axioms of a theory true, and interpretations are mappings of the vocabulary of a language onto the non-linguistic elements of the domain of interpretation.

Model theory is pursued in a metalanguage which talks *about* sets of models and the truth values of sentences in those sets of models. When a logician starts a paper "The language L consists of the sentences..." this much is metalanguage, but when it comes to proving theorems within the defined language, that is use of the object language. Proofs in model theory are proofs in a metalanguage, usually the language of set theory (or just plain English), which discusses sets of formulae and their truth values (i.e. they talk *about* models). This is made clear in the explanation of formula (1) which makes statements about *all models in which* .... A logic is most fundamentally defined model theoretically as a relation of semantic consequence.

Proof theory, in contrast, involves the specification of syntactic ways of defining logics. In proof theory, statements such as (2) occur:

$$P, \ P \supset Q \vdash Q \tag{2}$$

Single or double horizontal bars on the "turnstiles" are the only signs of when model theory or proof theory are being written, but the nature of the theories is very different. Proof theory is about the formulation of systems which capture syntactically the relation of logical consequence. Theorem proving *within* such systems employs the formally defined language of such systems, which is referred to as the object language. The modern con- ception of logic could be said to have been established by Godel's (1931) proof that there are model theories which cannot be captured in any proof theory. Syntax cannot capture some concepts of semantic consequence.

Formal proofs in a logic are conducted within the terms of proof theory. Syntax provides the mechanism for doing this. Neither proof theory nor model theory is about how results are computed – how proofs for target formulae are found. A logic, specified model- or proof-theoretically, is an infinite relation between premises and consequences. Only a theorem prover operating over a logic provides ways of computing results. Again, much of the insight of modern logic dates from Church's proof (1936), based on Godel's proof, that there are logics which are undecidable – logics for which there is no theorem prover that can take any arbitrary statement and decide whether or not that statement is a theorem. So there are logics which are not even specifiable in syntactic terms, and ones which though specifiable, are not "searchable" for arbitrary consequences of their specifications. These are not outlandish logics: in fact, some would say that all "interesting" logics fall into this latter category. Decidability is the exception rather than the rule.

When psychologists appeal to logic in relation to mental processing it is essential to remember these three "grades" of logical involvement. Most psychologists, particularly those of a cognitive science persuasion, assume that mental processes are to be given a computational formulation, and so it should be clear from the outset that they are committed to talking about deduction as theorem proving within proof theories which capture model theories.[3]

Unfortunately, this wedding-cake structure of logic has been obscured because elementary formulations of logic encourage the idea that they come with certain tacit implementations. One course on natural deduction systems and the student knows of one paper-and-pencil implementation of a logic or two. So, when psychologists argue from observations that one deduction is easier than another to conclusions that subjects are or are not "using" one or another proof theory, they have submerged all the issues about what implementation of the proof theory is assumed underneath tacit assumptions about their own pencil-and-paper strategies. Logics do not generally specify relative lengths of proof for theorems: theorem provers do.

Similarly, when psychologists rebel against *syntactic* proof processes and insist that processing is semantic, one must have careful recourse to this nested family of distinctions. In one sense of "syntactic", all computation is syntactic, and so *semantic processing* is oxymoronic. Computation manipulates representations by virtue of their physical characteristics, not by virtue of what they represent. But in this broad sense of syntactic, proving things within a set theory formulation of a model theory is a syntactic process – one manipulates syntactic representations of a set-theoretic language to get the answer. On a narrower sense of syntactic, one might well ask whether processing proceeds with regard to the syntax of one level of language, or whether it descends (or ascends?) to the syntax of a metalanguage to compute. This latter possibility gives a narrow sense to the distinction between syntactic versus semantic processing: this might be an important psychological issue, but one which one could only possibly be approached within a rigourous formulation of two levels of language, object- and meta-.

In fact, much of the psychological debate has been conducted about systems which are decidable (e.g. the categorical syllogism, which is a subset of the decidable first-order *monadic* predicate logic, and propositional logic which is also decidable [4]). In these small territories where the semantically specifiable can be captured by syntax and simple decision procedures for theoremhood can be taught in logic classes, there is no scope for distinguishing syntactic and semantic processing within the circumscribed meaning that is given to those terms above. One simply cannot say that behavioural data show that processing is semantic, because for any computational theory couched as a theorem-prover operating in set-theoretic terms in the metalanguage, there will be an object-level syntactic theorem-prover which mirrors its operation exactly in terms of manipulations of sentences.

This is very frustrating, if mathematical facts can be frustrating. The psychologist has learnt about natural deduction, in which one writes and rewrites sentences licensed by rules of inference and has learnt truth tables in which one manipulates truth values, rows of which represent the states of worlds. These two procedures have very different "feels". One is surely syntactic – about sentences – and the other is surely semantic – about models. What could be starker?

In order to see that the crucial distinction is not between syntax and semantics, consider how to turn the truth table into a proof-theoretic method (see table 3.1). All one needs do is to substitute the sentence P or not P in Table 3.1 wherever T occurs, and P and not P wherever F occurs, and then to treat each of the column entries as conjuncts within their rows which are treated as disjuncts. One then has a sentence, a very long sentence, which is true if the original formula is a theorem and is otherwise false. The semantics are mirrored by the syntax: a tautology stands for the value true; an inconsistency for the value false; each row of the truth table corresponds to a model and is now a conjunct of a larger proposition which expresses the fact that consequence is truth-in-all-models. A truth table, previously thought of as impeccably semantic, can be interpreted as a syntactic entity, a sentence.[5] Operations on the truth table (such as checking for the absence of F's in a column) can be mirrored by operations on clauses of the sentence.

Q	⊨	P	⊃	Q	Q	⊢	P	⊃	Q
T		T		T	$(((P \vee \neg P)$	⊃	$((P \vee \neg P)$	⊃	$(P \vee \neg P))) \&$
T		F		T	$((P \vee \neg P)$	⊃	$((P \& \neg P)$	⊃	$(P \vee \neg P))) \&$
F		T		F	$((P \& \neg P)$	⊃	$((P \vee \neg P)$	⊃	$(P \& \neg P))) \&$
F		F		F	$((P \& \neg P)$	⊃	$((P \& \neg P)$	⊃	$(P \& \neg P))))$
Truth table					Statement				

Table 3.1 Truth table in the meta language and isomorphic object-language statement.

Computationally, the two interpretations of what is going on are indistinguishable. In decidable systems such as propositional logic or the syllogism, syntax can *always* mirror the semantics; operations over sentences can always mirror operations over models.

Although there is no computational fact of the matter whether these representations should be thought of as in a set-theoretic language about models or in a proof-theoretic one, there is an important difference between this truth table style of theorem proving and a conventional natural deduction approach to the same proof. I will call the truth table approach *agglomerative* and the natural deduction one *analytic*. The former constructs one representation which agglomerates all the information carried by the target theorem and then processes this one representation:; the latter proceeds by following an analytic chain of abstractions embodied in particular proof rules and never arrives at a single representation which captures all the information.

There is no mystery why this distinction between agglomerative and analytic proof strategies should have been confused with the distinction between semantic and syntactic methods. Semantic methods quantify over models, and models are mappings of *whole* vocabularies onto *whole* domains. Truth tables are very "high-bandwidth" representations which grow exponentially with the number of atomic propositions in the vocabulary, but for the small problems for which they are tractable, they are susceptible to graphical search techniques which are conducive to human beings. They are important didactically because they bear a close relationship to the model theory which is the fundamental formulation of logic.

This distinction between agglomerative and analytic proof strategies is an empirical distinction. In fact, it is the distinction which I believe has driven the intuitions about styles of human deductive reasoning of the psychologists who have argued for "semantic processing". In computational terms, the distinction contrasts quite different implementations. A system with a large capacity for highly regimented tabular representations with certain complex search operations built in might well prefer the agglomerative style of theorem-proving. The next section explores what such an implementation might look like.

3.3 Empirical issues

Human beings are flexible processors of information and they certainly do not perform deductive reasoning even of such a limited subset of logic as the syllogism in one fixed way. There are children and adults, naive syllogizers and experts, people with pencil and paper and people without – a host of different reasoners in different contexts. The purpose of this section is not to establish that one implementation of the syllogistic subset of logic is the definitive account of these mental processes. The point is rather to show that one can take as read all of the data that has been taken as motivating a mental-models theory of syllogistic reasoning, and recast it within a theory that says subjects use a particular implementation of logic within their particular memory structure and processes, and that this recasting shows what is missing from the mental models account of reasoning. Implementations of computational theories require, above all, accounts of the memory resources available. In fact, if one accepts the theory of memory proposed here for implementation, it *explains* why subjects adopt the agglomerative strategy which mental models encapsulate. In the process, it becomes clear that mental models notation is much less distinct from some other notations than has been supposed (Lee, 1987; Stenning, 1991; Stenning and Oberlander, 1991a). Johnson-Laird's claim that Euler's circles suffer a combinatorial explosion (Johnson-Laird, 1983) rests on an unrealistic view of how the graphical systems are used. He assumes that they would be used in a totally agglomerative fashion in which all combinations of premiss diagrams are considered. Stenning and Oberlander show that under a reasonable interpretation of the strategies for their use, such as those described in logic textbooks, they are equivalent to mental models in their combinatorial range. Of course, mental models notation could also be employed in a totally agglomerative style of reasoning with the same consequences of inefficiency. The point is that there is no inherent difference between representing bindings of properties to individuals by placing predicate tokens in columns as opposed to positioning circles in relation to each other. Recasting the psychological problem as one of implementing logic does make it clear how implementations of both mental models and the graphical methods contrast with a conventional implementation of a natural deduction system.

In a larger perspective, the agglomerative style of theorem-proving is near one end of a continuum of approaches which has rule-rewriting systems at the other. A more serious empirical account of syllogistic reasoning would need to entertain subjects operating at different points on this continuum. In fact, it is possible to show how the use of strategies to reduce the number of models considered and the number of ways in which they are considered can gradually transform the agglomerative extreme into the analytic extreme (Stenning and Oberlander, 1991b). This may help to explain why graphical methods have formed such an important didactic starting point for teaching logical expertise.

What is needed to implement a theory of syllogistic reasoning based on agglomerative strategies? Most fundamentally, we need to specify what memory structures are involved: and the most basic memory requirement is a system which will keep track of collections of types of individual. In the theory of the syllogism, there are essentially seven types: three predicates F, G and H specify individuals which are F, G and H, ones which are F and G but not H, ones which are F not G but H and so on. The eighth type which are not F, not G and not H are background to the theory. This is not the only sort of memory we need, but it is very basic to the agglomerative style of theorem-proving.

So there are seven types of individual for any three content predicates. What we have to do is keep track of collections of them. There might be one of Type Seven, and one of Type Two in a model. It is never of any interest whether there is more than one individual of a type[6] so our collections need never have more than seven individuals in them. In fact, as we will see, we can do with considerably less.

We can imagine various representations for doing binding of attributes to individuals – sentences of a calculus, mental models, tables, Euler's circles, Venn diagrams – lots and lots of ways of doing it. The question for theories of human memory is how is the binding of properties within individuals achieved. This is not a question that has much interested developers of machine theorem-provers because in conventional architecture machines, binding is achieved by primitive mechanisms (fundamentally, loci and pointers) making them particularly adept at processing the strings of concatenated symbols which we are accustomed to using in doing pencil-and-paper logic. As a written proof proceeds, we can search back for lemmas already proved to reuse in applying rules of inference to generate new lemmas. Take away the pencil and pape, and our internal memory does not allow us to employ this strategy.

Lots of evidence points to the fact that models – determinate mappings from sets of terms onto the elements of models – have a special status in human memory. Determinate here means that each term denotes an identifiable element: distinctness (and identity) of reference are determined for all pairs of terms. When texts do not allow subjects to trace antecedents for anaphors they cannot construct these mappings and cannot remember the texts (Bransford and Johnson, 1972). The conventions of interpretation for indefinite introductions into texts, and subsequent reference to them ensure that such mappings can generally be constructed (Stenning, 1978). Where producers of texts diverge from the strict application of such conventions either through ignorance or for literary effect, they do so in circumscribed ways.

Not much work has been done analysing memory for mappings more complex than paired-associates. Stenning, Shepherd and Levy (1988) used a straight memory task where mappings of four binary choices of property were mapped onto two individuals. Individuals were always uniquely identified by profession, but could share or contrast on the other properties. Subjects read descriptions a sentence at a time in a self-paced task, answered some distractor questions and then recalled what they had read by picking descriptions off menus. Analysis of self-paced reading times and patterns of recall errors shows that subjects' memory for the bindings that make up these mappings are distributed over many facts about pairs of individuals. Stenning and Levy (1988) showed that this data could be simulated using a representation consisting of about 15 simple existential facts about a pair of individuals, which information is then *synthesized* into a description of the individuals by a PDP constraint satisfaction network (see

Figure 3.1). Corrupting the representation by flipping truth values of facts in the database lead to a pattern of errors resembling those people make. Although the details of the particular facts used in the database cannot be uniquely derived from this data, it can be shown that only a redundant distributed representation can give rise to the profile of errors people make.

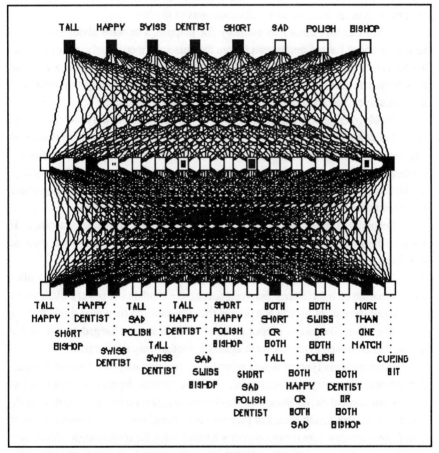

Figure 3.1 Representation and resolution in the PDP network.

What is essential here is not the details of the particular distribution of binding information in this model but the fundamental idea that binding of attributes to individuals in human memory is a high-level accomplishment achieved on the basis of constraint satisfaction applied to low-level data. Just such a system is required, as we have argued above, to make sense of a distinction between syntax and semantics. It can do this because the lower-level system is not implementing deductive reasoning at all: it is merely intended to explain how memory holds mappings which are collections of types of individuals defined in terms of a small number of properties (in this case four). At this level it computes over formal representations, though these are representations of things which are semantic with regard to the higher-evel process. This is analogous to manipulating the syntax of set-theory in order to compute results about sets of models.

What can this theory of memory for mappings explain about syllogistic reasoning style? Let me put the cart before the horse and motivate the use of such an account in a theory of reasoning before saying what else would be needed to incorporate it. Certain very general properties of constraint satisfaction networks are conducive to an account of agglomerative reasoning strategies.

Firstly, a constraint satisfaction mechanism can represent only one solution to one set of constraints at a time. In this case, one set of bindings based on one set of fragmentary facts about the pair of individuals. This is because although the micro-processes of computation are massively parallel, the macro-process is radically serial. Such networks only perform one relaxation at a time. Representing more than one model will entail performing more than one relaxation in *series*.

Secondly, a constraint satisfaction network can return only total mappings. If some of its input units are not set, it will still return a best-fitting total map of properties onto individuals.

Thirdly, the general computational properties of these models potentially offer an explanation of interference between successive models. It is very difficult to think about the pair of bishop and dentist that you saw and then next think about a pair that are just like them except for one property that has changed on one of the individuals, and then to change them again for another very similar pair.

Fourthly, this type of model potentially explains why we observe content-dependence of memory (and reasoning). Here the content-dependence of interest is not like the content-dependence that Manktelow and Over (this volume) discuss in which beliefs about truth values of premises or conclusions interfere directly. Such effects do occur but here we are concerned rather with the content-dependence that underlies the difference in memorability between artists, beekeepers and chemists, as opposed to reasoning with a's, b's and c's (Johnson-Laird, 1983). What a truly adequate parallel distributed memory storage and retrieval system would allow is the distribution of the binding mechanism over general knowledge about artists, beekeepers and chemists. It would offer an explanation as to why we can hold those in various combinations and in ways that we cannot hold a's, b's and c's.

People just get lost after two paragraphs when given that sort of material. The explanation is something that Johnson-Laird announces as a goal, but which mental models do nothing to provide.

So, what part would such a mechanism play in an agglomerative strategy of reasoning about syllogisms of the sort that mental-models theory represents? Figure 3.2 gives a schematic embedding of the memory model into the rest of the system. The memory mechanism is only doing a small part of the overall work, but its properties are what determine that an agglomerative strategy will be used.

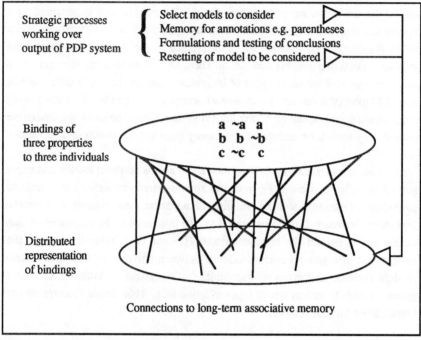

Strategic processes working over output of PDP system { Select models to consider
Memory for annotations e.g. parentheses
Formulations and testing of conclusions
Resetting of model to be considered

Bindings of three properties to three individuals

a ~a a
b b ~b
c ~c c

Distributed representation of bindings

Connections to long-term associative memory

Figure 3.2 A PDP network which retrieves the bindings of four binary properties to two individuals. The input layer (bottom) is a distributed representation of the set of bindings in the output layer (top). From Stenning and Levy (1988).

The output layer of the PDP model implements the "screen" on which this PDP mechanism holds a model. Other mechanisms must account for the selection of strategies and the easoning over the models, and we can suppose, for present purposes, that these are just as Johnson-Laird proposes. In particular, there will have to be a mechanism which can construct a model from premises, and reset the model to a different one as successive models are considered. The strategic part of the reasoning system has to be able to instruct the PDP system, "Consider a bishop and a dentist with such and such properties". So there's control from the top to the bottom. Other slave systems in working memory are involved in the strategy and tactics that reason over the models. But the centrepiece of the working memory is the system that holds the bindings that the top system is reasoning on, and it is only a hybrid system like this that can begin to explain the sorts of effect that mental models theory sets out to explain. Indeed it is these representations which have come to be known as mental models.

It now becomes clear that mental models are not at the extreme agglomerative end of the dimension we are concerned with. The extreme end is occupied by a system like truth tables (suitably adapted to the syllogisms' monadic predicate logic) which considers all possible models of the premisses, one at a time, and checks that they are models of a possible conclusion. There are 2^7-1 models (combinations with or without each of the seven types of individual), and so the "truth table" would have 127 rows of seven entries, each row corresponding to a model – a single truly agglomerated representation of the logical system. Even the most agglomerative graphical systems for reasoning abstract away from this extreme system in various ways.

Several devices in mental models notation allow abstraction over models and move mental models notation away from the agglomerative extreme. These include parenthesized elements and the handling of negation. As is usual with representational issues, one has to be careful to take into account the procedures which access and transform the representations. This can be brought out against the background of a general correspondence between columns of letters in mental models notation and types of individual.[7] Collections of columns therefore generally refer to collections of types of individual. This simple correspondence breaks down for four reasons:

1. The "closed world assumptions" under which mental models are interpreted: what is noted is mainly what is known to exist (but see below), and, for the purposes of inference, it is assumed that that is all that exists.

2. The negation notation in mental models allows several individual types to be represented by one column, at least during some stages of representation construction. So for example, c a b represents either an A which is not B, a non-A which is B, or both (see Inder, 1986, for a formulation of a "mental models" notation which avoids this somewhat idiosyncratic treatment of negation and fits the psychological data).

3. Parenthesized elements represent types of individual which are consistent with premises but not entailed to exist. Although the parentheses appear with only one letter, they apply to the individual represented by the whole column. Parentheses thus allow several models (with or without the individual-type represented by the parenthesized column) to be packed into one mental model representation. (See Stenning and Oberlander, 1991b, for a fuller discussion of abstraction over graphically represented models by such conventions, and Stenning and Oberlander, 1991a, for a discussion of the relation of mental models to graphical methods.)

4. Finally, the choice of representations for statement-types and the strategies for constructing models have the effect of cutting down the search space considered when compared to the extreme agglomerative method's search of 127 models. These strategies are analogues of theorem-proving strategies in the calculus: one of the most important tasks for a natural deduction theorem-prover is choice of assumptions, and this corresponds to choice of initial models to represent.

Mental models may not be at the extreme agglomerative end of representational strategies, but they are still quite far up that end when compared with natural deduction systems. Each mental model diagram carries a large amount of detail compared with each statement of the calculus. Of course, there is an issue here of how one counts "representations". Although calculus statements generally carry less information than mental models diagrams, there are generally more statements in proofs than there are models in a reasoning sequence. Natural deduction systems smear out the few diagrams into many statements and then generally prune the logically (though not psychologically) redundant assumptions. Figure 3.3, repeated here from Stenning (1991), illustrates this point by comparing an Euler's circle representation, a mental model representation and a proof of a syllogism in a natural deduction system.

Psychologically, the important point is that the strong claim in mental models theory, implicit in the graphical methods, and explained by the proposed constraint satisfaction implementation, is that a whole model, but only one model at a time, is represented in the process of reasoning. This is what gives empirical substance to the claim that human reasoning is agglomerative. This claim can be equally well expressed, at the level of notations, in a calculus, Euler's circles or mental models, but to become an empirical claim it must be backed by a strong theory of representation which distinguishes the notations (at least the agglomerative ones from the analytic ones).

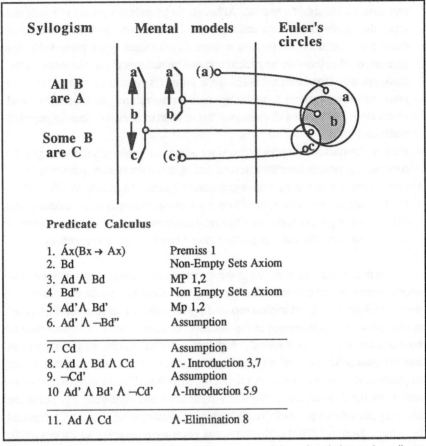

Figure 3.3 All B are A, some B are C, in mental models, euler circles and predicate calculus notations.

3.4 Conclusions

In the sense in which computational processing can be semantic, one cannot distinguish semantic and syntactic processes which implement decidable logics. If we are to give a computational account of human reasoning (and Johnson-Laird, 1983, insists we are), then even when giving accounts of reasoning within undecidable systems (such as polyadic first-order predicate calculus) we can only give accounts of decidable subsets, so even with undecidable systems, this argument bites just as deep (see Byrne and Johnson-Laird, 1990, for an attempt to diffuse these criticisms by moving to such systems).[8]

Some psychologists respond to these criticisms of mental models theory by suggesting that they may be of interest to logicians but are of no consequence to psychologists. The truth is the reverse. The important empirical distinctions are between different implementations of logics in human memory. These implementations may be very different than conventional machine implementations because human memory is very different from machine memory. The psychological study of reasoning in a computational framework cannot avoid centring on an account of memory implementation. Computations are defined in terms of memories and transformations on them. Not very much of existing memory theory is of help because it does not directly address knowledge representation issues such as attribute binding. Nevertheless, the important explanations of why we adopt the strategies we do, have to involve "low-level" accounts of how knowledge representation problems such as attribute binding are solved in human memory, and will require a new generation of memory theories. Recasting the problem as a problem of implementation has the further benefit for psychologists that it connects the study of human reasoning with the computational literature on logic programming. This literature at least makes it obvious that one can only implement limited subsets of logic, even if the subsets implementable on conventional machines are very different from those implementable in human memory. Even though there are large architectural differences between humans and conventional machines, this literature provides much general information about what aspects of logic are hard to implement, the efforts at parallel implementations being particularly interesting psychologically.

We have argued that using the concept of a mental model which is supposed to be distinct from a logical model has lead to confusion, and that this usage should be replaced by talk of psychological theories of how logics (and logical models) are implemented in human processes. This still leaves the term mental model available for the sort of extended analogies which people adopt in order to understand computers. I believe that in this latter usage, the term has a useful role to play.

It will not have escaped the attentive reader that this second concept of an extended analogy is operative in the use of the "mental models" systems we have been discussing which take their name from the first use. This is made most clear when an Euler's circle formulation of mental models notation is chosen, though Johnson-Laird's own discussion of how his diagrams are to be construed also talks of them as *analogical* representations. Circles are analogous to sets, and overlap of circles is analogous to the intersection of sets. Movements of circles are therefore analogous to sequences of overlappings. Sequences of overlappings are interpreted as disjunctions of cases. Thus concrete spatial and temporal relations are interpreted as abstract set-theoretic and logical concepts. The difference between the analogical components of systems like Euler's circles and the analogies used in HCI lies in how far the analogies can be taken (always the operative question with analogies). With Euler's circles one can specify exactly which aspects of the geometry of circles do not transfer: for example, absolute area and shape are not relevant. The closed curves must be interpretable as expandable, contractible and indeed distortable in order to capture the logic of sets. Even when this precise definition of the correspondence and non-correspondence of the vehicle and the cargo of an analogy can be laid down, the analogy may still play a crucial role in processing at the level of implementation. We have tried to establish just such an example here with syllogistic reasoning. If one has special apparatus, perhaps of perceptual origin, for processing two-dimensional representations, the analogy however explicitly formulated in logical terms still makes all the difference to processibility.

The moral to be drawn for HCI's use of "mental models" is perhaps that as long as the term is used for high-level analogies present in long-term knowledge or belief about correspondences between domains, little difficulty may result. When theories approach the stage at which computations over representations of these correspondences have to be specified in enough detail to be implemented in a fully specified computational process, then more caution is required – but then when that much progress has been made, we may expect to be in a rather good position to exercise such caution.

Notes

1. The support of the Economic and Social Research Council UK (ESRC) is gratefully acknowledged. The work was part of the research programme of the ESRC funded Human Communication Research Centre (HCRC).
2. For a historical discussion of the differentiation of these two approaches which is most revealing for cognitive scientists seeking an understanding of the conceptual relations between the theories, see van Heijenoort (1967).
3. Some psychologists resist the idea that their theories should be computational (notably Gibsonians), but I think that best sense can be made of such claims by interpreting them as rejecting particular types of computational architecture. In the very most general sense of computation which is at stake here, it is difficult to escape the notion that at least theories of reasoning are ultimately to be couched in

computational terms. In fact, the point of making the current argument is that by separating implementation of theorem-prover from specification of logic, one opens up the field to proposals for unconventional implementations like those Gibsonians have done much to support.

4. Monadic predicate logic has one-place predicates, but no relations relating pairs, triples or greater n-tuples of arguments. The latter only occur in polyadic predicate calculus. This divide is important in separating decidable from undecidable systems.

5. Barry Richards originally pointed this out to me.

6. This property of monadic predicate calculus is at the heart of the reason that it is a decidable system.

7. References to mental models notation will be to Johnson-Laird and Steedman (1978). The same observations, with minor adjustments for changes in notation, apply to other formulations.

8. Observe that almost the whole of the literature on logic programming, which attempts to implement fragments of polyadic first-order predicate calculus, is about one decidable fragment, namely Horn-clauses.

References

Braine, M.D.S. (1978). On the relationship between the natural logic of reasoning and standard logic. *Psychological Review 85*, 1–21.

Bransford, J.D. and Johnson, M. (1972). Contextual prerequisites for understanding: some investigations of comprehension and recall. *Journal of Verbal Learning and Verbal Behavior 11*, 717–726.

Byrne, R.M.J. and Johnson-Laird, P.N. (1990). Models and deductive reasoning. In Gilhooly, K.J., Keane, M.T.G., Logie, R.H. and Erdos, G. (eds), *Lines of Thinking. Volume 1*. Chichester: Wiley.

Church, A. (1936). A note on the Entscheidungsproblem. *Journal of Symbolic Logic 1*, 40–41, 101–103.

Gentner, D. and Stevens, A.L. (eds) (1983), *Mental Models*. Hillsdale, NJ: LEA.

Godel, K. (1931). Uber Formal Unentscheidbare Satze der Principia Mathematica und Verwandter Systeme, I. *Monatshefte fur Mathematik und Physik 38*, 173–198.

Inder, R. (1986). *The computer simulation of syllogism solving using restricted mental models*. PhD thesis, Centre for Cognitive Science, Edinburgh University.

Johnson-Laird, P.N. (1983). *Mental Models*. Cambridge: CUP.

Johnson-Laird, P.N. and Steedman, M.J. (1978). The psychology of syllogisms. *Cognitive Psychology 10*, 64–99.

Lee, J. (1987). *Metalogic and the Psychology of Reasoning*. PhD thesis, Centre for Cognitive Science, Edinburgh University.

Stenning, K. (1978). Anaphora as an approach to pragmatics. In Halle, M., Bresnan, J. and Miller, G.A. (eds) *Linguistic Theory and Psychological Reality*. Cambridge, Ma.: MIT Press.

Stenning, K. (1991). Modelling memory for models. In Ezquerro, J. and Larrazabal, J.M. (eds) *First International Colloquium on Cognitive Science*. Universidad del Pais Vasco. San Sebastian: Kluwer.

Stenning, K. and Oberlander, J. (1991a). *A cognitive theory of graphical and linguistic reasoning: logic and implementation*. Research Paper 20. HCRC, University of Edinburgh.

Stenning, K. and Oberlander, J. (1991b). Reasoning with words, pictures and calculi: computation vs. justification. In Barwise, J., Gawron, J.M., Plotkin, G. and Tutiya, S. (eds) *Second International Conference on Situation Theory and its Applications*. Kinloch Rannoch, Scotland, September 1990, Stanford: CSLI.

Stenning, K., Shepherd, M. and Levy, J. (1988). On the construction of representations for individuals from descriptions in text. *Language and Cognitive Processes 2*, 129–164.

Stenning, K. and Levy, J. (1988). Knowledge-rich solutions to the "binding problem": some human computational mechanisms. *Knowledge Based Systems 1*, 143–152.

Tarski, A. (1932). The concept of truth in formalized languages. In *Logic, Semantics, Metamathematics*. San Francisco: University of California Press.

Tulving, E. (1983). *Elements of Episodic Memory*. New York: Oxford University Press.

van Heijenoort, J. (1967). Logic as calculus and logic as language. *Synthese 17*, 324–330.

Chapter 4

The Logic of Logic

Andrew Rutherford

In Chapters 2 and 3, the notion of mental models is applied to the performance of logical problems. Here the term logic is used to connote reasoning in general, as well as the style of validated reasoning employed by logicians. As might be expected, the description of people's performance of formal logic in terms of mental models has developed almost exclusively in academic (as opposed to applied) psychology, with the impetus provided by Johnson-Laird. This particular focus is slightly ironic given Johnson-Laird's attribution of the conception to Craik (1943), who developed the notion in his applied work. Although Johnson-Laird (1983) states that the theory of mental models gives account of many aspects of mental life, such as semantics, comprehension and discourse, by far the largest amount of research developing and examining mental models theory has concerned deductive inference. Although consideration of logic problems with formal solutions may appear a rather dry enterprise, with apparently little relation to most of mental life, its study does provide unique theoretical advantages. Such logical problems are unlike many "real life" reasoning problems in having unequivocal solutions (cf. Manktelow and Over, this volume). Also, as logic has been studied and documented at least from the time of Aristotle, there is a considerable literature on the topic and so it might be thought, a considerable understanding of logic available to be tapped. Indeed, the two accounts presented by Byrne and Stenning illustrate the use of the cumulative knowledge of logic. Moreover, the important differences between these accounts reflects the difficulties of achieving a clear understanding of a well defined issue and forewarns of the theoretical hazards that may lurk in less prescribed areas.

In her chapter, Byrne reviews the mental model theory and formal rule accounts of propositional, relational and quantificational inference and much of the

MODELS IN THE MIND:
Theory, perspective and applications. ISBN 0-12-592970-6

experimental work she has performed to examine the adequacy of these accounts. Two major lines of argument are employed to support mental models theory in the comparison of deductive reasoning accounts. The first is that mental models theory is able to accommodate the empirical phenomenon of content-sensitivity in reasoning, as semantic procedures construct and manipulate mental models. Certainly, content-sensitivity is a difficult effect for formal rule theories to accommodate. Similarly, it is difficult for the particular schema account considered by Byrne, although alternative schema based theories seem able to accommodate this phenomenon (Rumelhart, 1980).

The common denominator of numerous schema theories is a conceptual framework that provides a basis for the implementation of sets or packages of organized processes. It is difficult to conceive of any processing account that will not need to be placed in the context of some such system. Although there have been notable attempts to specify the intra- and inter-organization of schemata (e.g. Norman and Bobrow, 1979; Rumelhart, 1980; Rumelhart, 1989; Rumelhart, Smolensky, McClelland and Hinton, 1986), most information-processing characterizations may be interpreted in this context (e.g. Johnson-Laird, 1983, p. 397–398).

Returning to the issue of content-sensitivity, it seems that mental models access the relevant world knowledge through the semantic procedures that construct and manipulate mental models. Unfortunately however, in mental models theory there is little description of such procedural semantics and certainly, there is no description of how such world knowledge exerts an effect. So, while mental models theory holds the promise of such an account, unfortunately it does not deliver it. Moreover, if the mental models notation is considered, it is difficult to see how such representations could incorporate particular and specific types of content information, without recourse to methods similar to those required by formal rule accounts (Rips, 1986).

The other major argument presented to support mental models theory is that it predicts correctly the relative difficulty of deductive inference problems. Difficulty is assessed by comparing two problems (A and B) in terms of the number of steps involved in formal rule account solutions of problems, with the number of mental models required to solve each of the same two problems. An experimental test is obtained by defining two problems where the formal rule account claims problem B to be most difficult and mental models theory claims problem A to be most difficult.

As the experimental results concord with the predictions of the theory of mental models, at the expense of the alternative accounts, Byrne's view that people make such deductions by manipulating mental models seems to have been corroborated. However, the analysis and description of logic provided by Stenning throws a spanner into the works of this eloquent hypothetico-deductive account.

The theory of mental models is based heavily on model-theoretic logic, particularly that employed by Montague (1974) to address semantics. However, Stenning emphasizes the difference between abstract specifications of what constitutes logic and the computational mechanisms that implement logic. The obvious parallel here is with Marr's (1982) separation of computational theory (what), and representation and algorithm (how). Stenning argues that while model-theoretic logic provides an abstract specification of what constitutes the relation of semantic consequence, it does not describe the computational mechanism necessary to do the logic. Similarly, while proof-theoretic logic (i.e. formal rule accounts) provides syntactic expression, again it is an abstract specification and does not describe a computational mechanism that could implement the logic. Stenning argues that the important psychological issue is how logic is implemented. Psychological claims based on logics expressed in model- or proof-theoretic terms of abstraction are misplaced because it is the nature of the implementation that has psychological consequence. A major result of this aspect of the account is that both mental model and formal rule theorists' claims of relative psychological difficulty based on comparisons of abstract model- or proof-theoretic logics are invalidated.

As operations on representations are carried out only on the basis of their physical nature, in a fundamental sense all computation is syntactic. Therefore, it is necessary to specify how, rather than just state that, some processing is considered properly as semantic. A distinction between levels of syntactic computation may provide a sense of syntactic and semantic processing. If computation occurs at a meta-language level (i.e. it is about the system), rather than at an object level (i.e. within the system), the term semantic might be used in its description. Nevertheless, for the decidable systems examined (and for the decidable fragments of undecidable systems), any implementation of model theory can be mirrored always by the proof-theory implementation. As any result could be the product of either implementation, still it will not be possible to distinguish between the latter sense of semantic and syntactic.

Stenning suggests that an empirical distinction between agglomerative and analytic styles of logic implementation may lie at the heart of the intuitive claim that semantic processes construct and manipulate mental models. With an agglomerative style of implementation, one representation is constructed to contain all (theorem) information appreciated. In contrast, with an analytic style of implementation, all the appreciated (theorem) information represented is separated out in a chain of proof rules. Agglomerative strategies may have been confused with semantic methods due to the similarity of agglomerative implementations to truth table representations, which often are used with model theory.

Stenning argues that agglomerative and analytic strategies are at opposite ends of a continuum. Originally, people may favour agglomerative strategies, but with practise and/or instruction, the advantages of an analytic strategy may be realized. However, it is possible that agglomerative and analytic strategies may differ in terms of the representational level at which they operate, with some "agglomeration" underlying some of the proof rules. Special processing apparatus of perceptual origin is speculated as the underlying reason for the natural propensity of agglomerative reasoning strategies. However, if this special processing apparatus was of perceptual origin, surely processing three-dimensional arrays, rather than two-dimensional arrays as suggested by Stenning, would be its forte. Another interesting issue is the extent to which agglomerative implementations entail or obtain advantage from intrinsic representational formats (Palmer, 1978). Intrinsic representations appear to concord with the representational aspect claimed of mental models, which is the maintenance of the relation-structure of the target entity.

Stenning claims that a basic requirement for implementing an agglomerative style of reasoning is a memory system that can maintain collections of types of individuals. Individuals are defined by their attributes and so what is needed is a memory system that is able to bind attributes to individuals. Of course, this is a trivial problem for conventional computing, but Stenning is attempting to provide a system that reflects human memory. Consequently, he opts for a PDP system in which to implement the agglomerative reasoning strategy.

Binding attributes to individuals is considered a high-level result based on low-level (PDP) operations. Stenning claims that such a hierarchy is necessary to distinguish between syntax and semantics: the low-level operations map the properties to individuals resulting in a representation that is interpretable semantically.

While this sort of system provides account of a number of reasoning phenomena, such as the difficulty of contemplating different possibilities simultaneously, also it offers an account of content-sensitivity. Stenning suggests that a complete PDP system would enable bindings to operate over world knowledge. Nevertheless, like the mental models account of content-sensitivity, primarily it is speculation.

Interestingly, given the initial degree of difference between the two accounts, the system described by Stenning provides at its top level a "screen" representation, which to a large extent concords with the notion of mental models presented by Byrne. However, Stenning's account makes it very clear that perhaps the most sophisticated part of a mental model system: the procedures that manipulate these representations and derive conclusions, remains to be specified. The theory and notation of mental models has been criticized for omitting this aspect from the account (e.g. Ford, 1985; Rips, 1986), but such criticism is disarmed if mental models, like Euler's circles, are taken as abstract specifications of what has to be represented and not how it is to be implemented.

The final topic addressed by both authors is the relationship between the sorts of model considered in this section and the mental models conceived in human-computer interaction (HCI) and human–machine systems (HMS). Keane, Byrne and Gentner (1991) suggest that the latter sort of mental model notion should be termed BBN models, as they were developed at Bolt, Berenek and Newman (BBN) Laboratories. However, while this terminology may be a boon to the BBN marketing department, it is probably of some chagrin to the workers from several Universities and particularly the commercial managers of Rank Xerox, who might feel they had a significant hand in the development of this mental model conception.

One of the major differences between the two sorts of mental model would appear to be the claims made for the representations they employ. While Johnson-Laird makes psychological claims concerning the maintenance of the relation-structure of the states of affairs represented, generally the mental model notions developed in HCI and HMS make weaker claims regarding the concordance between psychological representations and the representational formats employed in the hypothesized mental models.

On the representational issue, Stenning considers HCI (and presumably HMS) mental models solely as extended analogies. Briefly, he points out that the analogy employed to describe an entity can exert influence on the form of the computational account. Therefore, prior to implementing a computational account of an HCI or HMS mental model that makes strong psychological claims, the extent and nature of the analogy correspondence should be well understood.

A survey of the Byrne and Stenning chapters suggests that rather than presenting contradictory accounts, together they can provide a refined theoretical account and an empirical account of part of deductive reasoning. Yet, it seems that non-speculative process characterizations of empirical phenomena, such as content-sensitivity, continue to be elusive.

References

Craik, K.J.W. (1943). *The Nature of Explanation*. Cambridge: CUP.

Ford, M. (1985). Review: *Mental Models* by P.N. Johnson-Laird. *Language 41*, 897–903.

Johnson-Laird, P.N. (1983). *Mental Models*. Cambridge: CUP.

Keane, M.T.G., Byrne, R.M.J. and Gentner, D. (1991). *Mental models: two views*. Unpublished manuscript. Department. of Computer Science, Trinity College, Dublin.

Marr, D. (1982). *Vision*. San Francisco, Ca.: Freeman.

Montague, R. (1974). *Formal Philosophy: Selected Papers*. New Haven: Yale University Press.

Norman, D.A. and Bobrow, D.G. (1979). Descriptions: an intermediate stage in memory retrieval. *Cognitive Psychology 11*, 107-123.

Palmer, S.E. (1978). Fundamental aspects of cognitive representation. In Rosch, E. and Lloyd, B.B. (eds) *Cognition and Categorization*. Hillsdale, NJ: LEA.

Rips, L. (1986). Mental muddles. In Brand, M. and Harnish, R.M. (eds) *The Representation of Knowledge and Belief*. Tuscon: University of Arizona Press.

Rumelhart, D.E. (1980). Schemata: the building blocks of cognition. In Spiro, R., Bruce, B. and Brewer, W. (eds) *Theoretical Issues in Reading Comprehension*. Hillsdale, NJ.: LEA.

Rumelhart, D.E. (1989). Toward a microstructural account of human reasoning. In Vosniadou, S. and Ortony, A. (eds) *Similarity and Analogical Reasoning*. Cambridge, Ma.: CUP.

Rumelhart, D.E., Smolensky, P., McClelland, J.L. and Hinton, G.E. (1986) . Schemata and sequential thought processes in PDP models. In McClelland, J.L., Rumelhart, D.E. and the PDP Research Group, *Parallel Distributed Processing. Volume 2. Psychological and Biological Models*. Cambridge, Ma.: MIT Press.

Part 2

**Distributed Models
and Representations**

Chapter 5

Mental Models of Motion

Tony Anderson, Andrew Tolmie, Christine Howe, Terry Mayes and Mhairi Mackenzie

5.1 Introduction

In a classic volume on mental models edited by Gentner and Stevens, McCloskey (1983) reviewed research which, he argued, suggested that many adults entertain misconceptions concerning force and object motion. These misconceptions relate to both the nature of the motion and its causes, and even physics undergraduates have been shown not to be immune to such problems (e.g. McCloskey, 1983; McCloskey, Caramazza and Green, 1980). Essentially, McCloskey claims that subjects possess a coherent, but mistaken theory of the phenomena related to object motion, which has both explanatory and predictive value in common with the definitions of mental models (cf. Johnson-Laird, 1983).

McCloskey bases his claims on empirical evidence derived from experiments in which he presented subjects with a variety of dynamics problems in which they were asked to predict the path followed by moving objects under various conditions. For example, subjects were given a diagram which represented a side view of a metal ball sliding horizontally along the top of a cliff towards its edge, and were requested to draw the path the ball would follow after it went over the edge, ignoring air resistance (see Figure 5.1).

McCloskey found that the majority of the subjects' predictions were erroneous. In this example, Newtonian physics predicts (and strobe photography establishes) that the ball would fall through a perfect parabola; the path is parabolic as the result of uniform forward velocity interacting with accelerating vertical velocity. Most subjects, however, claimed that the ball would start with some forward motion and end its trajectory by falling vertically downward. Some subjects even claimed that the ball would initially travel in a horizontal path upon

MODELS IN THE MIND:
Theory, perspective and applications. ISBN 0–12–592970–6

leaving the cliff edge, with *no* initial downward component to the motion, until gravity took over and a straight downward path ensued.

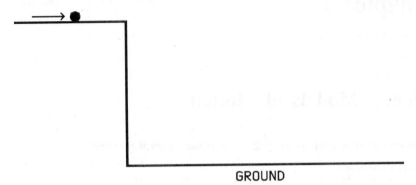

GROUND

Figure 5.1 An example of the type of problem presented by McCloskey to his subjects. The diagram shows a metal ball sliding along a (frictionless) clifftop, and the subject's task is to predict its motion after it slides over the edge of the clifftop by drawing the path that the ball will fall through until it hits the ground. Adapted from McCloskey (1983).

In addition to drawing the paths of objects in the various problems, the subjects were interviewed to obtain explanations for their predictions. The errors in subjects' predictions, and their associated explanations, imply (according to McCloskey) that "people develop on the basis of their everyday experience remarkably well-articulated naive theories of motion" (p.299). He claimed that the theories were remarkably consistent across individuals and resembled the pre-Newtonian impetus theory of motion. In the above example, this theory would predict that the ball, on leaving the cliff top, still contains (somehow) an impetus force which has to dissipate or be expended before gravity can exert its influence and pull the ball downward. Hence two types of path could result: either an initial curve downwards (as impetus and gravity interact) followed by a vertical segment (as gravity takes over), or a "straight out, straight down" path. These two possibilities indicate that subtle variations of a generic impetus theory are possible.

McCloskey's claim, however, that a naive impetus theory consistently underlies subjects' responses can certainly be challenged. In the first place, across the problems for which he presents data (McCloskey, 1983), impetus-based errors account for a highly variable proportion of responses across an undergraduate sample, ranging from 51% to 26%. Moreover, in one problem which was used (a ball falling from an aeroplane), the most common error (i.e. a vertical path) seems to be contrary to the predictions of an impetus theory.

Kaiser, Jonides and Alexander (1986) investigated a variation on the kind of force and motion problems used by McCloskey. They presented circular motion problems, with two different types of content: abstract (like McCloskey's problem of a ball being shot round a spiral tube) and familiar (such as water flowing round a coiled hosepipe). The task was to predict and explain the subsequent path of the object's motion after leaving the curved tube. It was found that familiar problems were more likely to be answered correctly, and that there was no tendency for subjects to transfer their learning from the familiar to the abstract task, the subjects citing any of a number of irrelevant reasons why the two problem types should be distinguished. This superiority of a concrete and familiar version of a task over an abstract version of the same task accords well with studies on reasoning. A good example of this phenomenon is Wason's (1966) selection task. Johnson-Laird, Legrenzi and Legrenzi (1972) found that a concrete and familiar version of this task was solved more frequently than the abstract version, despite being formally identical. Evans (1982) argues that the solution in the "concrete" case is not in fact reasoned out, but is instead directly derived from experience. Kaiser et al claim that the same is true for their physics problems. If the problem content is familiar, the subjects obtain the correct answer by reference to their experience of the world. If the problem content is unfamiliar, subjects bring their knowledge (or mis-conceptions) of physics into play, and derive a solution based on their impetus theory. Thus, there is evidence that the "naive theories" posited by McCloskey are somewhat limited in their application in practice.

An alternative view of subjects' conceptions of dynamics phenomena was articulated by diSessa (1988) in a paper aptly entitled "Knowledge in pieces". diSessa's basic claim is that intuitive physics is "a fragmented collection of ideas, loosely connected and reinforcing (and) having none of the commitment or systematicity that one attributes to theories" (p.50). Rather than a single, well-integrated impetus theory, subjects instead possess a set of *phenomenological primitives* or "p-prims", which are direct abstractions from experience, are primitive in the sense that they neither require nor provide any explanation, and are fragmented rather than well-integrated. For example, *force as a mover* is a p-prim: it is an abstraction from the act of throwing an object, and involves a directed impetus, a rapid pattern of effort followed by release of the object, and a result in the same direction as the impetus. diSessa posits that subjects possess several such primitive notions, and argues that different physics problems will invoke different sets of p-prims for the subject, and as a result, impetus-based responses will be given for some problems (those in which p-prims involving notions of impetus are invoked) but not for others. Thus in diSessa's account there is no overarching elaborated principle which subjects use to guide their responses, and it is possible for the set of primitives considered to vary from problem to problem.

We undertook a study in which we developed a set of paper-and-pencil problems similar to those used by McCloskey. We systematically varied both the mass of the object (having objects of relatively high mass or of relatively low mass) in the problem, and its initial forward velocity (which could also be either relatively high or relatively low), in all possible combinations, in each of linear, circular and pendular motion.

If McCloskey is correct in arguing that the erroneous trajectories (i.e. predictive responses) drawn by subjects when presented with these problems stem from coherent but mistaken theories or models of the causal factors involved, then individuals' predictive responses should tend to show characteristics which recur across specific problems, since these would derive from more general explanatory models. In particular, if a single, consistent naive impetus theory is held by a particular individual, then impetus theory-based responses should consistently be given regardless of the problem characteristics (high versus low forward velocity of the object, etc.).

If, on the other hand, diSessa's view is correct, subjects' predictive responses should be less consistent. Both mass and initial velocity have little or no bearing on the problem (e.g. free fall under horizontal linear motion results in a parabolically-shaped path regardless of whether the object involved is light or heavy, or is travelling rapidly or slowly – although this latter variable would influence whether a wide or a tight parabola resulted). However, the subjects' responses would be likely to vary as a function of these variables if there were no coherent underlying theory to aid prediction generation, but instead different combinations of p-prims were invoked with a corresponding variation in the salience of impetus.

In particular, it was hypothesized that certain combinations of mass and velocity would affect subjects' predictions in the following way: high mass and low forward velocity would render salient the vertical component of the free-fall motion, causing subjects to erroneously claim that the object would fall downwards vertically. Low mass and high forward velocity (e.g. a bullet being fired from a gun), on the other hand, would render forward motion more salient than vertical, resulting in the classic "impetus theory" response in which the object continues in a straight horizontal line for some distance, before gravity takes over and it then falls to hit the ground. If mass and velocity were commensurately great (either both high or both low in value), then they should be equally salient to the subjects and a more correct response (a forward parabola or some approximation to it) would result.

Furthermore, if predictive responses are based on p-prims, then they would not necessarily be related to any *explanation* of the object path provided by the subject; the latter could exist separately as more formalized but distinct knowledge.

5.2 The experiment

The sixteen problems we used involved the free fall of objects in independent linear (e.g. a ball rolling over a cliff edge), dependent linear (e.g. an aircraft dropping a crate of emergency food supplies), circular (e.g., a seat falling from a fairground Ferris wheel whilst it is rotating) or pendular (e.g. a conker falling off the end of a string whilst it is being swung) motion, with both the mass of the object involved and its initial velocity systematically manipulated. We presented these problems to 180 secondary school children aged between 12 and 15 years. Subjects completed individual booklets where for each problem they were requested to draw the path that they thought the object, already in motion, would follow under conditions of free fall. Unlike McCloskey's (1983) study, subjects were given no instructions with regard to the influence of air resistance. A further four items asked subjects to reflect on one specific problem for each of the four types of initial object motion, to attempt to identify and label the factors that would influence the path followed by the object, and to illustrate (via a force diagram) the direction in which these factors would cause the object to move, when taken independently.

Subjects' predictive responses to each problem were scored on two independent scales, one for the initial direction of the predicted motion and the other for the shape of the path. In both cases, the scoring scale was constructed by arranging the criterial features of a fully accurate response into a graded series. The subjects' responses were assigned a level or score on both dimensions according to the highest criterion that they met; a pass at a given level logically implied a pass at all lower levels. The subjects' responses to each problem were assigned a score between 0 and 3 according to the accuracy of the initial direction of the trajectory they had drawn (see Table 5.1 for details of the scoring scheme). Subjects' responses were likewise assigned a score on the second scale between 0 and 5 depending on the extent to which the trajectory drawn corresponded to the correct parabolic shape (see Table 5.2).

Responses to the four explanatory items were each scored on a scale from 0 to 6 according to whether the three relevant factors (initial velocity, gravity, and air resistance) had been differentiated, and whether these were shown as acting in the appropriate direction. Details of the scoring scheme are set out in Table 5.3.

Dimension 1: Initial direction.

SCORE	Corresponding criterial feature.
0	No non-vertical component illustrated, or no response given.
1	A non-vertical component is present.
2	The initial direction of motion is correct in general, i.e. within the correct quadrant.
3	The initial direction of motion is correct to within a few degrees.

Table 5.1 Details of the scoring system used for grading the initial direction component of the subjects' predictions.

Dimension 2: Shape of path.

SCORE	Corresponding criterial feature.
0	No non-vertical component is shown, or no response given.
1	A non-vertical component is present.
2	Both vertical and non-vertical components are interpretable as linear in nature, i.e. there is no path which can be accounted for only by a non-linear component or additional forces.
3	Vertical and non-vertical components interact as linear elements of a vector, i.e. they are not successive, either wholly or partially.
4	The vertical and non-vertical components are illustrated as exhibiting continuous change in their magnitude, i.e. there is no section in which both are effectively treated as constant; the path is a continuous curve.
5	Both vertical and non-vertical components show appropriate change in their magnitude, i.e. the magnitude of the non-vertical component decreases, and that of the vertical increases; the paths of the appropriate parabolic shape.

Table 5.2 Details of the scoring system used for grading the shape of path component of the subjects' predictions.

Response classification

SCORE   Corresponding criterial feature.

0   No response *or* no differentiation of factors other than in vague and non-explanatory terms.

1   No relevant factors differentiated.

2   Mixture of relevant *and* irrelevant factors.

3   One of the two main relevant factors (i.e. gravity and initial velocity, with or without wind resistance.

4   Both main relevant factors, with or without wind resistance, but not both shown as acting appropriately.

5   Both main relevant factors, shown as acting appropriately, either without wind resistance or with wind resistance not acting appropriately.

6   All three factors of importance, shown as acting appropriately.

Table 5.3 Scoring scheme for subjects' explanatory responses. Responses were scored according to the level of verbal explanation as well as to the diagrammatic representation of this explanation. Solutions to each problem were assigned a score between 0 and 6 according to the highest criterion that they met and a pass at a given level implied a pass at all lower levels of response.

The pattern of data obtained suggested that subjects' responses *are* affected by the salient physical characteristics of the problem rather than being the product of a single underlying unified "theory". There were statistically significant main effects of mass and velocity (massed together as a four-level factor) on the initial direction ($F_{(3, 522)} = 38.04$, $p < 0.001$) and also on the shape of path ($F_{(3, 522)} = 24.76$, $p < 0.001$) components of subjects' predictions (see Table 5.4).

Across all problem types, the subjects were likely to give a more accurate response if the mass/velocity variables were either both small in value or both large in value. If, on the other hand, one variable was high in value and simultaneously the other was low, the subjects were likely to give a less accurate response. This pattern is clearest in the case of the shape of path scores (see Table 5.4).

Note also that high velocity/low mass objects (e.g. the bullet fired from a gun) have higher scores on the initial direction dimension than the high mass/low velocity objects (e.g. the pirate treasure dropped from a galleon); this difference is statistically significant on a Dunn Multiple Comparison Test. Our scoring system for the initial direction dimension is such that impetus-based responses receive

ANDERSON ET AL

higher scores than purely vertical responses (see Table 5.1). The higher scores for high velocity/low mass objects than for low velocity/high mass objects suggests that the former are more frequently associated with impetus-based errors than are the latter, as predicted. However, these scores are mean values, and a potential difficulty is that the mean of a set of scores can, depending on their distribution, take a value which does not truly reflect the central tendency of the data.

Results

(i) Initial direction

		MASS		
		HIGH	LOW	MEAN
	HIGH	1.87^b	1.90^b	1.88
VELOCITY	LOW	1.75^c	2.13^a	1.94
	MEAN	1.81	2.01	1.91

(ii) Shape of path

		MASS		
		HIGH	LOW	MEAN
	HIGH	2.69^b	2.53^{bc}	2.61
VELOCITY	LOW	2.41^c	2.92^a	2.66
	MEAN	2.55	2.72	2.63

Table 5.4 The table show mean scores for all subjects across all problem categories (simple linear, disguised linear, circular and pendular) for each of the possible mass/velocity combinations, for both initial direction and shape of path scores. Scores with differing superscripts are significantly different.

We therefore undertook a separate analysis which involved categorizing the subjects' predictions as either possessing an initial horizontal component (which we predicted would be the preponderant error pattern in those problems in which forward velocity is high but mass is low), or as involving a substantial vertical component (which we predicted would be preponderant in those problems where object mass was high and forward velocity was low). In some cases, a single prediction by a subject contained both types of linear component; in such cases, both would be scored. It should be stressed that strict criteria for the scoring of these data were adopted. Only cases in which the linear components were truly vertical or truly horizontal (or within an angle of 2–3 degrees of horizontal or vertical) were accepted as instances. In one problem, for example, a person skiing moves rapidly down a slope, and then reaches a short upward slope before launching into space. As a result, his initial trajectory is at an upward angle of 30 degrees or so; a true impetus-based response would be to draw a straight line pointing upward at the same angle. However, such responses would not be counted in our coding scheme. As can be appreciated, the scheme results in a conservative estimate of the prevalence of both horizontal and vertical errors, and in particular, a conservative estimate of impetus-based responses.

The data were scored as mean proportions of all subjects' responses to all problems of a given mass/velocity combination (whether of independent linear, dependent linear, circular or pendular motion) which show a substantial (i.e. greater than or equal to a third of the total path length) horizontal or vertical linear component. We had predicted that these rectilinear errors would be fewest in problems in which mass and velocity were either both high or both low. The figures averaged across all of these problems (i.e. both high mass/high velocity and low mass/low velocity) are: horizontal linear errors occur in 3.5% of all problems on average, and vertical linear errors occur in 8% of all problems. We had predicted that vertical linear components would be more preponderant in the case of high mass/low forward velocity problems. The relevant figures are: vertical errors occur in 19% of such problems, whilst horizontal errors occur in 2%. Conversely, we had predicted that horizontal linear components would be more preponderant in the case of low mass/high forward velocity problems. The relevant figures for such problems are: vertical errors – 8%, horizontal errors – 14%. The correspondence between our predictions and these results is striking. The results confirm that our interpretation of the ANOVA results (that the higher initial direction scores for the high velocity/low mass objects compared to those of the low velocity/high mass objects are due to a greater preponderance of impetus-based errors in the former case) is correct. The figures are not due to a statistical artifice of using the mean. These results are, we would claim, more consistent with diSessa's "knowledge in pieces" account than McCloskey's.

However, further analyses suggested that diSessa's account may also be incomplete in its rejection of subjects' possession of coherent theoretical frameworks prior to the achievement of expert levels of knowledge. These analyses focused on the degree of correlation across problems between subjects' scores on firstly, their initial direction scores, secondly, their shape of path scores, and thirdly, their explanation level. Across the sixteen items for which predictive responses were made the mean inter-item correlation for scores on initial direction was 0.10, and for scores on shape of path it was 0.12, giving further evidence for a lack of consistency between subjects' predictive responses to different problems. In contrast, though, the mean inter-item correlation between subjects' explanation scores across the four relevant problems was 0.73, suggesting considerable consistency on this element of the task. The apparent contradiction of a lack of correlation between predictive responses and yet a high correlation between explanatory responses is clarified by an examination of the relationships between subjects' predictive and explanatory scores within specific problems. Within each of the four problems to which subjects made both predictive and explanatory responses there were in all cases significant positive correlations, ranging from 0.14 to 0.46, between scores on initial direction and shape of path, but in no case were scores on either predictive dimension significantly correlated with explanation scores (non-significant correlations of the order of 0.03 –0.08 being typical).

5.3 Discussion

The results from the ANOVA clearly suggest that mass and velocity do have significant effects on the subjects' responses to these problems. The results of the correlational analyses suggest that subjects' predictive and explanatory responses tapped independent knowledge stores. Elements of predictive responses to the same item appeared to be coordinated, but context-specific in terms of their degree of accuracy, implying that subjects made a series of low-level interpretations varying according to knowledge of the salient observable features. Explanatory responses did suggest the existence of models which generalized across problem type, but contrary to McCloskey's position, these models appeared to have little influence on predictive responses, at least at the (novice) levels of performance dealt with here. The implication is that predictive and explanatory knowledge can develop separately, although it might be supposed that ultimately their coordination would be a prerequisite for the attainment of expert levels of performance. Explanations rely on intuitive knowledge in the form of theories or models (as described by McCloskey), whereas predictions rely on a reconciliation of the principles in the model and the specific diSessa-type knowledge based on experience. In some cases, of course, only the knowledge from experience need be used to generate a prediction. A good example of this occurred whilst we were developing the set of problems used in the present experiment. Among the original

23 candidate problems which were pilot tested (some of which were not selected for use in the present study) was one in which subjects had to predict the trajectory of water going over a waterfall. More than 80% of all subjects correctly answered this problem, and high proportions of even the youngest children gave correct responses. Two reasons could account for this: firstly, subjects are more likely to have seen a waterfall than any of the situations in the other problems presented to them, and secondly, water, being a fluid, traces a path as it falls in a way that discrete objects do not. For both of these reasons, subjects are likely to have had experience of the problem content, and thus need only utilize that experience to generate an accurate prediction, in the manner described by Kaiser et al (1986). Generation of an explanation, however, would be a different matter.

Overall, our data indicate that there is an element of truth in both McCloskey's and diSessa's accounts. Of course, it could be argued that there are methodological difficulties with paper-and-pencil problems of the type used in our study. Are such items capable of tapping subjects' conceptions of physics phenomena, and if not, how best can they be tapped? It might be suggested, for example, that animation might improve subjects' scores on these problems. We have not tested this issue ourselves by directly comparing solutions from paper-and-pencil versions of a given problem with an animated counterpart. However, we would argue from other evidence that animation in itself is not enough to improve subjects' responses. The paper-and-pencil materials used in the present study were in fact a pre-test for a study on small-group peer interaction. Pairs of subjects worked together, and were presented with animated versions of the pre-test problems. At the same time, they each had their individual pre-test responses in front of them, and had to generate a joint prediction. All dyads were videotaped as they performed this task, and an examination of the videotapes revealed that working with a peer resulted in improvements in subjects' predictions, particularly if they contrasted their individual pre-test predictions and entered into discussions as to possible explanations for the phenomena. For the present purposes, it should be noted that subjects did not revise their pre-test predictions because of the animation; instead, subjects seemed happy to accept their pre-test predictions as a starting-point for jointly tackling the animated versions of the problems. What made a difference to their performance was the nature of the peer interaction that they engaged in, rather than a sudden realization brought about by the animated version of the problem that their pre-test predictions were in error.

Our data suggest that McCloskey's claims concerning naive theories of motion are weaker than he would have us believe: by examining the effect of mass and velocity on subjects' responses more systematically than he did, we obtained a diversity of subject responses which clearly undermine the notion of impetus theory, and furthermore, subjects' errors occurred in predictable patterns, patterns which his explanation would find it difficult to account for. However, there are undoubtedly other subtleties which his theory cannot satisfactorily deal with. There is evidence for this in the data from one of the problems that McCloskey himself used and that we modified and employed in the present study. The problem involved a low-flying aircraft dropping a ball (in the McCloskey version of the problem). A very common error pattern for this problem, found both by McCloskey and also in our data, is the claim by the subjects that the dropped object will fall vertically downward. McCloskey suggests that one explanation for such an error is that, because the object is carried by a moving body, it does not in itself possess impetus (only the carrying vehicle does). This explanation cannot be the whole story, because in a formally identical problem which we constructed (in which a burgee falls from the top of the mast of a slow-moving yacht), such "vertical" errors are outnumbered four to one by horizontal errors (which are very like McCloskey's impetus-based errors). It is possible that in the aircraft problem, the subjects adopt a frame of reference akin to that of an observer *inside* the aircraft. A "straight down" response is of course correct *from that frame of reference*. McCloskey does acknowledge the potential problems caused by frame of reference and suggests that the adoption of an internal frame of reference leads subjects to believe that carried objects have no impetus. We would argue that, rather than having a general belief that carried objects have no impetus, the subject's choice of a frame of reference and his or her subsequent response are very much a function of the salient properties of the individual problem they are dealing with.

Another possible objection to our methodology is that the problems we employed involved an externally imposed visual perspective (viewing the problem "side-on"), which, it could be argued, is unlikely to be the case in real life. Likewise, some problems may concern phenomena that are difficult or impossible for subjects to view in real life. In both cases, the sceptic would claim, it should be no surprise that the subjects get the answer wrong. We would argue, however, that a different visual perspective, e.g. an oblique viewpoint rather than a squarely "side on" view, as will often be the case in viewing a real-life phenomenon, will merely appear to compress the parabolic trajectory of an object as it falls, rather than change its shape radically. If subjects drew such a "compressed" parabola in our study, they would receive the same score in our scoring scheme as if they had drawn a correct parabola. If subjects are dealing with a problem which is difficult or impossible for them to have direct perceptual access to, then one could argue that their conception of the situation will be even more directly brought to bear than in the case in which they have had direct perceptual experience of the problem situation.

In addition, it could be argued that presuppositions are being made on our part concerning the comprehension by subjects of the physics of relative density, a complicated topic which most adults (never mind children) would fail to comprehend. Therefore it is not surprising that children should produce a variety of erroneous responses. Relative density *is* potentially relevant to this type of problem, but this argument is beside the point, for two reasons. Firstly, the objects chosen for inclusion in the problems in our study were, we would argue, heavy enough relative to air such that air resistance would not significantly affect the shape of the path. More marginal cases (e.g. a feather dropped in air) would be much more problematic for subjects and would in consequence result in an even wider variety of responses. Secondly, even accepting the argument that subjects do not fully understand relative density, in the absence of a complete understanding, subjects will, we would argue, be misled by irrelevant features of a problem such as the mass of the object in the problem, to produce different responses to formally identical problems. Their error patterns would in that case be predictable, and that is what our data show.

What the above objections (potential problems caused by using paper-and-pencil research methods, effects of visual perspective, possible difficulties arising from failure to comprehend relative density) do highlight is the fact that many variables are potentially at stake in these problems; this weakens McCloskey's case still further. Nevertheless, for the reasons outlined above, we would argue that our results do indeed warrant our conclusions, and that in consequence theoretical implications can be drawn.

5.4 Theoretical implications of the present study

The results from our experiment point to a dissociation between the knowledge underlying predictions and that underlying explanatory responses in our subjects, who were novices in the field of physics. Our data suggest that in novices, the mental model is only one component used in the generation of predictions. We would expect that in experts, the model plays a much more central role in the generation of predictions. This in fact squares well with Johnson-Laird's account. He (Johnson-Laird, 1983) suggests that the functions of what he describes as the "mental simulations" held by the novice to a domain (which permit predictive responses, but not explanations) are subsumed to the mental models developed as expertise increases, with these models gaining control over predictive responses. Our data indicate that, in this domain at least, it is possible for novices to have a better understanding of the forces at play in object motion than their predictive responses might be taken to imply (and, likewise, give predictive responses which seem *relatively* good yet possess a poor explanatory framework). For example, some subjects were able to draw correct parabolic trajectories for objects, yet were unable to distinguish either diagrammatically or verbally a single relevant factor which acted to produce that motion. Conversely, some subjects were capable of giving good explanations, listing all the relevant forces and showing them as acting appropriately, yet gave completely erroneous predictions. If simulations and models are coordinated only at the highest levels, this raises questions about research methodologies and operational procedures which rely on sampling predictive responses as a diagnostic of the elaboration of mental models.

Acknowledgements

The research reported in this chapter was funded by ESRC grant R000231287 to Anthony Anderson, Christine Howe and Terry Mayes. The authors wish to thank ESRC for their support, Liz Boyle for help with the data collection and analysis, and the staff and pupils of Holyrood and Knightswood secondary schools in Glasgow for their assistance with and participation in the study.

References

diSessa, A. (1988). Knowledge in pieces. In Forman, G. and Pufall, P.B. (eds), *Constructivism in the Computer Age*. Hillsdale, NJ: LEA.

Evans, J. St.B.T. (1982). *The Psychology of Deductive Reasoning*. London: Routledge.

Johnson-Laird, P.N. (1983). *Mental Models*. Cambridge: CUP.

Johnson-Laird, P.N., Legrenzi, P. and Legrenzi, M.S. (1972). Reasoning and a sense of reality. *British Journal of Psychology* 63, 395–400.

Kaiser, M.K., Jonides, J. and Alexander, J. (1986). Intuitive reasoning about abstract and familiar physics problems. *Memory and Cognition 14*, 308–312.

McCloskey, M. (1983). Naive Theories of Motion. In Gentner, D. and Stevens, A.L. (eds), *Mental Models*. Hillsdale, NJ: LEA.

McCloskey, M., Caramazza, A. and Green, B. (1980). Curvilinear motion in the absence of external forces: Naive beliefs about the motion of objects. *Science* *210*, 4474.

Wason, P.C. (1966). Reasoning. In Foss, B.M. (ed.) *New Horizons in Psychology 1*. Harmondsworth: Penguin.

Chapter 6

Representation and Interaction:
Are Mental Models All in the Mind?

Claire O'Malley and Steve Draper

6.1 What are mental models?

Talking about mental models can be a dangerous thing. There are so many various understandings of the term "mental model" in general, differences in taxonomies of mental models, as well as a diversity of terminology used to refer to different types of model (for a review see Rouse and Morris, 1986; Carroll and Olson, 1988). Some of the differences in the literature may derive also from the various contexts or applications in which mental models are studied (e.g. text comprehension, Johnson-Laird, 1983; human–computer interaction, Young, 1983; Kieras and Bovair, 1984; physics understanding, Gentner and Gentner, 1983). Some have concluded that mental models are no different to any other kind of representation (e.g. Rips, 1987).

Despite the confusion in the literature, the concept "mental model" is at least intuitively appealing as a way of distinguishing certain types of knowledge representation from others. The common sense notion of a mental model can perhaps be captured in the definition provided by Carroll and Olson (1988). In this view a mental model is "a rich and elaborate structure, reflecting the user's understanding of what the system contains, how it works, and why it works that way. It can be conceived as knowledge about the system sufficient to permit the user to try out actions mentally before choosing one to execute. A key feature of a mental model is that it can be "run" with trial, exploratory inputs and observed for its resultant behaviour " (Carroll and Olson, 1988, p. 51). This definition captures several things which seem to have intuitive appeal:

MODELS IN THE MIND:
Theory, perspective and applications. ISBN 0–12–592970–6

1. A mental model is different to a representation capturing isolated items of information; it is "a rich and elaborate structure", rather than a unitary proposition or production.

2. A mental model represents several different kinds of information, rather than one kind, "reflecting the user's understanding of what the system contains, how it works, and why it works that way".

3. For some people at least, a mental model is distinct from other kinds of information in that "it can be "run" with trial, exploratory inputs and observed for its resultant behaviour".

However, this last characteristic would not be a sufficient condition to distinguish the kinds of inference derivable from a mental model from the kind derivable from other types of representation. (Indeed, it is not entirely clear what it means to "run" a model.) Arguably, none of the criteria above would distinguish a mental model from any other kind of representation. The only point being made in using this definition is that it seems to capture the distinguishing features appealed to by most people when they talk about mental models.

Perhaps one of the aspects missing from this definition, or at least only implicitly entailed by it, is the notion that a mental model involves some degree of systematicity and coherence. According to some, what distinguishes these kinds of knowledge representation from others is that they are self-contained or closed systems, which allow users to simulate mentally the possible actions of a device and thereby predict its behaviour (Norman, 1983). This is would seem to be an important feature of models of computer systems at least.

Our intention in this paper is not to add to the confusion by providing yet another definition. We wish to suggest an alternative way of looking at knowledge representation in general, which, although it may not shed much light on what a mental model is or is not, may nonetheless be useful as a way of characterizing the function of certain types of knowledge representation in interacting with devices, whether they are machines or other types of artefact.

In this paper we address the nature of the knowledge employed by users when interacting with artefacts. Although, to a large extent, we will be using human–computer interaction as a domain, the intention is not to restrict the discussion solely to the use of computers. In this discussion we are interested in the extent to which users' knowledge about an artefact both supports and limits their success at using it, and the way in which the design of the artefact (e.g. the human–computer interface) affects the knowledge and beliefs which users acquire about it.

We focus on empirical findings from the domain of human–computer interaction which suggest, at first reading, that users do not appear to have coherent, internal representations of the system they are using. It is tempting to conclude from these findings that much of users' knowledge about a system is fragmentary and not the type of coherent, systematic representation entailed by most definitions of mental models. We suggest, however, that if one regards the user–computer dyad as an action system (cf. Clarke and Crossland, 1985), it is possible to see structure and coherence in the interaction. This is in the same spirit as Payne's suggestion that the interface should be regarded as a resource to be exploited rather than a gulf to be bridged (cf. Payne, 1990). In other words, instead of viewing the use of a computer system as a problem to be solved, where the user has to learn how to perform tasks, we should view interaction with the system as an opportunity for new forms of activity. This leads us to suggest that at least some forms of knowledge can be seen as distributed between users' internal representations and between representations embodied in the artefact itself and employed by users as external representations. Finally, we argue that HCI research needs to be directed towards looking at relations and interactions between people and artefacts rather than focusing on one or the other as isolated units (cf. Bateson, 1972).

6.2 Mental models versus knowledge-in-pieces

Although a common characterization of mental models (for example, of computer systems) is that they are coherent structural representations, in reality, users' knowledge about devices such as computer systems seems to be distributed and fragmentary (Hammond, Morton, MacLean, Barnard and Long, 1982; Carroll and Mack, 1985). They are often heavily context-dependent rather than being generalizable. Lewis (1986), for example, has shown how users may generate models or explanations of a command's function in a specific context but these explanations often do not predict the command's function in another context.

Research on conceptual understanding in other domains, such as physics, also bears this out. Whereas some researchers have characterized novices' intuitive knowledge of physics as consisting of a coherent and consistent set of ideas, which might be regarded as theories or models (e.g. Clement, 1982; McCloskey, 1983), others argue that intuitive physics consists of fragmentary knowledge which does not have the systematicity of a theory or a model (e.g. diSessa, 1983; 1988). However, Vosniadou and Brewer (in press) point out, with respect to children's understandings, that what may appear as contradictory and inconsistent from one point of view (i.e. the adult's or the expert's) may not be contradictory or inconsistent from the child's or novice's point of view. In a similar spirit we suggest that an understanding of the nature of the interaction between users and devices may provide us with a better understanding of what users' knowledge or mental models consists of. It may be that if one only looks at the user, what appears at first to be evidence for incomplete or fragmentary knowledge turns out to be much more coherent and systematic than if one looks at the user in interaction with the device. This is especially so with respect to display-based interaction, where much of the information needed for performing tasks is represented externally.

We suggest that the confusion and lack of evidence surrounding mental models may stem from a rather narrow view of the function of representations in guiding behaviour. There are several problems in assuming that understanding how to use a system must involve the internalization of all the information necessary to use it. In this respect theories of mental models (e.g. Young, 1983; Kieras and Bovair, 1984) seem to go hand-in-hand with assumptions about the goal-driven or plan-driven nature of activity. (Indeed, to some extent the concept of a mental model is required by the largely individualistic, constructivist paradigm dominating most of HCI, in order to explain certain types of behaviour – the approach of Card, Moran and Newell, 1983, is an example of this paradigm.) However, as Young and Simon (1987) argue, the behaviour of users is not the result of purely internal goal-directed activity, but more "the result of an interplay between ... goal-directed activity and the actual physical and functional settings ... that users find themselves in". This view is also seen in Suchman's work on situated activity (Suchman, 1987).

6.3 Distributed models

Another explanation for lack of evidence for structural models is provided by diSessa (1986), who points out that coming up with a single coherent view of a system may involve structural models and rules that are quite difficult to learn. If a system is to be used in a variety of ways, multiple models are likely to be developed.

In many situations users do not have a structural model from which the necessary knowledge for interacting with a system may be derived, nor do they have what Young (1983) refers to as functional models. Nevertheless these users perform quite well. This is possible because users can (in some situations) extract the information they need for interacting with the system from the environment.

So, skill at using a system may depend less on internalized representations, and the mental models underlying skilled performance may bear little resemblance to a "replica of the world" (Craik, 1943). Instead, users' knowledge may consist of information about how to interrogate the world for the information needed. For example, librarians do not have a representation of all the books in a collection "in their heads". They differ from other library users in their skill at using the information services to locate any book that might be wanted. This is one sense in which models can be distributed, i.e., distributed between knowledge "in the head" and knowledge "in the world" (cf. Norman, 1988).

diSessa (1986) has also talked about distributed models, but in a different sense: the sense in which knowledge may not be stored as a complete, coherent model, but may be distributed over several partial models (see also Collins and Gentner, 1983, on multiple models). This sense of distributed knowledge or multiple representations can be unpacked further. Firstly, users may have several models for different purposes (e.g. routine action versus debugging or error diagnosis and correction). Secondly, users may have several models for different aspects of the same device, especially if that device is complex. For example, the "cut-and-paste" operation of Macintosh applications requires the use of at least two sorts of model: one is a model of the clipboard, the other is a model of cutting and pasting. In fact there is a third model required to fully anticipate all states of the system – a model of the hidden buffer used in cutting and pasting. (For example, in word processors such as Microsoft Word, deleting text by using the "cut" command places a copy of the deleted text on the clipboard, which can be retrieved by using the "paste" operation. However, deleting text by backspacing is not retrievable using "paste", but in some cases it is retrievable using the "undo" facility.) In summary, several models may be needed where there are subcomponents to a device (especially a complex one) or where different uses of the device require different models (e.g. using the system versus diagnosing errors) or different types of model (e.g. functional versus structural).

6.4 Internal and external representations

In a study of how many commands users of the UNIX system knew, Draper (1985) found that even experts knew only a fraction. He suggested that the important characteristic of experts in such systems was not how much of the system they knew, but their skill in finding information when needed. Thus, in one sense the knowledge is left out in the world rather than being "in the head" – but this only works provided the user does have the knowledge about how to get the information. Norman (1988) discusses how many everyday tasks such as finding how to turn the lights on in a strange room depend upon an interesting blend of "information flow" and prior knowledge (a kind of generalized and distributed mental model). You can look for the switches, but you will look in only a few places where switches are usually placed. You recognize switches even though you do not know in advance exactly what they look like. In working out which switch to try, and which way to turn it you will draw on a blend of knowledge of conventions about on and off directions, physical actions for operating the switches, similarities between switch layouts and light positions, and so on.

Studies by Mayes, Draper, McGregor and Oatley (1988) and Payne (1991) suggest that users do not internalize much when they are working with display-based systems such as the Macintosh interface. The study by Mayes et al showed that even though users are looking at and using visual information from the screen, they seem unable to remember much detail about it. These studies raise the question of whether users *need* to remember much about an interface which supplies the information, or at least the prompts, needed to operate it. In general, the benefits of direct manipulation interfaces are purported to lie in the fact that users do not need to internalize many details in order to use the system.

However, the Mayes et al study did show marked differences between recall and performance in using the system. Users of display based systems clearly seem to know *something* – the question is, of what does that knowledge consist. Another issue is whether or not the methods used in the studies by Mayes et al and Payne are likely to reveal the kind of knowledge users have and what differences in knowledge there may be between more or less experienced users.

6.5 What gets internalized in using display-based interfaces?

In a follow-up study to those conducted by Mayes et al and Payne, we attempted to investigate in more detail the kind of knowledge employed in menu selection tasks by experienced users. In particular, the study was designed to investigate users' ability to recall menu items in context (i.e. to test "knowledge-in-use"). Our feeling was that the previous studies showing poor recall by users of MacWrite may have underestimated their knowledge of the system. In particular, we felt that some of this knowledge may have been inaccessible to subjects in free recall tests. So, rather than using free and cued recall measures as Mayes et al and Payne had done, we had users select target menu items where the names of headers and menu items had been masked by replacing them with 4-digit random numbers.

In designing this study we reasoned that, if users' representations of the system reflect the structure of the interface with respect to the task of finding a particular menu item (i.e. that the headers are always visible and a subset of menu items are only visible when a particular header has been selected), we would expect users to have more difficulty in selecting a menu item when the cues for finding the correct header have been altered. In this experiment the presence or absence of headers and menu items was manipulated in a task where users were asked to search for a particular menu item.

Subjects were experienced and regular users of MacWrite. However, since it was not clear whether or not they had equivalent experience with all of the menu items, subjects were given a 20-minute training session, followed by a 30-minute practice session, before being tested.

Subjects were then given a series of menu selection tasks using a simulated version of MacWrite. They were told that some of the headers and menu items had been replaced by random numbers. They were told to try and locate where the menu item should be and that they could only make one selection, after which they would be given the next task.

The simulation version of MacWrite was written in Hypercard. Although the menus worked in the same way as MacWrite menus, subjects were prevented from browsing by "walking through" the headers. To ensure that subjects made only one selection per task, each menu was revealed as the mouse button was pressed on one of the headers, and disappeared when the mouse button was released.

The menu selection tasks were presented under four separate conditions: all headers and menu items shown; only headers shown and menu items replaced with 4-digit random numbers; headers replaced by random numbers and menu items shown; all headers and menu items replaced with random numbers. There were 28 selection tasks in all, 7 tasks for each of the four conditions, so that each subject had to select 4 items from each menu. Subjects all completed the same tasks, but tasks and conditions were presented randomly. Subjects' times and selections were recorded automatically.

Since the study is reported in more detail elsewhere (Bibby, O'Malley and Waterson, in preparation), we will only report the main findings here. Results showed that subjects made significantly more correct selections of menu items when headers were present (mean=80%) than when they were absent (mean=36%; see Figure 6.1). However, when we looked at their performance in choosing the right header, rather than the menu item itself (see Figure 6.2), we found that subjects performance rose to a mean of 77%, even when the header was absent (compared with a mean of 85% when headers were present). The fact that there is only at most a 10% difference in the ability to select the correct header when it is present or absent and the chance hit rate is only 14% (there were 7 headers to choose from) suggests that users know the spatial location of the header more often than not.

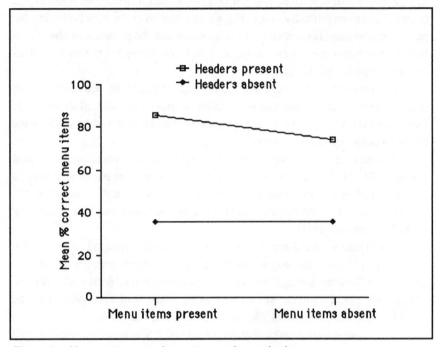

Figure 6.1 Mean percentage of correct menu item selections.

What is more surprising is that, when menu items were masked, subjects performance in selecting the correct item was 74% for cases where the header was present (see Figure 6.1). When the headers were absent, even though users could select the correct header 77% of the time (Figure 6.2), they could only select the correct menu item 36% of the time (Figure 6.1). As there were 56 possible menu items that they could have chosen from, they are still performing well above the chance level of approximately 1.8% correct. The drop in performance due to the absence of the headers suggests that headers are acting as cues for retrieving menu items.

These results show that users were surprisingly good at recalling menu items even when the names of the items had been masked, depending on whether a header was present or not. The results also suggest that users may be using memory for the spatial position of menu items to aid their recall. If this is so, then it may explain why free recall (e.g. questionnaire-based) methods tend not to reveal the knowledge that users have about using an interface. Although novices were not studied in this experiment reported here, results of another experiment (Bibby et al, in preparation) suggests that differences in knowledge between novice and expert users may be due to the strategy that each adopt in performing their tasks.

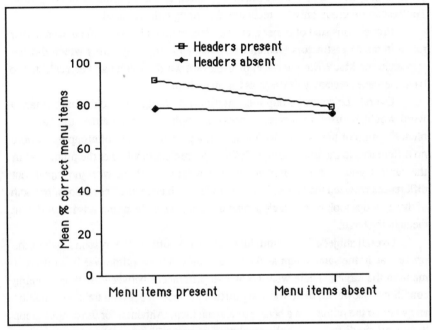

Figure 6.2 Mean percentage of correct header selections.

Hypotheses derived from analyses of the task of menu selection by Young, Howes and Whittington (1990) and Howes and Payne (1990) suggest that headers and items from the same menu should be closer semantically than headers and items from different menus. One measure of semantic distance is a recognition priming task. This suggests that there should be priming when the prime is from the same menu as the target, and priming should not occur if the prime and target are from different menus. In order to investigate whether or not users were employing spatial, rather than semantic memory for menu items, for one of the conditions we rearranged the menu items (though not the menu headers) so that the items were randomly placed under different headers.

Subjects in one condition (normal menus) used the normal MacWrite system, followed by a priming task. Subjects in another condition (scrambled menus) used the interface in which the menu items had been rearranged. Finally, a control group was given the priming task without interacting with the system. None of the subjects had used MacWrite or any other Macintosh-based word processing application prior to the experiment.

Subjects were given a 20-minute training session in the use of the word processing system, a 30-minute practice session, and a recognition priming task. For the control group only the recognition priming task was used.

Primes consisted of either menu headers or menu items. Targets were either menu items or distractors (semantically related computing terms which did not appear in the MacWrite interface, or irrelevant words which had been selected to have the same frequency of usage as the menu items).

Overall the control group took significantly longer to decide that the target word would be used in a word processing application than either the "normal menus" group or the "scrambled menus" group. For the control group there were no differences in the time taken to decide with respect to whether the prime was in the same menu or a different menu to the target. There were no significant differences between the "normal menus" or "scrambled menus" conditions, but both of these groups took significantly longer to decide when the prime was in a different menu to the target.

Overall subjects were more likely to give a correct YES response when the prime was in the same menu as the target than when the prime was in a different menu to the target. There were no overall differences between the three training conditions. However, there was a significant interaction between training condition and whether the prime was a header or a menu item. Although for the control group there were no differences in the number of correct YES responses when the prime was a menu header or a menu item, the "normal menus" group gave significantly more correct YES responses when the header was the prime and the "scrambled menus" group gave significantly more correct YES responses when a menu item was a prime.

The normal menu system had been designed such that semantically similar items appear in the same menu. However, only one complete menu can be seen at any time in interacting with the system. Both these properties suggest that users will pick up information about which headers and menu items are grouped together.

The finding that the control and "normal menus" groups gave significantly more correct responses when the prime was in the same menu as the target suggests that the semantic similarity of the menu commands (including the header) as designed into the system contributes to the way that users will select menu items. However, the "scrambled menus" group also shows this effect, despite the fact that semantic relations inherent in the interface were destroyed. One possible explanation is that the spatial contiguity of menu items is also an important determinant of what users will learn about the menu system they are using.

The second result of interest was an interaction between the training condition and whether the prime was a header or a menu item for the number of correct responses. In this case the control group showed no effect. The finding that the "normal menus" group gave more correct responses when the header was a prime suggests that the header is encoded in relation to each individual menu item beneath it. The finding that the "scrambled menus" group gave more correct responses when a menu item was a prime suggests that, since the semantic connections between the items have been removed, the spatial component that users learn is which menu items are close to each other.

Results from these studies suggest that users of display based interfaces internalize two kinds of information about menus: users can employ the semantic relationships between headers and menus to guide search, and they can also use information about the spatial location of the headers and menu items. The results suggest that semantic memory for menus is especially important for locating the correct header. Once the header is accessed, both or either the semantic or spatial memory for menu items can be used to locate the correct menu item. The results suggest that it is spatial memory that becomes important after the header has been accessed.

We would like to suggest the following explanation of these results. The task of menu selection can be broken down into three phases.

(i) Match the target menu item to the header. In normal use of the system, headers are always displayed, but menu items can only be revealed once the headers are accessed. This implies some pressure to internalize a mapping between headers and their respective menu items. This may be a semantic relationship, but the data suggest that it is not necessarily the semantic mapping inherent in the design that is being internalized. The data showed that subjects with the scrambled menu items performed equally well on a priming task as subjects who had learned the regular system. However, it seems that subjects with the scrambled menus take slightly longer to learn this mapping. Although this evidence is from novices, it does suggest that the mapping between headers and menu items is learned, rather than being inherent in the display.

Our findings suggest that experienced users have internalized some mapping between headers and menu items, since their level of performance was high when headers were shown, even though menu items were masked. The fact that there was no difference in correct response rate for the two conditions when headers were shown with and without menu items being shown suggests also that subjects have internalized some representation of the relative position of items within a menu.

(ii) Find the right header. Although subjects made fewer correct selections of menu items when headers were absent, analysis of the types of error made indicates that they were surprisingly good at selecting the correct header even when headers were masked. These errors are simply due to errors made in selecting the correct menu item. This also suggests that experienced users have internalized some representation of the position of headers along the menu bar, even though the fact that they are always shown in normal use would suggest no need for this. We suggest (tentatively) that internalization of these items speeds access for experienced users, although we do not have any strong evidence for this.

(iii) Find the right menu item. In normal use, menu items are only displayed once the correct header is accessed. The constraints of the display are also mirrored in our findings. Experienced users seem to be able to find the correct menu item, even when it is masked, as long as they have selected the correct header. This also suggests some spatial or positional representation for items within a menu. There is also some suggestive evidence in support of this from the priming studies. Novice users tended to make fewer errors in recognizing menu items when the header was the prime.

In summary, these findings suggest that experienced users seem to have internalized some representation of the spatial position of menu items, but this knowledge is only accessible once the correct header has been accessed. (It is tempting to suggest that there is a two-stage model of retrieval somewhere under here, analogous, if not consonant with Morton's model of headed records. See Morton, Hammersley and Bekerian, 1985.)

These studies show that experienced users do in fact internalize aspects of the display, to a much greater extent than is suggested by the studies reported in Mayes et al (1988) and Payne (1991). However, the nature of this internalization is not a single coherent representation that can be "run off" in one go to produce the correct response. In a sense, what users have internalized seems to be a function of the demands placed on them by the way in which the interface is designed. Users do not internalize everything. What they do internalize seems to be dictated by what the display is unable to provide, and what information is needed in order to access what the display is able to provide.

6.6 Discussion and conclusions

As was pointed out in the introduction, most theories of mental models (e.g. Young, 1983; Kieras and Bovair, 1984) assume that models are useful because they allow users to make inferences and generate procedures for performing tasks. These models only work if they are posited as coherent, self-contained, internalized representations. We suggest that, in interacting with display–based systems, users may not need to internalize all aspects of using the system, but they do need to internalize (i) information that the display does not provide, and (ii) knowledge required to interact with the display – including knowledge of how to access what is supplied by the display. This view may suggest why there have been some difficulties in establishing empirically the existence of coherent mental models in user–computer interaction. The kind of information users need to internalize, in the view we propose here, also fits with findings by Hammond et al (1982) on the fragmentary nature of users knowledge of systems, and with diSessa's "knowledge-in-pieces" notion (diSessa, 1988).

In the case of MacWrite menu selection tasks, users may store several disparate types of information which they then integrate with information supplied by the display in using the device (e.g. relative spatial position of certain items, semantic knowledge for other items). These representations may therefore be *differentially* susceptible to certain elicitation techniques (e.g. free recall, cued recall, recognition), which would explain the poor recall of users in the studies by Mayes et al and Payne. What is needed is a theoretical account of interactivity which will predict the distribution of knowledge/processing between user and artefact and can therefore be tested out experimentally. The D-TAG model described in Howes and Payne (1990) and the model described in Payne (1990) provide the beginnings for such a theory.

In conclusion, we propose that mental models may be characterized in terms of distributed representations, rather than as self-contained, coherent and internalized mental structures. There are two senses in which these representations may be "distributed". It may be that difficulties in establishing empirically the existence of coherent mental models (cf. Rouse and Morris, 1986) are due to the fragmentary nature of users knowledge of systems (cf. "knowledge-in-pieces", diSessa, 1988). In other words, knowledge may be distributed across several internal representations. This "knowledge-in-pieces" may also be explained by the second sense of distributed representations: representations may be seen as distributed between user and artefact. In other words, information represented at the interface or in other representational artefacts (e.g. diagrams – cf. Larkin and

Simon, 1987) can be seen as external memory aids which "fill in the gaps" in users' internalized representations when they interact with the system. In some cases, these external representations may be doing some of the computational work for the user (cf. Lave, 1988), obviating the need for the user to internalize all the inform-ation necessary to generate correct procedures online. As a consequence, display-based interaction can be characterized in terms of constraints imposed by the interface design on the distribution of these representations between users and artefacts (cf. Norman, 1991).

Winograd and Flores (1986) make use of Heidegger's concept of "breakdown" in discussing human–computer interaction. (Roughly speaking, this refers to when our attention is drawn to our actions.) We could regard the user's need to develop a mental model of a system as a case of breakdown, rather than "thrownness" (i.e. activity that is tacit and unproblematic), and hence as a symptom of its lack of usability. (On the other hand, this does seem to assume that mental models can only emerge as explicit, rather than tacit forms – see Bannon and Bødker, 1991). Mayes et al (1988) make a similar point in suggesting that the "memorability" of some user interfaces may be symptomatic of their lack of usability. Just as what is not said in a discourse is as interesting and informative as what is said, perhaps what users' do not internalize about the system they are interacting with is as informative for an understanding of HCI as what they do internalize.

As Winograd and Flores point out, Maturana and Heidegger both oppose the assumption that cognition is based on the manipulation of mental models or representations of the world. Learning and memory, for Maturana, do not depend on the indefinite retention of a structural invariant that represents an entity, but on the functional ability of the system to create, when certain recurrent conditions are given, a behaviour that satisfies the recurrent demands or that an observer would class as a re-enacting of a previous one. In this view then, a cognitive account should focus on the pattern of interactions which give rise to structure and the relationship of changes in structure to activity, rather than on describing putative invariant mental states which direct or guide behaviour.

There is a danger that this view could be read as behaviourist and anti-representationalist. This is not the position we wish to take. We take the view that people can and characteristically do construct and use internal representations, but only when necessary, not as a universal and necessary prerequisite for action. The view we are putting forward certainly includes the concept of (mental) representation. There may be such things as mental models, but they may not be the "normal" mode of cognition.

We suggest that the nature of mental representations should be described in terms of their functionality with respect to a given interaction. So, we should not expect to find many instances of mental representations which are structurally complete, coherent and "runnable". Acting in the world involves combining information already available in the environment (e.g. the computer interface) with some internalized representations in memory. What we need to internalize is a function of what is not already available to us. So, these internal representations are likely to appear as fragments or partial representations if one looks only at one unit in the interactional system (i.e. the user). The situation may be more subtle than this, since there will be cases in which information is only occasionally available in the environment. This may lead to the necessity for some redundancy in the distribution of representations in the interactional system.

Hutchins (1990) describes some of the advantages of redundancy in distributed cognition, in analysing cooperative activities involved in navigation. He notes that knowledge in cooperative tasks is often assumed to be distributed in an exhaustive and mutually exclusive way, and points out that this kind of distribution pattern is in fact rare, since it is so vulnerable to breakdown (i.e. if one member of the team fails to perform as required, the whole system breaks down). A more common distribution involves substantial sharing of task knowledge, although not complete overlap. Hutchins uses the expression horizon of observation to refer to the outer boundary of the part of the task that can be seen and heard by each team member. He points out that these horizons of observations are also affected by the physical arrangement of tools and other representational artefacts (charts, etc.). As Hutchins argues, these horizons of observation are important because they affect the extent to which members of the team can share their expertise and coordinate their tasks.

This view of distributed cognition may also have some implications for the nature of the differences between novice and experienced users, with respect to their knowledge of the system. Novices do not know enough about what the system can do to decide what needs to be internalized and what does not. Experienced users may turn out to "know" as little as novices on some measures (e.g. the recall measures used in studies by Mayes et al and Payne), but it may well be that they have reorganized their knowledge representation as a function of their experience with the system, so that some of the information internalized whilst learning to use the system becomes redundant and drops out of the representations necessary to interact with the system. In this case, we might predict that intermediate users actually know "more" than novices or experts.

However, we have to take care in interpreting findings such as these. Cases where experts perform worse than novices on some tasks have been noted in studies of programmers (e.g. Adelson, 1984), but only where tasks have been designed to suit the skills of novices rather than experts. There is also a good deal of evidence in developmental studies showing that young children can perform as well as older children, given the right tasks and conditions (e.g. Donaldson, 1978). However, as Thornton (1982) points out, "the argument for early competence has taken for granted that equivalent task performance is evidence for equivalent underlying processes". Her studies of children's classificatory skills show that whilst younger and older children may produce equivalent performance, there are very different processes underlying these procedures.

We can put the argument about user–computer interaction (or person-artefact interaction) as distributed cognition together with the developmental account given above, and consider user–computer interaction as a zone of proximal development, in Vygotsky's terms (Vygotsky, 1978). The user, in interaction with the artefact, creates new possibilities for action. This interaction is not just a division of labour, but also creates possibilities for learning and cognitive change as the user gains experience. However, this is not a case of simple assimilation. One common interpretation of the concept "zone of proximal development" (ZPD) would predict that users would internalize "more" as a function of experience (i.e. the interpretation that accompanies Wood, Bruner and Ross's (1976) accounts of scaffolding, where what one can do today with help, one can do tomorrow unaided, and an interpretation which has been criticized by Griffin and Cole, 1984). The ZPD creates new forms of activity (cf. Engeström, 1987). In this view, interaction with the system is not just a simple case of "cultural amplification" but of change (cf. Cole and Griffin, 1980). This is the point also made by Norman (1991) when he discusses how cognitive artefacts change the very nature of tasks in interactions.

The user–computer dyad, then, is not a simple sum of its parts, and the sense in which we are suggesting that the interaction be regarded as a form of distributed cognition is not one in which tasks are simply divided between user and system in an exclusive way. Studying users' representations in isolation from the interaction will not yield "part" of the cognitive representations present in the interaction; neither will analysis of the interface alone (as in the task analytic approach) yield another "part" of these representations. The interaction itself creates something qualitatively different. As Payne (1990) so aptly put it: it's time we looked HCI in the I.

References

Bannon, L. and Bødker, S. (1991). Beyond the interface: encountering artefacts in use. In Carroll, J.M. (ed.) *Designing Interaction: Psychological Theory at the Human-Computer Interface.* Cambridge: CUP.

Bateson, G. (1972) *Steps to an Ecology of Mind.* New York: Chandler.

Bibby, P.A., O'Malley, C.E. and Waterson, P. (in preparation). On knowing more than we think we do: recall and recognition of menus.

Card, S., Moran, T. and Newell, A. (1983). *The Psychology of Human–Computer Interaction.* Hillsdale, NJ: LEA.

Carroll, J.M. and Olson, J.R. (1988). Mental models in human–computer interaction. In M. Helander (ed.) *Handbook of Human–Computer Interaction.* Amsterdam: Elsevier (North-Holland).

Carroll, J.M. and Mack, R.L. (1985). Metaphor, computing systems and active learning. *International Journal of Man–Machine Studies 22*, 39–57.

Clarke, D.D. and Crossland, J. (1985). *Action Systems.* London: Methuen.

Clement, J. (1982). Students' preconceptions in introductory mechanics. *American Journal of Physics 50*, 66–71.

Cole, M. and Griffin, P. (1980). Cultural amplifiers reconsidered. In Olson, D.R. (ed.) *The Social Foundations of Language and Thought.* New York: Norton.

Collins, A. and Gentner, D. (1983). Multiple models of evaporation processes. *Proceedings of the Fifth Conference on the Cognitive Science Society.* Hillsdale, NJ: LEA.

Craik, K. (1943). *The Nature of Explanation.* Cambridge: CUP.

diSessa, A.A.(1983). Phenomenology and the evolution of intuition. In Gentner, D. and Stevens, A.L. (eds) *Mental Models.* Hillsdale, NJ: LEA.

diSessa, A.A. (1986). Models of computation. In Norman, D.A. and Draper, S.W. (eds) *User Centered System Design.* Hillsdale, NJ: LEA.

diSessa, A.A. (1988). Knowledge in pieces. In Forman, G. and Pufall, P.B. (eds) *Constructivism in the Computer Age.* Hillsdale, NJ: LEA.

Donaldson, M. (1978). *Children's Minds.* London: Fontana.

Draper, S.W. 1985). The nature of expertise in UNIX. In Shackel, B. (ed.) *Human–Computer Interaction Interact '84.* Amsterdam: North-Holland.

Engeström, Y. (1987). *Learning by Expanding.* Helsinki: Orienta-Konsultit Oy.

Gentner, D. and Gentner, D.R. (1983). Flowing waters or teeming crowds: mental models of electricity. In Gentner, D. and Stevens, A.L. (eds) *Mental Models.* Hillsdale, NJ: LEA.

Griffin, P. and Cole, M. (1984). Current activity for the future: the Zo-ped. In Rogoff, B. and Wertsch, J.V. (eds) *Children's Learning in the Zone of Proximal Development*. San Francisco: Jossey-Bass.

Hammond, N., Morton, J., MacLean, A., Barnard, P. and Long, J. (1982). Knowledge fragments and users' models of systems. IBM Human Factors Report No. HF071, IBM (UK) Laboratories, Hursley Park, Hampshire.

Howes, A. and Payne, S. (1990). Display-based competence: Towards user models for menu-driven interfaces. *International Journal of Man–Machine Studies 33*, 637–655.

Hutchins, E. (1990). The technology of team navigation. In Galegher, J. and Kraut, R. (eds) *Intellectual Teamwork: Social and Technological Foundations of Group Work*. Hillsdale, NJ: LEA

Johnson-Laird, P.N. (1983). *Mental Models*. Cambridge: CUP.

Kieras, D.E. and Bovair, S. (1984). The role of a mental model in learning to operate a device. *Cognitive Science 8*, 255–274.

Larkin, J. and Simon, H.(1987). Why a diagram is (sometimes) worth ten thousand words. *Cognitive Science 11*, 65–100.

Lave, J. (1988). *Cognition in Practice*. Cambridge: CUP.

Lewis, C.(1986). Understanding what's happening in system interactions. In Norman, D.A. and Draper, S.W. (eds)*User Centered System Design*. Hillsdale, NJ: LEA.

Mayes, J.T., Draper, S.W., McGregor, A.M. and Oatley, K. (1988). Information Flow in a user interface: the effect of experience and context on the recall of MacWrite screens. In Jones, D.M. and Winder, R. (eds) *People and Computers IV*. Cambridge : CUP.

McCloskey, M. (1983). Naive theories of motion. In Gentner, D. and Stevens, A.L. (eds) *Mental Models*. Hillsdale, NJ: LEA.

Morton, J., Hammersley, R.H. and Bekerian, D.A. (1985). Headed records: a model for memory and its failures. *Cognition 20*, 1–23.

Norman, D.A. (1983). Some observations on mental models. In Gentner, D. and Stevens, A.L. (eds) *Mental Models*. Hillsdale, NJ: LEA

Norman, D.A.(1988). *The Psychology of Everyday Things*. New York: Basic Books.

Norman, D.A. (1991). Cognitive artefacts. In Carroll, J.M. (ed.) *Designing Interaction: Psychological Theory at the Human–Computer Interface*. Cambridge: CUP.

Payne, S.J. (1990). Looking HCI in the I. In Diaper, D. Gilmore, D Cockton, G and Shackel B. (eds) *Human–Computer Interaction. Interact '90*. Amsterdam: North-Holland.

Payne, S.J. (1991). Display-based action at the user interface. *International Journal of Man–Machine Studies 35*, 275–289.

Rips, L.J. (1987). Mental muddles. In Brand, M. and Harnish, R.M. (eds) *The Representation of Knowledge and Belief*. Tucson, Az University of Arizona Press.

Rouse, W.B. and Morris, N.M. (1986). On looking into the black box: Prospects and limits in the search for mental models. *Psychological Bulletin 100*, 349–363.

Suchman, L.A. (1987). *Plans and Situated Actions: The problem of human–machine communication*. Cambridge: CUP.

Thornton, S. (1982). Challenging "early competence": a process oriented analysis of chidren's classifying. *Cognitive Science 6*, 77–100.

Vosniadou, S. and Brewer, W.F. (in press). Mental models of the earth: a study of conceptual change in childhood. *Cognitive Psychology*.

Vygotsky, L.S. (1978). *Mind in Society*. In Cole, M., John-Steiner, V., Scribner, S. and Souberman, B. (eds) Cambridge, Ma.: Harvard University Press.

Winograd, T. and Flores, F. (1986). *Understanding Computers and Cognition*. Norwood, NJ: Ablex.

Wood, D.J., Bruner, J.S. and Ross, G. (1976). The role of tutoring in problem solving. *Journal of Child Psychology and Psychiatry 17*, 89–100.

Young, R.M. (1983). Surrogates and mappings: two kinds of conceptual models for interactive devices. In Gentner, D. and Stevens, A.L. (eds) *Mental Models*. Hillsdale, NJ: LEA.

Young, R., Howes, A. and Whittington, J. (1990). A knowledge analysis of interactivity. In Diaper, D. Gilmore, D Cockton, G and Shackel B. (eds) *Human–Computer Interaction. Interact '90*. Amsterdam: North-Holland.

Young, R.M. and Simon, T. (1987). Planning in the context of human-computer interaction. In Diaper, D. and Winder, R. (eds) *People and Computers III*. Cambridge: CUP.

Chapter 7

Distributed Knowledge: in the Head, in the World or in the Interaction?

Peter A. Bibby

The previous two chapters have both made a strong case for reconsidering the status of mental models as multiple knowledge bases (Anderson et al, this volume) or representations (O'Malley and Draper, this volume). In Chapter 5 Anderson et al argue that McCloskey's work (McCloskey, 1983; McCloskey, Caramazza, and Green, 1980) may have overdetermined the status of "naive" theories of physics, imbuing the mental model concept with all the implications of a theory; a mental model is coherent and consistent giving rise to both explanations and predictions. On the other hand, Anderson et al believe that diSessa's work (1983, 1988) underdetermines the status of mental models. The theoretical concept of phenomenological primitives adequately prescribes the behaviour of people making predictions about what will happen in particular circumstances, but fails to account for the apparent consistency in peoples explanations of that behaviour, which of course is support for McCloskey's position. In order to explain this "dissociation" Anderson et al appeal to two different knowledge bases: the first contains a "naive" theory not dissimilar to the impetus theory that McCloskey subscribes to; the second contains the phenomenological primitives that diSessa describes.

In Chapter 6 O'Malley and Draper argue that it is not possible to construct a coherent theory of mental models in HCI if we continue to focus on only one part of the interactional dyad: the human or the computer. They point out that it is not possible to distinguish a mental model representation from any other kind of representation without appealing to the notion of "runnability", and that this is not a transparent concept. They go on to suggest several important distinctions that have previously been ignored when considering mental models. These are a) the user–

MODELS IN THE MIND:
Theory, perspective and applications. ISBN 0-12-592970-6

computer dyad should be viewed as an action system, b) some forms of knowledge can be seen as distributed between the user and the computer, c) much of the reasoning about a device is context dependent and situated and finally d) it is possible for the user to take different points of view of the problem at hand entailing the use of different knowledge "fragments" (the latter two points are also mentioned by Anderson et al in Chapter 5)

The major point to be extracted from these chapters is that knowledge can be seen to be "distributed" or "fragmented" or residing within different "knowledge bases", within the head of a user or between the user's head and the world. There seem to be three major problems that need addressing: the first problem is whether we can say that this distribution exists; second, if it does, how does this distribution of knowledge comes to function as it does; and third, can we decide what will reside in the head and what will reside in the world? Both these latter issues focus upon the ontogeny of mental models, that is their genesis and development.

According to Anderson et al different kinds of knowledge are used for predicting and for explaining. What might lead to this division? If we view such phenomena as explaining and predicting as essentially social in nature and thus language-based, we can obtain a clearer picture of the communicative functions of explanation and how this relates to the communicative functions of prediction. Antaki (1988) states that "people's explanations are coherent wholes, more or less well structured in and of themselves" (p.60). The notion of structure here is meant to suggest that "there is some network of (at its loosest) association or (at its tightest) logical implication among a certain set of views of the world" (p.63). There is no assertion made by Antaki about the relative accuracy of the explanations (with respect to some idealized expertise), only that they are coherent and structured. Antaki argues that this coherence in explanations comes in part from the explainer's commitment to look as if they understand what they are explaining. By using conventional devices, such as narratives (e.g. Gergen, 1988; Squire, 1990) or rhetoric (e.g. Billig, 1990) to present explanations, people may be presenting an argument which *seems* coherent. (The intended sense of rhetoric here is not the "empty phrases" interpretation which is commonly used as a derogatory accusation, but rather the sense in which rhetoric is the art of good communication.) A second and related point is that explanations can be seen as the adoption of particular discourses (e.g. Potter and Wetherell, 1987) and thus it is important to establish the communication function that such speech acts as explaining and predicting take within a particular discourse. In other words, people are doing things when they give explanations or make predictions and what they are doing cannot be understood simply in terms of the semantics of their utterances (Austin, 1962;

Searle, 1969), but rather in relation to the social and discursive context. When people are explaining they are trying to persuade others to believe their point of view or to justify that point of view to others.Toulmin (1958) argues that one way to achieve this, with the added consequence of perceived coherence, is the use of warrants and backings. A proposition which purports to describe some state of affairs about the world (a claim) is commonly supported by data and the warrant is the general rule by which the appeal to data can be said to support the claim. A backing, on the other hand, is the reason given for accepting a warrant. Explanations which fail to acknowledge the implicit structure in the use of warrants and backings will also fail to be coherent. They will not achieve the perceived status of a miniature theory about the world.

Predictions, on the other hand, do not serve the same social functions as explanations, although they do share the same linguistic base. Predictions do not require warranting and backing, and do not sit within the same kinds of discursive context. When making a prediction, people are not required to explain why they have come to the conclusion they have, rather they simply have to state their conclusion. In the work reported by Anderson et al, there is no requirement to justify a prediction, rather there is only a requirement to make the correct prediction, which implies that there is unlikely to be a simple dissociation in knowledge bases between predicting and explaining. On the contrary, the dissociation comes from the socio-linguistic context in which explaining and predicting take place. This leaves open the question of why the predictions seemed to be more correct than the explanations that subjects gave. Antaki (1988) argues that such beliefs as those that are used to make predictions about the physical behaviour of systems or machines, which are commonly held privately, would not be expected to alter in nature by being brought into a social arena. Explanations intended for the public arena, on the other hand can be seen to change because they require the use of additional knowledge for their justification. The dissociation between predictions and explanations need not be ascribed to a difference between knowledge bases, but rather through the status of these utterances in their communicative context. A claim for the fragmented nature of the knowledge that people have of physics is likely to be misguided by a need to present a representational theory of this fragmentation. The apparent fragmentation of knowledge, between phenomenological primitives and "naive" theories, is most likely due to a confusion between process and product. The process which underlies the generation of predictions and explanations may well be the same, but the product can only be understood in its socio-linguistic context.

The other sense of distributed exemplified by O'Malley and Draper is that knowledge can be seen to be distributed between the "head" and the "world" (Norman, 1988). One option advocated by many researchers is to consider the user as the major determinant of the interaction, and consequently demote the contribution that the artefact, the computer, makes to the interaction. It is the user's knowledge of how the system works that drives the interaction in a particular direction. Models such as GOMS (Card, Moran and Newell, 1983) implicitly assume that this is the case. What determines the course of the interaction is whether or not the user knows the appropriate methods for reaching a particular goal state. This approach has been challenged by Suchman (1987) who emphasizes the "situated" nature of interactions and demonstrates some of the problems of adopting a goals/plans analysis. An alternative which shares a similar assumption is the "mental model" approach, wherein it is not the users' knowledge of what methods to apply, but rather their knowledge of how the computer achieves a goal that directs the interaction with the computer. Both these positions regard the contribution of the artefact itself as minimal. This is clearly an unsatisfactory position, and as Payne (1991) points out, it ignores the "ecological" status of everyday interactions with computers.

Again we can appeal to the social nature of interacting with computers to gain an understanding of the meaning of "in the head" and "in the world". This works at two distinct levels. Firstly, the computer can be seen as a possible agent in an interaction (with the ability to make contributions to the interaction) and the interaction can then be viewed as a conversation (Payne, 1990). Secondly, the computer can be seen as an artefact which embodies the psychological claims of its designer/s (Carroll and Campbell, 1988) and as such is fundamentally social, in that the artefact has built in assumptions about the nature of other actors, the users.

Payne argues that in order to understand the nature of display-based inter-action with computers we have to adopt an analysis of the interaction as conver-sation, with the user and the computer both taking turns and making contributions (Clark and Schaefer, 1987; 1989). A contribution has two components: a presentation and an acceptance. A presentation is an utterance which carries the content of the contribution and acceptance follows with both participants establishing through collaboration that both have understood. Presentations and acceptances can take several turns and the overall function of these operations is to achieve a mutual grounding: the agreement that the communication of mutual beliefs has been achieved. Payne extends this analysis to include computers as possible participants by arguing that both the user and the computer generate "accounts" of the interaction. It is these accounts that establish the mutuality of the interaction.

The computer's accounts are established through the feedback that the computer gives the user about its present state. This analysis suggests that much of the interaction between the user and the computer cannot be said to rely simply on what the user knows but also on what the machine understands about the user's intentions. In this sense, it is within the conversation with the computer that meaning is established. In at least one way, the knowledge necessary to interact successfully with a computer is socially distributed.

The second way in which interaction can be seen to be social comes indirectly from the work of Carroll and Campbell (1988). Carroll and Campbell take the view that HCI is the study of an ecology of tasks and artefacts where tasks are the focus of the user's intentions and artefacts are the tools that are used to satisfy those intentions. Implicit within this view is that the artefact is a embodiment of psychological claims or more specifically socially constructed discourses (Bowers, personal communication). The consequence of the latter point of view is that it raises the thorny issue of how the discourses are structured for different groups, e.g. users, psychologists, HCI researchers or designers. It also raises the possibility that the claims made by the artefact are very different from those that the user may perceive. If the artefact has been structured in such a way as to embody the intentions of the designer(s) there is no guarantee that this will be how the artefact is understood by the user, since the user's discursive background is likely to be different. Instead of assuming that there is an immediate and successful transmission of intent from the user to the artefact, and vice versa, it is only possible to understand the intentions of the actors by examining the discourses within which those meanings reside. An example of such an analysis comes from the work of Radley (1990) who argues that artefacts can be seen as entities which entail "collective remembering" (Middleton and Edwards, 1990). As such, remembering is not seen as a process which resides within an individual, rather it is through the interaction with other agents or embodiments of agency that remembering takes places. Perhaps, we should not think of knowledge distributed between the "head" and the "world", but between different social agents, and as such, each agent is able to contribute to the meaning of an interaction.

It is arguable that understanding what it means for knowledge to be distributed can only occur if we accept the fundamentally social basis for cognition. If we are interested in understanding how cognitions (i.e. intentional states such as beliefs, desires, wants, etc.) are represented then we need a theory that acknowledges their social ontogeny and genesis.

References

Antaki, C. (1988). Structures of belief and justification. In Antaki, C. (ed.) *Analysing Everyday Explanation: A Casebook of Methods*. London: Sage.

Austin, J.L. (1962). *How To Do Things with Words*. Oxford: Clarendon Press.

Card, S.K., Moran, T.P. and Newell, A. (1983). *The Psychology of Human–Computer Interaction*. Hillsdale, N J: LEA.

Carroll, J.M. and Campbell, R.L. (1988). *Artefacts as Psychological Theories: The Case of Human–Computer Interaction*. IBM Research Report, RC13454.

Clark, H.H. and Schaefer, E.F. (1987). Collaborating on contributions to conversations. *Language and Cognitive Processes* 2, 19–41.

Clark, H.H. and Schaefer, E.F. (1989). Contributing to discourse. *Cognitive Science 13*, 259–294.

diSessa, A. (1983). Phenomenology and the evolution of intuition. In Gentner, D. and Steven, A. L. (eds) *Mental Models..* Hillsdale, NJ: LEA

diSessa, A.(1988). Knowledge in pieces. In G. Forman and P.B. Pufall (eds) *Constructivism in the Computer Age*. Hillsdale, NJ: LEA.

Gergen, M. (1988). Narrative structures in social explanation. In Antaki, C. (ed.) *Analysing Everyday Explanation: A Casebook of Methods*. Sage: London.

McCloskey, M. (1983). Naive theories of motion. In Gentner, D. and Stevens, A.L. (eds), *Mental Models*. Hillsdale, NJ:LEA.

McCloskey, M., Caramazza, A. and Green, B. (1980). Curvilinear motion in the absence of external forces: naive beliefs about the motion of objects. *Science 210*, 4474.

Norman, D.A. (1988). *The Psychology of Everyday Things*. New York: Basic Books.

Middleton, D. and Edwards, D.(eds) (1990) *Collective Remembering*. London: Sage.

Payne, S.J. (1990). Looking HCI in the I. In Diaper, D., Gilmore, D., Cockton, G. and Shackel, B. (eds), *Human–Computer Interaction. Interact '90*. Amsterdam: North-Holland.

Payne, S.J. (1991). Interface problems and interface resources. In J.M. Carroll (ed.) *Designing Interaction: Psychology at the Human-Computer Interface*. Cambridge: CUP.

Potter, J. and Wetherell, M. (1987). *Discourse and Social Psychology: Beyond Attitudes and Behaviour*. London: Sage.

Radley, A. (1990). Artefacts, memory and a sense of the past. In Middleton, D. and Edwards, D. *Collective Remembering*. London: Sage.

Searle, J.R. (1969). *Speech Acts: An Essay in the Philosophy of Language*. Cambridge: CUP.

Squire, C. (1990). Crisis, what crisis? Discourses and narratives of the "social" in social psychology. In Parker, I. and Shotter, J. (eds), *Deconstructing Social Psychology*. London: Routledge.

Suchman, L.A. (1987). *Plans and Situated Actions*. Cambridge: CUP.

Toulmin, S.E. (1958). *The Uses of Argument*. Cambridge: CUP.

Part 3

Mental Models in Human–Computer Interaction and Human–Machine Systems: Cognitive Skill and Cognitive Artefacts

Chapter 8

On Mental Models and Cognitive Artefacts

Stephen J. Payne

This chapter has modest aims: to explore some of the relationships between mental models and "cognitive artefacts" – tools designed to support cognition. I review some of the ideas in both literatures before discussing how, depending on their representational properties, cognitive artefacts can make different demands on their users' mental models.

8.1 Cognitive science and human–computer interaction

The field of human–computer interaction (HCI) has looked hungrily towards cognitive science for some applicable understanding of users' thought processes. Almost all research in the field takes improved design of computer systems as the ultimate motivation, for good reason, given the current structure of funding for the enterprise. Yet many researchers have openly claimed (or wished for) a reciprocal relationship, in which HCI research strengthens our understanding of theoretical issues in cognition (e.g Card, Moran and Newell, 1983, p.14; Landauer, 1987). How might the study of human interaction with computers enrich our general understanding of mental life, and how does the theme of this collection – mental models – bear on this possibility?

There are at least three reasons why the study of HCI appears well placed to contribute theoretical developments to cognitive science. First, many of the practical problems of HCI require an understanding of the user's complete task, from forming a goal, through acting on the world to interpreting the result. The commonplace psychological strategy of isolating a task component, such as word recognition, from the complex, meaningful task-context (of reading in this case) seems unlikely to bear fruit ripe for designers. The isolation strategy focuses research towards empirical competitions that can only be resolved in controlled

MODELS IN THE MIND:
Theory, perspective and applications. ISBN 0–12–592970–6

experiments, and away from engineering approximations that can predict aspects of complex behaviours in rich situations. Furthermore, it de-emphasizes the need for compatibility between separate theories of component processes. In HCI, it can speak only to those "low-level" details of the hardware interface, such as legibility constraints, which exert some influence independent of users' task strategies.

The literature on cognitive science has seen several pleas for integrative investigations of real tasks (notably Newell, 1973) as one way of trying to ensure that psychological knowledge cumulates into workable understandings of the ways in which the component processes of cognition are coordinated into meaningful action. The practical needs of HCI can help force the issue.

The second methodological advantage borne by HCI is that it provides the raw materials for ecologically valid intervention studies of task demands. One key to understanding the psychology of complete tasks is to understand how different task environments affect people's strategies, as Newell and Simon (1972) argued long ago. HCI affords the prospect of investigating this issue through detailed reflection on the consequences of existing designs (e.g. Carroll and Kellogg, 1989; Payne, 1991a) and through design experiments (e.g. diSessa, 1991).

The third reason to believe HCI could play an important role in the development of cognitive science is obvious and simple, yet largely neglected. Interacting with computers is an everyday cognitive activity for many people. If the human mind is a product of the tasks it performs and the resources it exploits, then understanding HCI is basic and essential. This argument gains force from the observation that computer systems are among many artefacts that routinely support cognitive tasks. Human cognition often, perhaps typically, involves a complex interplay between mental processes and artefacts. An ecologically valid cognitive science must understand the multifarious aspects of that relationship.

8.2 Artefacts in cognitive science

There is a rich tradition in cultural psychology that focuses on the importance of artefacts in shaping human thought (e.g. Bruner and Olson, 1977–78; Cole and Griffin, 1980; Vygotsky, 1978). However, with a few exceptions (such as Simon, 1969, and others whose work is reviewed below), this tradition has largely been ignored by current cognitive science, which has dealt almost exclusively with the unaided mind. In their everyday lives, people seldom undertake complex reasoning or decision–making tasks without turning to pencil and paper; yet in the scientist's laboratory, how many subjects have been permitted such luxuries?

What explains this state of affairs? There seems to exist an unspoken argument underlying traditional approaches to cognitive skill: only by looking at unaided skill can we see the mind in action. If we let people use tools, like pencil and paper, then our view of the mind will be confused by contingencies and circumstances that are outside the scope of psychology. But this argument is surely fallacious. I am reminded of James Gibson's critique of a perceptual psychology based entirely on studies of motionless heads (Gibson, 1979). You can't realize the crucial role of locomotion in vision unless you let your subjects move, and you can't realize the crucial role of artefacts in cognition unless you let your subjects use them.

There are signs that the neglect of the role of artefacts in thought is being overcome. For example, in research on human memory there is a call for theories which address "the role of memory aids and the factors governing their use" (Intons-Peterson and Fournier, 1986). And recent research on problem–solving and planning has focused on the use of diagrams, or on the mnemonic role of the external "display" (Larkin, 1989; Larkin and Simon, 1987). To provide a general introduction into some of the issues raised by a cognitive science of artefacts, I will begin by developing a taxonomy of cognitive artefacts, derived from the work of Donald Norman.

Norman (1991) defines a cognitive artefact as "an artificial device designed to maintain, display, or operate upon information in order to serve a representational function", and seeks to expose some fundamental aspects of such artefacts that affect the way they interact with human cognitive performance. One theme of Norman's work is to bring HCI back into the more general domain of cognitive ergonomics. Indeed, Norman (1989a) seeks to locate computer systems in a space of cognitive artefacts by offering a taxonomy of artefacts in terms of their representational properties.

Norman's tentative taxonomy utilizes just two distinctions. Some artefacts, like books or slide-rules, have only a surface representation that the user can perceive, whereas others, like tape recorders or computers, also have an internal representation, that the user cannot perceive. Some artefacts, like computers or slide-rules, are active, and can modify their symbols according to their content, whereas others, like books or tape recorders, are passive, and cannot. These distinctions lead Norman to propose a 2 x 2 classification of artefacts, with single artefacts belonging to one of the four categories.

In developing Norman's taxonomy, I prefer to make two distinctions which may be confused in the active/passive distinction. First, some artefacts allow the user to read and manipulate their representations, whereas others allow reading only. In the terminology of computer systems, we might say that some devices are read—write, whereas others are read—only. This is a fundamental distinction, as the properties of read-only artefacts are naturally much more limited. For example, it is generally only read—write artefacts that need internal representations. Almost all read-only artefacts have just surface representations. (The only exceptions that have been pointed out to me are some flexible information display systems, such as on-line timetables, or intelligent help systems and in fact many of these can be written to as well as read.)

For those read—write artefacts that do have internal representations, a second aspect of active/passive distinction is raised. All these artefacts will need some interface processes that translate between the internal representation and the surface form that users can interact with, but only some artefacts can perform computations that transform their own internal representations. For example, a simple tape recorder has an internal representation, of sound, and provides translation processes that allow this internal representation to be created and read. There are no processes that allow the internal representation to be modified. A word processor has an internal representation of text, which can not only be created and displayed but also modified.

Lastly, in this class of computing artefacts that can modify their internal representations, a distinction can be drawn between those artefacts that can make persistent changes to the external physical world, and those that cannot. In ordinary usage, a word processor does make persistent changes to the world (it prints documents), whereas a calculator or spreadsheet does not (the user simply reads off the desired result).

These distinctions provide a four-dimensional taxonomy of cognitive artefacts, shown in Figure 8.1. What use is this taxonomy? Later, I will argue that it exposes interesting aspects of the relationship between artefacts and mental models. Before that, we will use each of the distinctions made by the taxonomy to motivate a more general discussion of the psychologically important characteristics of cognitive artefacts.

Firstly, the taxonomy stresses the importance of reading and writing, using the terms in their most general senses: interpretation and manipulation of symbol systems. In using read—write devices, the general subtasks of reading and writing are tightly intertwined. The user "writes" to the artefact (perhaps literally, or perhaps by drawing, or by issuing a computer command with a mouse), and, immediately or later, reads the artefact's response (perhaps merely a record, perhaps some window on an elaborate computation). All read—write devices embody a surface representation that can act as an external memory, which human activity exploits by reading (rather than remembering) current problem states and, sometimes, recognizing (rather than recalling) the requirements and effects of operations (Larkin, 1989; Payne, 1991b).

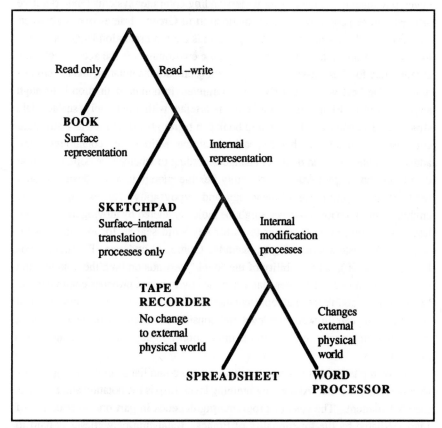

Figure 8.1 A taxonomy of cognitive artefacts (after Norman, 1989b).

Secondly, the taxonomy points out that artefacts often employ representations of representations, in a recursive structure. Although the taxonomy only distinguishes internal from surface representations, complex computational artefacts generally adopt several representational layers, from the bits up through the level of machine architecture to the operating system and programming language. How do human users process these layered representations?

Thirdly, the taxonomy highlights the important distinction between data and process in representational systems (Newell, 1981). Only some artefacts themselves represent computing processes, but the usability of all cognitive artefacts nevertheless depends on the interrelation between information structures and the processes through which the user can access and manipulate these structures.

This point has been developed by Green (1989; 1990) in his attempts to develop a general vocabulary for understanding computer systems (and cognitive artefacts more generally). A key distinction in Green's framework is between "notation" and "environment". The notation is the representation language which the user must understand and manipulate, the environment is the access tools that are provided for these tasks. Usability depends on both the notation and the environment. The best way to clarify the notation/environment distinction is through some examples. First, consider a book, an artefact with a read only, surface data structure. The notation of a standard book can be roughly described as a structure comprising a sequence of chapters, each containing sections, each containing pages, and so on. This notation does not change according to whether the book is on-line or off-line, but its properties are certainly flexible enough to allow design to alter readability, through use of headings and typography, for example. The environment of a book, however, might be radically altered by moving the book on-line. One might provide power tools for key-word search, for example, as the SuperBook system does (Egan, Remde, Gomez, Landauer, Eberhardt and Lochbaum, 1990). The usability of the "book" depends on both the notation and the environment. Note further that when the environment provides computational functions that modify internal representations, there is a layering of representational systems. One can drop down a level and consider the usability of the processing tools, in which case the SuperBook interaction language itself is treated as a notation.

To emphasize this point, let's consider a more familiar example, using Emacs to edit a Lisp program. At the programming level, Lisp is the notation and Emacs is the environment. The ease of programming depends in part on the structure of Lisp, mediated by the functionality of Emacs. Balancing parentheses is hard in some environments (such as pencil and paper), but some versions of Emacs help by providing special-purpose tools. At the editing level, Emacs is a notation, with a structure of its own that affects its usability – the organization of command names for example (see Green and Payne, 1984). The (minimal) environment for Emacs is the command-specifying functionality provided by the keyboard and display.

Finally, the taxonomy draws attention to the fact that even cognitive artefacts are sometimes designed to do physical work, and that users are therefore interacting with the physical world through the artefact. This mediating function of artefacts creates what Hutchins, Hollan and Norman (1986) call the gulfs of execution and evaluation.

8.3 Mental models

As everybody now knows (certainly if they have read through this collection to this point) the concept of a mental model in the psychological literature is confused and confusing. Intuitively, the idea is fairly clear: thinking involves the creation and internalization of simplified models of reality. Yet research under the same banner may appear to make very different theoretical commitments.

To bring some order to this confusion, I propose a simple analogical model for mental models research: a family of Russian dolls, each representing a theoretical position on mental models. At the centre of the family is the smallest doll, who makes the smallest theoretical commitment, which is merely that people's behaviour will often best be explained by appealing to the content of their memories – what they know and believe – independently of any mental mechanisms. This smallest doll's view may seem barely controversial, but it has led to an influential movement in cognitive psychology to consider the origin and nature of beliefs (particularly about the physical world), instead of focusing almost exclusively on the micro-structure of cognitive mechanisms. The well-known collection of Gentner and Stevens (1983) contains papers that share only the smallest-doll's position. As that collection testifies, the investigation of beliefs about specific content domains throws analogy into the spotlight. When people are trying to form understandings of obscure, invisible systems, such as the workings of an application program, they will often construct models by analogy with more familiar domains. Similarly, in technical discourse, ideas and understandings are often communicated through analogical models. By proposing a family of Russian dolls, I am attempting to exploit the same cognitive trick. The notion of theoretical commitment is mapped onto the nesting of dolls: larger dolls share the commitments of the dolls they embrace, but add new commitments of their own.

The second smallest doll, perhaps, adds the commitment that inferences are made by manipulating models according to their structural constraints. This commitment is widely shared among otherwise distinct approaches, for example by Newell and Simon (1972) and deKleer and Brown (1981). The key idea here is that the model's data structure is manipulated by special semantic operations, rather than general syntactic ones. In Newell and Simon's work, the axiomatic concept of a problem space is defined by a data structure and a particular set of operators. In deKleer and Brown's work, and in similar projects in artificial intelligence, reasoning is done by "mental simulation" of a symbolic structure of interconnected components.

Some readers may query my inclusion of Newell and Simon's problem space as an example of mental models theorizing (see also Payne, 1987a). It is true that in the earlier writings the term mental model was not used; yet the overlap in the ideas is clear, as is emphasized by Simon (1989) who explicitly paraphrases "problem space" with a "mental model of the task domain".

The next largest doll adds an insistence that mental models are structural analogues of the world they represent. This constraint distinguishes mental models from propositional descriptions in its insistence on a finite number of mental tokens to represent a corresponding number of objects in the world, and on the encoding of specific relations, such as "to the right of" rather than indeterminate descriptions like "next to". The quasi-homomorphism thesis of Holland, Holyoak, Nisbett and Thagard (1986) specifies just this structure-preserving commitment.

Finally, the largest mental models doll adds the idea that exactly the same kinds of model can be constructed by perceiving, imagining or reading. In particular, understanding text (whether discursive prose or logic-puzzle premises) involves utilizing world knowledge to form a model of the situation that is described in the text, i.e. that goes beyond the propositions in the text. This largest doll espouses Johnson-Laird's theory of reasoning and text comprehension (1983; see Byrne, this volume). For our purposes, the essential aspects of this theory are as follows:

1. Comprehension of text involves two mental structures: the verbal propositions and an analogical model of the state of affairs described by these propositions. (Johnson-Laird, 1983, reserves the term mental model for the analogical world-model, but in the face of the variety of usages in the literature, this specific sense is hard to maintain.) This hypothesis is promoted by several theories of text comprehension, including that of van Dijk and Kintsch (1983), who refer to the world-model as a "situation model".

2. Drawing inferences from text is done by constructing situation models and then inspecting these models to "read off" new propositions. Sometimes a single set of propositions will allow more than one model to be formed. In this case, demonstrative inferences can only be made by reconsulting the propositions and deliberately searching the alternative models for counter-examples.

Note how this theory of mental models assimilates the commitments of the smaller Russian dolls. It insists that situation models preserve the structure of the states of affairs they represent: it proposes that these models are manipulated according to the procedural semantics of verbal propositions, not by syntactic rules (aside from some very general search strategies); comprehension and reasoning are thus explained largely in terms of people's general knowledge of the world.

The strict inclusion hypothesis of the Russian dolls model appears to have some validity. No doubt the family is really larger than four, but useful models must simplify reality. Those theorists whose names I have associated with smaller dolls do not necessarily propose weaker theories; it is just that many of their commitments are not so directly tied to the concept of a mental model.

With this layered understanding of the psychological import of mental models, let us investigate its implications for the study of cognitive artefacts. The HCI literature has been a heavy consumer of the mental model concept, so that is where we will begin.

8.4 Mental models of cognitive artefacts

In most research on HCI, the term mental model is used at the level of the smallest Russian doll, making few a priori cognitive commitments. A great deal of research has demonstrated that people's use of computer systems is critically dependent on their beliefs about those systems, and several studies have focused attention on sources of beliefs, such as analogy with other systems (e.g. Allwood and Elliasson, 1987; Payne, 1991c).

Several workers have recognized a need to be more specific about the different types of knowledge recruited in HCI, leading to a useful and now commonplace distinction between procedural task–action mapping knowledge – how to work the system – and device models of "how the system works" (Kieras and Bovair, 1984). This kind of classification of knowledge types allows more specific questions, and may facilitate generalizations from one computer system to the next, but it is still neutral, theoretically, about the nature of mental models.

This neutrality does not imply that general research on mental models in HCI has been uninteresting. However, rather than review this research in detail, I will concentrate on the more ambitious approach, and describe an attempt to develop a notion of mental models of computer systems, and of cognitive artefacts in general, that makes several theoretical commitments.

First, let us note that Johnson-Laird's theory is, in fact, a mental models theory of interaction with a particular cognitive artefact, namely text (using the term broadly, to include spoken discourse). According to our representational taxonomy of cognitive artefacts, text, or at least prepared text that is being read (the domain of most of Johnson-Laird's work) is relatively simple, in that its representational roles are shared by all cognitive artefacts. This suggests that aspects of Johnson-Laird's theory might apply to all cognitive artefacts, but that the theory may need extending to cope with more complex representational properties.

The central, general aspect of Johnson-Laird's theory, I propose, is that the user of an artefact needs two mental representations – a representation of the artefact, and a representation of the world represented by the artefact. When the artefact is text, the first representation may be propositional and the second an analogical model, as specified by Johnson-Laird's theory. But this neat correspondence between content (artefact versus represented world) and type (propositions versus analogical model) does not exist for all artefacts; what remains constant is the need for twin representations. Consider using a map. This surely involves forming a mental representation of the map (which seems more likely to be imaginal than propositional), and a mental representation of the mapped area (which presumably is a Johnson-Lairdian mental model).

Moving to the other end of the taxonomy, in terms of representational complexity, consider computer systems. A key idea in understanding users' models of computer systems is due to Moran (1983). Moran notes that "a computer system is a conceptual world into itself", and that "the user must translate what he wants to do into the system's terms". These observations lead Moran to a technique for task analysis – ETIT analysis – which describes how "external tasks" defined independently of the system, are translated into "internal tasks" in the system's terms. For example, in some text editors, "delete sentence" might be translated into some combination of "cut line" and "cut string".

Moran's analysis, by treating tasks as atoms, suggests that the mapping problem only exists for artefacts that affect the physical world. But the mental models analysis suggests that it is general to all cognitive artefacts. In developing Moran's ideas, I have preferred to analyse the external and internal domains in terms of problem space theory, considering as primitives the conceptual entities and their interrelationship. The framework I have developed – the yoked state space (YSS) hypothesis – embraces the mental representations that are demanded by all kinds of cognitive artefacts, from maps to computer systems. The YSS hypothesis (Payne, 1987a; 1987b; Payne, Squibb and Howes, 1991) provides us with some convenient terminology. It states that users of an artefact must construct and maintain two separate state spaces: the device space, which represents the possible states of the device, and the goal space, which represents the possible states of the represented world. The user must also know the correspondence, or semantic mapping, between these two conceptual domains.

Let us now consider in turn the levels in our taxonomy of cognitive artefacts, to see if artefacts' additional representational properties demand more of their users' corresponding mental representations.

In using a read–only artefact, one can typically dispense with the mental representation of the artefact once the representation of the described situation has been constructed. Subsequent inferences, unless they are tricky, like those demanded by experimenters, can be made from the situation model only. This explains why memory for text tends to preserve gist rather than form (Johnson-Laird, 1970). However, when one is writing as well as reading, one needs to maintain both knowledge representations, as thinking and manipulation now must be done at both levels. The novelist, for example, must consider both plot and stylistics. The user of a computer system must maintain the device space and the goal space and the semantic mapping between the two. "Operators", like cut-string, are only available in the device space, but goals, like removing a sentence, are defined in the goal space, so that use of the artefact demands constant yoking of the two state spaces.

Artefacts which utilize internal, as well as surface representations will typically demand correspondingly richer mental models, in which the device space embraces aspects of the internal representation. If the surface representation only imperfectly reflects the internal representation (as is generally the case) then the state of the artefact can be changed in ways that are not reflected in the display. In these cases, the user's device space must explicitly represent features of the device's internal representation. To give a simple example, consider a multi-track tape recorder. From simply listening to the surface representation, it is impossible to tell on which track of the tape the internal representation is encoded. Nor will using the track-selection switch have any effect on the simplest pattern of use of the machine - whichever track is selected, the user can record and play back. To exploit the tape recorder fully, however, the user must understand the concept of track: he or she must develop a "figurative account" of the track-selection operation (Payne, Squibb and Howes, 1991).

In this instance, the mental demands of the artefact's internal representations seem rather simple. But as we move down the taxonomy to computer systems – systems that can modify their internal representations – the implications can become quite complex. Consider a simple computerized drawing package, such as MacDraw (for a more detailed analysis see Schiele and Green, 1990, and Payne, 1991a). Such packages provide the user with processes for creating and manipulating simple line drawings. The surface representation (the display) simply shows the current state of the line drawings, but to manipulate these successfully the user must know how this display (which corresponds almost exactly to the goal space) is represented internally, and in particular, how it is treated by the internal processes through which it is manipulated. To use MacDraw, for example, the user must realize that all line drawings are configurations of objects (circles, lines, rectangles, text are all types of object) and that, with the exception of text, parts of objects cannot be manipulated. If a square is drawn as a square, one cannot change the properties of one of its sides.

This example shows that processes that manipulate internal representations place demands on users' mental models, as the user must understand the conceptual structure of the parameters of these internal processes. We saw earlier that internal processes produce a layered structure of notations and environments, which also has implications for users' mental models. Users must construct yoked state spaces at each level of the notation/environment stack. To consider the Lisp/Emacs example, at the programming level, the user's goal space contains the objects of the problem domain, perhaps disks on the towers of Hanoi (to pick a classic programming assignment), and the user must figure out how these can be represented in the device space of lists and functions. While editing the program, the user must drop a level and treat lists and functions as the goal states which are represented in the Emacs device space of strings and characters. The informal observation that editing skill does not depend on the particular programming task suggests that the mental layering should be considered as two separate, but yoked state spaces that the user switches between, rather than a single tower of three state spaces which the user maintains as a working construct.

The final distinction in the taxonomy of cognitive artefacts concerns the relationship of the artefact's representations to the external physical world. In some cases, the modification of internal representations serves purely cognitive purposes, in others, changes to the representations in the artefact can exert persistent physical changes. However, in the mental models framework I have described, even artefacts that serve purely cognitive functions require that the user conceptualize a goal space and its relation to the device. Support for this conjecture is provided by a simple experiment (Payne, 1988).

Subjects were asked to learn to play a computer game, using an abbreviated command language to move a pointer on the screen, and to pick up and manipulate blocks in a 3-D space, represented on the screen as a cross-section and a plan view. One version of the game "Manipulation" was entirely abstract, users were simply moving patterns around. The other version, "Sea Mines" was introduced as commanding an underwater robot to rearrange the sea mines in an underwater combat space. In all other ways the two games were identical. The cover story manipulation affected the ease with which subjects learned the command abbreviations, and prompted different strategies of command usage. These findings suggest that subjects' goal space – their model of what the device represents – affects the way they solve problems in the device space, even when the goal space is entirely imaginary. I propose that all cognitive artefacts demand that the user constructs a model that explicitly represents the relationship between the artefact and some represented world, whether or not changes to that represented world have a physical manifestation.

8.5 Summary

The label "mental models" has been used to refer to psychological theorizing at many different levels. I have attempted to cast some order on this confusion by pointing to a gradient of theoretical commitments, whereby stronger versions of mental models theories embrace cumulatively more commitments. The most developed theory of mental models, that of Johnson-Laird (1983), can be considered as a theory about users' mental representations of artefacts that themselves perform a representational role.

A taxonomy of such cognitive artefacts has been presented. It has been argued that this taxonomy indexes the cognitive demands that the artefacts impose on their users. The content and use of mental models are sensitive to systematic variations in the representational properties of artefacts. If an artefact is written to as well as read from, then users must maintain their representation of the artefact alongside a model of the states of affairs it represents. If an artefact uses hidden, internal representations, then users must conceptualize aspects of those representations that are mapped imperfectly to the display. If an artefact provides processes that modify internal representations, then users must understand the conceptual entities that are parameters to those procedures.

The final distinction in the taxonomy, concerning the relation of the artefact to the physical world, may have no effect on the fundamental properties of mental models. However, this clearly does not imply that this distinction has no psychological import. Much of the psychology of cognitive artefacts remains to be discovered.

Acknowledgements

Thanks to Kevin Singley, and the editors for comments on an earlier draft.

References

Allwood, C.M. and Elliasson, M. (1987). Analogy and other sources of difficulty in novices' very first text-editing. *International Journal of Man–Machine Studies 27*, 1–22.

Anderson, J.R. (1978). Arguments concerning representations for mental imagery. *Psychological Review 85*, 249–77.

Bruner, J.S. and Olson, D.R. (1977–78). Symbols and texts as tools for the intellect. *Interchange 8*, 1–15.

Card, S.K., Moran, T.P., and Newell, A. (1983). *The Psychology of Human–Computer Interaction*. Hillsdale, NJ: LEA.

Carroll, J.M. and Kellogg, W.A. (1989). Artefact as theory nexus: hermeneutics meets theory-based design. *Proceedings CHI '89 Conference on Human Factors in Computing Systems*. New York: ACM.

Cole, M. and Griffin, P. (1980). Cultural amplifiers reconsidered. In Olson, D. (ed.) *The Social Foundations of Language and Thought*. New York: Norton.

deKleer, J. and Brown, J.S. (1981). Mental models of physical mechanisms. In Anderson, J.R. (ed.) *Cognitive Skills and Their Acquisition*. Hillsdale, NJ: LEA.

diSessa, A. (1991). Local sciences. In Carroll, J.M. (ed.) *Designing Interaction: Psychological Theory at the Human–Computer Interface*. Cambridge: CUP.

Egan, D.E., Remde, J.R., Gomez, L.M., Landauer, T.K., Eberhardt, J. and Lochbaum, C.D. (1990). Formative design-evaluation of SuperBook. *ACM Transactions on Information Systems 7*, 30-57.

Gentner, D. and Stevens, A. (eds) (1983). *Mental Models*. Hillsdale, NJ: LEA.

Gibson, J.J. (1979). *The Ecological Approach to Visual Perception*. Boston: Houghton-Miffin.

Green, T.R.G. (1989). Cognitive dimensions of notations. In Sutcliffe, A. and Macauley, L. (eds) *People and Computers V*. Cambridge: CUP.

Green, T.R.G. (1990). The cognitive dimension of viscosity: a sticky problem for HCI. In Diaper, D. Gilmore, D. Cockton,G. and Shackel, B. (eds) *Human–Computer Interaction. Interact 90*. Amsterdam: Elsevier.

Green, T.R.G. and Payne, S.J. (1984). Organization and learnability in computer languages. *International Journal of Man–Machine Studies 21*, 7–18.

Holland, J., Holyoak, K. Nisbett, R. and Thagard, P. (1986). *Induction*. Cambridge, Ma.: MIT Press.

Hutchins, E., Hollan, J. and Norman, D.A. (1986). Direct manipulation interfaces. In Norman, D.A. and Draper, S.W. (eds) *User Centered System Design*. Hillsdale, NJ: LEA.

Intons-Peterson, M. and Fournier, J. (1986). External and internal memory aids: how often do we use them. *Journal of Experimental Psychology: General 115*, 267–280.

Kieras, D.E. and Bovair, S. (1984). The role of a mental model in learning to operate a device. *Cognitive Science 8*, 255–273.

Johnson-Laird, P.N. (1970). The perception and memory of sentences. In Lyons,J. (ed.) *New Horizons in Linguistics*. Harmondsworth: Penguin.

Johnson-Laird, P.N. (1983). *Mental Models*. Cambridge: CUP.

Landauer, T. K. (1987). Relations between cognitive psychology and computer systems design. In Carroll, J.M. (ed.) *Interfacing Thought*. Boston, Ma.: MIT press.

Larkin, J. (1989). Display-based problem solving. In Klahr, D. and Kotovsky, K. (eds) *Complex Information Processing: The Impact of Herbert A. Simon*. Hillsdale, NJ: LEA.

Larkin, J. and Simon, H.A. (1987). Why a diagram is (sometimes) worth ten thousand words. *Cognitive Science 11*, 65–100.

Moran, T.P. (1983). Getting into a system: external–internal task mapping analysis. *Proceedings CHI 83 Conference on Human Factors in Computing Systems*. New York: ACM.

Newell, A. (1973). You can't play twenty questions with nature and win. In Chase, W.G. (ed.), *Visual Information Processing*. Hillsdale, NJ: LEA.

Newell, A. (1981). Physical symbol systems. In Norman, D.A. (ed.) *Perspectives on Cognitive Science*. Hillsdale, NJ: LEA.

Newell, A. and Simon, H.A. (1972). *Human Problem Solving*. Englewood Cliffs, NJ: Prentice Hall.

Norman, D.A. (1989a). Personal communication, Chappaqua New York.

Norman, D.A. (1989b). Cognitive artefacts. Paper presented at the *Kittle House Workshop on Psychological Theory and User Interface Design*, Chappaqua, New York, 19–22 June.

Norman, D.A. (1991). Cognitive artefacts. In Carroll, J.M. (ed.) *Designing Interaction: Psychological Theory at the Human-Computer Interface*. Cambridge: CUP.

Payne, S.J. (1987a). Methods and mental models in theories of cognitive skill. In Self, J. (ed.) *Artificial Intelligence and Human Learning*. London: Chapman and Hall.

Payne, S.J. (1987b). Complex problem spaces: modelling the knowledge needed to use interactive systems. In Bullinger, H.J. and Shackel, B. (eds) *Human-Computer-Interaction. Interact 87.* Amsterdam: Elsevier.

Payne, S.J. (1988). Metaphorical instruction and the early learning of an abbreviated-command computer system. *Acta Psychologica* 69, 207–230.

Payne, S.J. (1991a). Interface problems and interface resources. In Carroll, J.M. (ed.) *Designing Interaction: Psychological Theory at the Human-Computer Interface.* Cambridge: CUP.

Payne, S.J. (1991b). Display-based action at the user interface. *International Journal of Man–Machine Studies 35,* 275–289.

Payne, S.J. (1991c). A descriptive study of mental models. *Behaviour and Information Technology 10,* 3–21.

Payne, S.J., Squibb, H. and Howes, A. (1991). The nature of device models: the yoked state space hypothesis and some experiments with text editors. *Human-Computer Interaction 5,* 415–444.

Schiele, F. and Green, T.R.G. (1990). HCI formalisms and cognitive psychology: the case of task-action grammar. In Harrison, M. and Thimbleby, H. (eds), *Formal Methods in Human-Computer Interaction.* Cambridge: CUP.

Simon, H.A. (1969). *The Sciences of the Artificial.* Cambridge, Ma.: MIT Press.

Simon, H.A. (1989). The scientist as problem solver. In Klahr, D. and Kotovsky, K. (eds) *Complex Information Processing: The Impact of Herbert A. Simon.* Hillsdale, NJ: LEA.

van Dijk, T.A. and Kintsch, W. (1983). *Strategies of Discourse Comprehension.* New York: Academic Press.

Vygotsky, L.S. (1978). *Mind in Society.* Cambridge, Ma.: Harvard University Press.

Chapter 9

Mental Models in Cognitive Skill: The Example of Industrial Process Operation

Lisanne Bainbridge

9.1 Introduction

The term mental model is widely but often vaguely used. For example, industrial process operators are said to have a mental model of the process they control (steel works, oil refinery, etc.) . They use this in understanding how the process works and in deciding how to operate it. But authors are rarely specific about what these mental models are like. In the book edited by Gentner and Stevens (1983) all the authors use a mental model as an explanatory concept, but not one of them defines rigourously what they mean by the term. The aim of this chapter is to elucidate the complex notion of a mental model, and its place in cognitive skill.

What is a mental model in general? Early experimental psychology was almost exclusively concerned with tasks in which there was only one response to each stimulus. Cognitive psychology is concerned with understanding tasks in which a stimulus is processed in some way before a response is chosen; the brain of the person doing the task contributes something which is not in the original stimulus. For example, there is nothing explicit in "example" and "aelmpxe" which indicates that one is a word and the other is not, but the brain recognizes this and processes the two strings of letters in different ways. In many tasks, knowledge about structures or cause–effect relations which underlie what can be observed play a central part in cognitive processes. When doing a task which uses knowledge about the state(s) of a potentially changeable world, these structures of knowledge may be called mental models.

MODELS IN THE MIND:
Theory, perspective and applications. ISBN 0−12−592970−6

People studying mental models have a large range of interests, and this affects what they consider should be in a model. This chapter outlines some of the issues that someone studying mental models might be concerned with.

9.2 The dimensions of mental models

What are the main dimensions of the topic of "mental models", the issues that investigators are concerned with? I suggest that there are four main ones:

1. The part played by the "mental model" in cognitive processing,
2. The ways in which the knowledge is implemented,
3. The factors affecting what is in any one specific mental model,
4. The factors affecting what is in an investigator's model of a user's mental model.

These points will be explained in a little more detail in this section. The paper will then concentrate on user's/operator's mental models. For a wider ranging discussion of the term mental model, see Wilson and Rutherford (1989).

9.2.1 The contribution of mental models in cognitive processing

There has been a great deal of confusion because the term mental model has been used to refer to two different types of contribution to cognitive processing. If the term mental model refers in general to ways in which knowledge is used in cognitive processing, then this paper can also include other types:

(a) Knowledge of the permanent or potential characteristics of some part of the external world. This sort of knowledge is used in inferring what is happening in some part of the external world which cannot be observed directly, in predicting what is going to happen next, or in explaining or choosing what to do. It has always been called a mental model in the process control literature (e.g. Edwards and Lees, 1974), and by Gentner and Stevens (1983). Also it has been called long-term memory, or the knowledge base.

(b) Temporary inferred knowledge about the present or predicted state of the external world. In complex tasks, cognitive processes build up a structure of inference about what the available evidence means. This structure has been called a mental picture in the process control literature (e.g. Kraagt and Landeweerd, 1974), but because mental picture was often interpreted as implying a mental image this term has not been used recently. Johnson-Laird (1983) calls this temporary structure of knowledge a mental model which has caused confusion in process operator research. This knowledge has also been called short-term memory, operational memory, working memory, or the blackboard.

(c) Knowledge of the outcomes and properties (permanent or potential characteristics) of the user's own behaviour. It suggests that each working method has stored with it information which is used in deciding whether it is appropriate to use that method.

This chapter will distinguish between these three contributions to cognitive processing by calling them knowledge base, working storage and meta-knowledge (another term with multiple meanings) respectively.

9.2.2 Implementation of knowledge

Knowledge may be embodied in various forms, with various levels of accuracy. Many underlying mechanisms for knowledge representation have and are being suggested: propositions, production rules, frames, parallel-distributed processing, images, mental videos, etc. There is much debate in the psychological literature about whether different types of representational mechanism do exist in the brain or whether they can all be reduced to one. For practical purposes this issue can usually be side-stepped. For example, if some display format, perhaps a picture rather than a written description, can be used more easily by people doing a particular task, then this is more important than which of these representations might be fundamental in the brain.

9.2.3 Factors affecting a specific mental model

The knowledge that a specific person has about their task depends not only on the task aims, the device and environment, their training, and the amount and type of experience, but also on the emotional, social and cultural context, and on the individual's cognitive style.

9.2.4 The investigator's model of the user

The model which someone who is describing a user/ operator themselves finds most useful depends on their aim: whether this is to do elegant experiments, to simulate overt behaviour or underlying cognitive processes, or to make practical design recommendations, etc. In fact this is a recursive topic, as dimensions (1) to (3) also all apply to the investigator's model of the user's mental model.

It is important to consider dimensions (3) and (4) because any model must be a subset of what is potentially available to be represented. The most efficient subset to choose has a style and content of presentation which makes explicit what is most relevant, useful and usable in thinking about the current task, whether this is the task of the investigator or of the user. There is much unnecessary debate about models because investigators with one set of aims find models useless which were devised for other purposes (Bainbridge, 1986).

As there are many alternatives on each of these dimensions, the "problem space" of mental models is huge. This has at least three implications:

1. It accounts for knowledge elicitation difficulties, as any one method can access only part of all this,
2. It means that any one investigator is only concerned with a few cells of this space, and needs to be clear about which, to avoid unnecessary conflict,
3. In my view it means that it is not particularly useful to use the term mental model, as this is not sufficiently specific. Instead it is important to be clear about which of all these possibilities one is referring to.

9.3 The approach taken in this chapter

Of the above dimensions, this paper focuses on the uses of knowledge in cognitive processing. It will not debate the ways in which knowledge is represented, and it is not concerned with individual differences in mental models. It does present one investigator's model of the user/operator. As for the aims of this paper, there are five general points:

1. The data to be accounted for are verbal protocols and verbal reports collected from industrial process operators.
2. The methodological approach has been to ask what cognitive model is needed to account for the cognitive behaviour expressed. The model concentrates on cognitive skill rather than on problem solving.
3. Both process operation and modelling process operation are huge tasks, with thousands of variables. As the size of the task to be accounted for goes up, so the elegance and strength of the proofs given, and claims made, must go down. This means that, in this sort of modelling enterprise, the ideas are justified because they are useful rather than because they are completely testable.

4. This chapter is concerned with meta-theory, with suggesting general mechanisms which underly many applications, rather than with instantiating the details of any particular application.

5. Although the concepts are presented more explicitly than they often are in papers on mental models, they have not been programmed, so people who like fully specified models will find this frustrating. The aim of this paper is not to consider what can be done in the way of cognitive modelling within the limits imposed by any available computer tool, but rather to start to identify what are the requirements for a model of cognitive processes in complex tasks, and to present a model which is in sufficient detail to have practical implications.

9.4 An example of industrial process operation

Tables 9.1 and 9.2 show a short sequence of operator activity while diagnosing and responding to a process fault. The tables are adapted from an Operator Decision/Action Summary given by Pew et al (1981), who analysed what happened during the Prairie Island nuclear power station incident, after extensive discussions with the operators and other experts.

Table 9.1 shows the first information the operators received, and how they interpreted it. There are several possible reasons why a radiation alarm might go off, many of them more likely than the actual presence of radiation. Only the first line in Table 9.1 is information given on the process displays, the other items were all inferred by the operators, using their knowledge/ mental models of the process. The operators interpreted what was the actual state of the process, suggested what would confirm this interpretation, and directed their attention to checking for this confirmatory evidence. They actively looked for certain information, rather than just passively reacting to changes, and added goals to their task aims. Table 9.2 shows what happened seven minutes later, after the alarm had gone off again, another possible interpretation had been checked, and several other pieces of information had appeared on the displays. Again, the operators inferred what was happening inside the process. Given the displays they had, there was no way in which they could get direct information about a leak (rupture). They then worked by anticipation. They predicted what further changes would happen in the process, and predicted what automatic safety actions would be triggered off by these future changes. Next they predicted the effect of these automatic events, and chose and implemented actions to reduce the undesirable effects of the expected events. In this way they were using anticipatory control. They were not reacting by feedback to minimize an undesirable state which had occurred: they were anticipating, to try to prevent an undesirable future state from occurring.

INFORMATION AVAILABLE:	High radiation alarm on IR15 air ejector
COGNITIVE INFERENCES :	
Interpretation	Occasional spiking produces false alarms, assume this is a false alarm
Expectation	If not a false alarm, IR15 will alarm again
Intention	Monitor for further indications

Table 9.1 Prairie Island Nuclear Power Station Incident, Time 14:14 (adapted from Operator Decision/ Action Summary in Pew et al, 1981, p.B-12).

INFORMATION AVAILABLE:	Feed-flow/steam-flow mismatch in Steam Generator "A"
COGNITIVE INFERENCES :	
Interpretation	Air radiation alarms, plus rapid decrease of pressurizer level and pressure, plus mismatch, unequivocally confirm rupture probably in Steam Generator "A"
Expectations	Pressurizer level and pressure will continue to decrease. low pressurizer pressure will cause : - automatic reactor trip [shut-down] - automatic safety water injection
Intention	Minimize effect of reactor trip on power grid (sudden pull-off of power not desirable)
ACTIONS	Notify grid controller of planned reduction. commence load reduction.

Table 9.2 Prairie Island Nuclear Power Station Incident, Time 14:21 (adapted from Operator Decision/ Action Summary in Pew et al, 1981, p.B-12).

Modelling industrial process operation involves modelling the cognitive processes of interpreting incomplete data, and anticipating and planning actions with reference to expected events. In all these types of activity, having mental models of the process, enabling operators to know the relation between evidence and inference and to predict process behaviour, are essential.

9.5 The cognitive modules in process operation

This section gives more complete information about the modules of cognitive processing involved in process operation. The full supporting evidence is not given in detail. The activities which are proposed are sufficient to account for the data available on cognitive processes in four nuclear incidents (Pew et al, 1981; Woods, 1982), part of a steel-works (Bainbridge, 1974), gas distribution grid controlling (Umbers, 1979) and a commercial bakery (Beishon, 1969).

To analyse complex cognitive activity, it is necessary to distinguish between cognitive goals and task goals. For example a task/process control goal might be "keep the temperature at 200° C". Cognitive goals involved in meeting this task goal might be to find out: "what is the temperature now ?" Data on operators' moment-to-moment thinking (as reflected in verbal protocols) show that their thinking can be divided into a sequence of short units, each of which has a different cognitive goal.

This section outlines how these units or modules of cognitive processing have been identified, lists the modules, and suggests the main implications for mental models and cognitive processing in complex tasks such as process operation.

9.5.1 The notion of a "module" of processing

In Tables 9.1 and 9.2 the operators' cognitive activity was divided into a sequence of sections, and the cognitive purpose of each section was suggested.Table 9.3 gives another example, part of a verbal protocol from an operator controlling the availability of gas supplies (Umbers, 1976). The sequence of analysis has been to infer the cognitive goal underlying each piece of evidence about cognitive processing (phrase in the protocol). The sequence of cognitive activity is then divided into sub-sections, by grouping together all the items concerned with the same cognitive goal, and defining a new section when the cognitive goal changes.

These subsections have been called modules of processing because they seem to be independent, in the sense that they can occur in any order, though they are not independent in the sense that they do not relate to each other.

I'll give you a quick resumé of what the forecast was this morning, that is forecast estimate, and the estimate for this morning was 75 of MG [manufactured gas] and the NG [natural gas] send of 150 m.
                                    predict state

the stock aim on both MG is 62.6 and NG 180.7
                                    review goals

we have 3 plants at work, the 3b at C/hill, the 1c at Tipton, and No. 3 at W H, this gives us a total cum. make per hr. of 4.2 approx without B/ air
                                    review present state

B/ air will give us something in the region of – sorry, a correction to the total available without B/ air would be approx. 4.4 and there's 0.8/hr. of B/ air, so that we can in fact make 5.2 with full NG, this is something in the region of 129–130 for the day.
                                    review action availability and effect

we don't contemplate using this much
                                    evaluate

but there is the facility for taking NG off the reforming and putting Naptha in, which will give us another increase of something in the region 0.30-0.35/hr.
                                    review action availability and effect

so that we're not too badly off
                                    evaluate

if the weather forecast which they give for tomorrow has been mostly sunny and warm, with a max of 68 and a mean of 58° F.
                                    predict goals

we shall cope with the send on MG with what we've got quite admirably.
                                    evaluate

Note: Main text – verbal protocol from gas-grid controller.
          Bold italics – inferred cognitive goal of each protocol section.

Table 9.3 Adapted from Umbers (1976, p.321) study of gas-grid control, Time 22:07.

9.5.2 Proposed modules

The evidence that cognitive activity can be divided into subsections each with a different cognitive goal comes from verbal reports made by operators while actually doing a task, as in Bainbridge (1972), Umbers (1976, see Table 9.3) and Reinartz, 1989). This notion has then been used in inferring the modules used in cognitive activities which have been analysed and described in less detail by Beishon (1969), Pew et al (1981), and Woods (1982). This widens the number of task types accounted for.

In Table 9.4, the basic modules proposed are listed in bold type. This is only a preliminary list for discussion and to illustrate the arguments, as only a small range of tasks has been surveyed. In particular, the modules used in problem solving are not included. Not all these modules are needed in all tasks. The key concepts are:

1. Cognitive processing is done by modules each of which has a particular cognitive goal, which is to build up a temporary structure of information about the current state of the task.
2. The primary concerns of the cognitive processing, before choosing and making actions to operate the process are to infer and review the state of the process, and anticipate and plan future events and activities.
3. The modules refer to information which is available in knowledge bases, and already in working storage (i.e. to mental models) as well as to the environment.

9.6 Summary of knowledge bases and working storage

Table 9.4 lists the sources used by, and outputs of, the basic modules. It shows the working storage and knowledge bases referred to during cognitive processing, on the left. All the modules refer to the environment and to the previous output of the same module, so these have not been mentioned explicitly. The working storage output from the processing modules is shown on the right.

These types of working storage and knowledge base are not based on direct evidence. They are inferences, on the basis of observed cognitive activity, about what would be the working storage and knowledge bases needed to simulate this module of activity.

WS   previous state
           predicted events
           KB   stimulus -> identity
                      stimulus -> hypotheses, with test information
                      state -> response required procedures
                                IDENTIFY
                                            WS   further information needs
                                                    identity
                                                    predefined response(s).

WS   identity of recent changes
           previous state
           predicted events.
           KB   symptom -> cause hypoths, with test information
                      dynamic model/ scenarios
                                INFER/ REVIEW PRESENT STATE
                                            WS   present state
                                                    further information needs
                                                    predicted events,
                                                    both with timing, implications for
                                                    state inferences

WS   present state
           KB   scenarios
                                REVIEW/PREDICT EVENTS
                                            WS   predicted events, with timing
                                                    predicted effect

WS   present state
           predicted event
           proposed action
           KB   dynamic model
                                PREDICT STATE
                                            WS   predicted state/ effect, with timing

WS   present/ predicted state
           KB   product targets
                      plant constraints
                                REVIEW/PREDICT TASK GOALS
                                            WS   present/ predicted goals, with
                                                    timing

Table 9.4 Proposed processing modules with associated working storage (WS) and
knowledge bases (KB) on left : WS and KBs referred to during processing (all
modules refer to the environment), on right : WS produced by processing.

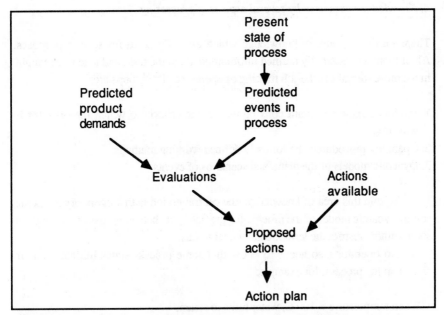

Figure 9.1 Main interdependencies between aspects of working storage.

9.6.1 Working storage

Figure 9.1 lists the main contents of working storage, and illustrates how one part of working storage depends on another. There are times when this whole structure has to be built up from scratch and in sequence, for example when the operators come on shift, or when there is an unexpected event such as a major fault. Otherwise, the existing working storage is referred to and revised as appropriate (this depends on working storage, but there is not space to go into this here).

9.6.2 The main knowledge bases used in well-established cognitive skill

The knowledge bases fall into two groups: those referred to by several process modules, and those which are referred to by only one module (for more details see Bainbridge, 1988.)

a) Knowledge bases used by several aspects of processing

There are three groups of knowledge which are referred to for several purposes. All of them are externally defined information about the task, and tend to be taught in the more formal off-the-job training of operators. The groups are:

1. Product targets and plant constraints, i.e. the criteria to which the operator is working,
2. Operating procedures, the formally defined working methods.
3. Dynamic models of the plant, and scenarios of events.

Within this area of knowledge, the central notion is that operators use some sort of dynamic model of the process for predicting its behaviour over time. Indeed some authors restrict the term mental model to this.

An operator also needs to know that some process states initiate a major change in the process, for example:

• When temperature > 100 C, water turns to steam.
• If pressure < x, automatic shut-down is initiated.
• When pH > y, product is precipitated, etc.

These are called a change in phase of the process, because different dynamic models are needed to predict how the process will behave, on each side of the discontinuity.

So it is possible to suggest that the operator's knowledge of the process has two levels, both of which are used in anticipation. First, a selection of dynamic models of process behaviour in various phases, for which the necessary components are illustrated in Figure 9.2. Second, knowledge of scenarios (see Figure 9.3) describing the sequence of events (phases):

1. During start-up, shut-down, or batch processing.
2. After a given fault has occurred.

b) Knowledge bases used by only one aspect of processing

The second group of knowledge bases are each used only by one processing module:

stimulus -> identity,
symptom -> underlying cause,
state -> response required,
effect required -> action with this effect,
action -> effect,
action -> required pre-conditions.

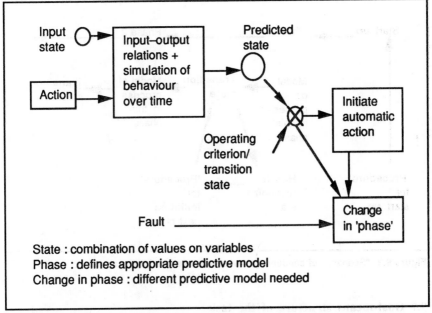

Figure 9.2 Components of dynamic model of process behaviour within one phase.

In each case, in well-developed cognitive skill these terms mean a specific action, identity, etc., not the use of a general principle to generate the answer. Interestingly, at least for this inferred evidence, these knowledge bases used by only one module are of the "association" type, i.e."if *x* then *y*", and need to be learned from repeated experience.

9.6.3 Knowledge bases used in problem solving

The above knowledge bases are used in cognitive skill, that is, when working methods and reference knowledge are well-established and readily available (see 9.6.2). When an appropriate working method and background knowledge are not known then problem solving is needed (Bainbridge, 1989b). It is generally assumed that operators then use information about the causal, functional and physical structures of the plant, and the goal structure of the task, to work out from first principles what is wrong, or what to do. Most reviews of operator knowledge focus on these types of knowledge, e.g. Rasmussen (1979), Bainbridge (1988), but there is not space to go into this here.

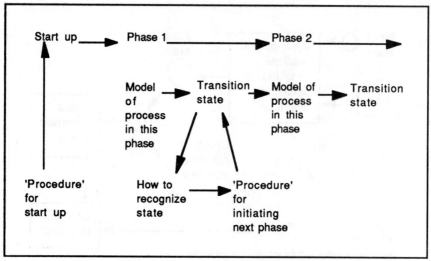

Figure 9.3 "Scenario" of sequence of events/phases in a batch campaign.

9.7 Goal-means structure of the task

Some aspects of the basic cognitive processing module have not yet been discussed. These include the need for the third type of mental model suggested: a skilled person's model of the properties of their own behaviour. Two main points will be covered in this section. First, the main features of the cognitive processing module and, second, the goal-means structure of the task, the need for choice between alternative methods of working, and the need for the third type of mental model.

9.7.1 The main features of the cognitive processing module

Figure 9.4 gives more detail about the suggested mechanisms in the basic cognitive processing module. There are six important features:

1. The aim of each processing module is to meet a particular cognitive goal, such as to find what is the present temperature, or to choose an action.

2. The "answer" is found (stepped arrow) by referring to the environment or to knowledge, or by further cognitive processing. This processing is carried out by modules at a lower level (see 9.5.2 and 9.6.1). Each module is somewhat like a complex slot in a "frame".

3. The modules actively search for the information they need, rather than passively responding to information at it arrives.

4. Finding the relevant answer is done within the context provided by existing working storage, represented by the left -hand of the two boxes.

5. The answer, represented by the right-hand box, itself becomes part of working storage. It either provides the answer for a superior goal, or it becomes part of the data used in later cognitive processing (see Figure 9.8). Working storage is therefore structured by its place in the goal/ module structure of the task. This provides a type of structured blackboard.

6. The modules communicate with each other via working storage, and are sequenced via working storage between the strategies on the basis of information about them.

9.5.2 The operators' knowledge of their own behaviour

The chequered arrow in Figure 9.4 represents the link between the goal and the method for meeting it. This acts as a reminder that it is not a simple link. It is not a simple link because behaviour is flexible, and it is easiest to represent this flexibility by goal-means independence (Bainbridge, 1975; 1978). A goal may be met by several methods: which of these to use will depend on details of the context. And a given method may be used in meeting several goals. So the goal-method link needs to include the choice of method.

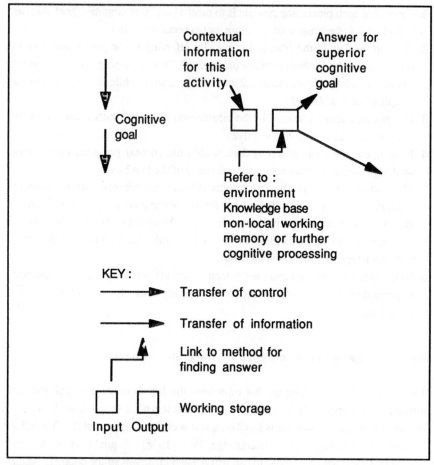

Figure 9.4 Components of basic processing module.

The suggested mechanism for this is that each method has stored with it data about its general properties: how long it takes, how accurate the result is, how much effort it needs, etc. On the basis of this information, the method is chosen which best fits the context. Figure 9.5 suggests, as an example, some dimensions of choice between topographic and functional strategies (Rasmussen and Jensen, 1974) in fault diagnosis.

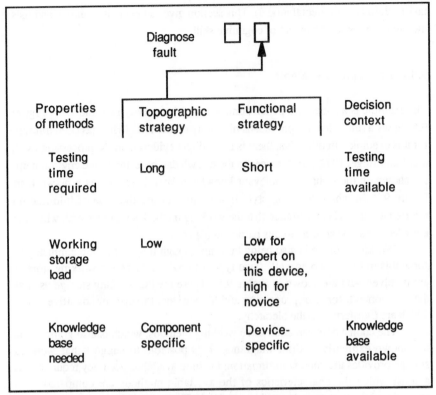

Figure 9.5 Topographic and functional strategies in fault diagnosis.

It is possible to suggest that one aspect of cognitive skill is that these data about working methods are ready available, so choosing appropriate behaviour is automatic/ unconscious (Bainbridge, 1978). The data, and the relevant dimensions of behaviour to consider, would have been learned from experience. This information could be considered as a third type of "mental model", of knowledge about the properties of one's own behaviour, an aspect of metaknowledge.

9.8 Processing and skill

The basic theme of this chapter is that the development of process operators' cognitive skill has built up an integrated cross-referencing structure, in which the goal structure/ working methods refer to knowledge about the process (a first type of mental model) and knowledge about one's own behaviour (a second type of mental model) to build up in working storage an overview of the current state of the task (a third type of mental model). This section gives an explicit example, and lists the implications for the nature of cognitive skill.

9.8.1 An explicit example

The example is a paper-and-pencil simulation of the activity in Table 9.1. Figure 9.6 shows a (three-level) goal-means hierarchy on the left. (This has been inferred for this example. In other data there is more direct evidence on the processing used, e.g. Bainbridge, 1972.) References to the knowledge base and to the environment are shown on the right. The relevant knowledge base is shown as a network in Figure 9.7, in which lettering style is used to indicate the type of information referred to. It has been assumed that the working method is more general, while the knowledge base is specific to this particular alarm.

Working storage is also being built up, though it would be too confusing to show this in Figure 9.6 as well. Two types of cross-reference in working storage are involved, and are shown in Figure 9.8. These are the working storage used as data, or context, for later processing and the answers to superior cognitive goals, which are transferred up the hierarchy.

The choice between alternative working methods, which is also going on, is not shown explicitly in these diagrams. It is possible to suggest that working storage provides the context information, i.e. time available, accuracy required, etc. against which the characteristics of the available methods are compared. An example where this choice would be needed in Figure 9.6 is at the point where the operators choose a method for selecting between hypotheses about the possible causes of the displayed information. In this example the operators used Reason and Mycielska's (1982) "frequency matching" strategy.

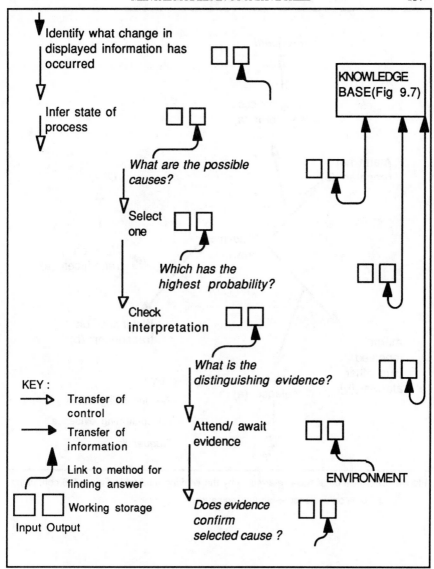

Figure 9.6 Working method for reacting to an alarm signal, with references to Knowledge base.

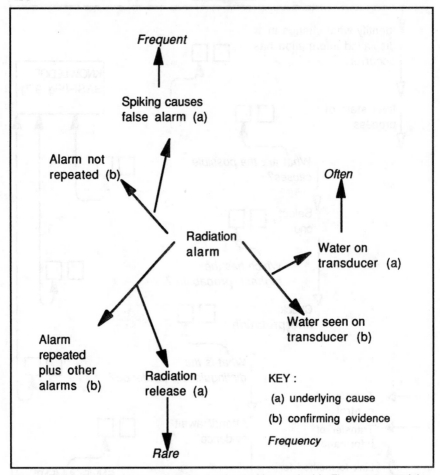

Figure 9.7 Knowledge base referred to by the working method in Figure 9.6 containing data on evidence -> underlying cause.

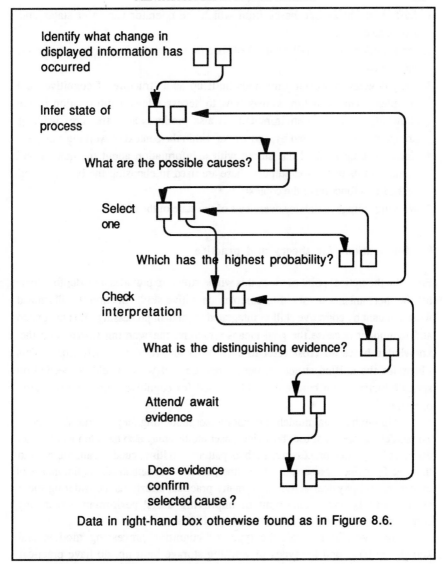

Figure 9.8 Cross-references in working Storage.

9.8.2 The components of cognitive skill

In summary, this model suggests that the main features of cognitive skill are well-developed working methods and mental models. Specifically, this consists of:

1. Sufficient knowledge bases from which the operator can infer states and anticipate events.
2. For 1:1 information, well-established specific knowledge bases can be accessed automatically.
3. Fully developed working methods built up as a structure of cognitive goal modules. This structure knows how to access relevant information in the knowledge bases and environment. It also produces and structures working storage which is activated by, and works within the context of working storage.
4. Each working method has stored with it information about the quality and quantity of its needs and outputs; these are used in choosing the best working method as a function of the context.
5. Working storage maintains overviews of the state of the task.

9.9 Implications for theory and practice

From the theoretical point of view, this whole structure provides a model for (some of) the mechanisms involved in complex cognitive skill. Section 9.6 illustrated what is meant by cognitive skill as integrated redundant processing. It is integrated and redundant because the goal-means structure, the working storage and the knowledge bases all cross refer to each other and reinforce each other. This illustrates the unified structure, but a great deal of work would be needed on specific instantiation before it could be used for cognitive modelling of users/operators.

Although mental models are part of user modelling they are not the whole. To predict all aspects of user behaviour, user models may also need to include other aspects of cognitive processing, such as pattern handling, cued recall, the time to translate from one representation to another, the non-mathematically optimum use of evidence, and physical activity. In many practical situations, considering these aspects will be more important in improving users' performance than any consideration of mental models (Bainbridge, 1989a).

However, in general, the types of cognitive processing module and knowledge base, and the types of working storage built up, do have practical implications. The main basis to these recommendations is that no part of a complex task is done in isolation, as is illustrated by the model.

Training, task analysis, and job aids such as displays, need to be oriented to helping the operators to build up the contextual overviews, and to work oriented to the future (Bainbridge, in preparation).

The types of knowledge base used are also relevant in training and in display format design. The content of the different knowledge bases, and their type and relevance to different aspects of processing, need to be considered in the design of training schemes (Bainbridge, 1990a). Display formats should be compatible with the type of knowledge represented (Bainbridge, 1990b). However, many recommendations about details of interface design for process operators do not need to be based on an explicit model of cognitive processes at the level of detail presented in section 9.6.1 (Bainbridge, 1989a; 1990b).

The need for the overviews, and the time taken to build them up from scratch, also have implications for job design. This is particularly true for the design of automated systems so that operators can either maintain an overview, or have time to build one up, and can maintain the cognitive skills needed, when expected to take over manual operation from an automated system (Bainbridge, 1983; in press).

Acknowledgement

Much of the research described in this paper was done while I was Visiting Research Fellow in the Ergonomics Workgroup, University of Twente, The Netherlands. I would like to thank Dr. Ted White and his colleagues for an excellent and happy research environment.

References

Bainbridge, L. (1972). *An analysis of a verbal protocol from a process control task*. PhD thesis, University of Bristol.

Bainbridge, L. (1975). The representation of working storage and its use in the organization of behaviour. In Singleton, W.T. and Spurgeon, P. (eds) *Measurement of Human Resources*. London: Taylor and Francis.

Bainbridge, L. (1978). Forgotten alternatives in skill and workload. *Ergonomic 21*, 169–185.

Bainbridge, L. (1983). Ironies of automation. *Automatica 19*, 775–779.

Bainbridge, L. (1986) . What should a "good" model of the NPP operator contain ? In *Proceedings of the International Topical Meeting on Advances in Human Factors in Nuclear Power Systems*, American Nuclear Society, Knoxville, Tennessee, April 21–24.

Bainbridge, L. (1988). Types of representation. In Goodstein, L.P. Anderson, H.B. and Olsen, S.E. (eds) *Tasks, Errors, and Mental Models*. London: Taylor and Francis.

Bainbridge, L. (1989a). Cognitive science approaches to process operation: present gaps and future requirements. In *Proceedings of the Second*

European Meeting on Cognitive Science Approaches to Process Control.
October 24–27, Siena, Italy.

Bainbridge, L. (1989b). Development of skill, reduction of workload. In
Bainbridge, L. and Ruiz, S.A. Quintanilla (eds)*Developing Skills with
Information Technology.* Chichester: Wiley.

Bainbridge, L. (1990a). A note on training sequences and simulator facilities for
industrial process operation. In proceedings of the meeting on *Operator
Training and Acquisition of Cognitive Skills.* School of Psychology,
University of Wales College of Cardiff, September 27–29.

Bainbridge, L. (1990b). Multiplexed VDT display systems. In Weir, G.R.S. and
Alty, J.L. (eds) *Human–Computer Interaction and Complex Systems.*
London: Academic Press.

Bainbridge, L. (in press). Will expert systems solve the operators' problems?
Behaviour and Information Technology.

Bainbridge, L. (in preparation). Cognitive context analysis.

Beishon, R.J. (1969). An analysis and simulation of an operator's behaviour in
controlling continuous baking ovens. Reprinted in Edwards, E. and Lees,
F.P. (eds) *The Human Operator in Process Control.* London: Taylor and
Francis.

Edwards, E. and Lees F.P. (1974). *The Human Operator in Process Control.*
London: Taylor and Francis.

Gentner, D. and Stevens, A.L. (1983). *Mental Models.* Hillsdale, NJ: LEA.

Johnson-Laird, P.N. (1983). *Mental Models.* Cambridge: CUP.

Kraagt, H. and Landerweerd, J.A. (1974). Mental skills in process control. In
Edwards, E. and Lees, F.P. (eds). *The Human Operator in Process Control.*
London: Taylor and Francis.

Pew, R.W., Miller, D.C. and Feeher, C.E. (1981). *Evaluation of proposed
control room improvements through analysis of critical operator decisions.*
Palo Alto, California: Electric Power Research Institute, NP-1982, Research
Project 891.

Rasmussen, J. (1979). *On the structure of knowledge – a morphology of mental
models in a man–machine system context.* Røskilde, Denmark: Risø
National Laboratory, Report M-2192.

Rasmussen, J. and Jensen, A. (1974). Mental procedures in real-life tasks: a case-
study of electronic trouble shooting. *Ergonomics 17,* 293–307.

Reason, J. and Mycielska, K. (1982). *Absent-minded? The Psychology of Mental
Lapses and Everyday Errors.* Englewood Cliffs: Prentice–Hall.

Reinartz, S.J. and Reinartz G. (1989). Verbal communication in collective control of simulated nuclear power plant incidents. In *Proceedings of the Second European Meeting on Cognitive Science Approaches to Process Control*, October 24–27, Siena, Italy.

Umbers, I. G.(1976). *A study of cognitive skills in complex systems*. PhD thesis, University of Aston.

Umbers, I.G. (1979). A study of the control skills of gas grid control engineers. *Ergonomics 22*, 557–571.

Wilson, J. R. and Rutherford, A. (1989). Mental models: theory and application in human factors. *Human Factors 31*, 617–634.

Woods, D.D. (1982). *Operator decision behaviour during the steam generator tube rupture at the ginna nuclear power station*. Westinghouse Research Report 82-1C57-CONRM-R2.

Chapter 10

Mental Models and Complex Tasks

Yvonne Rogers

During the 1980s when human–computer interaction and cognitive ergonomics were establishing themselves as subjects of study, both subscribed heavily to the theories, concepts and methods developed in cognitive psychology and cognitive science generally (see Long and Whitefield, 1989). The assumption behind this absorption was that since human computer interaction is essentially cognitive it made sense to describe and explicate the nature of users' tasks when using computer systems in terms of cognitive processes. In the beginning, models and theories were developed in HCI that were essentially modifications and often simplifications of models of human information processing (e.g. Card, Moran and Newell, 1983). The theoretical and practical limitations of these models, however, led a number of HCI researchers to look to alternative theories of cognition. The notion of mental models as conceptualized in the reasoning and knowledge literature was taken on board. Given that interacting with computers is essentially a complex task requiring various inferencing processes, the hope was that the concept could somehow provide the leverage with which to conceptualize more adequately the nature of this activity. In particular, many researchers saw this as an opportunity to model the dynamic aspects of the mental processes that occur during human–computer interaction. Although, much debate has since ensued a lot of it has been rather fruitless and counter-productive.

Part of the problem is that the mental model concept has been used in a rather ad hoc and arbitrary manner (Tauber, 1988). Also it has been used to describe idealized knowledge rather than actual knowledge use. A further problem has been the immense pressure to produce tools for designers before the theoretical foundations on which they are based have been developed sufficiently.

MODELS IN THE MIND:
Theory, perspective and applications. ISBN 0–12–592970–6

Researchers have come to realize that eliciting and subsequently modelling mental models is a very difficult and elusive task (see Part 5). The outcome of this research has been the development of a motley set of models, which use widely different terminology, are very confusing and lack the predictive power to be of any practical or explanatory value. In his chapter Payne points out that it must be acknowledged that human–computer interaction is a highly complex activity which needs to be unpacked in a methodical way with the appropriate levels of description and theoretical commitment. It could be argued, therefore, that one of the main reasons why current HCI research on mental models is limited is precisely because of its low level of theoretical commitment. The question is whether it is possible to move up a level – or add another Russian doll in Payne's analogy.

To distinguish between the various levels of theoretical commitment, Payne draws from cognitive psychological research, notably Johnson-Laird (1983). However, there are problems with coupling the study of mental models in HCI too closely with cognitive psychology theory. We need consider only the social and other contextual factors surrounding computer use to realize how different it is from the *basic* laboratory type verbal reasoning problems studied in cognitive psychology. While this approach may be appropriate for theory development in cognitive psychology, if HCI is to account for user interaction as it occurs in reality, then surely at this stage of our understanding it would be more illuminating to continue collecting and analysing data through inductive means. This view is implicitly supported by Bainbridge who makes the point that since operators tasks are highly complex it makes modelling the underlying mental processes also very arduous and complex. Therefore, the only way to manage this is to lower one's theoretical sights. Adopting such a "weak" approach is justified also on the grounds that it can be geared more towards practical uses. If the goals of the research are to build "pure" theories of the mental models then it can be argued that strict adherence to the scientific method is required. On the other hand, if the aims of the research are applied (as is purported in HCI) then it is questionable whether a high level of theoretical rigour is at all desirable.

Another problem stressed by Bainbridge is that the available concept-ualizations in the cognitive psychological literature are simply not geared towards explaining the complex cognitive skills that take place in the applied domain of industrial process operation. What is needed, therefore, is not to assimilate or simplify existing models and concepts of the cognitive processes but to extend and build on these. Indeed, Bainbridge, strongly advocates this approach and shows how this can be achieved in her chapter. Although concepts used for modelling language understanding such as "frames" for structuring knowledge, "blackboard" memories and "scenarios" for predicting events are useful in describing certain components of the operators behaviour, she points out that it is still necessary to develop further constructs which can model cognitive activities that cannot be accounted for by existing psychological concepts. Examples of such activities include the operators ability to simulate an external world that is in flux, the flexibility of their behaviour to act and react to these changes and their meta-knowledge in terms of the knowledge they have of the properties of their own behaviour. She also makes an important distinction between the largely "passive" process of understanding when reading (which has been the domain of mental models research in reasoning) and the more "interactive" processes of problem-solving during process operation in which the operators are required to control an external world through the application of strategies and plans.

Clearly, there are differences between the domains of cognitive psychology and HCI/HMS. Besides those types of task and levels of interactivity mentioned above, there is also the question of level of granularity at which to frame the topic of study. While it is acceptable for cognitive psychology to adopt a micro level of analysis, HCI is beginning to realize that it needs a macro level of analysis (see Forrester and Reason, 1990). Therefore, for how much longer can cognitive research in HCI piggy back on the conceptual and methodological machinery employed in cognitive psychology? Should it carry on in its current parasitic fashion, or should it attempt to adopt a more symbiotic relationship, as advocated by Payne, whereby the development of more extensive and refined models of user interaction should be pursued with the object of both furthering psychological theorizing and providing conceptual and practical tools in HCI. Alternatively, should HCI actually break away from the reins of cognitive psychology and in doing so look elsewhere for theories and methods that can provide the guidance and background in which to develop models that are more representative of the way people actually use computers in their lives?

It may be a little presumptuous to think that a *zeitgeist* within HCI research is the best solution but there does appear to be a feeling in the air that there is a need for a change of perspective which takes into account social and cultural aspects. For example, recent critiques by Suchman (1987), Forrester and Reason (1990) and Cooper (1991) of the cognitive framework have pointed out its many shortcomings and suggest that alternative methods, namely, ethnomethodology and discourse analysis are more appropriate tools to employ in the analysis of computers in use.

In order to determine which direction mental models research should go in HCI and HMS, it is a useful exercise to detail the caveats of existing models. In fact, both authors do this, discussing at length their analyses of the features which they consider have not been explicated in current theorizing on mental models. For Payne the most important issues which need unravelling are ones pertaining to the representational properties of the cognitive artefact and the users' conceptualizations of these. On the other hand, Bainbridge is concerned with the way different knowledge resources are recruited to solve the various types of tasks and problems which confront the operator of an industrial process.

Both see the distinction between the way the user thinks about a task and the way the system represents the task as having important implications for a person's mental model. For process operation, Bainbridge regards the difference between task goals and the cognitive goals required to achieve those goals as being critical. In her model she suggests that operators decide on the course of action to adopt by "running" through a series of cognitive modules, which have been recruited for the specific task goal in hand. The main cognitive processes which take place on line are to infer and review the state of the process and to anticipate and plan future events and activities. She models these activities by specifying the types of knowledge that are needed and how that knowledge is applied in the sense of its inputs and subsequent outputs in the "working storage".

In contrast to Bainbridge's very extensive model, Payne focuses more specifically on the translation process which occurs between the users' conception of the task in hand and their conception of the way the artefact represents the external task world. Based on in his "yoked state space" model, originally developed to explain users' interactions with devices, he has now applied it to the whole array of cognitive artefacts. Within this framework he distinguishes between the users' mental representation of the various states of the artefact (the device space) and their mental representation of the represented world (the goal space). His analysis shows that the extent to which users can switch smoothly between the two forms of representation depends on the type of artefact and the way it represents the system's internal and surface structure and processes. For complex artefacts it can mean the user having to conceptualize the task at a number of different representational levels. This is assumed to make greater demands on the users' mental models.

On another level both authors consider the dynamic interplay between different levels of representations and knowledge. Bainbridge proposes that in order to capture this, what is required is a third mental model. By a third mental model she is in fact refering to an aspect of meta-knowledge, i.e. knowledge about one's behaviour. However, at what point during an operators task does such a reflexive level of understanding come into being is not discussed. Neither is how this relates to the underlying automatic cognitive skills and modules. Taking Rasmussen's

(1986) Skill-Rule-Knowledge framework conscious and analytic processes are assumed to occur at the knowledge-based level when operators are confronted with novel situations as opposed to familiar routine tasks. However, Payne argues that in order for users to successfully perform a task using a cognitive artefact they need *to know* the mappings between their goals and the way the artefact can achieve those goals.

If we are to eludicate further the way in which people switch between different levels of representations and how this is brought about more attention must be given to the meta-cognitive dimension.

References

Card, S. K., Moran, T. P. and Newell, A. (1983). *The Psychology of Human–Computer Interaction.* Hillsdale, NJ: LEA.

Cooper, G. (1991). Context and its representation. *Interacting With Computers 3*, 243–253.

Forrester, M. and Reason, D. (1990). HCI "intraface model" for system design. *Interacting with Computers 2*, 279–296.

Johnson-Laird, P. (1983). *Mental Models.* Cambridge: CUP.

Long, J. and Whitefield, A. (1989). *Cognitive Ergonomics and Human-Computer Interaction.* Cambridge: CUP.

Rasmussen, J. (1986). *On Information Processing and Human–Machine Interaction: An Approach to Cognitive Engineering.* Amsterdam: Elsevier.

Suchman, L. (1987). *Plans and Situated Actions.* Cambridge: CUP.

Tauber, M. J. (1988). On mental models and the user interface. In van der Veer, G. C., Green, T. R. G., Hoc, J-M. and Murray, D. M. (eds) *Working with Computers: Theory versus Outcome.* London: Academic Press.

Part 4

Mental Models and Instruction

Chapter 11

Mental Models, Instructions and Internalization

Peter A. Bibby

11.1 Introduction

Interacting with computers is an everyday occurrence for many people. Computers are used in offices and in industry, in the home and in the world of entertainment. However, noticing that more and more users exist tells us nothing about how users get started in their interactions with the computer, nor how they improve in using the computer. One major concern is how users acquire their knowledge of computers, and how the product of the acquisition of this knowledge helps them to interact successfully with the computer.

One kind of knowledge that the computer user often needs to gain is knowledge of how the computer achieves the goals that the user has. Probably the most common way of achieving this initial understanding is through instruction. Instruction can be provided through tutoring or through reading a manual. It is the consequences of the latter method of acquisition which is the concern of this chapter. Specifically, how the knowledge of the systems functioning is represented to and by the user, both in terms of the content and the structure of instructions.

Generally speaking instructions provide the user with a representational "scaffolding" (Wood, 1988) from which they can build a better understanding of the system. The information is initially represented externally and needs to be internalized if the user is to be able to interact with the system without continual reference to that external representation. There are two major factors which relate to this problem. The first involves the appropriateness of the content of the

MODELS IN THE MIND:
Theory, perspective and applications. ISBN 0–12–592970–6

instructions and the second is how this information should be presented and then internally *re*-presented.

Several questions follow from these higher level issues. Is knowledge of the operating procedures for achieving the users' task goals important or should the user be provided with information which allows them to infer what the procedures are for achieving the task goals (e.g. Kieras and Bovair, 1984)? Should the information in the instructions be explicit and verbalizable or should it simply allow users to develop a tacit skill (e.g. Berry and Broadbent, 1984)? Should the information be presented diagrammatically or sententially, and what are the consequences of these different modes of presentation for the user (e.g. Larkin and Simon, 1987)? These issues of content, structure and representation are intimately interlinked and it is unlikely that we can consider them independently without misconstruing the importance of each. I wish to argue that research in human–computer interaction (HCI) has attempted to consider these issues separately from each other and has consequently misrepresented the complexity of the use of instructions.

11.2 Mental models and instructions in HCI research

With respect to the content of instructions, providing users with operating procedures is useful in as much as they are easily learnt and effective for completing simple tasks. They can also form the basis for causal reasoning about what other unspecified operating procedures may be (Lewis, 1988). However, this kind of reasoning, although enabling generalization about other possible operating procedures, is neither constrained by any additional knowledge nor informed about the sensibleness of such generalizations with respect to the overall functioning of the system. The assumption behind simply providing operating procedures is that the skill of computer use is construed as knowing the available methods for achieving goals. However, Brown (1986) argues that the operating procedures for manipulating the system need to be semantically rationalized, which is to say that the user understands the reasons for and the interrelationships between the operations that form the procedure. Brown claims that a mental model of the system and its functioning provides "the most stable and robust basis for such an understanding". Thus, one way of viewing the knowledge needed to interact successfully with a computer is to view the user as having an appropriate "mental model". Instructions can be a source of this information. This is not to say that other sources of information are not important.

Given this point of view, research into mental models can be seen as an attempt to investigate those very abilities that skill-as-method theories (Payne, 1988) ignore, particularly the detailed domain knowledge which informs, influences, and constrains cognition. Skill-as-method theories in HCI, the most highly developed and tested being the GOMS (Goals, Operators, Methods and Selection Rules) model of Card, Moran and Newell (1983), portray skilled computer use as depending upon the representation of a collection of methods for achieving goals and selection rules for deciding which is the most appropriate method at any given time. Critics (e.g. Carroll and Campbell, 1986) have pointed out that this kind of analysis ignores the conceptual problems that novices have. Furthermore, it ignores the kind of reasoning that experts in other fields tend to use. In general experts can be seen to use very specific chunks of information or schemas to solve problems in familiar situations (e.g. Chase and Simon, 1973; Lesgold, 1984). This is very reminiscent of Card et al's (1983) view of expert performance in using a computer. However, in uncommon circumstances the very same experts are able to reason about the problems on the basis of their knowledge of the deep causal structure of the domain (e.g. Kuipers and Kassirer, 1984). This knowledge of the deep structure, a highly sophisticated model of the domain, is lacking in skill-as-method theories. Mental models are useful because they enable or even entail reasoning about the functioning of a device, and this constrains and informs about the possibility of making sensible actions when interacting with the device.

What is a mental model? Although this seems a simple question, the divergent opinions expressed in the literature indicate that it does not have a simple answer. Carroll and Olson (1988) argue that a mental model is a rich and elaborate structure that reflects the users understanding of what the system contains, how it works and why it works this way. Carroll and Olson, divide mental models into three separate categories called "surrogates" (Young, 1983), "metaphors" (Carroll and Thomas, 1982) and "glass box" machines (Du Boulay, O'Shea and Monk, 1981).

A surrogate is a model of the system that mimics the input/output functions without assuming that the way the surrogate fulfils this role is the same as the processing in the target system. The surrogate behaves the same as the target system, but it does not have the same causal structure. It is this aspect of the surrogate that is most worrying. Why go to the trouble of developing a surrogate model which, as Young (1983) points out, is likely to be as complicated as an exact model of the system if it does not allow you to understand a systems behaviour, only predict it? An exact representation of the internal mechanics of the system will allow the user to do all the processing that a surrogate maintains, with very little extra effort, if any, and also sustains additional processing.

The metaphor model is a direct comparison between the target system and some other system. It is thought that the user can utilize their knowledge of another domain to aid their understanding of the system they are faced with. Being able to operate a system on the basis of expectations derived from other systems is no doubt a useful strategy and consequently several common metaphors have been used in instruction manual for computer systems.

For example, the typewriter metaphor has been studied by several investigators (Bott, 1979; Carroll and Thomas, 1982; Douglas and Moran, 1983). It is not the place here to provide a full analysis of how metaphors work, but simply to note that they do seem to have been used as a basis for constructing a mental model of a system (for a review of metaphor in HCI see Carroll, Mack and Kellogg, 1988). Young (1983) points out that although metaphors are useful, the problem with studying metaphors as models is that it simply changes the focus of research. Instead of finding out what a user knows about a system, the researcher has to establish what the user knows about the system on which the metaphor is based. Worse still, once this is identified, a process has to be applied which allows the user to take the knowledge from the known domain to the target domain, an additional cost which may not be worthwhile.

Finally, the glass box models lie in the middle of a continuum from surrogates to metaphors. The glass box model share the mimicry quality of surrogates whilst offering a semantic basis for understanding the system, as do metaphors, by providing information about the internal processing and mechanics of the system. Mayer (1976) describes how a glass box mimic aids users learning to program in a BASIC-like language. Unlike metaphors, a glass box model is provided through instruction, whereas metaphors can be spontaneously generated by the user. These models combine the advantages and disadvantages of both surrogates and metaphors.

Are mental models of computer systems really able to aid learners to learn, to help find solutions to problems or to support other kinds of reasoning about a system? There is increasing evidence that mental models of computer systems fulfil all three roles. Halasz and Moran (1983) report an experiment in which subjects were either given information about the internal states of a reverse polish notation calculator or they were given just procedures for operating the calculator. The results indicated that although there was no difference between the two groups on the performance of problems that resembled examples given in the instruction manual, for problems that required novel operator sequences, the group who had a greater understanding of the internal processing made fewer errors and took less time.

Bayman and Mayer (1984), in a similar study, gave different instructions to three groups of calculator users. One group received a diagram on the internal registers of the calculator arranged in a line, alternating between operator and number registers. A second group were given a diagram which presented the internal registers as a stack of number registers with a single operator register to the side. The last group were given no description of the internal registers. They hypothesized that the diagrams would encourage the development of a mental model that represented the internal states of the calculator, and this would lead to more "sophisticated" performance and fewer errors. It was found that the instruction groups used different strategies to solve arithmetic problems and that the instructions supported behaviour that was less prone to error.

A set of three experiments by Kieras and Bovair (1984) sought to explicate these results. In this case, subjects were presented with the problem of operating a simple control panel device. In the first experiment, one group of subjects learned by rote a set of operating procedures for the device, and a second group had to learn the operating procedures, but they had previously been given a diagram which represented the relationships between the device components and the device topology, i.e. how the components fitted together. This diagram was thought to provide the basis for the construction of a mental model of the device (a device model). It was found that the device model group learned the procedures more quickly, when later tested for recall had retained them more accurately, and used them more adaptively than the rote learners. A second study, based on verbal protocols taken of subjects using the control panel revealed that the device model group were able to infer the procedures from the diagram of the internal working of the control panel, and this afforded better recall. Kieras and Bovair suggested that it might not be the knowledge of the internal mechanics that was important, rather, the fact that more information was provided allowed for richer encoding and thus encouraged better retention of the operating procedure information. A final study demonstrated that simply giving more information was not a sufficient condition for improving performance, rather specific information about the functioning of the components and the device topology was essential as only this information supports direct and simple inferences about the behaviour of the device.

The major conclusion to be drawn from this research is that a user's knowledge of a system's behaviour is useful when it either is or supports the creation of a mental model of that system. However, much of this research has not considered how this knowledge has found itself inside the user's head. A common thread in this research is that the mental model that has been shown to be useful has often been derived from instructions. The internally represented product of the instructions is seen to be synonymous with a mental model. This leads to two major misconceptions about the status of mental models and their relationship to instructions. Firstly, the simple assumption underlying these studies that users in the model-instruction groups acquire a mental model of the device's workings, whereas users who receive only procedural instructions have no such mental model may be inappropriate. This latter assumption is particularly problematic since Shrager and Klahr (1983) have shown that users are able to construct a model of a device's workings in the absence of any instructions at all. A second and equally unfortunate misconception is that the representational form of the instructions is not an important factor when considering the status of the internal representation of the mental model in the mind of the user. None of the above studies has directly examined the implications of the structure of the instructions focusing solely on their content. This is the issue I wish to address in the next section.

11.3 Instructions and internalization

Bibby (1989; Bibby and Payne, 1990) has attempted to address the question of the structure of instructions through the combination of two important theoretical ideas, the first from Larkin and Simon (1987) and the second stemming from the issues of knowledge acquisition and change that face developmental psychology. The first illuminates a fundamental property of representations of knowledge, by defining two distinct equivalence relations that can exist between different representations .

> Two representations are considered to be *informationally equivalent* if all the information in one is also inferrable from the other, and vice versa.   Each could be constructed from the information in the other. Two representations are *computationally equivalent* if they are informationally equivalent and, in addition, any inference that can be drawn easily and quickly from the information given explicitly in one can also be drawn easily and quickly from the information given explicitly in the other, and vice versa. (Larkin and Simon, 1987, p.67).

Larkin and Simon (1987) use this distinction to throw light on the behavioural implications of differing external representations. In particular, they used it to explain why diagrams are sometimes so much more useful to problem solvers than are written descriptions. They argue that representations consist of data structure and programs which are used to make inferences on the basis of those data structures. Diagrams and sentential representations can be distinguished both on the basis of the associated data structures and programs. The sentential data structure represents the data elements in a single sequence. On the other hand, the diagrammatic data structure represents elements which can be indexed by two-dimensional location. The programs that operate over these two kinds of data structure vary along three kinds of processing: search, recognition and inference. They conclude that diagrammatic representations have the following advantages over sentential representations:

1. Diagrams can group together relevant information reducing the need for large amounts of search when trying to make problem-solving inferences.
2. Diagrams avoid the need to match symbolic labels by utilizing location information to group information about elements of the representation.
3. Diagrams support perceptual inferences which are extremely easy for human beings.

They argue that sentential and diagrammatic representations may be informationally equivalent but they are unlikely to be computationally equivalent. Their analysis provides some understanding of the results in the device model literature. It is often the case that the device model information is presented as a diagram whilst other information is provided by a variety of sentential representations. This other information is then shown to be inferior to the device model information in so far as it helps the user operate the device. The problem here is that the advantages for the diagrammatic device model representations may not be due primarily to the presence of information which supports inferences about the device, but rather due to the way in which that information is represented and how that form of representation supports inferences. It is not the aim here to suggest that diagrams are necessarily the most appropriate representation from which to derive a mental model, rather that different instructional representations may lead to the development of different internal representations of a device from which a mental model can develop.

The second idea is that much cognition utilizes public, external symbolic systems. This idea goes back at least as far as Piaget (e.g. Piaget and Inhelder, 1969) and Vygotsky (1936) who claimed that "the functional use of a new sign is preceded by a stage of 'naive psychology', i.e. by a period of mastering the external structure of the sign" (Vygotsky, 1936/1987, p.93). A more recent statement of the idea is due to Rumelhart, Smolensky, McClelland and Hinton (1986) who exemplify it nicely with reference to the processes of "mental" arithmetic. When thinking through a sum like 247 x 46 (without using pencil and paper), you may construct a model in your mind's eye of the visual stages that accompany pencil and paper solutions: the external symbolic conventions are made available in the mind's eye as an internal tool for thought.

This position has a long history in developmental psychology and is discussed in detail by Wood (1988). Indeed, it can be viewed as a major problem for theories of cognitive development. Unfortunately it is difficult to find an operationalized account of this process which can provide answers to questions about what knowledge is internalized; in what circumstances is a particular kind of knowledge internalized; what is the form of the resulting representation; and what changes occur to representation through the its use?

What is needed is a conception of "internalization" that can be operationalized to provide a more explicit understanding of the role of instructions in the development of a mental model of a device. Bibby and Payne use Larkin and Simon's definitions of representational equivalence allowing them to offer just such a conception:

> An external representation is internalized if not only the informational but also the computational character of the external representation is shared by the mental representation (Bibby and Payne, 1990, p.6).

This definition suggests that when different external representations which show computational differences are internalized these difference will continue to be evident in the corresponding mental representations and the ensuing behaviour. The internalized representation of the instructions can be viewed as just one tool which supports reasoning about a device.

This position sits well with present computational theories of skill acquisition such as ACT* (Anderson, 1983) and SOAR (Rosenbloom and Newell, 1986). Both these theories suggest that declarative representations exist in the minds of users which form the basis for any consequent problem solving. Although these two theories posit different fundamental mechanisms for the continuing development of a skill, in particular ACT* relies on knowledge compilation and SOAR relies on chunking, both can view the internalization process as the building of a new declarative base on which to reason about a device's behaviour and operation.

11.4 Evidence for the internalization of instructions

Research by Gilmore and Green (1984) can be interpreted as offering some support for this idea of internalization. Working on the comprehensibility of programming notations, they showed that differences in the comprehensibility of programs can arise because the mental operations demanded by some tasks are harder in certain notations, even though the different notations represented the same algorithm. In the current terms, the different expressions of the same algorithm are computationally different even though informationally equivalent. Further, Gilmore and Green demonstrated that the mental representation of a program preserves some of the features of the original notation; a comprehended program is not merely abstracted information stored in memory, but reflects the structure of the source of that information. The pattern of responses to questions about the remembered program paralleled the pattern of responses when the written program was available for consultation, suggesting that remembered programs were internalizations of the written form, in just the sense we have introduced.

Mayer and Greeno (1972) taught the concept of binomial probability to subjects using two different methods. The first method emphasized the formula for calculating probabilities and the second method focused on the meanings of the variables used in the formula. Using transfer tasks as a measure of performance they found that there were structurally different outcomes in the pattern of learning with respect to which instruction method had been used. Although they interpreted their results in terms of the connectedness of cognitive structure, an equally plausible account is provided by the internalization hypothesis.

Bibby and Payne (1990) have investigated this notion of internalization and its consequences with respect to different kinds of experience operating a simple device and the ensuing mental model representation. They provided different groups of users with an elaborated version of the knobs, dials and indicator light control panel device used by Kieras and Bovair (1984). Users were then given a general introduction to the device which explained what it was used for. In addition, users were given different instructional descriptions of the device which either explicitly stated the topology of the device (a power flow diagram) or allowed them to infer the topology (a set of operating procedure or a fault-diagnosis look-up table). These instructions where informationally equivalent with respect to a pair of tasks in the sense that they allowed the users to complete those tasks successfully. The first task was to identify a faulty component and the second task was to re-position an incorrectly positioned switch to make the device work successfully. A task analysis with respect to each of the different instructions suggested that the group with the power flow diagram would find the switch positioning task harder than the fault finding task; the group with the look-up table would also find the switch positioning task harder than the fault-finding task; the group using the operating procedures would find the fault-finding task harder than the switch positioning task. It was predicted that if users internalized the instructions then the different computational properties of those instructions would become apparent when completing the tasks.

The experiments reported by Bibby and Payne aimed to test the consequences of instructions and their interaction with the experience of operating a simple device. First, they tested whether users internalized the external instructional descriptions of a simple device. Users were allowed to refer to the instructions whilst solving five examples of both the fault finding and switch positioning tasks. After this the instructions were removed. The performance crossover between the instructions and tasks predicted on the basis of the task analysis was present when the instructions could be consulted and it remained after they had been removed. Bibby and Payne argued that this was evidence for internalization. However, Lewis (1988) argued that the performance crossover may not be due to the instructions per se but to the different experiences using the instructions to solve the tasks. In order to overcome this criticism, later experiments (Bibby, 1989) did not allow the subjects to refer to the instructions when solving the tasks. Exactly the same performance crossover was found providing stronger evidence for internalization.

A second experiment tested whether extended experience of operating the device would nullify the initial computational differences between different instructional materials. The results offered no support for this hypothesis. Bibby and Payne argued that the robustness of the products of internalization suggests that users may labour for a considerable period under the computational costs of instructional materials that are poorly related to tasks.

The third experiment reported in Bibby and Payne tested whether users could learn to compensate for the computational disadvantages of instructional materials if they have enough experience of solving the tasks that reveal those differences. They found that with extended experience of the fault finding and switch positioning problems the differences between the instruction groups dissipated. It was concluded that users do indeed compensate for the inadequacies of instructional materials. A fourth experiment wherein the performance crossover which had dissipated with extended practice on the tasks reappeared when users were confronted with similar, but novel tasks. These results allowed Bibby and Payne to distinguish between three possible explanations for the dissipation of the performance crossover: (1) a user's knowledge base may no longer contain the internalized representations of the instructions; (2) the users have developed task-specific strategies for solving the tasks; and (3) subjects may be using strategies that are relatively worse or better for the different tasks but the speed up in execution times has swamped the effects. It seems that the initial internalization of instructions remains available to subjects. Secondly, the similarity of the novel tasks to the practised tasks offered support for the second explanation over the third. If users stick with the same strategy throughout their practise on the first two tasks, this strategy would surely transfer to the new tasks, making it unlikely that the crossover effects would be visible.

Bibby and Payne argued that their experiments on internalization demonstrated the utility of internalization as a construct. Furthermore, they argued that internalization has much more widespread significance than just pointing out the effects of different instructions. For example, Johnson-Laird (1983) provided evidence that analogical mental representations, i.e. those which share the relation structure of the state of affairs they are representing, are used in human reasoning. However, the notion of structure, which underlies the definition of analogical representations, and of mental models in the sense intended by Johnson-Laird, is not transparent. Another way of defining types of representation is in terms of the inferences that they support. Simon's notions of informational and computational equivalence allow the precise specification of a relationship between representing and represented worlds. It is surely true that internalization, the preservation of computational differences in the mental representations of external forms, denotes a more limited idea than Johnson-Laird's mental models but it does provide a lever on the problem of how instructions affect behaviour.

11.5 Internalized instructions and mental models

As defined and tested by Bibby and Payne (1990) internalization is a theoretical construct which provides an understanding of the outcome of providing particular instructional representations of a device. However, internalization provides no direct description of the representation of the content of the mental model. Since we want a full understanding of the nature and function of mental models of devices and the outcome of using instructional descriptions we need to establish what is being represented, how it is represented and what changes in representation occur, if any.

Revisiting the research on mental models, a common assumption has been that the ontology of the device, i.e. the objects that make up the components in the device, and the flow of control, i.e. how the different components interact with each other are two crucial, interacting contents that support the usefulness of the mental model (de Kleer and Brown, 1981, 1983; Kieras and Bovair, 1984; Williams, Hollan and Stevens, 1983; Collins, 1985). Kieras and Bovair (1984) provide the most explicit statement of this position. They concluded that both the knowledge of the components and how they were connected were essential in so far as they enabled inferences about operating procedures.

Greeno (1983) has pointed out that the ontology of the mental model by itself may be an important factor in the effectiveness of the mental model. Falzon (1982) provides support for this position in a study of air traffic controllers who thought of their task in terms of aircraft "separations", whereas an alternative viewpoint could consider the essential aspect of the problem as the aircraft "positions". Essentially, Greeno's position is that the mental representation used to solve a problem consists of a set of "conceptual entities", the ontology, and a set of "procedures" aimed at transforming the problem into the desired state, the solution. Different representations of the same problem arise since a given element can be coded as a conceptual entity, which is available for use in a procedure, or as an attribute associated with a conceptual entity, which are not directly accessible to the procedure. The advantage of this position is that given the same device, different "ontologies" can exist, and they support different inferences more or less efficiently.

Bibby (1989) reports an experiment which asked users to write a set of instructions for a new user after they had had different amounts of experience interacting with the same control panel device. The results were divided according to their implications for device ontologies or task-specific strategies. The scripts provided two kinds of information that supported the suggestion that the different instruction groups have different device ontologies. The first piece of evidence is that the two groups showed a preference for describing the device either in terms of the switches that direct power through the system, or the components through which the power flows; the second comes from the information that was generated about the strategies used to solve the tasks, with the one group depending primarily on the state of the switches and the other group depending on the component(s). (Here I am assuming that the problem solving strategy is a re-description of a particular problem solving episode. In terms of the SOAR architecture it is the consequence of searching through a problem space. With respect to the ACT* architecture it is the outcome of applying productions in a particular sequence.) It seems likely that the different instructions led the groups to consider the device from different viewpoints. In other words, the conceptual entities that form their representation of the device are different.

Concerning the development of task-specific strategies it was clear that the strategies that were reported for solving the problems differed according to the amount of practice the user had interacting with the device. When users had a small amount of practice solving the tasks they described strategies that are mechanical in their application. For a fault-finding task there was a tendency to check all the possibilities in a sequential manner until a broken component was identified. The users who had more practice on this task described strategies that required far less work. They developed ways of restricting the amount of search that was necessary to isolate the broken component. Thus, there is a shift to more efficient strategies. This shift mirrors the well-documented shift from weak to heuristic search (e.g. Newell and Simon, 1972; Anzai and Simon, 1979; Langley, 1987; Larkin, 1981).

However, the picture is more complex than it may initially seem. For the general information about the device, there was an interaction between the instructional materials and references to components or switches. One group were more likely to refer to the switches than the components when describing the device, whilst the other group were more likely to refer to the components than the switches. The general descriptions of the strategies followed a similar pattern. One of the groups with a small amount of practice described a strategy that relied on looking at the position of the switches and checking to see if the associated component was working. The other group in this practice condition described a strategy which relied on looking at the components one at a time and checking to see if that component's indicator light should be illuminated. The users with an increased amount of practice could also be separated according to which instruction group they belonged. One group described a strategy which reduced the amount of search by using route information. It was no longer necessary to check all possibilities, rather only those that followed a particular sequence needed to be checked. The other group used information about which indicator lights should be lit given particular antecedent conditions. This strategy also reduced the amount of search necessary to identify a faulty component, but did so in a different way. It seems that the change from mechanical, inefficient strategies to search reducing strategies does not solely depend on simply having more practice on this task, but also on what the initial strategy is. In general this depends on what instructions are made available to the user prior to interacting with the device.

11.6 Modelling the use of instructionally derived mental models

Bibby (1989) developed an ACT*-like production system model of the development of the task-specific strategies using the processes of knowledge compilation (composition and proceduralization, Anderson and Neves, 1981) and found that these learning mechanisms were unable to account for the observed improvement in problem solving procedures. Given that SOAR, an alternative, but equally ambitious computational model of skill development uses a chunking mechanism (Laird, Newell and Rosenbloom, 1987) which is very similar to ACT*'s composition it is unlikely that modelling the observed phenomena in SOAR would significantly improve matters.

The main reason behind the failure of ACT* and SOAR's learning mechanisms follows from the fact that users, rather than just "stringing" a number of productions together into larger production rules, also seem to discover and delete redundancies in the rules. For instance, a user may discover that a test used to determine the truth of one condition in a production rule can also be used to determine the truth of a different condition. An example would be the case in which the subject discovers that of two components only one can be active at any given time. Therefore, a rule whose antecedent contains two conditions that (i) the first component is active and (ii) the second component is not active contains some redundancy.

An interesting and related empirical observation was that subjects whose model is appropriate for the task at hand seem to discover more redundancies than those whose model is not appropriate. These results therefore lead to an additional claim about the role of mental models: they provide the basis from which users can reason about their problem solving procedures and through this process a component of expertise is developed in terms of the generation of task-specific problem solving strategies. However, the relationship between the mental model and the task-specific strategy is complex. The mental model serves to eliminate condition redundancies in the problem solving procedures that novices have, but this depends on the degree to which the model is suited to the task. When a model matches the task well, all the condition redundancies in a problem solving procedure are eliminated. However, when the model is only poorly suited to the task, only a subset of the condition redundancies are removed. The degree of model-task match is an important factor in this ability to improve problem solving procedures. This is of course a specialization of the AI truism that a good representation will considerably improve problem solving performance (an observation empirically supported by van Baalen and Davis, 1988 and Clarke and Reichgelt, 1990).

The dual role of mental models, both in the construction of task-specific problem solving strategies and in the elimination of redundancies in such strategies has immediate implications for computational models of learning and practice. For example, the best known models of the construction of task-specific problem solving strategies, ACT* and SOAR, do not allow for explicit reasoning about problem solving procedures on the basis of the declarative knowledge, in this case the mental model. ACT* provides a model of learning that has no mechanism for the interaction between declarative knowledge (the mental model) and procedural knowledge (the problem solving strategy). Once a successful problem solving strategy has been developed then knowledge compilation takes place and the outcome of this process is no longer available for further assessment. Similarly chunking in SOAR does not enable further reasoning about possible changes in problem solving procedures. If a successful route through a problem space has been identified and chunked there is no further role for declarative knowledge. This model of the usefulness of declarative knowledge, i.e. that the knowledge that the mental model constitutes is useful only in the initial stage of the development of problem solving procedures, is at odds with Bibby's results.

11.7 Summary and conclusions

The work reported here suggests that there are at least three different components of skilled computer use which develop on the basis of people using instructions. In the first instance, user's are able to internalize instructional descriptions of devices. In doing so the mental representation of those instructions maintains the computational properties of the form of the instructions. This does not imply that user's simply create a mental image of the instructions in their mind's eye, although that is certainly a possibility. A variety of representational systems, such as a propositionally based system would be able maintain the computational structure of instructions by formal redescription. Second, user's develop a description of the device which represents both the ontology and the topology of the device. It is not the case that users who are explicitly given this information are the only users to be able to generate this information. At the moment it is not known how users develop this representation of the device, but the form of the ontological description of the device is closely related to the instructional materials that users are given. Finally, a third component of skilled computer use is the task-specific strategies. These strategies develop on the basis of using the internalized instructions to solve problems on the device. However, different instructions can lead to compiled strategies with more or less redundant operations built into them. By using the knowledge of the ontology and topology of the device users are able to eliminate condition redundancies. The number of redundancies that are eliminated is closely related to this knowledge and some descriptions of the ontology make available more information than other descriptions.

How does this fit with the present diversity of opinions expressed in the HCI literature? It is not difficult to conclude that different mental models can be based on different kinds of descriptions or representations of a system. However, it seems unlikely that users would restrict themselves to utilizing one of the many possible representations. Indeed, it is almost impossible to conceive of a situation where just one kind of representation, surrogate, metaphoric or glass-box would be solely adhered to by a user, and that a user would resist utilizing alternative representations. I suggest instead that a mental model is not one thing, but a combination of several interacting component representational structures. Indeed, it is possibly this quality that gives the idea of mental models its dynamism. The requirement that several representations having to interact encourages a view of knowledge use as a active process, avoiding representational systems which are essentially passive. Mental models can be considered as the outcome of this dynamic use of representations.

If we characterize the mental model as the interactive use of several representations we can achieve a conceptualization of the role of instructions. Instructions are external representations which are internalized by the user. The internalized representations provide just one of the possible representations which can be viewed as constituting the user's mental model. Other representations can be constructed by the user on the basis of their previous experience of other similar systems and through their experience of interacting with the system. It is also possible that through the use of these representations, more representations can be constructed. I want to suggest that mental models are not unitary representations, but what we know as mental models are the outcome of using multiple representations. At the same time, it may be the case that with sufficient experience of using these multiple representations that a unitary representation of a device or system can be constructed, and this may be added to the knowledge base that is viewed as the mental model.

Acknowledgements

This research was supported by an SERC/CASE award with British Telecom as the industrial sponsors. I would like to thank Steve Payne for his support and encouragement while this research was carried out at Lancaster University. I would also like to thank Claire O'Malley, David Gilmore, David Wood, Han Reichgelt and John Bowers for their invaluable discussions of earlier versions of this chapter .

References

Anderson, J.R. (1983). *The Architecture of Cognition.* Cambridge, Ma.: Harvard University Press

Anderson, J.R. and Neves, D.M. (1981). Knowledge compilation: mechanisms for the automatization of cognitive skills. In Anderson , J.R. (ed.) *Cognitive Skills and their Acquisition.* Hillsdale, NJ: LEA.

Anzai, Y. and Simon, H.A. (1979). The theory of learning by doing. *Psychological Review 86,* 124–140.

Bayman, P. and Mayer, R.E. (1984). Instructional manipulation of users' mental models for electronic calculators. *International Journal of Man–Machine Studies 20,* 189–199.

Berry, D.C. and Broadbent, D.E. (1984). On the relationship between task performance and verbal knowledge. *Quarterly Journal of Experimental Psychology 36A,* 209–231.

Bibby, P.A. (1989). *Knowledge of Devices: The Role and Representation of Mental Models of Devices.* PhD Thesis. University of Lancaster.

Bibby, P.A. and Payne, S.J. (1990). *Learning about devices by internalizing instructional descriptions.* IBM Research Report RC15522. IBM T.J. Watson Research Center, Yorktown Heights, NY.

Bott, R. (1979). *A study of Complex Learning: Theory and Methodology.* CHIP REPORT '82, Centre for Human Information Processing, UCSD.

Brown, J.S. (1986). From cognitive to social ergonomics and beyond. In Norman, D.A. and Draper, S.W (eds), *User Centred System Design.* Hillsdale, NJ: LEA.

Card, S.K., Moran, T.P. and Newell, A. (1983). *The Psychology of Human–Computer Interaction.* Hillsdale, NJ: LEA.

Carroll, J.M. and Campbell, R.L. (1986). Softening up hard science: reply to Newell and Card. *Human–Computer Interaction 2,* 227–249.

Carroll, J.M., Mack, R.L. and Kellogg, W.A. (1988). Interface metaphors and user interface design. In Helander, M. (ed.) *Handbook of Human–Computer Interaction.* Amsterdam: Elsevier.

Carroll, J.M. and Olson, J. (1988). Mental models and human–computer interaction. In Helander, M. (ed.) *Handbook of Human–Computer Interaction.* Amsterdam: Elsevier.

Carroll, J.M. and Thomas, J.C. (1982). Metaphor and the cognitive representation of computing systems. *IEEE Transactions on Systems, Man and Cybernetics 12*, 107–116.

Chase, W.G. and Simon, H.A. (1973). The mind's eye in chess. In Chase, W.G. (ed.) *Visual Information Processing*. New York: Academic Press.

Clarke, P. and Reichgelt, H. (1990). Explorations in representation change. Technical Report. AI Group. University of Nottingham.

Collins, A. (1985). Component models of physical systems. In *Proceedings of the Seventh Annual Conference of the Cognitive Science Society*. Hillsdale, NJ: LEA

de Kleer, J.K. and Brown, J.S. (1981). Mental models of physical mechanisms and their acquisition. In Anderson, J.R. (ed.) *Cognitive Skills and their Acquisition*. Hillsdale, NJ: LEA.

de Kleer, J.K. and Brown, J.S. (1983). Assumptions and ambiguities in mechanistic mental models. In Gentner, D. and Stevens, A.L. (eds), *Mental Models*. Hillsdale, NJ: LEA.

Douglas, S.A. and Moran, T.P. (1983). Learning text editor semantics by analogy. In *Proceeding of CHI'83 Human Factors in Computing Systems Conference*. New York: ACM.

Du Boulay, B., O'Shea, T. and Monk, J. (1981). The black box inside the glass box: presenting computing concepts to novices. *International Journal of Man–Machine Studies 14*, 237–249.

Falzon, P. (1982). Display structures: compatibility with the operators' mental representation and reasoning processes. In *Proceedings of the Second European Annual Conference on Human Decision Making and Manual Control*. University of Bonn, Germany.

Gilmore, D.J. and Green, T.R.G. (1984). Comprehension and recall of miniature programs. *International Journal of Man–Machine Studies 21*, 31–48.

Greeno, J.G. (1983). Conceptual entities. In Gentner, D. and Stevens, A.L. (eds) *Mental Models*. Hillsdale, NJ: LEA.

Halasz, F.G. and Moran, T.P. (1983). Mental models and problem-solving in using a calculator. In *Proceedings of CHI'83 Human Factors in Computing Systems*. New York: ACM.

Johnson-Laird, P.N. (1983). *Mental Models*. Cambridge: CUP.

Kieras, D.E. and Bovair, S. (1984). The role of a mental model in learning to operate a device. *Cognitive Science 8*, 255–273.

Kuipers, B.J. and Kassirer, J.P. (1984). Causal reasoning in medicine: analysis of a protocol. *Cognitive Science 8*, 363–385.

Laird, J.E., Newell, A. and Rosenbloom, P.S. (1987). SOAR: An architecture for general intelligence. *Artificial Intelligence 33*, 1–64.

Langley, P. (1987). A general theory of discrimination learning. In Klahr, D., Langley, P., and Neches, R. (eds), *Production System Models of Learning and Development.* Cambridge, Ma.: MIT Press.

Larkin, J.H. (1981). Enriching formal knowledge: a model of learning and cognition. In Anderson, J.R., (ed.) *Cognitive Skills and their Acquisition.* Hillsdale, NJ: LEA.

Larkin, J.H. and Simon, H.A. (1987). Why a diagram is (sometimes) worth ten thousand words. *Cognitive Science 11*, 65–99.

Lesgold, A.M. (1984). Acquiring expertise. In Anderson, J.R. and Kosslyn, S.M. (eds) *Tutorials in Memory and Learning: Essays in Honour of Gordon Bower.* San Francisco, Ca.: Freeman.

Lewis, C. (1988). Why and how to learn why: analysis-based generalization of procedures. *Cognitive Science 12*, 211–256

Mayer, R.E. (1976). Some conditions of meaningful learning for computer programming: advance organizers and subject control of frame order. *Journal of Educational Psychology 67*, 725–734.

Mayer, R.E. and Greeno, J.G. (1972). Structural differences between learning outcomes produced by different instructional materials. *Journal of Educational Psychology 67*, 331–350.

Newell, A. and Simon, H.A. (1972) *Human Problem Solving.* Englewood Cliffs, NJ: Prentice Hall.

Payne, S.J. (1988). Metaphorical instruction and the early learning of an abbreviated-command computer system. *Acta Psychologica 69*, 207–230.

Piaget, J. and Inhelder, B. (1969). *The Psychology of the Child.* Routledge: London.

Rosenbloom, P.S. and Newell, A. (1986). The chunking of goal hierarchies: a generalized model of practice. In Michalski, R.S., Carbonell, J.G. and Mitchell, T.M. (eds) *Machine Learning,* Volume 2. Los Altos, Ca.:Morgan Kaufman.

Rumelhart, D.E., Smolensky, P., McClelland, J.L. and Hinton, G.E. (1986). Schemata and sequential thought processes in PDP models. In Rumelhart, D.E., McClelland, J.L and the PDP Research Group, *Parallel Distributed Processing.* Vol 2. Cambridge, Ma.: MIT Press.

Shrager, J. and Klahr, D. (1983). Learning in an instructionless environment: observation and analysis. In *Proceedings of the 1983 CHI Conference on Human Factors in Computing.* New York: ACM.

van Baalen, J. and Davis, P. (1988). Overview of an approach to representation design. AAAI-88. San Mateo, Ca.: Morgan Kaufman.

Vygotsky, L. (1936/1986). *Thought and Language: Newly Revised and Edited by Alex Kozulin.* Cambridge, Ma.: MIT Press.

Williams, M.D., Hollan, J.D. and Stevens, A.L. (1983). Human reasoning about a simple physical system. In Gentner, D. and Stevens, A.L (eds) *Mental Models.* Hillsdale, NJ: LEA.

Wood, D. (1988). *How Children Think and Learn.* Oxford: Blackwell.

Young, R.M. (1983). Surrogates and mappings: two kinds of conceptual models for interactive devices. In Gentner, D. and Stevens, A.L. (eds) *Mental Models.* Hillsdale, NJ: LEA.

Chapter 12

Mental Models as Multi-record Representations

Simon C. Duff

12.1 Introduction

Research into human–computer interaction (HCI) has suggested, in agreement with basic theoretical research in other areas (e.g. reasoning, vision) that there are internal mental structures which develop during learning, and which support knowledge use during problem solving. In the case of HCI they contain knowledge about how computers and software are used and what they do. Such structures are often referred to as mental models. One of the aims of HCI has been to investigate the role of mental models and such work has been carried out from a number of perspectives, which have attempted to understand the role of knowledge content and structure, and thus mental models, during interaction (e.g. Hammond, Morton, MacLean, Barnard and Long, 1982; Frese and Albrecht, 1988; Duff, 1989). It has not always been possible to demonstrate that possessing a particular model results in behavioural effects, though there are examples: the work with reverse Polish Notation calculators of Halasz and Moran (1983) and the work of Kieras and Bovair (1984), concerned with controlling a starship firing system. One reason why many of the early studies were not able to demonstrate any effects was the choice of task, which often was something that subjects would already be familiar with to an extent (e.g. Foss, Smith and Rosson, 1982). Here, the fact that the subjects' prior knowledge concerning the task would reduce the overall differences between model and no-model groups, would lead to the experimental manipulation of presence or absence of a model being less effective. The prior knowledge would endow all subjects with some level of task and device model, a factor which has been identified as important for contributing to the development of an individual's

MODELS IN THE MIND:
Theory, perspective and applications. ISBN 0-12-592970-6

mental model (Chi and Ceci, 1987; Feigenbaum, 1988), allowing them to develop new cognitive structures through the use of metaphors (Carroll and Thomas, 1982).

An assumption that appears to be made in much mental model work is that models are unitary structures which encompass the user's knowledge about a particular device. Wickens (1984), on reviewing the process control literature, suggests that mental models are specific to a particular system. However, some recent studies by Duff (1988; 1989), carried out with the intention of looking more closely at the role of knowledge in learning about a system and analysed using Barnard's (1987) framework of nteracting cognitive subsystems (ICS), suggest a more flexible view of the representation of mental models. These studies required groups of subjects to learn control operations for various systems (e.g. process control plants, air-traffic control systems) under differing constraints (e.g. order uncertainty – a given set of controls must all be used in a preset order, item uncertainty – a selection from a larger set of controls must be used) and given instructions of the operating procedures in different forms (knowledge form), for example, as lists of action sequences, or with the reasons behind the operating procedures. Subjects' abilities to make use of this knowledge were later tested under novel conditions. The overall effects can be summarized as follows: knowledge form plays a role in accuracy and speed of action execution both during learning and problem solving. Knowledge which describes relationships between system components, and the reasons for these relationships (how-it-works or figurative knowledge), leads to mediocre accuracy during learning, but improves performance in novel situations at the cost of speed. Knowledge which provides lists of operating procedures (how-to-do-it or operative knowledge) leads to faster and more accurate performance during learning, but poor accuracy under novel conditions. Learning via exploration (i.e. no operative or figurative knowledge given) leads to fast action execution, accuracy dependent on the extent to which general principles and heuristics can be abstracted from the device.

Cognitive task analysis (CTA) was performed using ICS to investigate the theoretical basis of the above findings. CTA depends on analysis at increasingly finer levels of detail, identifying the tasks subjects have to perform, how they are performed, and the various sources of knowledge which may be available. In this way it is possible to propose how the differences between experimental groups come about due to differences in learning strategies invoked, knowledge available and cognitive processing involved, and on the basis of these hypotheses, to make a number of predictions regarding the effects of new experimental manipulations. The outcome of studies testing these predictions will provide some indication of whether the analysis performed has identified the important psychological factors determining behaviour in these situations, and so uncover more details about mental models.

12.2 Interacting cognitive subsystems (ICS)

ICS distinguishes between different cognitive subsystems which are proposed to have specific functions and process certain specific representations of knowledge. Most important for consideration here are three types of subsystem, each dealing with a different representation. The first subsystem deals with the surface structure form and content of verbal material (morphonolexical – MPL), the second with the underlying meaning of verbal material (propositional – PROP) and the third with relevant inferential connections within broader, schematic knowledge structures (implicational – IMPLIC). What a user knows about a system will be reflected at each of these levels. The different types of representation can be called upon strategically to help a user decide what to do, and the precise properties of performance will depend upon the particular composition of mental representations and their inherent properties. This suggests that mental models are not unitary bodies of knowledge. Rather, they should be considered as being based on a range of representations containing different forms of knowledge.

Through CTA, the following can be said about the knowledge provided in earlier experiments (Duff, 1988; 1989). Figurative knowledge describes a system in terms of propositional and semantic relationships (PROP and IMPLIC processing required), from which inferences must be drawn. The consequences of the relationships determining action selection must be processed. Operative knowledge describes a device with simple verbal material (MPL processing required), relying on the reuse of recent memory records for its usefulness. As action sequences are described, little inferential processing is required, so relationships, heuristics etc. are unlikely to develop. Knowledge derived from exploration describes a device via surface and inferential representations (MPL, PROP and IMPLIC processing required) dependent on the extent to which general principles about the device can be abstracted. To reduce cognitive load, exploratory learning acts to identify heuristics to constrain behaviour.

Duff's earlier studies (1989; 1989) show that the differences in subsystem used to develop a mental model of the device strongly influence the strategies which subjects invoke in order to carry out the tasks under learning and problem solving conditions. In addition, the knowledge contained within the various subsystems develops over time, both in the quantity of knowledge which is represented, and the extent to which this knowledge becomes integrated with other relevant knowledge.

Within Barnard's approach, an important feature of the subjects' knowledge is represented through the concept of a common task record (CTR). It is the content and structure of the CTR which influences user behaviour as it details "what must be done" to achieve a certain goal, describing the device at the propositional level as a series of structures which are related. It indicates the complexity and flexibility of the information, and thus how it may be able to constrain the use of knowledge whilst carrying out a task. Barnard (1987) argues that users will rely on the propositional CTR for the execution of tasks. However, where this is insufficient to resolve uncertainty concerning a specific sequence of actions, surface structure representations and schematic knowledge may be called into play. In many settings, users provided with only operative knowledge of the steps in a procedure will be able to determine what to do largely on the basis of very simple propositional and surface structure representations. Inferential representations will only be required to tackle novel tasks. Users given only figurative knowledge will have to actively construct propositional and surface representations of what to do, via inference. Likewise, users left to explore a device will have to determine the relevant propositional and surface structure representations, but without the benefit of the constraints embodied in figurative knowledge. The general framework suggests that users will tend to rely on the type of knowledge representation that most readily enables them to determine what to do. If the users only have figurative knowledge, but no operative knowledge, they must use inference to determine the relevant propositional and surface structure for task execution. If the instructional material is operative and specifies the action sequence, inferential processing would not be a necessary requirement.

This analysis points to two factors which can be manipulated through the provision of knowledge:

1. The strategies which may be invoked during learning.
2. The location of knowledge as suggested by ICS, which describes the device and is available for use.

It would seem that giving users both operative knowledge of task procedures and igurative knowledge about how the device works should provide them with a mental model that is best able to support accurate and fast task performance. However, if it is assumed that users typically rely on the specific form of mental representation that can be used most readily to execute a sequence of actions, then a counter-intuitive prediction can be arrived at. Consider a device which requires the resolution of order uncertainty for its accurate control. If users are provided with sufficient figurative knowledge of device constraints for them to infer action sequences and added to this is some operative information about the sequence itself, then they will make less use of inferential processing because some of the necessary information is available without inferential processing. As the amount of operative knowledge added to figurative knowledge is increased, so the need for inferential processing will effectively decrease. The direct consequences of this should be three-fold. Firstly, users will increasingly rely on surface structure and simple propositional representations, the effect of this being reduced ability to solve novel problems. Secondly, the CTR that develops at the propositional level will not in itself reflect the structure implied by the figurative knowledge, and hence the specific pattern of performance errors should change. This is because the CTR representation constrains interaction through the structure of device knowledge. For example in figurative cases where the knowledge describes a relationship between different pairs of controls, the CTR will not describe relationships within individual pairs, thus errors would be expected to occur more often on commands that are to be used first in a pair (e.g. whilst resolving order uncertainty), than on the second member of a pair. This is because the knowledge effectively ties down the within pair orders, but not the between pair orders. When the use of operative information supersedes this, the structure of knowledge describing pairs of controls will break down, so errors will begin to occur in later positions also. Thirdly, since inferential processing of a similar but less constrained nature is involved in exploratory learning, we should expect an analogous pattern of overall performance to that for figurative knowledge but at a lower level of accuracy.

12.3 Method

These basic predictions were tested using a between groups design on a system which required users to learn ordered sequences of actions in a three component minimal office system. The three components were file operations, record operations and system operations. To control each component successfully, a pair of action sequences had to be performed, one requiring six actions and the other eight. The system was displayed on an Apple MacIntosh and constructed within HyperCard, the actions available in each sequence appearing as an array of named icons. Three groups of subjects had to learn each of the sequences (six in total), and were subsequently tested with a number of problem solving tasks. The groups differed in the knowledge they received prior to attempting each separate sequence of actions. The operative group received instructions detailing command operations, e.g."...3. Check, 4. Start, 5. Close ....." the names corresponding to the icon names, and the numbers to the actions position in the sequence. The figurative group received text which would in principle allow them to infer the order in which controls should be used within pairs, but not between pairs. Thus, in an eight action sequence such as 1(A:B) 2(C:D) 3(E:F) 4(G:H), figurative knowledge would not describe the required orderings between pairs 1 and 2, but would between actions A and B, e.g."Files must be checked before the filing operation is started to ensure that there are files for this process to operate on". The third group were told to explore each component of the device to discover the correct action sequences. For each separate component, figurative and exploratory groups received additional operative knowledge. For one pair of action sequences, no additional operative knowledge was provided, and for the remaining two pairs of sequences, there was increased operative knowledge. Such a design allows the performance of the figurative and exploratory groups to be assessed in relation to the performance of the operative group on identical task material, providing a clear view of the effects of additional operative knowledge.

Within each pair of command sequences, there were a series of positional and semantic regularities to determine the extent that such information would be abstracted under various conditions. That is, command names or command meanings were shared between paired lists for each component of the minimal office, which might be used to predict command positions in the sequences. This was important in the case of the exploratory group, whose main strategy has been proposed as the abstraction of generalities.

The experiment took place in two phases: learning and problem solving.

12.3.1 Learning

Subjects practised each of the command lists three times in succession after having received the applicable knowledge, studied it, and had it removed. The order in which lists were presented, and the list/knowledge pairings were balanced to reduce effects of any possible interactions between specific lists. Pairs of lists (in each component) were practised consecutively in order that the generalizations which applied, and the changes in knowledge conditions, were not separated. To overcome positional practice effects, on each of the three trials the positions of commands within the icon array varied randomly.

12.3.2 Problem solving

The problem solving stage comprised three trials in which the entire device was controlled. Each command list was performed once. Pairs of lists were not presented together and presentation was counterbalanced by list, knowledge type and number of commands required. In these problem trials, the set of commands which were available was reduced. Thus, the knowledge which subjects had received would need to be interpreted to account for controls missing from the learned sequence.

Condition 1 was essentially a replication of earlier comparisons between operative, figurative and exploratory learning. In condition 2, the exploratory group received additional operative knowledge describing the half of the command sequence positions (those which could not be predicted from the system generalities). The figurative group received additional operative knowledge for 50% of the figuratively described controls. In condition 3, the exploratory group received additional operative information about sequence positions of commands which could be predicted from system generalities. The figurative group received approximately 75% of additional operative information.

12.4 Results

User responses were logged as was the time taken to select each command. Figures 12.1 and 12.2 show the learning data as commands per required action and time per action decision, respectively. During initial learning, the provision of additional amounts of operative knowledge for the figurative and exploratory groups clearly facilitates accuracy of performance. In condition 1, these groups behave at the same levels as during previously reported studies (Duff 1988; 1989) and performance is reliably less accurate than for the other tasks ($F_{2,42} = 38.05$, MSe = 2.04, p<0.0001).

For the time data, there is also evidence of an increase in speed associated with presence of additional operative knowledge. Speeds of command selection for figurative and exploratory groups in condition 1 are slowest ($F_{2,42} = 80.5$, MSe = 94, p<0.0001).

During the problem solving phase, the overall pattern changes markedly in line with the predictions. Figure 12.3 and 12.4 show how the provision of operative knowledge to exploratory and figurative groups influence their behaviour. Increasing operative knowledge reduces figurative group problem accuracy for

both sequence lengths while resulting in less accurate exploratory group behaviour
($F_{2,42}$ = 19.87, MSe = 1.2, p<0.0001)).

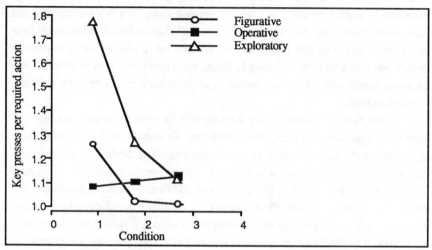

Figure 12.1 Learning data – key presses per required action by knowledge type and condition.

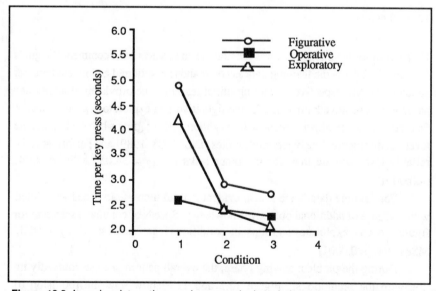

Figure 12.2 Learning data – time per key press by knowledge type and condition.

Time data show an associated decrease in command selection time, probably indicating that the amount of inferential processing is reduced ($F_{2,42} = 35.8$, $MSe = 39.9$, p<.0001). Figure 12.5 shows the error pattern, by serial position, for the command sequences involving six operations. The patterns for the sequence of eight operations is the same. The data shows how figurative knowledge constrains behaviour when it is used to develop a CTR (condition 1). More errors are made on controls that are described first in a pair, suggesting that the mental representation has developed to reflect the relational knowledge given in figurative instructions. Where additional operative knowledge is provided (commands so described are marked *), it is clear that the neatly structured pattern of errors does not occur, suggesting that surface information was being used preferentially during learning. Relational information present in the initial figurative information is not reflected in the representation used to support performance. However, those controls which are described as pairs still show the error pattern of more errors on the first member of the pair.

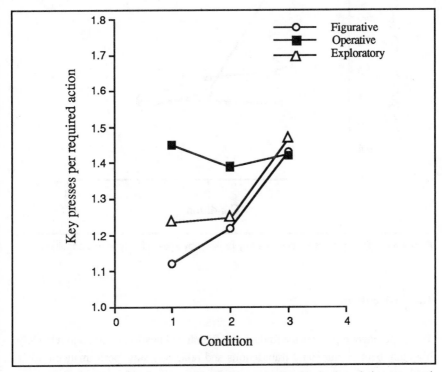

Figure 12.3 Problem data – key presses per required action by knowledge type and condition.

The pattern of data for the operative group does not match that of the figurative group. More errors are made on later commands in the sequence, indicating that this representation supports a primacy effect. In line with the predictions, the error data for the exploratory group shows a similar pattern as the operative group in the six sequence case in condition 1. With eight actions, and the benefit of the use of generalities between pairs of command lists, this pattern breaks down, greater accuracy attributed to where the generalities exist. In condition 2, a similar pattern emerges, though the differences between commands are reduced by the presence of operative knowledge describing non-inferential command positions. In condition 3 this pattern no longer exists, and generalities are no longer of any more benefit.

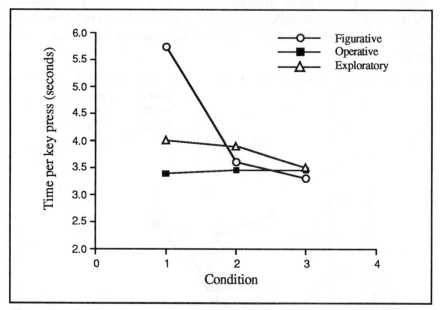

Figure 12.4 Problem data – time per key pressed by knowledge type and condition.

12.4 Discussion

This experiment replicates the finding that figurative knowledge results in relatively high numbers of command transactions and relatively slow performance during learning, and the development of knowledge structures that facilitate performance on novel tasks.

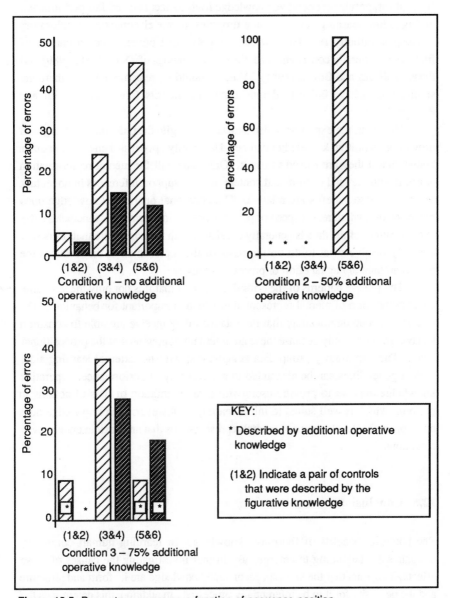

Figure 12.5 Percentage errors as a function of sequence position.

By contrast, providing operative knowledge leads to accurate and fast performance during initial learning, the accuracy dropping in novel contexts. Exploratory learning is initially fast, but obviously highly error prone. Such a pattern of findings is generally consistent with the earlier findings of Duff (1988; 1989) and those of Kieras and Bovair (1984). But, it should be remembered that there are studies which have failed to demonstrate such effects (e.g. Foss, Smith and Rosson, 1982).

However, the experiment also shows how fragile the potential advantages of providing figurative knowledge can be. Users only appear to benefit from such knowledge if they are forced to use it. Only then will the mental representation develop with the kind of form and content that can support inferences in novel task settings. These benefits are relative. The additional operative knowledge does reduce errors and increases speed of performance during learning. Nonetheless, the overall pattern of the data is generally consistent with the conjecture that users will mentally resolve what-to-do on the basis of the representation that reduces the overall amount of mental effort or processing activity.

The precise patterns of the error data suggest that it is not only the structure, but also the form of mental representation which is important for behaviour. The figurative group demonstrate that the relations they receive are able to constrain behaviour, presumably because these are internally represented at the propositional level. The exploratory group data suggest that with no external learning aids, system generalities can be abstracted to aid accuracy of performance. Operative knowledge appears to provide users with a representation of lists of actions to perform, which is well suited to initial learning. However, such knowledge does not support the development of mental representations that are flexible under novel conditions.

12.5 Conclusions

The potential benefits of figurative knowledge for learning human–computer dialogues are beginning to emerge. By further investigating the causes of these effects, it appears that the key aspects of such knowledge are its form and structure and the necessity for it to be inferentially processed. In addition, this determines the level at which the mental representation is instantiated, contributing towards the flexibility and, as suggested by earlier work, the memorability of the information. Analysing such data using ICS strongly suggests that the idea of a single mental representation of a device is incompatible with the range of performance which can be found. It is more the case that there are internal representations at different cognitive levels, which are responsible for describing the device in different ways, and which are constantly evolving. As each subsystem is considered to distinctly record and represent different kinds of knowledge, all of which may be sufficient, independently or combined, to lead to accurate task performance, this suggests that mental models are based on a collection of varied, interconnecting records of knowledge, the exact specifications of which are dependent on the specific factors present during learning. The hope is that the particular effects presented here, and the reasoning about their causes, go some way towards developing and understanding the precise relationships that hold between performance, mental processing and the structure and content of knowledge relevant to system use.

References

Barnard, P.J. (1987). Cognitive resources and the learning of human–computer dialogs. In Carroll, J.M. (ed.) *Interfacing Thought*. London: MIT Press.

Carroll, J.M. and Thomas, J.C. (1982). Metaphor and the cognitive representation of computing systems. *IEEE Transactions on Systems, Man and Cybernetics SMC-12*, 107–116.

Chi, M.T.H and Ceci,S.J. (1987). Content knowledge: its role, representation and restructuring in memory development. *Advances in Child Behaviour 20*, 91–142.

Duff, S.C. (1988). Device knowledge and the rReduction of action uncertainty. Paper presented at ECCE 4, Cambridge, England.

Duff, S.C. (1989). Reduction of action uncertainty in process control systems: the role of device knowledge. In Megaw, E. (ed.), *Contemporary Ergonomics*. London: Taylor and Francis.

Feigenbaum, E.A. (1988). What hath Simon wrought? In Klahr, D. and Kotovsky, K. (eds) *Complex Information Processing*. Hillsdale, NJ: LEA.

Foss, D. Smith, P. and Rosson, M. (1982). The novice at the terminal: variables affecting understanding and performance. Paper presented at the Psychonomic Society meeting, Minneapolis, Mn, USA.

Frese, M., and Albrecht, K. (1988). The effects of an active development of the mental model in the training process: experimental results in a word processing system. *Behaviour and Information Technology 7*, 295–304.

Halasz, F.G and Moran, T.P. (1983). Mental models and problem solving in using a calculator. In *CHI' 83 Conference Proceedings: Human Factors in Computing Systems*. Boston, Ma.: ACM.

Hammond, N., Morton, J., MacLean, A., Barnard, P. and Long, J. (1982). *Knowledge fragments and users models of systems.* IBM Research Report HF071. IBM (UK) Laboratories, Hursley Park, Hampshire.

Kieras, D. and Bovair, S. (1984). The role of a mental model in learning to operate a device. *Cognitive Science 8,* 255-273.

Wickens, C.D. (1984). *Engineering Psychology and Human Performance.* Colombus, Oh.: Merrill.

Chapter 13

Mental Models and Instructional Use

Yvonne Rogers

In the preceding two chapters we have seen how the two authors have explored representational issues surrounding instructional use. Both adopt a minimum level of theoretical commitment to the concept of mental models, regarding it essentially as the product of multiple knowledge representations. Rather than attempt to operationalize mental models per se, primarily the focus of their research has been upon the nature of mental representations that develop through the use of various types of external information and practise with either computer systems or mechanical devices. Viewed from this perspective, the notion of mental models is considered in terms of the consequences of mental representations for performance with a device or system. This contrasts with the reasoning approach taken by Byrne (this volume) in which the term is used to explain on-line construction and manipulation of mental models and that taken by Anderson et al (this volume) in which the emphasis is on the predictive nature of mental models.

To infer the characteristics of the mental representations that develop through instructional use, Duff and Bibby have adopted the experimental approach. Various performance measures were collected which were found to be related to the type and quantity of instruction provided to the subjects. For example, in one of Bibby's experiments the group of subjects given instructions that explicitly showed how the knobs, dials and indicators were related to each other on the device (described as topological knowledge) found it harder to reposition an incorrectly placed switch than to identify a faulty component. In contrast, the group of subjects given only a set of operating procedures found the opposite to be the case. Based on these findings, Bibby infers that the mental representations developed in the various experimental conditions were systematically different due to the different computational properties of the instructions. In other words, the speed and ease by which

MODELS IN THE MIND:
Theory, perspective and applications. ISBN 0–12–592970–6

inferencing can be achieved from the various types of external instructions is assumed to be preserved during the process of internalization in which mental representations are constructed. This explains why subjects found it easier to perform the task when there was a match between instruction type and task type than when there was a mismatch, presumably because the internalized knowledge is either appropriate or not for the task. Similar claims are made by Duff about the distinctiveness of mental representations constructed from different instructional material.

It is interesting to speculate why the computational properties of an external representation should be preserved during learning and skill acquisition and, furthermore, why it should be the case that the internalization effect should persist even through extensive practice with the device. Intuitively, it seems improbable that external representations, in the form of instructions, can cause such permanent mental imprinting. In particular, the idea that exposure to the printed word or a diagram can be so instrumental in shaping people's understanding and performance seems unlikely if we consider the immense problems that they have in the real world when trying to understand and follow instructions. Furthermore, the instinctual desire just to abandon instructions in favour of getting on with the task by trying out the system suggests that hands-on experience will play a much more significant role in determining the user's mental representations of the system. It seems strange therefore, that within the context of the experimental situation the pervasive experience of practice does not override or alter the pre-existing mental representation induced by the instructional material. Whilst acknowledging that in general, user's performance will eventually improve through practise, Bibby proposes that such changes are the result of task-specific strategies emerging and execution times speeding up, rather than any fundamental changes to the initial mental representations.

If we accept these theoretical claims as being true, then it suggests that written instructions could be very powerful tools. An obvious implication is that it should be possible to design instructions that enable the user to develop appropriate mental representations to perform their tasks. However, the danger is that if the instructions are inappropriately designed, a user will develop an inadequate mental representation that will be difficult to change. In support of this notion, Bibby's second study showed that even after much practise, users had great difficulty operating the device when given instructions that did not match the task they were to perform. Only after extensive practise did the users compensate for their knowledge deficiency.

Therefore, it seems that the provision of inadequate instructions can cause lasting problems. Duff proposes that users may try to overcome such deficiencies in knowledge by recourse to inferencing. He suggests that while the how-to-do-it or procedural type instructions enable the user to make a relatively easy transition between reading the instructions and actual performance, the how-it-works type instructions require the user to deduce certain inferences before being able to perform the task. The assumption is that telling someone how to do something in a step-by-step manner will make it quicker and easier to learn. Conversely, making users work something out for themselves will be much more taxing and time-consuming. The pay-off for extra effort is that it will enable the users to develop strategies that subsequently can facilitate the solving of novel problems. However, such a transfer effect will not be available to the group receiving just the how-to-do-it instructions. The underlying message, therefore, is that it is more effective in the long run to understand the internal structure of a system.

In the real world most people are likely to have access to a variety of knowledge resources and use a number of learning methods. For example, hands-on experience, practice and the use of analogy are other ways by which knowledge can be internalized. Prior knowledge also plays a critical role. Thus the acquisition of knowledge and the transition through to performance can be seen as the interplay between various internal and external knowledge resources. To account for the effects of these other resources Bibby and Duff stress the importance of viewing the construction of mental models as resulting from multiple mental representations. Hence, the theory purports that whilst the various forms of knowledge may be internalized as distinctive mental representations, subsequently they are utilized interactively.

The obvious advantage of having different levels and forms of knowledge to draw from is that it provides the user with an assortment of mental representations from which to think and reason about the problem in hand. However, a potential disadvantage of having multiple representations is that as many of them are likely to be incomplete, unstable and easily confused with each other (Norman, 1983), it may lead the user to make incorrect judgements and predictions resulting in erroneous performance with the device. The issue of consistency across representations needs to be addressed if we are to accept the characterization of mental models as being multiple representations. Furthermore, it is important to consider how the construct of mental models can be used to specify the dynamics of the way the various knowledge sources are recruited.

One of the problems which always has plagued the empirical approach to the study of mental representations is that the findings only ever can be indirect insights. It is one thing to discover that people adopt different strategies and make different errors given different sets of instructions; it is another to ascertain theoretically just how text or diagrams that constitute the external instructions are translated into differing internalized knowledge structures. For example, having read a set of procedural instructions or studied the way different entities on a diagram are connected for a given device or system, in what way is this internalized and moreover, how is this knowledge then utilized by the user when attempting to carry out a subsequent task using that device or system?

The authors attempt to tackle these issues by recourse to existing computational models of the mind. Duff draws from the modular architecture known as Interacting Cognitive Subsystems (Barnard, 1987) which describes how a number of subsystems operate in specific domains of processing. He uses the architecture as a framework in which to define the constraints of the different types of knowledge. Bibby goes one step further and attempts to model the use of internalized instructional representations through an adaptation of the production system model of ACT*. The advantage of attempting to model systematically mental models through computational means rather than other forms of textual explanations is that it requires a greater degree of theoretical rigour. A problem with using existing static modelling techniques , as indeed Bibby points out , is that they were not designed to model the more dynamic processes commonly attributed to mental models. A consequence is that the existing notation is too restricting and inappropriate to enable the mental processes, particularly explicit reasoning, to be represented adequately. What is needed therefore, if we are to gain anything from using modelling tools as explanations of mental models (which are approximations of reality only) are more flexible models (be they computational or other) that can represent the translation processes which occur between the initial exposure to external instructions and the subsequent application of knowledge when using a device or computing system. Also, such a model needs to be able to take into account previous knowledge and experience.

What do these studies tell us at a practical level? For instance, is it preferable to give people who are learning a new device or system procedural type instructions which match the tasks they need to perform to achieve their goals (presuming we know what they are), or should we provide them with instructions that convey knowledge about the internal and external structure of the system? Is it preferable to spoon-feed people or make them do most of the inferencing? Or is the ideal solution one in which the different types of knowledge are appropriately combined to give the user the best of both worlds. Duff discusses the problem of providing various combinations of how-it-works knowledge with how-to-do-it knowledge, suggesting that provision of both might not be the optimal solution. His reasoning is based on the assumption that it is better to encourage users to do a certain amount of inferencing otherwise their understanding will remain at a surface level and hence, it will limit their ability to solve novel problems. Interestingly, his results show the opposite: that adding how-to-do-it type of knowledge to the how-it-works knowledge enables users to learn more quickly with fewer errors. He concludes that users are somewhat reluctant to think for themselves and will only use the how-it works knowledge if really forced. It seems that the principle of operation is to do only what is necessary. The result that providing structural knowledge of the system may not be an effective method of instruction supports several other findings which have shown that explicit teaching of principles, fundamentals and theories does not necessarily enhance performance (e.g. Rouse and Morris, 1986).

As for offering advice for the design of instructions, the two authors have not been forthcoming. In contrast with the more applied, prescriptive-based research, which Carroll and his colleagues have carried out on the design of minimalist instruction (e.g. Carroll, 1990), the focus of Bibby's and Duff's research has been largely theory-oriented. In particular, the emphasis has been on characterizing the nature of mental models as a theoretical construct in relation to instructional use rather than for pedagogical concerns. The extent to which there can be any cross-fertilization between the theoretically-based treatment of the concept of mental models and its application within the context of instruction remains to be seen.

References

Barnard, P.J. (1987). Cognitive resources and the learning of human–computer dialogues. In Carroll, J. M. (ed.) *Interfacing Thought*. Cambridge, Ma.: MIT

Carroll, J.M. (1990). *The Nurnberg Funnel: Designing Minimalist Instruction for Practical Computer Skill*. Cambridge, Ma.: MIT.

Norman, D.A. (1983). Some observations on mental models. In Gentner, D. and Stevens, A. L. (eds) *Mental Models*. Hillsdale, NJ: LEA.

Rouse, W.R. and Morris, N.M. (1986). On looking into the blackbox: prospects and limits in the search for mental models. *Psychological Bulletin 100*, 349–363.

Part 5

Methods for Eliciting Mental Models in Human–Computer Interaction and Human–Machine Systems

Chapter 14

Searching for Mental Models in Human–Machine Systems

Andrew Rutherford and John R. Wilson

14.1 Introduction

The notion of a mental model may be traced back at least to the ideas of the psychologist Kenneth Craik (1943). Unfortunately, Craik's premature death curtailed the development of the mental model notion in academic psychology, where it remained dormant for nearly forty years until its resurrection by Johnson-Laird (1983). However, during this time, motivated by an attempt to understand peoples' capabilities and difficulties in operating machinery and systems that were becoming more and more complex, a similar notion was proposed and developed in applied psychology and ergonomics/human-factors.

Within the broad class of work termed ergonomics, some of the earliest references to operator mental models or conceptual models may be found in the human–machine systems (HMS) literature on continuous process control (e.g. Edwards and Lees, 1973; 1974; Veldhuyzen and Stassen, 1977). Further developments of the mental model notion in HMS can be found in the work of Rouse and his colleagues in the USA (e.g. Rouse and Morris, 1986) and the Risø group in Europe (e.g. Goodstein, Anderson and Olsen, 1988; Rasmussen, 1979; 1986).

The microprocessor revolution of the 1970s and 1980s enabled the construction of computers with more power, greater efficiency and less size, at considerably reduced cost. This provided the computer technology suitable for a rapid and prolific expansion to serve both the genuine and media-hyped information handling demands of contemporary society; in commerce, industry, leisure and of course, armaments. As systems were enhanced to deal with the increasing number of delegated tasks, they inevitably became more complex machines. Nevertheless, despite their greater complexity, because they had taken over so many functions it was no longer viable for experts to be in direct control of all their operations. An anomaly had been created: computer users of diminishing sophistication were required to operate computer systems of increasing complexity.

As computer products that proved difficult to use might fall into disrepute and business futures might be tied to the success of a computerization programme, the anomaly that provided ideal conditions for inefficient, erroneous and perhaps even disastrous computer use became the focus of increasing worry for both computer manufacturers and user groups. As a result, considerable financial support became available in the move to develop more usable systems. The availability of research funds, as well as the appreciation that computers were being used to perform cognitive tasks (Landauer, 1987) drew academic psychologists to the inter-disciplinary area of human–computer interaction (HCI).

It is increasingly difficult to justify differentiation between a field of HCI and one of HMS. Increased use of distributed information systems in continuous process control, the advent of computer aided design/manufacture (CAD/CAM) and computer aided production management (CAPM), and the communality of input, output and dialogue issues have meant a shared interest in human factors relevant to computer systems use. As the fields of HCI and HMS have converged, common theoretical requirements have made the mental model notion a valuable and frequently encountered theoretical construct. Unfortunately however, the separate development of the mental model notion in certain component disciplines of HMS/HCI has resulted in the use of a single term that has a number of interpretations.

14.2 The scientific status of the mental model concept

The term mental model has been applied to a various assortment of notions ranging from an image or mental picture (e.g. Lindgaard, 1987, p. 4; Oschanin, 1966 cited by Moll, 1987; Rouse and Morris, 1986, p. 355), to an analogy (e.g. Collins and Gentner, 1987), to qualitative simulations (e.g. de Kleer and Brown, 1983), to a particular representational format (Johnson-Laird, 1983), to an abstract mapping of properties and relations onto individuals (Stenning, 1990) and even to task-action mappings (e.g. Tauber, 1988). In turn, the variety of mental model conceptions have given rise to many different approaches to their study. Methods employed in the attempt to identify mental models have included interviews (e.g. diSessa, 1983; Kempton, 1986), questionnaires (e.g. Collins and Gentner, 1987; Gentner and Gentner, 1983), through multivariate statistical analyses of similarity ratings (e.g.

Kellogg and Breen, 1987), to partial (e.g. Johnson-Laird, 1983) and complete computer simulations (Forbus, 1983; Kuipers and Kassirer, 1984). While the utility of some of these accounts has been criticized (e.g. Briggs, 1988; Wilson and Rutherford, 1989), the plethora of differing views on the essential character of mental models and the various approaches to their identification, which provide a number of types of mental model description that are of dubious compatibility (although see Carroll and Olson, 1987 for an attempt at some reconciliation), indicate that the nature of the concept is not established uniformly throughout the pertinent scientific communities.

Some years ago Richard Young commented,

the notion of a mental model.remains a hazy one, and there are probably as many different ideas about what it might be like as there are people writing about it. (Young, 1983, p. 35)

More recently, Yvonne Waern has stated,

The concept of mental model as currently used by researchers in the field of human–computer interaction is prescientific. It is used to explain observations and to stir imagination, rather than to test hypotheses. There is no agreement on the definition of the model, on what it refers to or how it functions in the thought processes of the individual . (Waern, 1987, p. 277)

So despite its relatively long history (and the theoretical approach of Johnson-Laird, Byrne and their associates), the mental model notion appears to be stuck at an early phase of theoretical development. Given such a situation, it seems natural to ask why this is so. Is there something special about such theoretical notions that makes them particularly difficult to develop, or might it be that the mental model concept lacks substance or theoretical utility?

The utility of the mental model notion over the concept of background knowledge has been questioned (Rouse and Morris, 1986) and delineated (Wilson and Rutherford, 1989) and, as psychology knows well, in the philosophy of science there are difficulties with entities that cannot be observed directly. However, questions regarding the utility of the mental model notion over the concept of background knowledge appear to be the result of a lack of theoretical development rather than its cause and other theoretical developments in psychology have been unhampered by the non-observable nature of mental activity. Therefore, it seems unreasonable to attribute the current state of mental model theory in the applied sphere to these issues. Instead, it appears that the lack of development of the mental model concept in the applied sphere may be due primarily to the sort of questions that applied research asks, and the consequence this has for theoretical development.

Rom Harre states,

> A theory must serve as the basis for explanation, it is not just a codifying device. In order to fulfil this demand, a theory must describe the means by which the phenomena it explains come about. A theory must refer to the mechanisms of nature, not just to the quantitative results obtained by studying those mechanisms in action . (Harre, 1985, p. 24)

However, in applied research it is often determination of the quantitative result that is the main goal. Typically, the point of interest is whether there is a benefit or effect of a particular manipulation and if so, its extent. Of course, it would be ridiculous to claim that explanation is not of interest, but this is not the assertion. The claim is only that the emphasis is shifted from explanation to the quantitative result. If there were no shift in emphasis, then applied research and pure research would be indistinguishable.

Contrary to Waem's claim, within the HMS/HCI literature the mental model notion has been used to generate testable hypotheses, which have been examined by experiment (e.g. Bennett, 1982; Borgman, 1986; Halasz and Moran, 1983; Kay, 1987; Katzeff, 1988; Kieras and Bovair, 1984; Zhang and Wickens, 1987). Nevertheless, if the hypothesis testing that Waem intends is of the classical variety, where the hypotheses are developed from ideas concerning mechanism, as referred to by Harre, then her claim remains valid. Although hypotheses are generated and examined in these and other mental model studies, usually they are restricted to predictions of superior performance given appropriate but unspecified mental model operation. However, appropriate mental model operation is presumed as a consequence of the experimental procedures, which actually involve presenting subjects with different instructions, training or other information formats.

As most mental model studies do not assess predictions based on descriptions of mental model mechanisms, the form of explanation provided by most current mental model conceptions cannot be equivalent to that which characterizes a full theory. Instead, most mental model studies provide a description of conditions under which the particular mental model concept appears to be useful. These studies not only contribute to the accumulation of information that informs the mental model notion, but also define phenomena that must be accommodated by subsequent mental model theories. In many respects, such studies provide a sort of natural history of mental models.

Any standard description of the scientific method (e.g. Keeton, 1980; Villee, 1977) presents as the initial stage natural observation and exploratory examinations, which provide information that is employed by creative inductive processes for hypothesis and eventually theory development.

In Figure 14.1 an idealization of the cyclic scientific method is presented as a flow chart. There is little doubt that the least understood part of the scientific method is the nature of thought at its origin. From some unspecified source, perhaps based on seminal observations, ideas are formed and raise questions that informal and exploratory studies are constructed to provide information on. This data forms the input to an inductive process that develops a (provisional) model of the situation under consideration.

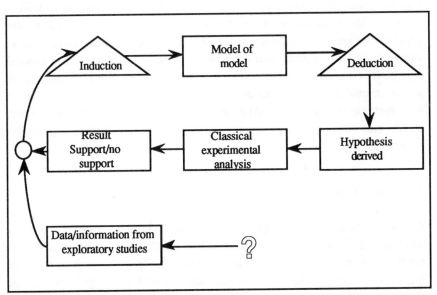

Figure 14.1 The cycle of the scientific method.

One of the difficulties with the mental model concept is its use of the term model. As this term is used frequently in theoretical discussions to designate the nature and status of theoretical constructs, discerning the intended meaning of the term can be problematic. In the present context, the inductive process should aim to provide a theoretical construct (a model) of the particular theoretical notion (the mental model).

From the provisional model of the mental model, deductive processes may provide predictions or hypotheses that can be tested by experiment. This is the classic stage of the scientific method. Although inaccurate and misleading, the theoretical construct (i.e. the model) often is termed a hypothesis and so this stage is frequently referred to as a hypothetico-deductive analysis. On the basis of the experimental results, which introduces the topic of assessment criteria such as statistical analyses attempt to provide, it is decided whether there is support for the experimental hypotheses, and so in turn, support for the theoretical model. This information feeds into the subsequent inductive process and the cycle of the scientific method continues.

So rather than being prescientific, as stated by Waern, the current phase of the development of the mental model concept appears to concord with the initial stage of the scientific method. Certainly, more sense can be made of the mental models literature if the majority of mental model studies are regarded as explorations of the mental model notion, rather than as exemplars of the classical deductive experimental approach. At this stage, exploring the mental model concept under various approaches is useful in that it allows comparison of alternative theoretical perspectives and empirical methods. The information provided by these initial studies should lead to a state of theoretical development where the classic implementation is appropriate. At present therefore, the majority of mental model studies may be considered as providing the input to the inductive stage of the scientific method.

14.3 Induction

Lately, psychologists have begun to investigate the human reasoning processes involved in science (Langley, Simon, Bradshaw and Zytkow, 1987) and induction (Holland, Holyoak, Nisbett and Thagard, 1986). Holland et al employ the term induction to refer to inferential processes that expand knowledge in the face of uncertainty. However, this is a very broad definition of induction and, indeed, it has the consequence of placing most of the topics in the psychology of thinking under the heading of inductive processes.

In contrast, philosophical considerations of inference have provided further and more precise distinctions and associated terms. In this tradition, based on the work of Peirce (1934; 1935; 1958), Addis (1987) provides a useful synopsis of types of inference: abduction is the creation of new distinctions or hypotheses to account for data, adduction is support for abduction (although this is not mentioned by Addis) and deduction is the redescription of information contained in a system of facts and hypotheses. On the basis of this account, induction is restricted to the assessment of truth, or the validity or utility of hypotheses. It may be appreciated that within such a scheme, induction requires the prior existence of a hypothesis. It is the specification of what constitutes an adequate test (but not its execution) and the comprehension of the result of this test that are the products of the processes of induction.

The description of inference favoured by Peirce and Addis has certain advantages, such as identifying distinctly the process whereby new information enters the system. However, it is common now for induction to be regarded as a combination of abduction and adduction; the creative generation of models/ hypotheses with the evidential basis for such ideas cited. Paradoxically, while the meaning of induction as described by Peirce has faded, the definition of deduction provided by Peirce remains in use. Nevertheless, to concord with the majority of the literature, the commonly employed sense of induction will be used here.

In the history of the philosophy of science, one group, termed inductivists, asserted that a finite and discrete set of principles describes completely the scientific method. Clearly, if this were the case, identification of these principles would remove much of the difficulty of science. Moreover, if rules of induction were to be developed on the basis of these principles, science should become an essentially transparent procedure, which might be automated. However, the set of principles advocated, accumulation, induction and instance confirmation, have been criticized heavily, not least for being totally unrepresentative of the actual practice of science (Harre, 1985).

However, another more contemporary group has considered induction and has had automation as a specific goal. This group comprises members from the area of machine learning and their approach will be discussed in the context of the following section on expert system knowledge acquisition.

14.4 Modelling knowledge for expert systems

At first thought, there may not appear to be much in common between knowledge acquisition for expert systems and exploratory studies to identify mental models. However, both activities have the problem of extracting relevant information from a person (knowledge elicitation) and subsequently, constructing some pertinent representation based on this information. Nevertheless, despite this communality, there has been little interaction between the two areas. It might be surmised that this is in part due to a perceived mismatch in the formality between the two areas at data collection and model representation. Mental modellers may falsely have regarded the data collection procedures of knowledge elicitation as lacking formal rigour in comparison with their experimental approach, while knowledge engineers may have regarded the mental model representations presented in the literature as too informal compared with the implementation formalisms used in expert systems.

However, irrespective of the reasons for a lack of communication between the two areas, developments in the theoretical perspective of knowledge acquisition for expert systems have emphasized their similarity. In particular, it has been recognized that representing relationships between domain elements cannot support the form and depth of reasoning required for many problems (Shadbolt and Burton, 1989). To achieve this, causal models of the processes that give rise to object relations and influences are required. If expert systems manifest the knowledge of experts, then their knowledge implementation must reflect accurately the experts' mental models of the knowledge domain. Consequently, it is advocated that knowledge acquisition is the modelling of expert knowledge and not the extraction or mining of expert knowledge, as is often presumed even by advanced acquisition systems (Breuker, 1987; Breuker and Wielinga, 1987; Morik, 1987; 1989). Knowledge elicitation should be considered an integrated part rather than an independent phase of expert system construction, not least for influencing the representational format chosen for the implementation. Indeed, Morik stresses the interactive nature of the modelling process, claiming that the model of expertise develops over the period of knowledge elicitation as the experts adapt to the explication of their own expertise.

One of Morik's aims is the design of expert knowledge acquisition systems that provide support to knowledge domain modelling by employing machine learning techniques to perform parts of the knowledge modelling autonomously. Morik (1989) categorizes approaches to machine learning in terms of a description of a cycle of knowledge domain modelling that she compares with the standard scientific method. This is pertinent and interesting as it suggests that there are well defined and understood methods that express the inductive stage of the scientific method as depicted in Figure 14.1.

Morik lists concept identification in terms of properties, regularity discovery, hypothesis generation on the basis of derived laws, enhanced problem solving by chunking, rule refinement through conflict resolution, analogy, theory formation and even automatic experimental design, as activities that are the focus of research in machine learning (see Morik, 1989, for details and references). Nevertheless, while the current techniques may offer useful tools for various aspects of expert system construction, this work is at a relatively early stage of development. Despite the impressive sounding titles, the means of carrying out such activities are often very primitive and consequently, there are problems which restrict the applicability of these techniques.

Many of the activities listed by Morik are founded on machine learning research which has focused on inductive or similarity based learning techniques that employ statistical regularities in a set of examples to generate rules. The equivalent use of the terms induction and similarity based learning gives some indication of the restricted aspect of induction under study in machine learning research in comparison with the connotative range of the term as used in the discussion of the scientific method.

The best known induction algorithm is ID3 (Quinlan, 1983; 1986a). This algorithm provides rules in the form of decision trees on the basis of a set of examples. However, ID3 has been criticized for allowing the input order of examples to affect the rules that are generated by the ID3 algorithm and for being unable to separate causality from correlation, with the result that erroneous causal rules may be induced (Bramer, 1987; Hart, 1987). Moreover, those rules which are produced may not be "brain compatible". This means that the rules cannot be understood nor checked by mental application to any example set (Shapiro, 1987).

In general, contemporary inductive techniques require a large number of examples for useful operation. Also, it is important that, as far as possible, the examples should be free of noise, that is incorrect or incomplete data. The presence of noise in learning examples can cause serious problems for inductive systems. Inductive algorithms that cope with noise are the focus of much research activity (e.g. Niblett, 1987; Quinlan, 1986b).

Furthermore, a major problem for any knowledge representation system are the restrictions placed on the system by the representational format used in the system description or implementation. For instance, the examples upon which the induction algorithms operate must be formulated in a machine-acceptable manner. This is determined by the particular representational format(s) employed by the system. The rules that are induced from examples of such a type also will conform to the restrictions of the representational format selected for the system, and so the choice of the examples' representation will determine the potential result of the inductive algorithms (Morik, 1987; 1989). Therefore, induction is constrained not only by the quality of the information employed to manifest the domain knowledge, but also by the information that is able to be captured by the representational format.

Moreover, not only is considerable noise likely to be present in data collected at the initial stages of any scientific enquiry, but at this stage it may not be clear what constitutes noise. Indeed, this points to one of the important differences between induction to aid expert system construction and induction within the scientific method. As machine induction attempts to replicate expertise, it is able to employ what Shapiro (1987) terms an oracle. This may be a teacher or an exhaustively computed database that determines whether each example satisfies its inducted classification. In contrast, the products of scientific induction do not have such an accessible and well defined set of criteria. Instead, the products of scientific induction are judged by criteria that philosophers of science still struggle to describe and continue to debate, but which include concordance with the real world, as assessed by observation or experiment.

Due to the difficulties caused by noisy data and its possible interaction with the important limitations imposed by representational formats when the range of representational requirements are unknown, it is extremely doubtful that the current machine learning approach could define the initial inductive stage of the scientific method as applied to mental model description or indeed, any other domain.

14.5 A methodological overview

Although several partial or brief reviews of methods used to identify mental models are available in the literature (e.g. Briggs, 1988; Moll, 1987; Rouse and Morris, 1986), it is the intention to describe and assess here a greater range of methods in more detail than has been done before. Prior to this however, some of the difficulties and limits that have been attributed specifically to mental model identification will be considered.

14.5.1 Mental model identification problems

In a review of mental models research, Rouse and Morris (1986) assess the prospects and limits of accounts of mental models. As part of their argument, they categorize four approaches to the identification of mental models. The approaches they list are: empirical inference, empirical modelling, analytical modelling and verbal reports. Although the fourth category is described more accurately as a form of data, it encompasses much of the mental models research concerned with higher level cognition. The three other categories would appear to be subsumed by the classical experimental approach. From such a division and Rouse and Morris's discussion of these classifications, it becomes clear that their account of mental models is based heavily upon, if not biased by the theoretical notion of mental models as developed in the area of manual/supervisory control. This is rather ironic as one of Rouse and Morris's admonishments concerns the distortion of mental model accounts introduced by the subjective perspective of the experimenter. Rouse and Morris remark that:

> researchers' mental models affect their conceptualization of others' mental models. (Rouse and Morris, 1986, p. 353)

As they acknowledge, this is a topic that bedevils all of science. However, it is far from accepted that psychology is more afflicted by such distortions or biases than other scientific disciplines. Indeed, it could be argued that psychology is likely to be less prone to this than other disciplines, by virtue of the fact that there is greater awareness of such influence and that in psychology this is a topic of study (Harre, 1985).

Many of the problems highlighted by Rouse and Morris are well considered issues, as they are inherent in all psychological investigation, rather than solely with respect to mental model identification methods. For example, there is nothing novel about the metaphysical status of the mental model theoretical entity and its relationship to the methods that may be applied to examine it. All cognitive and most other psychological accounts make similar metaphysical claims and are addressed by similar methodological approaches. Likewise, Rouse and Morris raise the issue of identifying the true mental model. This topic equates with the issue of truth in the philosophy of science and again it is an issue which has been considered extensively, as it pertains to all scientific research and not just mental models.

One of the major differences between the mental models implied by Rouse and Morris and those presented in the cognitive literature is the separation of "cue selection" and "response execution" from the mental model. This separation provides the rationale for the claim that inferences from empirical studies can be indirect only, because the data taken to reflect mental model operation are most likely to be confounded by perceptual and response processes. Moreover, they claim that an account of mental models that incorporates cue selection would:

> obscure important interactions between cue utilization and cue combination mechanisms. (Rouse and Morris, 1986, p. 356)

Several points need to be made with respect to these claims. The first is that virtually all psychological investigations, from psychophysics to social psychology, must overcome various forms of potential confounding. Examination of any aspect of mind necessarily involves coping with a dynamic, interactive, biologically and socially determined system. Only very basic (encapsulated) psychological operations lend themselves to the methodological compartmentalization employed in the physical sciences (for discussion of encapsulated processes, see Boden, 1988). In psychology therefore, it is not usually possible to isolate empirically the processes of interest to a particular study, nor in most cases is it theoretically wise to presume to do so. In other words, it is the norm for psychologists to have to devise ways of minimizing the influence of a vast range of variables in any investigation. This is one reason for the emphasis on experimental design in psychology courses and why good psychological investigation and theory building is so difficult.

Second, it is far from clear exactly what should be lost and why this should be lost from an account of mental models that incorporates the determination of cues. A clear specification of the mental model processes involved in cue selection should be no more obscure than any other form of account. Once clear descriptions of mental model operation are provided, it becomes an empirical issue as to which account best accommodates the pertinent experimental data.

A third point relates to the claim that when such confounding is unlikely to occur, empirical modelling, which is the algorithmic specification of the relationship between stimulus and response, can be done with regression and time series analyses of the input–output relations. However, there is not a simple relationship between a statistical model, such as might be described by the methods of data analysis mentioned by Rouse and Morris, and a psychological model or theory (Cummins, 1983).

The fundamental limits of mental model identification claimed by Rouse and Morris are based on their theoretical and methodological account. Therefore, questioning the insight and validity of this account also must question their claims regarding such limits. However, this is not to say that mental models are easily identified.

Norman (1983) provides a concise account of several important issues concerning research on mental models. Indeed, so concise is his presentation that the aspect of it to be addressed here is contained completely within the second footnote. Here Norman warns of the difficulties of determining the nature of mental models through people's verbal reports.

Verbal accounts can be misleading for several reasons. They may be incomplete and/or erroneous because people may not have conscious access to the cognitive structures that determine their behaviour and because genuinely, they may have a particular belief, but do not act in a concordant manner. Also, as Norman describes, the demand structure of the situation may "force" people to provide reasons for their behaviour when they did not base their actions on any particular conscious reason. However, given the social situation, people are likely to provide the answer they presume the experimenter wants to hear. Consequently, mental model identification methods must be designed and applied to cope with such circumstances.

Given the amount of discussion in the literature concerning the problems of determining the nature of mental models, it may be appreciated that researchers working in this area consider it to be a difficult task. Nevertheless, the endeavour is not only worthwhile in terms of the theoretical development and practical advantages it provides, but also attainable in terms of continually closer approximations to what might constitute the reality of a mental model.

14.5.2 Mental model information elicitation methods

In the present context, methodology refers not only to different approaches, such as experimental and naturalistic study and design paradigms, but also to the different manners of analyses of the behavioural data elicited and recorded. Presented below is a simple diagram that outlines the features that determine the degree of formality of mental model identification studies.

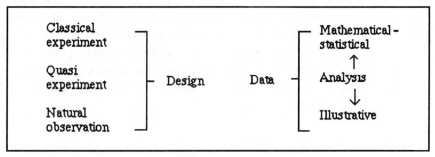

Figure 14.2 Features determining the formality of mental model identification studies.

On the left of Figure 14.2 distinctions are made in terms of the logical structure (i.e. design) of the study. Although three labels are used, probably it is better to think of a continuum of formality along which potential studies may be located, with the labels employed identifying three areas on this continuum. This feature defines the first order formality of the study.

On the right of Figure 14.2 a distinction is made in terms of the type of analysis carried out on the study data collected. Again it is best to think in terms of a continuum of analysis formality, with the simple identification and reporting of comments or acts from protocols to illustrate theoretical claims at one end and various mathematically based analyses located towards the other end of the continuum. This feature determines the second order formality of the study.

a) Classical experimentation

This is the standard methodological approach in psychology. The classical experimental method obtains its power to identify causality by implementing control procedures. Unfortunately, this can make it an unwieldy tool for use in the field. Classical experimental methods are designed to assess the product of hypothetico-deductive logic applied to theory. However, as most current mental models research appears to be directed to the goal of eliciting information to provide some insight into the mental model form rather than trying to determine which set of hypothetical mental operations is supported by the data, induction, rather than deduction appears to be the aim of current data analysis. Therefore, classical experimentation is inappropriate for much current mental models research not only because of the practical difficulties of application, but primarily because of the method's specific theoretical purpose (cf. Evans, 1988).

Several mental model studies have employed designs that reflect the classical experimental approach (e.g. Bennett, 1982; Borgman, 1986; Halasz and Moran, 1983; Katzeff, 1988; Kay, 1987; Kieras and Bovair, 1984; Zhang and Wickens, 1987). However, while these studies have provided information on conditions, including instructions and training, which are presumed to influence mental models, they do not provide information on the mechanism that manifests such effects (see Bibby; Duff, this volume).

b) Quasi-experimental and naturalistic approaches

Given the preceding argument, it should be expected that the majority of mental model studies would employ less formal methods than classical experimentation. Also, it is not uncommon for several different methods of eliciting mental model information to be employed within one study. In many studies, the formality of the data analysis replaces the formality of the design in importance. This latter aspect is considered in section 14.5.4.

c) Interviews

Interviews can vary between two types: structured or unstructured. Structured interviews are of a prescribed format, which should ensure that the information required of interviewees is elicited. A major problem with interviews is that only information that can be expressed verbally may be obtained. Information may be represented in forms that cannot be interrogated successfully by language processes. In such situations, the demand structure of the task may result in spurious rationale for behaviour (Norman, 1983). Moreover, as interviews are most likely to occur after task performance, it is probable that they will be prone to retrospective distortions (for further discussion see Bainbridge, 1979).

A number of studies have used this method as their primary source of mental model information. In most cases the style of interview carried out is described as "in depth", but unfortunately no further information regarding the interview is provided (e.g. diSessa, 1983; Kempton, 1986; McCloskey, 1983).

d) Questionnaires

Questionnaires are written, structured interviews and so share the limitations described above for interviews. In mental model studies relatively short questionnaires are employed frequently, but typically as an adjunct to other methods of eliciting mental model information, for confirmation, or as a means to group subjects (e.g. Collins and Gentner, 1987; diSessa, 1983; Gentner and Gentner, 1983; Williams, Hollan and Stevens, 1983).

e) Thinking-aloud protocols

This is the most popular method of eliciting mental model information as evidenced by the number of studies that employ this approach (e.g. Clement, 1983; Govindaraj and Su, 1988; Katzeff, 1990; Larkin, 1983; McCloskey, 1983). Nevertheless, as the thinking-aloud is in terms of a verbal account, again the information that can be captured using this method is restricted to that which may be verbalized (cf. interviews and questionnaires).

Generally, the validity of such verbal reports relies on a model of verbalization presented by Ericsson and Simon (1980, 1984). In contrast to critics who question the validity of such verbal protocols (e.g. Nisbett and Wilson, 1977;

Nisbett and Ross, 1980), Ericsson and Simon claim that valid verbal protocols may be obtained by avoiding retrospectively generated protocols and instructions that might lead subjects to attempt to explain their thoughts, rather than just report them. Moreover, provided subjects give account of only that information in short-term memory (more accurately working memory, Baddeley, 1990), and this information is represented verbally, the primary problem-solving task and the concurrent verbalization task will not interfere with each other (for further discussion see Bainbridge, 1979; Praetorius and Duncan, 1988).

Russo, Johnson and Stephens (1989) have distinguished between reactive and non-veridical invalidity of verbal protocols. A verbal protocol is considered to be reactive if it alters primary task performance and a verbal protocol that does not reflect the primary task performance is regarded as non-veridical. Four types of task were used by Russo et al in an experimental examination of protocol reactivity. Unfortunately, the pattern of reactivity observed, even with the relatively simple tasks employed, did not concord with Ericsson and Simon's model predictions. Russo et al concluded that the theoretical understanding of verbal protocol generation is not adequate to assure the absence of reactivity without an empirical check.

f) Constructive interaction

This method of eliciting information from people has been employed in several mental model studies (e.g. Garrod and Anderson, 1987; Miyake, 1986; O'Malley, Draper and Riley, 1985). O'Malley (1987) lists a number of features of successful joint problem-solving which are manifest using a constructive interaction method. These features are:

1. A greater possibility of alternative perspectives or interpretations as a result of two people addressing the problem.
2. With another person providing perspectives or interpretations there is less chance of "cognitive hysteresis" (Lewis and Norman, 1986).
3. Alternative perspectives or interpretations encourage articulation, dis-cussion and criticism of views.
4. As a consequence of 3 the normally implicit rationale of the subjects is made explicit,.
5. Dialogue is an integral part of the subjects' task, rather than being additional to the primary problem-solving task, as is the case with individual thinking-aloud methods.

Few would dispute these specific claims. However, the potential implications of the final claim require consideration. There is a suggestion that constructive interaction is superior to the thinking-aloud method because the verbalizations produced by subjects are an inherent part of the task.

Given the criticisms of the validity of verbal reports produced by the thinking-aloud method, it might be expected that the superiority of the constructive interaction method would be founded on a lack of reactivity and assured veridicality. Nevertheless, even with a constructive interaction method, subjects may verbalize their thoughts to the other subject only concurrently or retrospectively. Therefore, any concurrent verbalization of thoughts is open to exactly the same criticisms of reactivity and non-veridicality that are levelled at verbal reports obtained using the thinking-aloud method. In addition, as subjects determine the time at which they verbalize their thoughts, validity cannot be enhanced by ensuring concurrent, as opposed to retrospective production. Consequently, it would seem that the criticisms directed at the thinking-aloud method regarding protocol validity are as, if not more, pertinent to the method of constructive interaction.

Moreover, when a constructive interaction method is employed, the subject's task is not just to solve the problem presented, but to team up with another person and solve the problem. Obviously, in these circumstances dialogue will be an integral part of the task because the constructive interaction method makes it so. In other words, the subject's task in constructive interaction is significantly different from the subject's task in the individual thinking-aloud method.

O'Malley (1987) discusses some of the implications of the fact that the verbalizations provided by subjects are for the purpose of communication in a social context. She concedes that the differing task demands between constructive interaction and individual thinking-aloud methods may result in different psychological strategies being employed. For example, subjects may be more interested in showing their ability to debate a point rather than persuade the other person of the accuracy of their view (Antaki, 1985). In such circumstances, the constructive interaction method might reveal less of the nature of the subject's understanding of the problem and more of the subject's reasons for being believed. However, it is difficult to imagine subjects being able to argue their case without some, if not considerable, expression of their understanding of the problem.

A more damaging critique of constructive interaction as a method for eliciting information pertinent to individuals' mental models is the view that to be able to communicate with the other person, individual subjects may have to modify their account of their understanding of the problem and its solution. O'Malley refers to Freyd's (1983) "shareability hypothesis", which asserts that the requirement to share information results in certain constraints on that information. This raises the possibility that people may construct and employ communicational artefacts to achieve meaningful exchanges. Such communicational artefacts would be modified versions of their actual understanding determined by their conception of the current shareability constraints (presumably their understanding of the other person's understanding).

Although the social context of cognition and the influence this exerts on mind cannot be denied, it is quite another matter to suggest that only mental models which represent such common understanding exist. If this were so, the notion of constraints on what can be shared would not arise. Consequently, the use of the constructive interaction method to provide information for the description of individuals' unique mental models should be considered carefully.

Lastly, it should be mentioned that the social aspect of the constructive interaction method requires that another factor is considered. This is the social compatability of the two subjects to be placed in the constructive interaction situation. From experience, it is not difficult to think of two people that would destructively, rather than constructively, interact. Without a formal means of assessing people's compatibility for joint problem-solving, subject pairings and their outcomes are dependent on the experimenters' best guesses.

14.5.3 Data

The level in Figure 14.2 labelled design data refers to the type of data elicited and recorded in the studies carried out. A host of different types of subject behaviours have been employed in mental model studies. The data collected across studies (and often within studies) have ranged from accuracy and latency of responses (e.g. Bennett, 1982; Kay, 1987), to a complete record of computer interaction (e.g. Moll, 1987), to complete recordings of all overt behaviour on video (e.g. Miyake, 1986; for discussion of such an approach see Laws and Barber, 1989). The relatively new term applied to the recording of aspects of subjects' behaviour is the protocol. Originally, this term was restricted to the record of verbal productions, but now it is applied generally (Byrne, 1982) and has been used to describe behaviour recorded as pictures, diagrams, videos and computer interaction logs.

With present-day technology making so many forms of recording relatively easy to employ, there is a tendency to record more behaviour than will be employed in the analyses that provide the basis for the psychological inferences. Moreover, as a variety of different types of dependent variable measure may be extracted, it is not unusual for the potential amount of data available for analysis to seem overwhelming. If the protocol is a passive record of some of the subjects' overt behaviour (e.g. computer interaction log) or indeed, all of the subjects' overt behaviour (e.g. video recording), a major source of potential error is the data extraction procedure. Data errors may occur as a function of a theoretical misconception, or more simply as transcription errors.

14.5.4 Data analysis

As described earlier, the data analysis employed in mental model studies may be placed on a continuum of formality. However, if this were done, it would be observed that many studies congregate at the ends of the formality continuum. At one end, the form of data analysis tends to be the selection of examples from the data for illustration, while at the other end, sophisticated multivariate analyses are employed. Both of these forms of data analysis reflect the exploratory nature of the majority of studies. Illustrative examples of subjects' behaviour are presented to support particular mental model interpretations derived from the data, while multivariate analyses are used to infer structure from the recorded data, which is related to the mental model.

Despite the tendency of many studies to adopt analyses of polar formality, several other approaches are evident. For example, Bailey and Kay (1986; 1987) have suggested a graphical means of describing the structure of verbal data, while a number of computer based systems have been developed to facilitate the analysis of verbal protocol data (e.g. Sanderson, James and Seidler, 1989). Some of these systems have the specific goal of aiding the induction of mental models (e.g. Kowalski and VanLehn, 1988). Kuipers and Kassirer (1984) too have described a means of analysing verbal protocols. Their goal is to develop a qualitative causal (mental) model based (although not exclusively) on the objects and relations identified from subjects' protocols.

The mathematical theory of rough sets also has been used in the determination of a mental model in terms of production rules (Mrozek, 1989). The definition of a problem space in terms of production rules is the basis for the SOAR approach to problem solving (e.g. Laird, Newell and Rosenbloom, 1987). This may be considered as providing a description of mental models in terms of a particular processing mechanism (Simon, 1989).

The approach adopted by Katzeff (1990) and Sanderson, Verhage and Flud (1989) was to employ task analysis to identify partially subjects' mental models.

In the former case, the information provided by the system was compared with that required for an appropriate mental model and on the basis of discrepancies, subject difficulties were predicted. In the latter case, appropriate control actions to achieve specified goals were identified and on this basis subject difficulties were predicted. In both cases, subject performance was compared to the predictions derived from the mental models developed from the tasks.

The statistical analyses employed to identify structure are often referred to as psychological scaling techniques. Analyses from this category that have been applied to mental model studies include cluster analysis (e.g. Baggett and Ehrenfeucht, 1988; Kellogg and Breen, 1987), multi-dimensional scaling (e.g. Cooke and McDonald, 1987) and conceptual network production (e.g. Cooke and McDonald, 1987; Cooke and Schvaneveldt, 1988).

Although these techniques are applied to identify structure, it is important to distinguish the structure of the data expressed by the statistical analysis and the representational structure of the mental model. The raw data are best regarded as an abstraction of the product or output of the mental model operation. It would appear to be a very simplistic and dubious claim that data structure and mental model representational structure are equivalent. Rather, it would seem that the data structure identified by such analyses describes sets of relationships and communalities, which are a consequence of the mental model operation. Such data descriptions must be given account in terms of the mental model operation, rather than presented as the account of the mental model. Mathematical equations do not provide psychological accounts (Cummins, 1983).

Another heading for such statistical analyses is data reduction techniques. Such data analysis methods attempt to provide summaries of the data submitted. When it is considered that not only is the data analysis reducing the amount of information describing the mental model operation, but also that the task which provided the original measures probably taxed only a part of the mental model operations available, it can be appreciated that the structure revealed by the statistical analysis is unlikely to provide an accurate reflection of the nature of the mental model.

14.6 General assessment

As described earlier, there is a close relationship between knowledge acquisition for expert systems and mental model identification. However, in contrast to the few reviews of mental model identification methods, the expert system literature provides several practical "how to do knowledge acquisition" type accounts (e.g. Hart, 1986; Kidd, 1987), as well as a number of general reviews of knowledge elicitation methods (e.g. Evans, 1988; Gammack and Young, 1985; Hoffman, 1987; Shadbolt and Burton, 1989; Slater, 1988; Welbank, 1983). Consideration of such methods (Rutherford and Wilson, 1991) reveals mental model information elicitation methods to be a subset of knowledge elicitation methods. The use of a subset of knowledge elicitation methods to elicit mental model information reflects the different objectives of the two spheres of work. The elicitation methods used in mental models research are biased towards those which are most likely to provide procedural information and insights into process control structure. In contrast, the form of knowledge representation employed in many expert systems is such that declarative information is implemented most easily. However, as the requirement for causal models to enable more sophisticated problem solving increases, the differences between knowledge acquisition for expert systems and mental models research are likely to diminish.

However, the most popular method of eliciting procedural information, namely concurrent thinking-aloud, does not yet rest on an assured theoretical base. Indeed, the particular limitations, biases and potential errors associated with any information elicitation method must be considered seriously, along with the specific goals of the study, when making a choice regarding which information elicitation method to employ. Unfortunately, the current theoretical understanding of the processes underpinning such information elicitation techniques does not allow a simple identification of a "best" method.

In those studies where mental models are induced from subjects' responses, the route from the mental model information elicited by the various methods to the hypothesized mental model remains opaque. Experimenters employ intuitive rather than formal procedures to suggest possible mental models. Such opacity is not surprising therefore, as so little is known about the creative and inductive processes underlying model or hypothesis generation. In contrast to knowledge modelling for expert systems, there has been little progress in providing some formal basis to the path from data to hypothesized mental model (Rutherford and Wilson, 1991). The attempt to utilize the formality of multivariate statistics has foundered at the gap between the mathematical model and the psychological model, with a tendency to imply erroneously that the former is equivalent to the latter.

Perhaps more important than the failure to describe the inductive route from the information elicited by the various methods to the hypothesized mental model is a general lack of clearly specified candidate mental models. Ideally, such a mental model should be specified with sufficient clarity that it could be programmed and its predictions determined. However, it is likely that intuitive induction provides intuitive candidate mental models, which are not described easily in the formal manner advocated.

One danger in exploratory studies of mental models is that preconceptions of likely mental models may be confirmed only and never rejected. This may come about as a result of the informal choices available regarding pertinent data, methods of eliciting such data and the form of the data analysis. At each step the choice made may constrain the alternatives such that only the preconception that gave rise to such choices can describe the result. For example, Baggett and Ehrenfeucht (1988) considered the conceptualization of assembly tasks, which they hypothesized to be organized as a hierarchy of sub assemblies. The order of asking for components for assembly was coded in terms of component proximity/distance and examined using hierarchical cluster analysis. Not surprisingly, hierarchical clusters were determined and this finding was taken as corroboration of the hypothesis that conceptualizations (mental models) of assembly are organized in a hierarchy of sub assemblies.

Mental model accounts that are induced opaquely from data or even transparently from invalid data, or that conform to preconceptions are problematic primarily when they are in error. Therefore, if serendipity is not to be relied on, it is important to assess the accuracy of the hypothesized mental model. Consequently, there is a need to follow up exploratory studies, which should provide clear (and ideally, programmed) descriptions of hypothetical mental models, with tests of predictions based on these hypothesized models. In other words, in mental models research, given the successful completion of the first stage (as defined above), there is a need to move to the classical stage of the scientific method.

Acknowledgements

This work was supported by the ESRC/SERC Joint Committee (Grant Reference GR/F/07705).

References

Addis, T.R. (1987). A framework for knowledge elicitation. In *Proceedings of the First European Workshop on Knowledge Acquisition for Knowledge-Based Systems*. Reading University, 2–3 September.

Antaki, C. (1985). Ordinary explanation in conversation: causal structures and their defence. *European Journal Of Social Psychology 15*, 213–230.

Baddeley, A.D. (1990). *Human Memory: Theory and Practice*. Hove, Sussex: LEA.

Baggett, P. and Ehrenfeucht, A. (1988). Conceptualizing in assembly tasks. *Human Factors 30*, 269–284.

Bailey, W.A. and Kay, E.J. (1986). Toward the standard analysis of verbal data. *Proceedings of the IEEE International Conference on Systems, Man and Cybernetics*. October 14–17, Atlanta, Georgia.

Bailey, W.A. and Kay, E.J. (1987). Structural analysis of verbal data. In Carroll, J.M. and Tanner, P.P. (eds) *Proceedings of CHI and GI 1987*. Toronto, Canada, 5–9 April.

Bainbridge, L. (1979). Verbal reports as evidence of the process operator's knowledge. *International Journal of Man-Machine Studies 11*, 411-436.

Bennett, K.B. (1982). The effect of display design on the user's mental model of a perceptual database system. Ph.D. dissertation, Catholic University of America, USA.

Boden, M. (1988). *Computer Models of Mind*. Cambridge: CUP

Borgman, C.L. (1986). The user's mental model of an information retrieval system: an experiment on a prototype online catalogue. *International Journal of Man–Machine Studies 24*, 47–64.

Bramer, M.A. (1987). Automatic induction of rules from examples: a critical analysis of the ID3 family of rule induction systems. In *Proceedings of the First European Workshop on Knowledge Acquisition for Knowledge Based Systems*. Reading University, 2–3 September.

Briggs, P. (1988). What we know and what we need to know: the user model versus the user's model in human-computer interaction. *Behaviour and Information Technology 7*, 431–442.

Breuker, J. (ed.) (1987). *Model-Drive Knowledge Acquisition Interpretation Models*. Deliverable Task A1, ESPRIT Project 1098, University Of Amsterdam.

Breuker, J. and Wielinga, B. (1987). Knowledge acquisition as modelling expertise: the KADS methodology. In *Proceedings of the First European*

Workshop on Knowledge Acquisition for Knowledge Based Systems. Reading University, 2–3 September.

Byrne, R. (1982). Protocol analysis in problem solving. In Evans, J.St.B.T. (ed.) *Thinking and Reasoning.* London: Routledge.

Carroll, J.M. and Olson, J.R. (1987). *Mental Models in Human–Computer Interaction.* Washington DC: National Academy Press.

Clement, J. (1983). A conceptual model discussed by Galileo and used intuitively by physics students. In Gentner, D. and Stevens, A.L. (eds) *Mental Models.* Hillsdale, NJ: LEA.

Collins, A. and Gentner, D. (1987). How people construct mental models. In Holland, D. and Quinn, N. (eds) *Cultural Models in Language and Thought.* Cambridge: CUP.

Cooke, N.M. and McDonald, J.E. (1987). The application of psychological scaling techniques to knowledge elicitation for knowledge-based systems. *International Journal of Man–Machine Studies 26,* 533–550.

Cooke, N.M. and Schvaneveldt, R.W. (1988). Effects of programming experience on network representations of abstract programming concepts. *International Journal of Man-Machine Studies 29,* 407–427.

Craik, K.J.W. (1943). *The Nature of Explanation.* Cambridge: CUP.

Cummins, R. (1983). *The Nature of Psychological Explanation.* London: MIT Press.

de Kleer, J. and Brown, J.S. (1983). Assumptions and ambiguities in mechanistic mental models. In Gentner, D. and Stevens, A.L. (eds) *Mental Models.* Hillsdale, NJ: LEA.

diSessa, A. (1983). Phenomenology and the evolution of intuition. In Gentner, D. and Stevens, A.L. (eds) *Mental Models.* Hillsdale, NJ: LEA.

Edwards, E. and Lees, F.P. (1973). *Man and Computer in Process Control.* London: The Institution of Chemical Engineers.

Edwards, E. and Lees, F.P. (1974). *The Human Operator in Process Control.* London: Taylor and Francis.

Ericsson, K.A. and Simon, H.A. (1980). Verbal reports as data. *Psychological Review 87,* 215–251.

Ericsson, K.A. and Simon, H.A. (1984). *Protocol Analysis: Verbal Reports as Data.* Cambridge, Ma.: MIT Press.

Evans, J.St.B.T. (1988). The knowledge elicitation problem: a psychological perspective. *Behaviour and Information Technology 7,* 111–130.

Forbus, K.D. (1983). Qualitative reasoning about space and motion. In Gentner, D. and Stevens, A.L. (eds) *Mental Models.* Hillsdale, NJ: LEA.

Freyd, J.J. (1983). Shareability: the social psychology of epistemology. *Cognitive Science 7*, 191–210.

Gammack, J. and Young, R.M. (1985) . Psychological techniques for eliciting expert knowledge. In Bramer, M. (ed.) *Research and Development in Expert Systems.* Cambridge: CUP.

Garrod, S.C. and Anderson, A. (1987). Saying what you mean in dialogue: a study in conceptual and semantic coordination. *Cognition 277*, 181–218.

Govindaraj, T. and Su, Y.-L. (1988). A model of fault diagnosis performance of expert marine engineers. *International Journal of Man-Machine Studies 29*, 1–20.

Gentner, D. and Gentner, D.R. (1983). Flowing waters or teeming crowds: mental models of electricity. In Gentner, D. and Stevens, A.L. (eds) *Mental Models.* Hillsdale, NJ: LEA.

Goodstein, L.P., Anderson, H.B. and Olsen, S.E. (1988). *Tasks Errors and Mental Models.* London: Taylor and Francis.

Halasz, F.G. and Moran, T.P. (1983). Mental models and problem solving in using a calculator. *CHI'83 Conference Proceedings: Human Factors in Computing Systems.* Boston, Ma.: ACM.

Harre, R. (1985). *The Philosophies of Science: An Introductory Survey.* Oxford: Oxford University Press.

Hart, A. (1986). *Knowledge Acquisition for Expert Systems.* London: Kogan Page.

Hart, A. (1987). Role of induction in knowledge elicitation. In Kidd, A.L. (ed.) *Knowledge Acquisition for Expert Systems.* New York: Plenum Press.

Hoffman, R.R. (1987). The problem of extracting the knowledge of experts from the perspective of experimental psychology. *AI Magazine 8*, 53–66.

Holland, J.H., Holyoak, K.J., Nisbett, R.E. and Thagard, P.R. (1986). *Induction: Processes of Inference, Learning and Discovery.* Cambridge, Ma.: MIT Press.

Johnson-Laird, P.N. (1983). *Mental Models.* Cambridge: CUP.

Katzeff, C. (1988). The effect of different conceptual models using reasoning in a database query language. *International Journal of Man–Machine Studies 29*, 37–62.

Katzeff, C. (1990). System demands on mental models for a full text database. *International Journal of Man–Machine Studies 32*, 483–509.

Kay, D.S. (1987). Using cognitive models of the user to design computer instruction. Ph.D. dissertation, Yale University, USA.

Keeton, W.T. (1980). *Biological Science* (3rd edition). London: W.W. Norton and Company.

Kellogg, W.A. and Breen, T.J. (1987). Evaluating user and system models: applying scaling techniques to problems in human–computer interaction. In Carroll, J.M. and Tanner, T.T. (eds) *CHI and GI 1987 Conference Proceedings*. New York: ACM.

Kempton, W. (1986). Two theories of home heat control. *Cognitive Science 10*, 75–90.

Kidd, A.L. (1987). (ed.) *Knowledge Acquisition for Expert Systems: A Practical Handbook*. New York: Plenum Press.

Kieras, D.E. and Bovair, S. (1984). The role of a mental model in learning to operate a device. *Cognitive Science 8*, 255–273.

Kowalski, B. and VanLehn, K. (1988). CIRRUS: inducing subject models from protocol data. In *Proceedings of the Tenth Annual Conference of the Cognitive Science Society*. Montreal, Canada. 17–19 August.

Kuipers, B. and Kassirer, J.P. (1984). Causal reasoning in medicine: analysis of a protocol. *Cognitive Science 8*, 363–385.

Laird, J.E., Newell, A. and Rosenbloom, P.S. (1987). SOAR: an architecture for general intelligence. *Artificial Intelligence 33*, 1–64.

Landauer, T.K. (1987). Relations between cognitive psychology and computer system design. In Carroll, J.M. (ed.) *Interfacing Thought: Cognitive Aspects of Human–Computer Interaction*. London: Bradford/MIT Press.

Langley, P., Simon, H.A., Bradshaw, G.L. and Zytkow, J.M. (1987). *Scientific Discovery: Computational Explorations of the Creative Process*. London: MIT Press.

Larkin, J.H. (1983). The role of problem representation in physics. In Gentner, D. and Stevens, A.L. (eds) *Mental Models*. Hillsdale, NJ: LEA.

Laws, J.V. and Barber, P.J. (1989). Video analysis in cognitive ergonomics: a methodological perspective. *Ergonomics 32*, 1303-1318.

Lewis, C.H. and Norman, D.A. (1986) . Designing for error. In Norman, D.A. and Draper, S.W. (eds) *User Centered System Design: New Perspectives in Human Computer Interaction*. Hillsdale, NJ: LEA.

Lindgaard, G. (1987). Who needs what information about computer systems: some notes on mental models, metaphors and expertise. (Branch Paper 126), Clayton, Australia: Telecom Australia Research Laboratories.

McCloskey, M. (1983). Naive theories of motion. In Gentner, D. and Stevens, A.L. (eds) *Mental Models*. Hillsdale, NJ: LEA.

Miyake, N. (1986). Constructive interaction and the iterative process of understanding. *Cognitive Science 10,* 151–177.

Moll, T. (1987). On methods of analysis of mental models and the evaluation of interactive computer systems. In Frese, M., Ulich, E. and Dzida, W. (eds) *Psychological Issues of Computer Interaction in the Work Place.* Amsterdam: Elsevier.

Morik, K. (1987). Knowledge acquisition and machine learning-the issue of modelling. *Proceedings of the First European Workshop on Knowledge Acquisition for Knowledge Based Systems.* Reading University, 2–3 September.

Morik, K. (1989). Sloppy modelling. In Morik, K. (ed.) *Representation and Organization in Machine Learning.* Berlin: Springer-Verlag.

Mrozek, A. (1989). Rough sets and dependency analysis among attributes in computer implementations of expert's inference models. *International Journal of Man–Machine Studies 30,* 457–473.

Niblett, T.B. (1987). Constructing decision trees in noisy domains. In Bratko, I. and Lavrac, N. (eds) *Progress in Machine Learning.* Wilmslow: Sigma Press.

Nisbett, R.E. and Wilson, T.D. (1977). Telling more than we can know: verbal reports on mental processes. *Psychological Review 84,* 231–259.

Nisbett, R.E. and Ross, L. (1980). *Human Inference: Strategies and Shortcomings of Social Judgment.* Englewood Cliffs, NJ: Prentice Hall.

Norman, D.A. (1983). Some observations on mental models. In Gentner, D. and Stevens, A.L. (eds) *Mental Models.* Hillsdale, NJ: LEA.

O'Malley, C.E., Draper, S.W. and Riley, M.S. (1985). Constructive interaction: a method for studying human-computer interaction. In Shackel, B. (ed.) *Human- Computer Interaction - Interact'84.* Amsterdam: North- Holland.

O'Malley, C.E. (1987). Understanding explanation. Cognitive Science Research Paper, Serial No. CSRP 088, The University of Sussex, School of Cognitive Sciences, Arts Building, Falmer, Brighton BN1 9QN.

Peirce, C.S. (1934). Pragmatism and pragmaticism. In Hartshorne, C. and Weiss, P. (eds) *Collected Papers of Charles Sanders Peirce.* (Book 3, vol. 5). Cambridge, Ma.: Harvard University Press.

Peirce, C.S. (1935). Scientific metaphysics. In Hartshorne, C. and Weiss, P. (eds) *Collected Papers of Charles Sanders Peirce.* (Book 3, vol. 6). Cambridge, Ma.: Harvard University Press.

Peirce, C.S. (1958). Science and Philosophy. In Burks, A.W. (ed.) *Collected Papers of Charles Sanders Peirce.* (Book 4, vol. 7). Cambridge, Ma.: Harvard University Press.

Praetorius, N. and Duncan, K.D. (1988). Verbal reports: a problem in research design. In Goodstein, L.P., Andersen, H.B. and Olsen, S.E. (eds) *Tasks, Errors and Mental Models.* London: Taylor and Francis.

Quinlan, J.R. (1983). Learning efficient classification procedures and their application to chess endgames. In Michalski, R., Carbonell, J. and Mitchell, T. (eds) *Machine Learning: an Artificial Intelligence Approach.* Palo Alto: Tioga Press.

Quinlan, J.R. (1986a). Induction of decision trees. *Machine Learning 1*, 81–106.

Quinlan, J.R. (1986b). The effect of noise on concept learning. In Michalski, R.S., Carbonnell, J.G. and Mitchell, T.M. (eds) *Machine Learning: An Artificial Intelligence Approach, Volume II.* Los Altos, Ca.: Morgan Kaufmann.

Rasmussen, J. (1979). On the structure of knowledge – a morphology of mental models in a man–machine context. Report M-2192. Risø National Laboratory, Røskilde, Denmark.

Rasmussen, J. (1986). *Information Processing and Human–Machine Interaction.* Amsterdam: North-Holland.

Rouse, W.B. and Morris, N.M. (1986). On looking into the black box: prospects and limits in the search for mental models. *Psychological Bulletin 100*, 349–363.

Rutherford, A. and Wilson, J.R. (1991). Methodologies for identifying mental models of selected advanced manufacturing technologies: Part 1. Research report for the SERC/ESRC Joint Committee. (Grant Reference GR/F/07705).

Russo, J.E., Johnson, E.J. and Stephens, D.L.(1989). The validity of verbal protocols. *Memory and Cognition 17*, 759–769.

Sanderson, P.M., James, J.M. and Seidler, K. (1989). SHAPA: an interactive software environment for protocol analysis. *Ergonomics 32*, 1271–1302.

Sanderson, P.M., Verhage, A.G. and Flud, R.B. (1989). State–space and verbal protocol methods for studying the human operator in process control. *Ergonomics 32*, 1343-1372.

Shadbolt, N.R. and Burton, A.M. (1989). Knowledge elicitation. In Wilson, J.R. and Corlett, E.N. (eds) *Evaluation of Human Work: A Practical Ergonomics Methodology.* London: Taylor and Francis.

Shapiro, A.D. (1987). *Structured Induction in Expert Systems.* Wokingham: Turing Institute Press/Addison-Wesley.

Simon, H.A. (1989). The scientist as problem solver. In Klahr, D. and Kotovsky, K. (eds) *Complex Information Processing: The Impact of Herbert A. Simon.* Hillsdale, NJ: LEA.

Slater, W.J. (1988). Human factors in knowledge acquisition. In Helander, M. (ed.) *Handbook of Human–Computer Interaction.* Amsterdam: Elsevier.

Stenning, K. (1990). Modelling memory for models. In Ezquerro, J. and Larrazabal, J.M. (eds) *First International Colloquium on Cognitive Science.* Universidad del Pais Vasco. San Sebastian: Kluwer.

Tauber, M.J. (1988). On mental models and the user interface. In G.C. van der Veer, T.R.G. Green, J-M. Hoc and D.M. Murray (eds) *Working with Computers: Theory versus Outcome.* London: Academic Press.

Veldhuyzen, W. and Stassen, H.G. (1977). The internal model concept: an application to modelling human control of large ships. *Human Factors 19,* 367–380.

Villee, C.A. (1977). *Biology.* (7th edition). London: W.B. Saunders Company.

Waern, Y. (1987). Mental models in learning computerized tasks. In Frese, M., Ulrich, E. and Dzida, W. (eds) *Psychological Issues of Human–Computer Interaction in the Workplace.* Amsterdam: Elsevier.

Welbank, M.A. (1983). A review of knowledge acquisition techniques for expert systems. British Telecom Research, Martlesham Heath.

Wilson, J.R. and Rutherford, A. (1989). Mental models: theory and application in human factors. *Human Factors 31,* 617–634.

Williams, M.D., Hollan, J.D. and Stevens, A.L. (1983) . Human reasoning about a simple physical system. In Gentner, D. and Stevens, A.L. (eds) *Mental Models.* Hillsdale, NJ: LEA.

Young, R.M. (1983). Surrogates and mappings: two kinds of conceptual models for interactive devices. In Gentner, D. and Stevens, A.L. (eds) *Mental Models.* Hillsdale, NJ. LEA.

Zhang, K. and Wickens, C.D. (1987). A study of the mental model of a complex dynamic system. In *Proceedings of the Human Factors Society 31st Annual Meeting.* Santa Monica, Ca.: Human Factors Society.

Chapter 15

User's Models of Computer Systems

Martina-Angela Sasse

15.1 Introduction

One of the truisms of human–computer interaction (HCI) states that users of
complex devices – such as computer systems – build and use some form of mental
representation of those devices. These representations are often called mental
models. Unfortunately, the term mental model has been applied to a variety of
related but distinct representations, e.g. the designer's model of the system or the
psychologist's model of the user. Nielsen (1987) has drawn up a taxonomy of the
different representations for which the term has been used. The research described
in this paper deals exclusively with representations of computer systems held in the
mind of the user. Following the distinction introduced by Norman (1986), I will
refer to them as users' models.

Knowledge about users' models – how they are constructed and applied, and
which models lead to successful user–system interaction – could make a significant
contribution to the design of systems and the instructional materials that accompany
them (Carroll and Olson, 1988), since such knowledge could be employed to
design systems and training materials in such a manner that they support the
construction of an adequate user's model, for instance through linguistic cues or
visual representations.

A substantial number of theoretical and empirical research contributions in
this area have been published from the early eighties to date. In their recent review,
however, Carroll and Olson (1988) state that:

1. Research on user knowledge is scattered.
2. Analytical methods and techniques for representing users' models are sparse if
   growing.

MODELS IN THE MIND:
Theory, perspective and applications. ISBN 0–12–592970–6

3. The reported effects of different models on user performance are still inconclusive.

Carroll and Olson conclude their review with a list of eleven identified "research needs", a programme of (mainly empirical) research on users' models that would help to fill existing gaps and integrate currently scattered knowledge into a theory. The work described in this paper consists of a series of five empirical investigations, which between them address several of these research needs. The first set of goals was to try and elicit models from users to establish whether people do employ user's models, what they consist of and what the behavioural correlates of such models are. The studies observed people using commercially available software which was reasonably complex. Once collected, the data will be used to find a way of describing actual user knowledge in a non-mechanistic form and create a complement to sequence/method representations. This could, eventually, contribute to a body of knowledge and/or tools which help to design systems and training materials which support "good" users' models.

This chapter consists of two parts. Firstly, a discussion of methodological problems connected to eliciting users' models and secondly, a detailed description of the different experimental setups that were designed to elicit user's models, and a discussion of their advantages and disadvantages. The in-depth analysis of the data obtained from this study, and work on a way of representing the users' models, is still in progress.

15.2 Users' models and their behavioural correlates

15.2.1 Previous studies

Experimental studies on users' models in HCI have been published since the mid-eighties. As Norman (1983) said in a prophetic footnote, it is not easy to discover what a user's model is like. As with other cognitive phenomena, users' models are not directly observable. We can only try to infer what models users hold from their observable behaviour. Previous studies have tended to employ performance measures as indicators to determine whether subjects had acquired a model or not, or whether one type of model was more effective than another. Two or more groups of subjects would be taught to use a system, and their performance compared afterwards. Typically, one group will be taught about the system in terms of a model, whereas the other group(s) are taught differently (e.g. procedures or examples).

In a review three of these studies (Kieras and Bovair, 1984; Borgman, 1986; Frese and Albrecht, 1988), Sasse (1991) argued that they suffer from the problems of (1) over-interpretation of performance data, (2) lack of ecological validity, (3) small sample size and (4) the possibility of alternative explanations.

a) Over-interpretation of performance data

Differences in performance between "model" and "no model" groups are used to determine whether a user's model had been effective. It is assumed that if users are taught a system in terms of a certain model, they will acquire and employ it. It is, however, important to try and elicit users' models to determine whether differences in performance are due to a difference in model, or another factor in the experimental setup: the instruction material given to the control group(s) might be so limited that poor performance is inevitable, or there might be a huge difference in the time subjects spent with an instructor.

The results of one study which did make an attempt to elicit the subjects' models, in addition to the performance shown on a benchmark test, shows that performance results cannot be used as the sole indicator for users' models. Borgman (1986) trained two groups of subjects to use a library database system. The model group instruction material drew upon the analogy of a card-index catalogue, whereas the control group received only procedural instruction on how to retrieve entries. The performance results seemed to confirm her hypothesis that while there would be no performance differences on simple retrieval tasks, the model group would out perform the control group on a set of complex transfer tasks, as a result of the model. When Borgman asked the subjects to describe the system and how it worked, she expected those in the model condition to describe the system in analogy with a card catalogue and the subjects in the no-model condition to state less complete and correct models. She found, however, that most subjects held some sort of model of the system, regardless of the training condition. Only 4 out of 28 subjects specifically referred to the system in analogy to a card catalogue - and one of them had been trained in the no-model condition.

This study illustrates that the relationship between performance data and the user's model is not necessarily straightforward. People often do the right things for the wrong reasons and users performing well on a benchmark task can hold the most appalling misconceptions. The construction of a user's model is, like all learning, a fundamentally active process. Users who are taught a device without reference to a model will construct one of their own and subjects who are taught certain models will not necessarily adopt them. The construction of a user's model also depends on previous knowledge and experience, as the study by Briggs (1988) showed.

In summary, performance data should not be used as the only evidence in studies on users' models. If we want to determine what users' models are like, we need to collect qualitative data.

b) Lack of ecological validity

Often, results from studies on users' models cannot be generalized because of a lack of ecological validity, which stems from three main sources: the types of subjects, the devices used and the experimental scenarios.

The users in the studies reviewed were all "novice" or "naive" users and undergraduate students. The experimenters not only established that none of the subjects had ever used a system similar to the one in the study, but recruited subjects with little or no experience of computer use. Studies with novice users focus on a particular stage of model building and use. While it is certainly desirable to establish how models are constructed and employed by novice users, theories of users' models have to cover all groups of users: even novice users are novice users only for a certain period of time. Some of the difficulties users have in their very first interaction with a particular system are simply orientation problems, such as finding the right keys. In a study by Briggs (1988) with naive users, 35% of all total breakdowns in user–system interaction were due to errors or slips in key selection, which can be expected to decrease as familiarity with the system increases. Real-life systems can be complex and require a certain amount of learning and practice. Studying models of users who have progressed passed the learning stage helps to identify misrepresentations which persist even with prolonged use and impair usability.

The experimental scenarios in studies on users' models are often designed to establish a high degree of internal validity. Experimenters tend to structure user–system interaction tightly and to control or eliminate all possible other influences. This is a difficult goal to achieve. Even when user–system interaction is tightly structured, users will create different situations in the course of the interaction, and different interactions and responses will be required from the experimenter. Studies which place the user in a less restrictive and artificial setup might yield more reliable observations.

Finally, experimenters sometimes use artificial devices (e.g. a lights and switches panel in Kieras and Bovair, 1984) for users to work with. Results gained from experiments with these devices are difficult to generalize because the devices are not as complex as real-life computer systems and users have to develop a model without a meaningful task context. People using computers formulate their tasks in terms of the external task domain, and then reformulate the task into the system's terms (Moran, 1984). We can therefore assume that the external task domain has some influence on the users' model, at least in the initial stages of interaction. Moreover, one of the classic experiments on mental models (Wason and Johnson-Laird, 1972) showed that subjects' performance on an abstract reasoning task could be improved dramatically by presenting the same (equivalent in terms of formal logic) task in a concrete, meaningful context (cf. Manktelow and Over, this volume). Subjects operating artificial devices cannot employ previous knowledge, experience and terminology in the same way that a user familiar with office work might employ them when using a word processor or a spreadsheet. Even when experimenters try to create a more meaningful context (Kieras and Bovair, 1984, described their device as a "Starship Enterprise phaser-bank"), it remains doubtful whether their findings can be generalized to use of systems in work contexts.

c) Small samples

The problems with using performance data to test hypotheses about users' models are aggravated in studies with small samples.

In the study by Frese and Albrecht (1988), a set of performance data was collected to compare the effect of three different types of training on users' models on a total of 15 subjects (5 in each group). The authors concede that the groups are rather small and describe the tests employed as "not very conservative", but do nevertheless conclude that results of the study prove their hypothesis (that "active" acquisition of a user's model, through exploration and making mistakes, leads to a better user's model) to be correct.

d) Alternative explanation

The study by Frese and Albrecht (1988) is an example where factors other than the users' models might have influenced their performance. The problem originates from the design of the training for the different groups, the level of interaction between subjects and experimenters. In the control groups, subjects followed written instructions. The experimenter intervened and interacted with the subjects only when they made a mistake. In the "active" condition, subjects were given no written material. They were encouraged to generate and test hypotheses, which then were "elaborated with the guidance of the experimenter down to the keystroke level". Essentially, it is possible that the differences were due to the effect of personal tuition versus learning through written instruction.

15.2.2 Behavioural correlates of users models'

a) Thinking-aloud techniques and verbal protocols

Thinking-aloud techniques have been extensively employed in HCI. Users are encouraged to verbalize their thoughts and conclusions while they are interacting with a system. This encouragement is often given by the experimenter throughout the session in form of questions or prompts. Subjects may be asked, for instance, to explain their own behaviour, reason about the system's behaviour , or reason about errors. The sessions are usually recorded on audiotapes or videotapes and a written protocol of the interaction is generated on the basis of these. The scientist can then attempt to derive a conceptualization of a user's model from the explanations.

Norman (1983) states that these protocols may be informative, but are always incomplete: people cannot give complete verbal accounts of their thought processes. The cueing or construction of a user's model is a subconscious process, and we cannot expect verbal accounts of subconscious processes. If we ask a user to verbalize these processes, the very shift from subconscious to conscious processing can change the nature and content of the processes we are trying to tap. Such accounts can actually yield erroneous information, since asking subjects to think aloud changes the demand structure of the situation: users probably tend to rationalize their behaviour if they have to explain it, or tend to tell the experimenter what they think s/he wants to hear, or might be guided by subtle verbal and non-verbal cues given by the experimenter.

Thinking-aloud is obviously highly artificial behaviour, but we can remove some of this artificiality by making the explanation of models a necessary part of a higher-level task.

b) On-line protocols

Norman (1983) advocates on-line protocols which record the behaviour of users and system during the interaction, because they are more "reliable" than explanations gathered from the users. It is quite obvious, however, that a conceptualization derived from an on-line protocol of user–system interaction will not yield much information about a user's model. After all, on-line protocols record the user's and the system's behaviour – the experimenter will have a record of what the user did, but know nothing about why they did it. Conceptualizations construct-ed on this basis reflect guesswork on behalf of the experimenter about a user's model rather than a good approximation of the model.

Having some record of system behaviour is essential for the interpretation of a user's verbal protocols. But a record of the screen display which can be linked to the user's behaviour (verbal and otherwise) is, to my mind, sufficient. Such accounts help to illuminate utterances like, "I'll try to move this thing over here" . Videotaped accounts of user–system interaction are a good way to capture essential, higher-level data.

c) Performance data

Most performance data in research on users' models are collected through benchmark tests. After some initial training (on the basis of which the user is supposed to have constructed a model), the subjects are asked to perform a set of tasks. The most common measurements taken are; time taken to complete a task and/or subtasks, frequency and types of errors efficiency of task completion (rating by experimenter), efficiency of training (time/error ratio, transfer task) and retention rate.

The tasks presented to the subjects in benchmark tests are designed to test knowledge users are assumed to have acquired in the training phase. Such tests are applied mainly to compare the performance of users that have been trained by different methods and are assumed to have constructed different models as a result of the training. However, performance alone cannot be seen as proof that the user does hold a certain model.

Performance time may be an "objective" measurement and easy to obtain, but tells us very little about a user's model. There is no strong theoretical link between a user's model and the time it takes them to complete a task. There is, however, a strong correlation between time and errors, since incorrect actions and recovery obviously cost time.

Errors are among the most informative data about users' models, if some analysis is performed on them. Unfortunately, most of the experimental studies on users' models in HCI count errors rather than analysing them. Possible types of analysis are qualitative/explanatory analysis, or a classification of errors. We can apply a general classification (e.g. Norman, 1988), or devise a classification suitable to describe the system used. It makes sense to adapt some of the categories from a general classification, and distinguish between slips and errors and apply categories well-known in HCI, such as mode-errors (Monk, 1986), if appropriate. On the basis of error analysis, we can try to identify missing representations or misrepresentations that the user holds and try to build a conceptualization of their model. It is, however, not always easy to determine exactly which inappropriate representation caused a particular error. Scenarios where the experimenter can try to prompt the user to comment on the error (e.g. What did you think the system would do?) can yield valuable insight in this respect. One of the drawbacks of error analysis is that while we can learn a lot about models constructed by users who make errors, there is very little information to be gained about models held by competent users.

Some experimenters (Kieras and Bovair, 1984; Frese and Albrecht, 1988) ask subjects to perform a transfer task. The procedures that have to be applied to solve a transfer task are not explicitly presented to the users, but can be "inferred" from the material presented during training. The ability of users to infer new procedures is seen as a crucial test of the appropriateness of their users' models. Transfer tasks have been used extensively in psychological research on learning and are a useful method to establish whether users have developed general understanding of how a system works, such as a model, or are just executing well-learned procedures.

Retention of information over time is a measurement that has been employed by Kieras and Bovair (1984) and Frese and Albrecht (1988). The argument for retention rate as a performance measure is that it should be easier to remember information that has been integrated in single, coherent, plausible models. Frese and Albrecht simply counted the number of commands remembered, whereas Kieras and Bovair asked subjects to perform another benchmark test on the device they had been trained on before. Again, additional qualitative information, such as which items subjects remember (not just how many) and why, would shed more light on whether users' models are employed and in which form.

15.3 Five scenarios for investigating users' models

One of the aims of the study was to explore the use of different experimental scenarios to elicit users' models: this avoided the problems with setups as presented in the previous section. In designing these studies, I have also tried to put into practice a suggestion by Young (1983), who suggested that information about users models can be collected by (1) observing users using the system, (2) asking users to explain the system, (3) users asking users to predict the behaviour of the system, or (4) observing users learning the system. After a brief description of subjects and the general setup, an account of each study is given, commenting on the strengths and weaknesses of the scenario employed.

Subjects. The users were students at the University of Birmingham, taking a subsidiary course in computing. Out of a total of 32, between 21 and 26 students volunteered to take part in the individual sessions. The samples were nearly balanced with respect to gender and the age of the students was between 18 and 34. Most of the students had no computing experience whatsoever when they started the course.

General procedure. Each of the five studies observed the users interacting with a computer system – three applications and a programming language on an Apricot microcomputer, and one application on an Apple Macintosh. Prior to the experimental sessions (with the exception of the last) the users were taught to use the applications in hands-on tutorials and workshops (2 hours per week). All tutorials and workshops were run by the author, who also designed all training materials and exercises, following the idea of minimalist instruction (Carroll and Mack, 1985). At the end of the training for each application, the users were asked to attend individual experimental sessions. All experimental sessions were recorded on videotape. One camera recorded the user, a second camera recorded the computer screen. A microphone recorded the users' verbal comments. The pictures from the two cameras were mixed and recorded on the same tape.

15.3.1 Observing users using a system

The first study observed 22 users editing a document on a word processor (Wordstar). The experimenter (the author) sat next to the user, answering questions the user asked and prompting them throughout the course of the interaction. The experimenter tried to follow a certain "script" throughout the interaction by applying the following rules.

When a user asked the experimenter how to solve a certain task, the experimenter would not answer by telling the user the procedure in the first instance. Instead, the experimenter would ask a question like; "How did you delete (insert, underline) a word (sentence, paragraph) in the exercises in class?" Only when it was clear that the user could not remember the procedure, would the experimenter tell the user how to solve the task.

Whenever a user made an error, the experimenter would wait to see if the user would comment on the error, try to recover from it, or try again. If the user did not say or do anything following the error, the experimenter would try to prompt the user to comment on the error, and how to recover and perform the task. Whenever the user made a comment that indicated they were referring to some kind of user's model, the experimenter would encourage the subject to elaborate their statement.

This experimental scenario led to a fairly similar structure across the individual user–system interactions and seemed to elicit much detailed information. The disadvantage of the scenario was that some users clearly felt under pressure to perform. This was partly due to the fact that the experimenter and the course tutor were the same person, even though assurances were given that the sessions would in no way be used to assess the user's performance for the practical credits. The disadvantage of prompting from the experimenter was highlighted in this study: it occasionally seemed to interfere with the users' problem solving processes. Furthermore, it was difficult to elicit knowledge from the more competent users. While errors provided the experimenter with good opportunities for prompting, prompting without errors seemed to be "unnatural" and made users more self-conscious, an observation in line with Norman's (1983) assertion about the change of demand structure.

15.3.2 Users explaining a system

In the second study, the 26 users were asked by the experimenter to teach another person (a co-experimenter) how to use the spreadsheet software (Open Access) they had been learning in the previous weeks. The experimenter suggested that the "learner" (co-experimenter) should operate the keyboard and that they should try to teach him what knowledge they thought was necessary to use the spreadsheet. The experimenter would then leave the room and watch the session on a monitor in the adjacent control room. The users were told that they could call for the experimenter if they got into a situation from which they were unable to recover and continue. This teaching back scenario is based on an observational technique called constructive interaction (Miyake, 1982) and a variant of the thinking aloud approach. The idea is to study two people who try jointly to solve a problem, capitalizing on the fact that communication of knowledge takes place naturally between the two participants. Therefore, the technique avoids the change in demand structure (O'Malley, Draper and Riley,.1984, but cf. Rutherford and Wilson, this volume). The success or failure of this scenario obviously depends to a large extent on the skills and behaviour of the co-experimenter. The subjects have to be fully convinced that the "learner" does not know anything about the system - otherwise they are not motivated to communicate their knowledge to the coexperimenter. The co- experimenter very cautiously tried to prompt the users by demanding explanations whenever appropriate. Some users tended to give entirely procedural instructions. Demanding explanation for those procedures is a good way of encouraging them to verbalize the models that the procedures are derived from and also to check whether they hold a model at all.

This teaching back scenario worked extremely well in terms of conceptual knowledge elicited and is probably best of all the approaches described here. Most of the users enjoyed the task, and communicated a great deal with the co-experimenter. This illustrates the benefit of a "natural" context for the interaction. A great deal of knowledge can be elicited from the more competent users. The disadvantage of this scenario is that when less competent subjects do get into a situation from which they cannot recover and have to call for the experimenter, the result is a considerable disruption in the interaction.

15.3.3 Users predicting the behaviour of a system

Twenty-six users participated in the third study, which asked them to predict the behaviour of a Prolog program. The experimenter presented them with a short Prolog program on the computer, consisting of a knowledge base and one rule. The users could also refer to a printout of the program. The study consisted of three sets of tasks. To start with, the experimenter asked the user to type in a number of Prolog queries and predict the answer the system would return before entering the question. The experimenter then presented a few questions in natural language and asked the user to construct Prolog queries to find the answer to these questions. The user then proceeded with queries. If the query did not return the predicted answer, the experimenter again asked the user to work out what was wrong with the query. Lastly, the experimenter asked the user to construct a rule and add it to the program. The user was then asked to explain what the rule would do and to run a few queries to check if the rule worked as intended. If the rule did not work, the experimenter encouraged the user to find out why.

The study yielded quite a good insight into the users' understanding of Prolog. The first task elicited more from the less competent users, since like in the first scenario, errors made by the user provided a good opportunity to discuss the workings of the system. The second and third tasks provided a better chance to review the models held by the more competent users, since it allowed the observation of problem-solving behaviour. The interaction was fairly structured, but less artificial than in the first study. Predicting the behaviour of a system and asking users to make changes to the system is a good way of checking whether the user holds a representation which could be described as a surrogate model of the system.

15.3.4 Users describing and using a system

The fourth study was not directly based on Young's (1983) suggestion, but tried to illuminate the relationship between knowledge that users hold and their performance. Twenty-one users participated in this study and the system in question was a database (Open Access). First, the experimenter asked the user to explain what a database system is. She checked whether the users knew the basic terminology and commands of the SQL type query language. Then the experimenterpresented the user with a database file (a customer record) and three tasks.

This experimental study yielded some interesting observations. While most of the users had no problem whatsoever in performing the three tasks, very few of them knew the terminology or could describe the basic concepts accurately. They remembered the commands of the query language and knew how to apply them, but could not explain what the commands actually did.

The interaction process in this scenario is highly structured, but does not provide the experimenter with many opportunities to elicit users' models. It might be more appropriate for testing specific hypotheses about users' models and performance. The observations made in this study suggest that the users certainly did not hold a surrogate model of the system. The fact that they were, nevertheless, able to operate the system and solve the tasks indicates that they might have developed something akin to a mapping model.

15.3.5 Observing users learning a system

In the final study, 22 users were asked to explore a word processor (MacWrite) in a one hour session. The "observing users learning a system" approach was left for the last of the five studies, since the six month course should have allowed the users to acquire some relevant background knowledge, i.e. a set of relevant models that could be applied to the learning of a new system. Since all studies on users' models so far concentrated on novice users learning a system, it seemed more interesting to observe users who had some experience with computer systems learning a system.

The experimenter introduced the user to a co-learner (co-experimenter) and asked them to work together to find out how the word processor worked. This scenario is a further variation of the constructive interaction technique which was also employed in the second study. Applying a straightforward constructive interaction approach would have paired two users to explore the system. In view of the fact that all the other studies observed one user per session, I decided to vary the approach and pair each user with a contrived co-learner. This change in the approach counteracts the possible danger of one partner taking charge and dominating the interaction, in which case there would be little knowledge elicited from the less dominant partner.

The experimenter suggested that the user should operate the keyboard, while the co-learner should consult the manual whenever the user felt that they needed some specific information about the system. As with the teaching back scenario in study 2, the success or failure in eliciting users' models depends largely on the skill and discretion of the co-experimenter. If the co-experimenter is perceived as having knowledge about the system, the user will rely on the more expert "co-learner" to feed them the procedures which have to be employed to solve the task, and not contribute very much to the interaction. In a bid to avoid such a situation arising, the co-experimenters were briefed to be interested, but not over-helpful. They were not to respond too quickly when the user asked a question and always had to look the answer up in the manual. When they had located the relevant text, they were to give a vague answer rather than an exact procedure in the first answer to a question (e.g. they answered, "It's got something to do with the ruler when the user could not work out how to change the margin").

The scenario worked quite well in terms of verbal responses elicited from the users. The interaction was, through the provision of a series of tasks, more tightly structured than in the other constructive interaction scenario (study 2). Most of the users enjoyed the sessions and were quite confident in exploring the system. A detailed analysis should give information about how the use of the previous word processing system influenced the way they approached this one.

15.4 Conclusions: scenarios for empirical studies on users' models

The scenarios based on the constructive interaction technique (Studies 2 and 5) seem to be most effective for eliciting users' models, but require more resources and preparation than the highly structured approaches. It is, however, effort well spent if structure and content of the knowledge elicited are to be used for a conceptualization of the users' models.

The structured approaches seem to be more suited to testing specific hypotheses about users' models, rather than eliciting them. Highly structured scenarios like the one in Study 1 are restrictive and artificial. While they are easier to set up and analyse, researchers using this approach have to be aware that they might be trapping users' models rather than tapping them. Predicting the behaviour of a system and asking the user to make changes (Study 3) is a good method to test whether the user holds a surrogate model of the system. Contrasting users' conceptual knowledge about a system, and their ability to use the system to perform tasks (Study 4) is a method that could be employed to test for mapping models.

In the analysis, it turned out that concentrating on users' errors and their recovery procedures was most fruitful for a reconstruction of users' models. This leaves us with a problems as to how to elicit models from competent users. Here, the constructive interaction technique seems the only promising approach to elicit data for reconstruction of the users' model.

References

Borgman, C.L. (1986). The user's mental model of an information retrieval system: an experiment on a prototype online catalogue. *International Journal of Man–Machine Studies 24*, 47–64.

Briggs, P. (1988). What we know and what we need to know: the user model versus the user's model in human–computer interaction. *Behaviour and Information Technology 7*, 431–442.

Carroll, J.M. and Olson, J.R. (1988). Mental models in human-computer interaction. In Helander, M. (ed.) *Handbook of Human–Computer Interaction*. Amsterdam: Elsevier.

Carroll, J.M. and Mack, R.L. (1985). Metaphor, computer systems, and active learning. *International Journal of Man–Machine Studies 22*, 39–57.

Frese, M. and Albrecht, K. (1988) The effects of an active development of the mental model in the training process: experimental results in a word processing system. *Behaviour and Information Technology 7*, 295–304.

Kieras, D.E. and Bovair, S. (1984). The role of a mental model in learning to operate a device. *Cognitive Science 8*, 255–273.

Miyake, N. (1982). Constructive interaction. Technical Report No. 13. Institute of Cognitive Science, San Diego, University of California.

Monk, A. (1986). Mode errors: a user-centered analysis and some preventative measures using key-contingent sound. *International Journal of Man–Machine Studies 24*, 313–327.

Moran, T.P. (1984). Getting into a system: external-internal task mapping analysis. In Janda, A. (ed.) *Human Factors in Computing Systems. Proceedings of the CHI'83 Conference*, Boston, Ma., 12–15 December, 1983. Amsterdam: North–Holland.

Nielsen, J. (1987). The spectrum of models in software ergonomics. In *Proceedings of the Fifth Symposium on Empirical Foundations of Information and Software Science*, Røskilde, Denmark, 23–25 November, 1987.

Norman, D. A. (1983). Some observations on mental models. In Gentner, D. and Stevens, A. L. (eds) *Mental Models*. Hillsdale, NJ: LEA.

Norman, D. A. (1986). Cognitive engineering. In Norman, D.A. and Draper, S.W. (eds) *User–Centered System Design*: Hillsdale, NJ: LEA.

Norman, D. A. (1988). *The Psychology of Everyday Things*. New York: Basic Books.

O'Malley, C.E., Draper, S.W. and Riley, M. (1984). Constructive interaction: a method for studying user–computer user–interaction. Technical Report C-015. Institute of Cognitive Science, San Diego, University of California.

Sasse, M. A. (1991). How to t(r)ap users' mental models. In Tauber, M.J. and Ackermann, D. (eds) *Mental Models and Human-Computer Interaction 2*. Amsterdam: Elsevier.

Wason, P.C. and Johnson-Laird, P.N. (1972). *Psychology of Reasoning* Cambridge, Ma.: Harvard University Press.

Young, R.M. (1983). Surrogates and mappings: two kinds of conceptual models for interactive devices. In Gentner, D. and Stevens, A.L. (eds) *Mental Models*. Hillsdale, NJ: LEA.

Chapter 16

Capturing Mental Models

Yvonne Rogers

The two chapters in this part critically review the mêleé of methods that have been used to identify mental models in human-computer interaction and human–machine systems research. Rutherford and Wilson provide an overview of the types of methods, data and analysis that are available, while Sasse focuses more specifically on the techniques that have been used in various HCI user model studies. Both chapters discuss the limitations of the methods, highlighting the numerous difficulties that researchers face in attempting to elicit and describe mental models. Central to this research is the problem of deciding how to select the most appropriate methodology given the multitude of possibilities. As Rutherford and Wilson point out, it is not possible to simply select the "best" method or set of methods. Instead, the relationship between data collection, data analysis and representation must be considered carefully, together with an appreciation of the weaknesses of each method and the specific goals of the study.

To overcome the methodological dilemma Sasse proposes that a battery of methods is employed to enable empirical data to be collected on users' explanations, predictions and descriptions of aspects of various systems as well as users' overt performance. However, the problem with casting the net so wide is that the sheer quantity and diversity of data obtained can become unwieldy. Sasse's solution is to take the comparative approach, where the merits of each method are evaluated in terms of their utility and outcome. However, her commentary falls short of any theoretical discussion. The question of whether one form of data is more valid than another, in terms of how well it reflects the underlying cognitive processes, is not addressed, nor is the question of how the assortment of data can be analysed and subsequently abstracted at a higher level of representation.

Clearly, there is a need for a systematic methodological framework to guide the process of mental model elicitation and representation. Rutherford and Wilson

MODELS IN THE MIND:
Theory, perspective and applications. ISBN 0–12–592970–6

suggest that it might be helpful to consider some of the methods used and developed in the area of knowledge acquisition, as it too is concerned with extracting information from a person for subsequent modelling. However, they fail to mention that the field of knowledge acquisition suffers from similar methodological muddles. Moreover, the problem appears to be even more exacerbated, as a result of wholesale borrowing from psychology, epistemology, machine learning and general artificial intelligence (AI). As commented by Shaw and Woodward (1990), this approach has resulted in "the knowledge acquisition area resembling a patch-work quilt whereby methods and techniques are strung together in a pragmatic rather than systematic fashion" (p.180). Indeed, current prescriptive advice to knowledge engineers is not to worry about *which* system to adopt, given that there are so many, but just to ensure that *some* system is adopted and that it is made explicit in the documentation process (Cordingley, 1989).

On the other hand, Shaw and Woodward (1990) argue for the need to develop a general methodological framework for knowledge elicitation methods. Importantly, they propose that such a framework should be able both to clarify the assumptions underpinning each method and also to classify their structures. To this end, they have developed a preliminary framework which links psychological theories of cognitive processing with knowledge elicitation tools. Somewhat ironically, they have turned to Norman's (1983) and Johnson-Laird's (1983) conceptualization of mental models to provide their representational scheme and operational definitions. One of the main requirements of the framework is the importance attached to preserving the modelling processes that the expert employs when solving a problem or communicating knowledge throughout the data collection–analysis–implementation cycle. This is all very well, except that the researcher needs to determine what the modelling processes are in the first place, so the problem of elicitation and representation again are brought back into the mental models court!

To facilitate the "smooth" transition between the different stages of the modelling cycle, various "intermediate" and "mediating" representations have been developed in the applied field of knowledge acquisition. Both are intended as conceptual aids for the expert, so that the knowledge elicited can be validated and confirmed. An example of the former is a diagram. On the other hand, a "mediating representation" is a more specific kind of notation developed to synthesize knowledge from talk with experts (Johnson, 1989). It achieves this by mediating between verbal data and standardized knowledge representation schemes found in AI software environments (e.g. systematic grammar networks). However, such verification aids are not used explicitly within mental models research. The question remains whether the methodological process of elicitation/analysis/ representation would benefit from introducing such reifying aids or conversely, whether they would interact with the various constraints imposed by each of the representational formats resulting in the creation of even more noisy data (cf. Rutherford and Wilson).

Within applied research it is widely recognized that there needs to be systematic monitoring between the different stages of transferring and translating empirical data into other representational forms. In contrast, in basic research such monitoring is more of a tacit process. Often, it is taken for granted that in virtue of their training and expertise, basic researchers are suitably equipped to perform the various empirical and computational analyses. However, studies of how cognitive scientists interpret and re-present the various representational forms (i.e. models, protocols, diagrams) from a sociology of scientific knowledge/technology perspective suggest otherwise. For example, Woolgar (1988) discusses the "methodological horrors" that confront scientists when they attempt to determine what is happening in a laboratory experiment and how they make sense of the data. In attempting to manage the raw data, he argues that the criteria of acceptability of what the data constitutes and, subsequently, what the data can be best represented as, is achieved largely through the researchers, reliance upon a chain of unquestioned assumptions. Moreover, Woolgar advocates that these assumptions are not uniquely determined by the phenomena themselves but instead they are the result of social, historical, psychological and other factors interceding between the phenomenon and its description.

It appears that the cognitive science's solution to such methodological horrors is not to acknowledge them as a form of practical reasoning that should be explicated as systematic practices (cf. Suchman, 1988 and Johnson's "mediating representation" procedure), but rather to try to eliminate them by developing and refining methods that have more rigour and theoretical commitment. Based on Marr's (1982) important contribution to theoretical psychology, stating the need to distinguish between computational, algorithmic and neural levels of analysis, attempts have been to develop mental model theories in such terms (e.g. Johnson-Laird and Byrne, 1991). Furthermore, a unified theory of cognition is being developed (Newell, 1991) to provide a set of general mechanisms that are intended to simulate the full range of cognition at the computational and algorithmic levels. The cognitive architecture that has been constructed for this purpose is SOAR (Laird, Newell and Rosenbloom, 1987). Its power over other computational architectures is claimed to reside in its universality, uniformity, its use of general mechanisms and its interaction effects that result from using a combination of weak and strong search methods. In turn, these mechanisms provide it with the flexibility to evaluate the experimental data that exists in cognitive psychology in a coherent and systematic way (see Rosenbloom, Laird, Newell and McCarl, 1991). If the mechanisms in SOAR fail to match the known empirical data in psychology, a deficiency in the SOAR theory is presumed and further refinement of the mechanisms is undertaken. Certainly SOAR looks impressive and indeed, it may overcome some of the pitfalls that beset less rigorous forms of cognitive modelling. However, in a recent review, Norman (1991) points out a number of problems with the fundamental assumptions underlying the SOAR architecture. These include the tenuousness of adopting the notion of a uniform computational architecture, a single form of learning and a single long-term memory system, especially in view of recent neuropsychological evidence and connectionist modelling which would appear to contradict such claims. In relation to mental models, SOAR assumes that their construction and manipulation is a form of problem solving that operates as a search within a uniform problem space. However, such a view is extremely limiting. Indeed, Norman poses the question of whether it is appropriate to view reasoning, analogizing, deducing and inferring solely in terms of a single representational and a single processing structure. Bibby (this volume) also discusses the inadequacies of SOAR for representing explicit reasoning about problem-solving procedures on the basis of a mental model.

Therefore, the danger of representing mental model construction and manipulation in the SOAR architecture is its over-simplification of the underlying cognitive mechanisms. Moreover, Marr's (1982) criticism (originally expressed with regard to production systems) that such study is examination of a processing mechanism and does not address the important issue of the nature of the computational problem also seems appropriate. Given the paucity of alternative computational architectures that might be more suitable for this purpose, it is difficult to know how to resolve the methodology/theory dilemma. On the one hand, should more rigourous and systematic computational methods of analysis and representation be pursued, while acknowledging that it is necessary to incorporate more untestable assumptions in the underlying theory? Or, on the other hand, do we focus on developing and refining empirical methods which are better able to deal with "noise", but at the expense of diluting the explanatory power of the theory? Furthermore, what of the more pragmatic approaches (cf. Sasse, this volume; Cordingley, 1989) where the emphasis is not so much on developing a theoretical account, but rather an account geared towards practical ends such as improving the user interface and designing more usable knowledge systems? Of course the shaping of future methodologies will depend on the goals (and funding) of the research but the problem of data collection, analysis and representation will continue to be fundamental to all.

References

Cordingley, E.S. (1989). Knowledge elicitation techniques for knowledge-based systems. In Diaper, D. (ed.) *Knowledge Elicitation: Principles, Techniques and Applications*. Chichester: Ellis Horwood.

Johnson, N.E. (1989). Mediating representation in knowledge elicitation. In Diaper, D. (ed.) *Knowledge Elicitation: Principles, Techniques and Applications*. Chichester: Ellis Horwood.

Johnson-Laird, P.N. (1983). *Mental Models*. Cambridge: CUP.

Johnson-Laird, P.N. and Byrne, R. (1991). *Deduction*. Cambridge: CUP.

Laird, J.E., Newell, A., and Rosenbloom, P.S. (1987). SOAR: an architecture for general intelligence. *Artifical Intelligence 33*, 1–64.

Marr,D. (1982). *Vision*. San Francisco: W.H. Freeman.

Newell, A. (1991). *Unified Theories of Cognition*. London: Harvard University Press.

Norman, D.A. (1991). Approaches to the study of intelligence. *Artificial Intelligence 47*, 327–346.

Norman, D.A. (1983). Some observations on mental models. In Gentner, D and Stevens, A.L. (eds) *Mental Models*. Hillsdale, NJ: LEA.

Rosenbloom, P.S., Laird, J.E., Newell, A. and McCarl, R. (1991). A preliminary analysis of the SOAR architecture as a basis for general intelligence. *Artifical Intelligence 47*, 289–325.

Shaw, M.L.G. and Woodward, J.B. (1990). Modelling expert knowledge. *Knowledge Acquisition 2*, 179–206.

Suchman, L.A. (1988). Representing practice in cognitive science. *Human Studies 11*, 305–325.

Woolgar, S. (1988). Time and documents in researcher interaction: some ways of making out what is happening in experimental science. *Human Studies 11*, 171–200.

Part 6

Social and Pragmatic Factors

Chapter 17

Obligation, Permission and Mental Models

Ken I. Manktelow and David E. Over

17.1 Introduction

This chapter is concerned with empirical research on understanding and reasoning with rules of obligation and permission. These are prime examples of normative, *deontic* concepts. Deontic reasoning, of the sort of interest here, takes place when we think about what we must, ought to, or may do rather than about what was, is, or will be the case. As will become clear, attempting to explain deontic thinking leads one to range across the boundaries of several, usually disparate areas of research, including those on deduction, social cognition, subjective utility, and subjective probability. We engage in deontic reasoning when we try to answer questions like the following. "Should I give up smoking?" This is a question about a possible obligation in prudential morality. "May I reject the null hypothesis on the basis of these results?" This is a question about a possible permission in the normative theory of hypothesis testing. "Ought I to pay the poll tax?" This is a question about a possible legal or ethical obligation.

Deontic reasoning is obviously a fundamental part of human thought; and research on normative theories of thought and action has gone on for thousands of years, thanks to which we have such subjects as logic and the law. However, experimental research on actual deontic reasoning, of the sort ordinary people conduct every day, is of quite recent origin. In fact, cognitive psychology has tended to ignore this type of reasoning, in spite of its intrinsic importance. But very recently, research on a famous paradigm of conditional reasoning has forced cognitive psychologists to study it seriously, and to propose schema theories of how it takes place. One of the main aims of the present discussion is to describe how this has come about. The other is to argue that the theory of mental models is a more fundamental way of trying to explain ordinary deontic reasoning than schema theories are.

MODELS IN THE MIND:
Theory, perspective and applications. ISBN 0−12−592970−6

Cognitive psychologists have had to investigate deontic reasoning because of their interest in whether the particular content of a reasoning problem, independent of its logical form, can affect the way people try to solve it. We shall therefore begin with a brief review of the relevant areas of research on content effects in human reasoning, and the major schema theories which have been proposed to explain them. This will lead on to a detailed consideration of the use of mental models theory in explaining deontic thought, using empirical work as evidence.

17.2 Content effects on reasoning

The very idea of problem content having an effect on thinking has had profound theoretical repercussions, as several recent reviews have noted (e.g. Evans, 1989; Johnson-Laird and Byrne, 1991; Manktelow and Over, 1990a). This is because, according to classical views of reasoning, the mind may be held to contain content-independent rules of inference. Strictly speaking, then, all deductive reasoning of the same logical form should take the same course. In fact, this does not happen: what the problem is about, independent of its logical form, has enormous influence on how people think about it.

Although work on content effects in reasoning initially concentrated on syllogisms (see Evans, 1989 and Newstead, 1989 for recent reviews), most of the evidence for the recent upsurge in content-dependent theories of reasoning has come from work on another experimental paradigm, Wason's selection task. Since we shall be reporting research using this problem, we shall outline its general structure before going on to the theoretical and empirical work resulting from its use.

The selection task dates from the 1960s (e.g. Wason, 1968), and was originally presented in what came to be known as *abstract* form. What this means is that these early tasks had little familiar content, consisting of materials such as letters and numbers or coloured shapes, and supposed relationships between these which were not found in ordinary experience. Subjects were given a statement about cards couched in the form of an *indicative* conditional: *if p then q*. For instance:

If a card has a vowel on one side [p] then it has an even number on the other side [q].

Each card had a letter on one side and a number on the other; sometimes subjects were allowed to examine a set of such cards before attempting the task. Four cards were placed before the subject. Each showed one of four separate logical possibilities: p made true, i.e a vowel present (symbolically, the p card); p made false, i.e. a consonant present (the $\bar{p}$ card) q made true, i.e. an even number indicated (the q card); and q made false, i.e. an odd number indicated (the $\bar{q}$ card). The subject's task was to select only those cards which might show that the target conditional was false.

The correct answer is to select the p and $\bar{q}$ cards, since only those cards could potentially bear the combination of values which would falsify the conditional: a card with a vowel on one side but an odd number, and not an even one, indicated on the other side.

Since only around 10% of subjects arrived at this conclusion (see Wason and Johnson-Laird, 1972), a lot of work went into finding out not only why this task seemed so difficult, but also how it could be changed to make it easier. One way of doing the latter was to substitute more realistic, familiar, or "thematic" materials. During the 1970s, a number of reports appeared in which subjects produced high levels of correct responses with thematic versions of the task (see Griggs, 1983 for a review). However, in the 1980s the picture became complicated by the discovery that not all thematic contents facilitated the correct response in this way: some did, some did not.

Plainly, people's performance on the selection task was determined by their existing knowledge, and thus research became concerned with characterizing the knowledge which would allow people to get the task right under some conditions. As people did not have to have experience of the exact problem content, only familiarity with its fairly general type (Griggs, 1983; Johnson-Laird, 1983), an obvious candidate was schema theory. Schemas embody fairly generalized, but still domain-specific knowledge which enable inferences to be made: the script theory of Schank and Abelson (1977) is a well-known example. (See Manktelow and Over, 1990a, on schema theory.)

As far as the selection task is concerned, it is possible to conceive of more or less general schematic knowledge which people could be evoking in getting it right. An example will demonstrate this. Probably the most reliable content in bringing about high levels of correct responding (you can use it in class demonstrations with confidence) is the "Sears" problem developed by D'Andrade and first reported in Rumelhart (1980). In this, subjects imagine they are workers in a department store, and have been given the following *rule*:

If any purchase exceeds $30, then the receipt must have the signature of the departmental manager on the back.

The cards have now become receipts with the amount on one side and space for a signature on the other, and subjects can see four: one for over \$30 (p), one for under \$30 ($\bar{p}$), one which has been signed (q) and one which is unsigned ($\bar{q}$). When asked which they should choose to check whether the rule has been violated, most people choose the correct combination of the large receipt and the unsigned one. What kind of knowledge has brought about this performance? Some might suggest general experience with department stores, but there are even more general possibilities.

Note that we have called the conditional statement in this version of the task a rule. That is, the conditional here is stating a regulation which is supposed to govern people's behaviour. In technical terms, this particular example is a *conditional obligation:* it states what people must do, in the sense of what they should or ought to do, given some condition. Researchers have often used "rule" to describe the very different kind of indicative conditional found in abstract versions of the selection task, but this has led to confusion, and we shall use the word only in its proper deontic sense. With this point clear, we should ask whether some kind of general ability to reason with rules –to engage in deontic thinking, in other words – accounts for the facilitation of correct responses in this second selection task.

Since the mid 1980's, increasing empirical research has supported the view that people do have fairly general knowledge of how to engage in deontic reasoning. The decisive step was taken by Cheng and Holyoak (1985; Cheng, Holyoak, Nisbett, and Oliver, 1986). Their work also has the merit of having stated the first schema theory of anything which could be called deontic reasoning.

17.3 Schema theories of reasoning

Although we are going to argue that schema theories cannot fully explain ordinary deontic reasoning, without the postulation of mental models, it is necessary to review here the major schema theories of recent years. This is partly to point out the limits of this approach, and partly to do justice to the influence that these theories have had on our own work on deontic thinking. We shall consider first the theory of pragmatic reasoning schemas which was introduced by Cheng and Holyoak, and then the theory of Darwinian algorithms proposed by Cosmides (1989). Our aim is to point out the components in each which have contributed to the formulation of deontic reasoning which we set out below.

Cheng and Holyoak (1985) argue that we acquire schemas for deontic thinking by induction from ordinary experience. They consider the case of what they take to be permission rules. The essential relation in thinking about permission is, they contend, that between an action and its precondition. For them a *permission schema* consists of the following production rules:

1. If the action is to be taken, then the precondition must be satisfied.
2. If the action is not to be taken, then the precondition need not be satisfied.
3. If the precondition is satisfied, then the action may be taken.
4. If the precondition is not satisfied, then the action must not be taken.

Any problem clearly marked as one concerning permission is said to evoke this schema. As far as the selection task is concerned, the activation of rule 1 will result in the choice of the p card, and the activation of rule 4 will result in the choice of the $\bar{q}$ card, since those rules dictate actions. Rules 2 and 3 do not, and hence will not lead to any selections.

This theory was tested by Cheng and Holyoak with an implicitly deontic scenario. They asked subjects to imagine that they were immigration officers checking forms, with the object of making sure that:

If the form says ENTERING on one side, then the other side includes cholera among the list of diseases.

When a rationale was given stating that the point of this so-called permission rule was to prevent disease, the predicted pattern was produced by the majority of subjects: they chose the cards showing ENTERING (p) and not showing cholera ($\bar{q}$).

We have our doubts about this analysis (including its terminology), which we shall reveal as we go along. But we wish to stress immediately a point whose full significance has been missed in the literature. There is a difference between this immigration problem and the Sears problem, on the one hand, and the abstract type of problem, on the other. In the latter case, the subjects' task is to pick just those cards that might show whether an indicative conditional, in our example about a supposed link between vowels and even numbers, is true or false. But in the former sort of case, the subjects' task is to pick just those cards which might indicate whether a rule has been conformed to or violated. This point is related to one we made earlier: only in the former case are we dealing with a proper rule, a deontic statement. Such a rule is an attempt to regulate behaviour, and thus it can be accepted as true, by department store workers or immigration officials, but still violated *by people's actions*. In complete contrast, the assertion of an indicative conditional is just an attempt to describe a matter of fact. It would be meaningless to say that an indicative conditional truly described some state of affairs, but had been violated by someone's behaviour.

There are two reasons why this point should be fully explored and taken account of. The first follows immediately from the fact that the above indicative conditional, in the abstract task, is not a proper rule: it is a kind of non-deontic conditional. It and the two deontic conditionals do not have the same logical form, i.e. they cannot all be simply given the form *if p then q*. The logical form of the deontic conditionals could only be adequately represented in a deontic logic. It would be too easy and quick to argue, though many researchers have tended to do so, that the different responses in the three tasks above establish, *on their own*, that reasoning is affected by content. We cannot, in fact, say that the abstract task is of the same logical form as the deontic tasks, but that the latter differ from the former in specific content. We must go a little more slowly and carefully in our argument that reasoning is determined by content and not logical form.

The second reason for keeping the difference between the abstract tasks and the deontic ones in mind is that, by doing this, we are led to ask what does make a deontic conditional true or false. A travel agent may say to us, "You must be inoculated against smallpox if you enter that country." But a more experienced travel agent might reply, "No, that is false. What is true is that you must be inoculated against cholera if you are to enter that country." Ordinary people understand such statements; they would be unable to grasp the less fundamental difference between conforming to a rule and violating it if they did not. After all, one cannot be said to conform to or violate a false deontic conditional, such as the one just given about smallpox inoculations. But Cheng and Holyoak do not ask the fundamental question of what it means to say that a deontic conditional is true or false, and, as we hope will become clear, that is a serious limitation of their schema theory.

Before we say more about this limitation, we want to consider the views of Cosmides (1989). Though she is a schema theorist, she has influenced us, and her views are a good introduction to our own. She contends that subjects in Cheng and Holyoak's experiment produced the correct answer because their materials evoked a different sort of schema, the empirical consequences of which just happened to coincide in this particular case. Cosmides' schemas are called Darwinian algorithms, the name arising from her proposal that they are a product of our evolutionary rather than our learning history.

Cosmides argues that the survival of the human species crucially depends on the dynamics of social exchange. The fundamental relation in social exchange, which we must all be sensitive to in order to cooperate, is expressed in this type of rule:

If you take a benefit then you pay a cost.

The corollary of the understanding of rules of this sort is that people will equally well grasp what it is to break them, and hence to cheat, which is to take a benefit without paying the appropriate cost. Society could not function if people could cheat with impunity. It is obvious how this would translate into the form of the selection task: if four cards showed cases of taking a benefit (p), not taking a benefit ($\bar{p}$) paying a cost (q) and not paying a cost ($\bar{q}$) detecting the cheater would result in selecting the required p and $\bar{q}$ cards. Thus Cheng and Holyoak's subjects could have been detecting the cheaters: the persons who might have gained the benefit of entering a country without paying the cost of having a cholera inoculation.

Like Cheng and Holyoak, Cosmides does not tell us what makes a supposed rule true or false in the first place. The analyses of both Cheng and Holyoak and Cosmides seem to be directed towards answering the *pragmatic* question of what it is to conform to or violate a deontic conditional, which is already accepted as true. But this leaves more fundamental problems untouched: the *semantic* problem of saying what it is for deontic conditionals to be true or false, and the *epistemological* problem of explaining how people discover, or try to discover, whether these conditionals are true or false. Why are people cheaters if they enter the country without a cholera inoculation, but not if they enter without a smallpox inoculation? The country has laid down the one deontic conditional as a rule and not the other. Why does it accept the one as true and the other as false? What enables the subjects in the selection task to understand why the country has accepted the one as true? Cosmides does not address these questions, but by emphasizing the importance of benefits and costs in deontic reasoning she gets closer to an answer to them than Cheng and Holyoak do. We shall see why this is so by bringing out more of the difficulties with the views of both Cheng and Holyoak and Cosmides. By moving beyond their work to semantic and epistemological questions, we hope to establish the need for an account of deontic reasoning based on mental models.

17.4 Troubles with schemas

Cosmides could be interpreted as making a strong claim, namely, that the facilitation of correct answers on a selection task is reliably produced only when the rule expresses the benefit—cost relationship she specifies. This claim has been disputed both by Cheng and Holyoak (1989) and ourselves (Manktelow and Over 1990a, b). It would be falsified by finding a version of the task which produces the facilitation effect but which does not include such a rule. We have already used an example, the Sears problem, which does not appear to express a benefit—cost relation in the way Cosmides usually speaks about her concept. Strictly, Cosmides' analysis would have to read the rule there as stating a relation between the "benefit" of receiving a large receipt and the "cost" of having it signed. This does not seem to be the right way to talk about the matter, but we should not reject entirely the idea of costs and benefits in this scenario. The subjects in that scenario are asked to imagine that they are department store workers, and of course, there would be benefits or costs for these workers depending on whether they did the job properly or improperly.

The problem with the strong claim can definitely be seen in a version of the task we have used in previous work (Manktelow and Over, 1990b; see also Cheng and Holyoak, 1989). Here subjects were given the following rule:

If you clean up spilt blood, then you must wear rubber gloves.

Cards showed whether people had (p) or had not ($\bar{p}$) cleaned up blood, on one side, and whether they had worn gloves (q) or not ($\bar{q}$), on the other. Subjects reliably picked out the correct cards: those showing someone who had cleared up blood and someone who had not worn gloves. Cleaning up blood could hardly be described as a benefit for which one has to pay the cost of wearing gloves.

We therefore reject the strong claim: the data are simply against it. However, it is possible to generalize Cosmides' case about benefits and costs, and to argue that what is important in interpreting deontic rules is the *expected utility* of conforming or not conforming to them. Given the scenarios in which they are embedded, there is clearly a greater utility in conforming to the Sears rule (it is generally in one's interest to do one's job properly) and the medical rule (it is certainly in one's interest to avoid the risk of disease) than in not conforming to them. Our work (Manktelow and Over, 1990b) on deontic selection tasks, with conditional obligations, suggests that there will be facilitation of correct responses when there is a great difference in expected utility between conforming to the obligations and violating them. If this is so, then we do have a good reason for concluding that deontic reasoning is content-dependent. The significant factor for facilitation is not the logical form of the conditional obligation, but rather what its special content, in a particular context, tells us about differences in utility between conforming to it and violating it. We also predict that, as this difference in utility decreases, so will facilitation.

Our account of these deontic selection tasks fits in well with the fundamental semantics of obligation and permission. (We cannot go into the technical details of the exact semantics we most favour here. For the general approach, see Jackson, 1985, and Manktelow and Over, 1990a.) We can illustrate this by describing the following way of trying to *discover* whether a conditional obligation is true or false. Suppose we are nurses in a hospital who are trying to decide whether to accept the above conditional about spilt blood as true or false. We know that we are going to have to clean up spilt blood at some stage, and we imagine that we are just about to do so. We compare in our minds what would follow if we were to use rubber gloves with what would follow if we did not. We see that we would be protected from nasty diseases in the former case, but not in the latter, and consequently we much *prefer* the former to the latter. This strong preference allows us to speak, more technically, of the former case as having greater utility than the latter. That being so, we accept the conditional obligation as true, and take care not to violate it. Subjects in a selection task based on this conditional would also be able to go through this reasoning and grasp why it was important not to violate that rule.

This way of describing the epistemological process of discovering the truth of a conditional obligation is, we contend, very natural and seems to fit ordinary experience; and it could hardly be more natural than to use mental models in a technical account of this process. For us, however, the really significant point about the theory of mental models here is that it provides a way of accounting for the semantic understanding of conditional obligations. Not only that, but it is a way that directly relates to the formal semantics of these conditionals. This refers to possible states of affairs, and preferences among these; and mental models can be taken simply as attempts to represent these states for the purpose of making decisions based on the preferences.

The main limitations of the theories of Cheng and Holyoak and Cosmides stand out even more now. Their schemas provide no way of accounting for the semantic understanding of any deontic statements, and no way, therefore, of relating this understanding to performance on the selection task. In particular, Cheng and Holyoak's production rules themselves contain unanalysed deontic terms, such as "may", "must", and "need not". Their syntactic schemas provide no account of how people understand these terms, although perhaps this problem could be overcome by supplementing their view with mental models and subjective utilities. They would then have a deeper explanation of some important aspects of their experiments. For example, recall that facilitation of correct responses seemed to result from telling the subjects that the immigration rule about cholera is "to ensure that entering passengers are protected against disease" (Cheng and Holyoak, 1985, p.401). Here again is the clear difference in utility between being protected from a serious disease and not being so protected.

Interestingly, Cheng and Holyoak found *some* facilitation in a fairly abstract selection task. In it, the subjects were asked to suppose that they were authorities checking whether people were obeying a regulation about an abstract precondition P for taking some action A. But notice that utility differences are *fairly* strongly suggested even by this general description. We generally prefer to do what legitimate authorities require of us, either because we are reasonably moral agents, or because of the sanctions most authorities can exercise if we do not do what they say. And of course, authorities themselves lay down regulations on the basis of their preferences.

There is some potentially misleading terminology in Cheng and Holyoak's work. What they call "permission" rules are, in fact, conditional obligations, stating what one must do given certain circumstances. Their immigration rule is clearly an implicit conditional obligation. People entering the country are obliged to have a cholera inoculation, though Cheng and Holyoak prefer to say that having this protection is a "precondition" for getting permission to enter. But conditional permissions, correctly so-called, have a different logical form, stating what one *may* do, given some condition. An example would be the statement that one may enter the country if one is a citizen of it. Perhaps because the terminology has been misleading, proper conditional permissions have been neglected in the literature, but we have recently run experiments on them (see Manktelow and Over, 1991). These experiments, which we shall discuss in the next section, demonstrate how important it is to investigate, and integrate in one theory, the full pragmatic and social context of deontic reasoning, as well as the semantics and epistemology of deontic statements. They also give empirical backing to our argument for using the theory of mental models to account for deontic thought.

17.5 Studies of reasoning with conditional permissions

In this chapter, we have been interested in deontic statements about thought and action. Deontic statements are admittedly more general than this, but certainly their role in the attempt to regulate thought and action is far and away their most important. When they are fulfilling this role, we can usually distinguish two interested parties (which might actually be individuals or groups of people). We shall term these parties the *actor* and the *agent*. The actor is the person (or group) whose behaviour is the target of some rule; previous research has almost always concentrated on this person's actions. The agent is the person (group, organization, institution, or whatever) who states the rule. Naturally, both parties have their own preferences and so subjective utilities; and that can mean that they can have different interests in whether a rule is conformed to or not. The best way of illustrating this is to describe our experiments (they are reported in full in Manktelow and Over, 1991).

In the first experiments we used a scenario which we thought would readily evoke real-life utilities in our subjects. It concerned a mother (the agent) laying down the following permission rule for her son (the actor).

If you clear up your room, then you may go out to play.

It is easy to imagine why a mother would assert this as true. Supposing that her son clears up his room, she has no reason to prefer his not going out to play to his doing so, i.e. for her the utility of his going out to play is then at least as great as that of his not going out to play. (Note the difference between the truth conditions for this conditional permission and those for a conditional obligation.) In addition, most subjects would naturally think that mothers generally prefer tidy rooms to untidy rooms, while little boys generally prefer going out to play to being kept indoors. These views would not, of course, come from knowledge of the semantics of the conditional permission, but rather from familiarity with mothers, sons and the kind of context in which rules like our example are laid down. Yet another point which would normally be inferred in this kind of context, without further information, is that the only way the boy can get permission to go out is by clearing up his room; that also would be inferred by pragmatic and not semantic considerations. Now, on the basis of all this, we can see that there is more than one way in which each party can fail to conform, in some sense, to the rule as a whole. There are, in fact, four possible cases, two for each party:

1. The agent (mother) sees p is true but does not allow q (she is unfair to or cheats her son).
2. The agent does not see p is true but allows q (she is weak or is unfair to herself).
3. The actor (son) makes p true but does not do q (he cheats or is unfair to himself).
4. The actor does not make p true but does q (he cheats his mother).

Thus it should be possible to elicit completely opposite response patterns in a selection task, depending on which social role and possible violation are in question. Using these scenarios, we looked at cases 1 and 4, i.e. at opposite patterns resulting from the different social perspectives. In one experiment (case 1), subjects were asked to think about the behaviour of a mother suspected by her son of not keeping her side of the bargain: they imagined that their younger brother was complaining to them about her unfair treatment of him. Four cards showed whether the boy had tidied his room (p) or not ($\bar{p}$) on one side, and whether his mother had let him out to play (q) or not ($\bar{q}$) on the other. Which cards could show whether the mother had been unfair? Under case 1, it was predicted that subjects would tend to choose the p and $\bar{q}$ cards. These were the results (N = 27).

p	$\bar{p}$	q	$\bar{q}$
26	5	5	19

These results are statistically significant ($\chi^2 = 24.05$, p<0.01); the predicted combination was chosen by 17 subjects.

In another experiment, we tested case 4. This time, 19 subjects were asked to think about the behaviour of the boy. They thought about his actions from the point of view of a working mother giving her son a rule about tidying his room while she was out: had he broken the rule? In this case, a the prediction was that they would choose the $\bar{p}$ and q cards - the reverse of the usual "facilitated" pattern. The results were:

p	$\bar{p}$	q	$\bar{q}$
2	15	17	4

Again, these results were significant ($\chi^2 = 18.21$, p<0.01), with 13 subjects choosing the predicted combination.

These findings clearly confirm our analysis of the influence of subjective utilities and social roles in determining people's deontic judgements. However, there are two possible objections, which were addressed in another experiment. Firstly, we did not test cases 2 and 3. Secondly, in using highly familiar scenarios concerning family interactions, it was possible that we were simply eliciting people's memories of actual experiences, and not getting them to think at all. We therefore designed another set of scenarios using more artificial content.

These tasks were inspired by the Sears problem: they concerned a rule given by a shop to its customers:

If you spend more than £100, then you may take a free gift.

Because it was unlikely that the subjects would have had experience of such circumstances in their lives, the utilities were made explicit in the task instructions, e.g. the gifts were said to be very attractive. The cards were said to show how much had been spent on one side: £120 (p) or £55 ($\bar{p}$), and whether the gift had been claimed (q) or not ($\bar{q}$) on the other side. The four possible cases of failing to conform to this rule, with their attendant predictions for the task, were as follows:

Case 1: The shop takes enough money but does not issue the gift: $p\bar{q}$

Case 2: The shop does not take enough money but issues the gift: $\bar{p}q$

Case 3: The customers pay enough but do not take the gift: $p\bar{q}$

Case 4: The customers do not pay enough but do take the gift: $\bar{p}q$

Tasks in all four conditions were identical, including the rule itself, except for a couple of clauses in the background story specifying the perspective in question. The results are given in Table 17.1. Once again, it can be seen that the predicted responses were significantly more frequent, and in all four cases the predicted combinations of cards were chosen by most subjects, no other being produced more than twice.

These data strongly confirm the predictions resulting from an analysis of deontic reasoning in terms of subjective utilities and social roles. These patterns would not have been predicted by Cheng and Holyoak's theory; in its present form, it can neither represent social roles nor take account of subjective utilities. Cosmides' social contract theory might have predicted some of the responses to individual scenarios (e.g. cases 1 and 4), but as it stands, her scheme is neither general enough in its account of subjective utilities nor of social roles. However, we do not want to discuss here detailed extensions to existing proposals, but rather to argue that an adequate theory of deontic reasoning should include mental models.

Case 1: The firm cheats the customers

p^* $\bar{p}$ q $\bar{q}^*$

12 2 1 10 $\chi^2 = 14.84$, p<0.01

Case 2: The firm cheats itself

p $\bar{p}^*$ q^* $\bar{q}$

4 11 12 0 $\chi^2 = 14.63$, p<0.01

Case 3: The customers cheat themselves

$p^*\bar{p}$ q q^*

10 2 2 10 $\chi^2 = 10.67$, p<0.02

Case 4: The customers cheat the firm

p $\bar{p}^*$ q^* $\bar{q}$

2 12 13 0 $\chi^2 = 19.96$, p<0.001

Predicted patterns are indicated by (*) in each case.

Table 17.1 Frequency of card selections under four conditions using the rule *If you spend more than £100, then you may take a free gift.*

17.6 Modelling the semantics and pragmatics of deontic understanding

In this chapter we have argued, theoretically and from experimental evidence, for two crucial components in the understanding of deontic conditionals: subjective utility and social roles. Neither of these factors is fully taken account of in existing schema theories. Furthermore, we have seen that the factors are not independent, but interactive: each social role has its own attendant subjective utilities, dependent on preferences among the outcomes of possible actions. Expected utilities determine, in context, which deontic conditionals are accepted as true, and who benefits and who loses if these are conformed to or violated in different ways. Our experimental evidence has supported the view that people have a reliable grasp of how these factors need to be combined in good deontic reasoning.

Actually, this reasoning is even more complex than we have so far made explicit. The implicit factor in what we have said, which calls for much research in its own right, is that of subjective probability, i.e. a person's assessment of how likely, rather than how desirable, relevant outcomes are. This factor can affect which rules are said to be true in the first place. The medical rule about spilt blood provides an example. Nurses working in an AIDS ward would tend to accept this rule and regulate their behaviour by it: not only is a possible outcome of violating it highly undesirable, but also too likely for comfort. On the other hand, most parents would reject the rule as one to be followed after an accident their child has had in the kitchen with a broken glass. The possible outcome of a life-threatening disease is just as undesirable in this case, but far less likely.

Good deontic thinking requires adequate mental representation of all the semantic, pragmatic and social factors we have mentioned. Our research so far confirms that people can do this in selection tasks. It is interesting to note that some recent research by Girotto and his colleagues (Girotto, Blaye, and Farioli, 1989; Girotto, Light, and Colbourn, 1988; Light, Girotto and Legrenzi, in press) also confirms that even young children are proficient at making certain deontic judgements. Since good deontic thinking is so intimately connected with successful behaviour, in the sense of getting us what we most prefer to have, perhaps this was only to be expected on evolutionary grounds. But what kind of cognitive theory should we have of this kind of thinking?

Our argument is that mental models must be used in a full account of the rich and complex nature of ordinary deontic thought. As we have already said, the fundamental point for us is that mental models are a way of accounting for semantic understanding. Johnson-Laird (1983) introduced mental models to try to explain how people could discover valid, truth-preserving inferences. We have pointed out in previous work (Manktelow and Over, 1987 and 1990a) that his is essentially a model theoretic, i.e. a semantic, approach to this problem, unlike the syntactic one of postulating the existence of content-independent mental inference rules. More recently, Johnson-Laird and Byrne (1991) have extended this approach, in their own way, to try to account for people's understanding of non-deontic conditionals.

Consider the following non-deontic conditional:

If you cut yourself on that bloody glass, then you will get AIDS.

What would make this conditional true in some circumstance? The best answer (going back at least to Stalnaker, 1968) seems to be that it is true if you do get AIDS in the nearest possible state (or states) of affairs in which you do cut yourself on the glass. (By using "nearest" here one means to rule out possibilities in which, for example, AIDS is not a contagious disease. See Manktelow and Over, 1990a, on the semantics of conditionals.) How would we discover that that is the case? Here the best answer goes back to Ramsey (1931) and is closely related to the semantics just given. Roughly, what we appear to do is to take the antecedent of the conditional as a supposition, add to it what seems to be relevant and compatible with it from our beliefs, with minimal changes, and then try to discern whether the consequent follows. If it does, then we conclude that the conditional is true. Clearly, we could redescribe this process in the terminology of mental models, and then that way of presenting the matter would also have the great virtue of being directly and intimately related to the semantics of the non-deontic conditional.

The next step would be to extend the theory of mental models to cover deontic thought. This thought, we hold, depends on an ability to work out, in the way we have just described, the truth or falsity of non-deontic conditionals. We must first get some idea of what would follow in certain possible outcomes before we can express preferences among them, and so decide what we must or may do. In other words, we need to set up mental models, representing possible outcomes of actions, before we can say which ones we prefer and come to deontic conclusions. Sometimes it would be necessary for the mental models to represent *explicitly* what our preferences and the consequent utilities were, as when we were reasoning about money, but that could certainly be done.

Mental models could also be expanded to take account of the pragmatic and social factors not represented in current schema theories. That is, they could be used to represent the different parties to deontic contexts and their differing utilities. That would make the pragmatic and social representation cohere well with the underlying semantic representation. Much more difficult admittedly, is to see how to use mental models back at the semantic level to deal with subjective probabilities. But any other theory would also find this a problem, and perhaps some kind of weighting of mental models would be the way forward. Here more than anywhere else, we see the need for research on conditional reasoning to be related to what is conventionally conceived as a very different body of work, that on subjective probability and utility.

There is a final point about using mental models to account for deontic reasoning. It may be a fact that cutting ourselves on some contaminated glass will give us AIDS. Such facts of nature can make non-deontic conditionals, such as our last example, *objectively* true or false. But few of us think that deontic statements are objectively true or false. After all, hypochondriacs or masochists may prefer having a disease to good health, and we cannot prove them wrong scientifically. Consequently, the concept of truth for deontic statements must be a subjective one, and so it is when it is explained in terms of those other subjective concepts, individual utility and probability. But that implies that mental models are not only a subjective way of trying to discover the truth of deontic statements, they are part of what it to say that these statements are true in the subjective sense. It is therefore impossible to imagine that any theory of deontic thought could ultimately do without them.

References

Cheng, P.W. and Holyoak, K.J. (1985). Pragmatic reasoning schemas. *Cognitive Psychology 17*, 391–416.

Cheng, P.W. and Holyoak, K.J. (1989). On the natural selection of reasoning theories. *Cognition 33*, 285–313.

Cheng, P.W., Holyoak, K.J., Nisbett, R.E. and Oliver, L.M. (1986). Pragmatic versus syntactic approaches to training deductive reasoning. *Cognitive Psychology 18*, 293–328.

Cosmides, L. (1989). The logic of social exchange: has natural selection shaped how humans reason? Studies with the Wason selection task. *Cognition 31*, 187–276.

Evans, J. St B.T. (1989) . *Bias in Reasoning: Causes and Consequences*. Hove, Sussex: LEA.

Girotto, V. Blaye, A. and Farioli, F. (1989). A reason to reason: pragmatic basis of children's search for counterexamples. *European Bulletin of Cognitive Psychology 9*, 297–321.

Girotto, V., Light, P.H. and Colbourn, C. (1988). Pragmatic schemas and conditional reasoning in children. *Quarterly Journal of Experimental Psychology 40A*, 469–482.

Griggs, R.A. (1983). The role of problem content in the selection task and THOG problem. In Evans, J.St B.T. (ed.) *Thinking and Reasoning: Psychological Approaches*. London: Routledge.

Jackson, F. (1985). On the semantics and logic of obligation. *Mind 94*, 177–196.

Johnson-Laird, P.N. (1983). *Mental Models*. Cambridge: CUP.

Johnson-Laird, P.N. and Byrne, R.M.J. (1991). *Deduction*. Hove, Sussex: LEA

Light, P.H., Girotto, V. and Legrenzi, P. (in press). Children's reasoning on conditional promises and permissions. *Cognitive Development*.

Manktelow, K.I. and Over, D.E. (1987). Reasoning and rationality. *Mind and Language 2*, 199-219.

Manktelow, K.I. and Over, D.E. (1990a). *Inference and Understanding*. London: Routledge.

Manktelow, K.I. and Over, D.E. (1990b). Deontic thought and the selection task. In Gilhooly, K., Keane, M., Logie, R. and Erdos,G. (eds) *Lines of Thinking(Vol. 1* Chichester: Wiley.

Manktelow, K.I. and Over, D.E. (1991). Social roles and utilities in reasoning with deontic conditionals. *Cognition 39*, 85–105.

Newstead, S.E. (1989). Interpretational errors in syllogistic reasoning. *Journal of Memory and Language 28*, 78–91.

Ramsey, F.P. (1931). *Foundations of Mathematics*. London: Routledge.

Rumelhart, D.E. (1980). Schemata: the building blocks of cognition. In Spiro, R.J., Bruce, B.C. and Brewer, W.F. (eds) *Theoretical Issues in Reading Comprehension*. Hillsdale, NJ: LEA.

Schank, R.C. and Abelson, R. (1977) . *Scripts, Plans, Goals and Understanding*. Hillsdale, NJ: LEA.

Stalnaker, R.C. (1968). A theory of conditionals. In Rescher, N. (ed.) *Studies in Logical Form*. Oxford: Blackwell.

Wason, P.C. (1968). Reasoning about a rule. *Quarterly Journal of Experimental Psychology 20*, 273–281.

Wason, P.C. and Johnson-Laird, P.N. (1972). *Psychology of Reasoning: Structure and Content*. London: Batsford.

Chapter 18

The Presence Phenomenon and Other Problems of Applying Mental Models to User Interface Design and Evaluation

Bob Leiser

18.1 Introduction

My aim in this chapter is to identify some of the problems in applying mental models to user–computer interface design and evaluation. As a consultant I cannot use the theory unless I can persuade prospective clients that it is of value to them. Although it has its uses as it stands, I would not attempt to sell the notion of mental models as a complete approach to design and evaluation.

The idea of a single theory underpinning user interface design and evaluation is appealing. For this reason I describe the shortcomings I see with mental models as applied to user interface design and evaluation in the hope that this will prompt research and development of the field in an applied direction. My concern is with a range of aspects of human–computer interaction which cannot be accounted for with the current view of mental models. In particular, my work in speech and natural language interfaces has led me to worry about a phenomenon I have called "presence" which is not addressable in the currency of mental models.

Firstly I will describe the two predominant views of what a mental model is and the advantages and limitations of each. I will then recount some of the general difficulties I see in applying mental models, making particular reference to the phenomenon I call presence.

I will argue that presence cannot be regarded as a particular type of belief, nor as a specific type of perceptual phenomenon and so must be given special consideration where it may occur. I will go on to discuss problems that presence poses for the use of mental models in the study of human-computer interaction and some of the work which needs to be done to overcome them.

Returning to a more general level I will summarize the problems I see in using mental models, and present a shopping list which defines what I want from the theory before I feel it can be used as the basis for a unified approach to user interface design and evaluation.

18.2 Mental model theories and their shortcomings

18.2.1 Two different views of users' mental models

It is clear from the many conferences and publications which address the topic called mental models that there are a number of different interpretations of the term. Inevitably, everyone who uses the term is convinced that their use of it is the appropriate one and that other uses are based on misunderstanding of the term or adaptations of the concept. Rather than describe all of the uses of the term here, I will discuss the two most common interpretations of it.

The interpretation of mental models which I was taught first and most comprehensively is Johnson-Laird's. The view of this as the 'correct' interpretation is reinforced by the title of his main work on the subject *Mental Models* (Johnson-Laird, 1983). Johnson-Laird sees a mental model as the set of possible representations of the available information. For a user interface this would consist of a set of representations of the relationship between user actions and system responses. Because the model consists of a set of representations, there is scope for inconsistency between them.

Much more common in the study of human–computer interaction is the view of a mental model as a kind of *internalized flowchart* of a system's functionality. This would be a list of beliefs such as if I press <return>, the last thing I typed gets interpreted and acted upon, he <escape> key takes me out of whatever I'm doing. The user refers to this list when trying to figure out how to carry out a task or when predicting the likely results of some action.

Both views have their appeal. Johnson-Laird's, by its definition as containing a set of possible representations, allows for internal inconsistency in a mental model. Thus the user may apply two mutually incompatible beliefs at different stages of interface use.

The internalized flowchart approach is easier to grasp, making it easier to explain and justify its application. A mental model of this type is easier to draw or describe, but by the same token may omit inconsistencies; the features which are often essential in explaining or predicting user behaviour.

18.2.2 Problems in applying mental models

The ultimate test of a theory in a consulting context is whether it can be demonstrated as having potential value to clients. Their primary intention is to have a problem solved and generally feel no charitable inclination to give a new theory or technique a chance to prove itself. When the client is concerned with the development or evaluation of software it would be necessary to be able to present the theory as a working tool, which is applied in a systematic way and which produces tangible results. This has been a major motivating factor in the development of user interface design checklists, methodologies for incorporating human factors in the software development cycle, and task analysis.

However strongly motivated the human factors practitioner is, it will always be necessary to be able to present mental model theory in this kind of packaged form to justify its use. At present this is not possible. Mental models provide us with a convenient way to look at an interface design or evaluation problem, but remain for internal consumption only. I will now describe some of the problems which I feel preclude the use of mental models as a tool:

a) The user's mental model is hard to get at

No standard methodology has been accepted and packaged as a validated tool. Techniques developed by individual researchers for their own purposes tend to be limited in their applicability to other domains and lack validation in other domains or even in the domain to which they were originally applied. Acceptance as a validated tool is critical: whatever you think of their relative merits and validities, it is easier to persuade someone to pay you to apply an Eysenck Personality Inventory (EPI: Eysenck and Eysenck, 1963) than some new technique you have developed yourself and which few people have heard of.

b) The process of eliciting a mental model obscures its internal inconsistencies

When a user has become a little familiar with a system, their mental model will be mostly accurate in so far as it leads to effective interaction. It is the inaccurate remainder of the model which leads to breakdowns in interaction and which is thus the bit of real interest because it highlights areas where improvement is required. Amongst these will be inconsistencies; beliefs about the system which contradict each other and so cannot both be true and in turn must lead to errors. Inconsistencies, then, are an important part of the model which an investigator must be aware of.

The internalized flowchart type of mental model cannot represent the sort of internal inconsistency that makes a mental model worth examining. Although Johnson-Laird's notion of mental models allows representation of internal consistencies in the user's model of the interface, there is a problem in eliciting and representing this information simply because it is internally inconsistent.

The easiest way to illustrate the difficulty in capturing a mental model which contains inconsistencies is to give an example. Until a few years ago, my geographical knowledge of the north of England was very limited. Never having spent any time travelling in that area, I had no idea where cities like Bradford, Manchester and Leeds were in relation to each other. Had I been asked to indicate on a map where I thought Manchester was and later, in different contexts, to do the same for Leeds and Bradford, it is likely that I would put all three in the same place. This is because of the lack of detail in my mental model, and because the time separation between the events did not allow me to impose the consistency which I know must exist, i.e. three cities cannot all be in the same place. By asking the questions in the right way, an inconsistency in my mental model was revealed. Had I been asked to perform the same task in an experiment one afternoon, I would have been forced to place the cities in different locations. This placement would be done perhaps on logical grounds or arbitrarily, but I would not allow an inconsistency to appear in my answer; I am not capable of representing such an inconsistency to myself let alone anyone else.

This is the problem with explicit methods of eliciting user's mental models; when required to express their beliefs directly users cannot express internal inconsistencies of this sort. Thus an explicit method cannot capture them. You cannot devise a way of eliciting inconsistencies without having some suspicion about what they are; only by suspecting that my mental model of the north of England has three cities in the same place could anyone devise the specific conditions under which to ask me the questions which would reveal the inconsistency.

c) Mental models are explanatory, not predictive

Mental models are never identified in their purest form. They are identified by the symptoms they produce in the system user. As such they tend to be explanatory (of the phenomena which reveal them) rather than predictive (except perhaps of related symptoms in other aspects of system functionality which have not yet been observed). In this role, mental models provide a fire-fighting technique rather than a design tool.

d) The process of elicitation may be more informative than the model itself

The process of eliciting a user's mental model inevitably leads the psychologist to stumble upon user interface problems. Thus by the time it is elicited (as far as this is possible) its usefulness is often complete. While this is not a problem in itself, it perhaps suggests that we should be placing more emphasis on the process of identifying a user's mental model than the form and nature of the model itself.

e) Mental models do not account for all aspects of user–system interaction

The last and most critical shortcoming of current approaches to the use of mental models is that they are not complete. They do not account for a number of crucial aspects of user–computer interaction which need to be addressed in any comprehensive interface evaluation or design. Generally speaking these are aspects of interaction which are not attributable to belief. Three such aspects which I will now discuss are alarms, screen layout and the main subject of this chapter, presence.

Alarms

A user's different reactions to various types of alarms cannot be attributed to beliefs. The superior effect of a bell over a computer-generated beep is not due to belief but to phenomena much nearer the level of perception.

Screen layout

Here different comprehension of information presented visually may arise as a result of colour use and grouping. While not as low level as the phenomena determining reactions to alarms, the phenomena acting here are certainly at a cognitive level lower than belief. A user may react differently to the same piece of information presented in different styles. In particular the perceived force of an instruction or recommendation may be largely a result of the style of presentation. This phenomenon cannot be accounted for in terms of beliefs.

Presence

Lastly and of most interest here are the user reactions which arise as a result of human-like features of the interface. A car which talks produces a very different user reaction from one that simply flashes a light to signify the same state of affairs. This class of phenomena, which I have called presence, is what I'll now go on to discuss in detail.

18.3 Presence: examples and characteristics

A number of examples can be cited which present a view of computer systems not as socially neutral but as capable of varying along a continuum which might loosely be called sociability by which I mean capability of eliciting user reactions which are learned from their experience of interacting with humans.

18.3.1 The computer as socially neutral

At the neutral end of the scale we can see the computer eliciting behaviour which is different from that elicited by a human counterpart as a result of its lack of social features. Following a suggestion from Slack and Van Cura (1968) that computers might be more successful than human interviewers in collecting information that the interviewee found embarrassing, Lucas, Mullin, Luna and McInroy (1977) compared the responses of clients with alcohol dependence to questions about how much they had drunk in the past week using human and computer interview techniques. In the human interview, the questions were asked by a psychiatrist, while in the computer interview questions were presented on a computer screen and the interviewee responded by pressing appropriate keys. In the computer interview they confessed to drinking around 33% more than in the human interview. The suggested account for this was that the computer facilitated honesty because the immediate threat of disapproval one would fear from a human was absent.

It is important to note that the respondents knew the psychiatrist would have access to their responses. So the effect was not the result of belief about who would get to know what they said. It was the absence of the social immediacy which led them to report their drinking more honestly. Unfortunately Lucas et al did not state the exact form of questions asked by the computer, so it is impossible to tell whether this was controlled between conditions.

To provide a more exacting comparison, I carried out a more carefully controlled study where subjects' responses to EPI lie scores were compared across parallel forms of the EPI. One version was administered by a human interviewer and the other by a computer. In both cases subjects were only required to respond "yes" or "no". Lie scores under the computer administration were significantly lower than those in the condition where responses were given to a human, confirming the hypothesis that the physical presence of a human leads respondents to fake good to a greater extent that when a machine is collecting the responses.

These two studies show the computer in the role we typically associate it with: that of a socially neutral machine which cannot elicit reactions which a human will. Further along the sociability dimension there are examples which show the computer exerting influence on users in a way normally thought to be exclusively human.

18.3.2 Social reactions to the computer

a) Convergence

Convergence is a phenomenon observed in human dialogue whereby each speaker tends to adopt features of the other's speech. Convergence is observed in features as diverse as frequency of pauses, speech rate and frequency of interruptions (Giles and Powesland, 1975). Current accounts of convergence are socially based (e.g. Giles, Mulac, Bradac and Johnson, 1987). We would expect, therefore, that a dialogue with a socially neutral partner would not show convergence. But converg-ence has been observed in human–computer dialogue.

I first had a hint of such a possibility in my early work in speech interface design. The first speech interface I ever used was speaker-dependent, requiring each user to train the system by recording templates of each of the command words. Training was carried out as follows:

System:	Please repeat each word after the tone. Train <tone>
User:	Train
System:	Directory <tone>
User:	Directory
System:	Setup <tone>
User:	Setup

.

.

.

| System: | And lastly, Finish <tone> |
| User: | Finish |

This dialogue design caused two problems for the system user. In saying "Setup", the speaker who had recorded the system messages placed stress on the first syllable. Users showed a tendency to use the same intonation when responding to that prompt during training, although some users preferred to stress the second syllable when they used the command in their subsequent use of the system. They had converged on the pronunciation of the prompt, then reverted to their preferred pronunciation, which caused some recognition problems.

Another problem occurred with the command "Finish". Because it was last in the training session, the speaker who recorded the prompts had naturally adopted a falling intonation. This was also converged upon by users with the result that their subsequent utterances of the word as a command provided poor matches with the recorded template.

I first attempted to provide a formal demonstration of convergence in human–computer dialogue in the context of a research project on development of a natural language database querying system. A central feature of this project was its approach of identifying and exploiting phenomena observed in human–human dialogue for use in human–computer dialogue. It was felt that considerable improvement in the natural language interaction could be achieved if users of a natural language database querying system would converge to the terms and structures used by the system in its outputs: appropriate design of system outputs would lead to convergence towards terms and syntax most easily understood by the system.

To investigate the feasibility of such a technique we ran a "Wizard of Oz" study which is reported in detail in Leiser (1988; 1989a). In essence the study was as follows: subjects were told they were interacting with a natural language database querying system. They were required to make queries of the system in order to access information missing from a table they were given. In response to each query, the experimenter playing the role of the computer presented a paraphrase of the query. This was constructed using a carefully controlled set of terms and syntactic structures. Subjects had to confirm that this was what they meant before the answers were provided. The design incorporated controls to eliminate any effect of pre-existing user bias towards particular terms or structures and also eliminated any possible account for results in terms of subjects' being reinforced for using the desired terms and structures in their subsequent queries.

Analysis of subjects' responses revealed a gradual adoption of the terms and structures used by the system in the paraphrases of queries. Here the subjects were responding to the outputs of the system as they would to a human dialogue participant in so far as they were converging on characteristics of its output. The controls employed eliminate the possibility that this was a result of learning contingencies: it seems to have been the result of automatic application of strategies learned from human–human dialogue.

b) Human-like modes of interaction between humans and computers

A number of examples can be cited where the same information has a different effect on the user depending on whether it is presented by some mechanical device or via some output medium which has certain characteristics which can be regarded as human.

Replacing beeps with voice warnings

Informal evidence of user reactions being affected by human characteristics in system output can be found in situations where a simple "beep" indication is replaced by a spoken message, although the meaning of the indication remains the same. When such a change was made in the Austin Maestro's seat belt warning, users found the new spoken warning much more irritating than the original simple "beep". The reasons for this have not been formally investigated but it may be due to a feeling approaching betrayal when what at first is alerting and interesting because of its distinctly human nature transpires to be a mere automaton, just as the "Have a nice day" you hear so often in the States loses its charm when you realize it is not a heart-felt greeting to a weary traveller but an automatic response to all clients which has been designed to create the impression of friendliness.

Whatever the reasons, it is clear that changing the indication from an undisguisedly mechanical one to a human-like one lends the system presence, which changes the user's reaction significantly.

Talking to machines instead of typing

Voice input is also regarded as special by users. Although they have no difficulty in grasping the concept of communicating with what is a social void via a keyboard, people find talking to a machine an uncomfortable experience, initially at least. This seems to be because you cannot model the listener in the way that you are used to doing in conversation with humans. Every aspect of conversational speech from content to intonation is influenced by the speaker's mental model of the listener. When one has no assumptions whatsoever about the listener, talking becomes very difficult. Using a keyboard for the first time, there are also no tacit assumptions about the receiver, but there are also no communication-by-typing habits which rely on feedback from the receiver and which would have to be unlearned or modified.

As well as causing problems in the use of speech recognition interfaces, the discomfort which arises when trying to talk to a listener who you cannot model accounts for the high "slam-down" rate in conventional telephone answering machines; although they know that what they say will be eventually heard by a human, callers have difficulty in speaking to a void. Thirty-four per cent of callers avoid this situation by hanging up immediately when confronted by an answering machine (Furner, 1987). By giving the dialogue the human characteristic of asking a series of relevant questions, Furner persuaded 80% of callers to provide all the required information where only 25.6% did so with a conventional machine.

These examples provide evidence that adding the human characteristics of accepting speech input rather than keyboard input and engaging in interactive dialogue rather than one-sided dialogue make enormous differences to the user's performance which cannot be accounted for in terms of beliefs. The differences are due to presence which is the result of the addition of human characteristics.

Making the user rather than an external object the subject of interaction

The vast majority of user–computer interaction scenarios consist of collaborative manipulation of an object which is neither the interface itself nor the user; a document, a spreadsheet, a character in an adventure world for example. Any reference to the user by the computer is incidental, arising usually through the need to resolve ambiguities or illegal input. Dialogues of this sort are emotionally safe, seldom eliciting any emotional reaction from the user except in cases of repeated ambiguous or illegal input. The affective paucity is due to the subject matter rather than the fact that a computer assumes one half of the interaction. The situation is very different when the user becomes the object of the interaction. There is a wealth of anecdotal accounts of user interaction with ELIZA, Weizenbaum's (1966) simulation of a psychiatrist engaged in psychoanalytic interview of a client, played by the user. Here the subject of interaction is explicitly the user and many become heavily engrossed in the dialogue and emotionally upset at the experience.

So again we see the user's reactions to the computer heavily influenced by something other than beliefs. Users are in no doubt that they are interacting with a machine. The system's chosen subject of interaction lends it presence, which has a major impact on the user.

18.3.3 Implications of presence for human–computer interaction

a) Characteristics of presence

There are a number of points that should be made about presence to distinguish it from other concepts and to further define it.

Presence is not the phenomenon whereby users of computer equipment refer to it using terminology normally reserved for referring to human activity ("It thinks that was the filename you just typed" or "It knows who you are from your login"). These terms are just convenient metaphors to describe the situation; try thinking of any term used in computing which is not a metaphor, or a dead metaphor. This user reaction is not a social reaction, just use of a convenient human metaphor.

Presence is not the same as anthropomorphism either. Anthropomorphism refers to the explanation and prediction of behaviour by attribution of human characteristics: it is concerned with belief, either that the system has human capabilities or that it can be usefully treated as if it does, human performance providing a convenient and familiar model of behaviour compared to a void or a complex alternative. Presence does not operate at the level of belief in the way that anthropomorphism does, although some examples of presence might be described as anthropomorphic (e.g. reacting more quickly to a spoken warning message if the phrasing and intonation imply urgency). Presence is an over-learned reaction, not based on belief but on life–long habits learned through experience of interaction with humans.

The continuum described above of relationships which may exist between a computer and a human user has a parallel in human-human communication. Rutter, Stephenson and Dewey (1981) described a continuum they called "cuelessness" on the basis of their observations of humans in dialogue in a number of constrained communications scenarios. These included use of blind subjects, audio only communication, communication where both participants were in the same room but visually separated by a curtain and, as a control, face-to-face communication. They found differences in the degree of task-orientation, depersonalization and spontaneity of the conversation arising from these manipulations. These could not be attributed singly to visual communication or to physical presence but were accounted for by the combined influence of the two, cuelessness.

In simple terms, cuelessness, like presence is an aspect of a communications situation which determines the nature of the relationship between the two participants. In the case of cuelessness, the relationship is between two humans, whereas in the case of presence, the relationship is between a human and a computer, the aspects affecting this relationship are all features of the computer, and only the human's participation in the dialogue is affected.

It is not clear how far this high level parallel would survive under detailed examination, but it may be useful to look at the research on cuelessness to identify some factors which may determine the level and likely effects of presence in a human-computer dialogue.

b) Effects of presence

When presence arises by chance in an interface its effects are more likely to be harmful than beneficial. "Social" reactions are complex because they are learned from interaction with humans who are complex. Thus the learned reactions which arise as a result of Presence will be more complex than those appropriate to human-computer interaction because the computer's interpretation is limited compared to the human's. This may have two consequences. The system may fail to interpret an input which has been shaped in some way by presence (e.g. a spoken input shaped by convergence on the intonation of the computer's spoken prompt) or the user may expect different reactions to two inputs which differ in some aspect not discernible by the computer (e.g. if a speech input/output device uses different volume levels to indicate the degree of urgency in the content of an output, the user may adopt a similar technique in providing command input – the system would either not discern the difference or fail to hear the softer version).

c) Exploiting presence in user interface design

Presence can be harnessed and exploited to improve interaction between the user and the computer. I have described the possibilities of exploiting reactions to presence in detail elsewhere (Leiser, 1989b). Three examples are described below:

1. Because users of a speech interface converge on the pronunciation of system outputs, these can be recorded in such a way as to improve recognition performance; the rate, pitch and intonation should be close to that of the ideal for input.
2. If a natural language dialogue system uses terms and syntax which are within its own range of coverage, convergence on the part of the user will lead to improved comprehension of input.
3. If spoken warning messages are produced with intonation and phrasing appropriate to the urgency, reliability etc. of their content, the user's reactions are more likely to be appropriate than when deadpan intonation and standardized phrasing are used, as the user will naturally react in a manner appropriate to the style of presentation. This is a simple extension of the general principle that natural stimulus–response pairings should be used in any interface situation.

18.4 The way forward for mental model theories

Presence and the other phenomena listed above have a number of implications for the exploitability of mental models in user interface design and evaluation.

The theories of mental models are still close to the conceptual stage. They have not been developed into a set of tools in the same way as learning theory spawned a set of tools for behaviour modification among other things. Any theory at this stage lives on borrowed time as far as widespread acceptance in applied fields is concerned; there is a danger that it gets the image of being something that "people have been going on about for years but nothing useful has ever come of". Serious development is needed soon.

We need a way of getting at a user's mental model of a system. Such a technique would have to meet four requirements;

1. Some degree of consensus on its validity.
2. Ability to capture internal inconsistencies in a user's model.
3. Easily administered.

4. Easily replicated results.

A way of predicting a user's mental model is required. Studies of users' mental models are inevitably post hoc; a system has been built, and users are invited to interact with it and then provide data which help the experimenter to determine what their model of the system is. This allows adjustment of the design to avoid any problems arising from an inappropriate mental model of the system. It would be preferable to be able to predict the average user's mental model from the user interface specification, perhaps by a walk-through procedure, so that user difficulties can be eliminated prior to costly implementation.

Were there such a method of predicting users' mental models and from these, their behaviour would require extensive validation prior to wide acceptance. Furthermore the value of the validated method would need to be demonstrated in a meaningful way, showing perhaps how problem X had been identified prior to implementation of system A whereas the similar system B which did not use the method only came upon the problem many months and pounds of implementation costs later.

If mental model theories are to be useful in an applied sense they need to be extended to encompass a wider range of phenomena than they can at present. Among these must be those described above: they are alarms, screen layout and presence. No doubt there are others which potential users of mental models could identify.

Postscript

Finding myself in the unusual position of the one who is demanding solutions rather than being asked to provide them, I have placed an intentionally tall order. My primary motivation, however, has been to point out what I feel is needed to turn the theory of mental models from an interesting idea into a valuable tool.

Acknowledgements

Thanks to Peter Mason of YARD Ltd who made many useful suggestions in the process of quality assurance of this paper. This paper is dedicated to George Leiser, my father, who died during its preparation.

References

Eysenck, H.J. and Eysenck, S.B G. (1963). *The Eysenck Personality Inventory.* London: University of London Press.

Furner, S.M. (1987). Rapid prototyping as a design tool for dialogues employing voice recognition. In Laver, J. and Jack, M.A. (eds) *Proceedings of European Conference on Speech Technology, Volume 2.* CEP Consultants Ltd, 26–28 Albany Street, Edinburgh, EH1 3QH.

Giles, H. and Powesland, P. F. (1975). *Speech Styles and Social Evaluation.* London: Academic Press.

Giles, H., Mulac, A., Bradac, J.J. and Johnson, P. (1987). Speech accommodation theory: the first decade and beyond. In McLaughlin, M. L. (ed.) *Communication Yearbook 10*, 13–48. Beverly Hills, Ca.: Sage.

Johnson-Laird, P. N. (1983). *Mental Models.* Cambridge: CUP.

Leiser, R.G. (1988). Improving natural language understanding by modelling human dialogue. In *Putting the Technology to Use: Proceedings of the 5th Annual ESPRIT Conference.* Amsterdam: North-Holland.

Leiser, R.G. (1989a). Exploiting convergence to improve natural language understanding. *Interacting with Computers 1*, 3.

Leiser, R.G. (1989b). Improving natural language and speech interfaces by the use of metalinguistic phenomena. *Applied Ergonomics 20*, 168–173.

Lucas, R.W., Mullin, P.J., Luna, C.B.X. and McInroy, D.C. (1977). Psychiatrists and computers as interrogators of patients with alcohol-related illnesses: a comparison. *British Journal of Psychiatry 131*, 160–167.

Rutter, D.R., Stephenson, G.M. and Dewey, M.E. (1981). Visual communication and the content and style of conversation. *British Journal of Psychology 20*, 41–52.

Slack, W.V. and Van Cura, L.J. (1968). Patient reaction to computer-based medical interviewing. *Computers and Biomedical Research 1*, 527.

Weizenbaum, J. (1966). ELIZA – A computer program for the study of natural language communication between man and machine, *Communications of the ACM 9*, 36–45.

Chapter 19

Social and Pragmatic Issues for Mental Model Accounts

Andrew Rutherford

Both of the chapters in this part deal with topics where there is a requirement for further development of mental model accounts. Although pragmatic and social issues are raised in other chapters, Manktelow and Over, and Leiser, through consideration and discussion, emphasize such theoretical issues much more than the authors of any other chapter.

Manktelow and Over present a very lucid argument for placing the study of deontic logic firmly within the sphere of mental models research. They present theoretical analysis and empirical evidence which supports the view that an adequate account of deontic thinking must accommodate mental representation of not only semantic, but also pragmatic and social factors. They claim that given such requirements, it is natural to use the mental models framework to provide an integrated account.

In their analysis of the nature of deontic thought, Manktelow and Over highlight a number of issues that previous accounts have neglected. However, Manktelow and Over argue that these issues must be addressed if a full account of deontic thinking is to be presented. For example, according to Manktelow and Over, the tendency to regard abstract and concrete versions of deontic problems as formally equivalent has led to spurious claims concerning the effect of problem content and has deflected attention from the true nature of deontic reasoning. They claim that a real deontic problem is one in which the law stated prescribes, but may be violated by people's behaviour. In contrast, abstract problem rules describe arbitrary matters of fact. Therefore, these rules do not describe real-world states of

MODELS IN THE MIND:
Theory, perspective and applications. ISBN 0-12-592970-6

affairs and consequently, the rules have no meaningful correspondence with people's behaviour.

Through consideration of how a person might conform to or violate a deontic conditional, Manktelow and Over's analysis begs the question of what makes a deontic conditional true or false? In part, it is the ability of mental models to provide such a semantic account (in contrast to the pragmatic accounts provided by Cheng and Holyoak, 1985; Cosmides, 1989) that Manktelow and Over regard as useful. However, the issues raised by Stenning in chapter three, regarding the relationship between semantics and syntactic mechanisms suggests that such provision is not so readily at hand.

Manktelow and Over describe subjective utility and social roles as two interactive factors that are crucial to an understanding of deontic reasoning. Neither of these factors are mentioned by the existing schema models. Social roles define the subjective utilities that determine which deontic conditionals are accepted as true, as well as the different consequences of conforming to or violating the deontic conditionals. This account relies on a determination of subjective probability, that is a person's estimate of how likely something is to happen. For deontic statements therefore, the concept of truth is a subjective one, depending upon subjective utility and subjective probability. Manktelow and Over assert that subjects in a selection task are able to engage the same epistemological method of determining the truth of a conditional obligation as a person in a real deontic situation. Therefore, the data from their reported experiments can be claimed to strongly confirm the predictions of their analysis of deontic reasoning in terms of subjective utilities and social roles. These are results which would not have been predicted by Cheng and Holyoak's account, nor could the account provided by Cosmides accommodate the full range of results. However, although Manktelow and Over criticize two schema-ased models, it is worth bearing in mind that it is the specific nature of the accounts that have been criticised and not the schema framework which contributes to mental model theory (see chapter 4).

One disappointment of Manktelow and Over's chapter is that they seem to have been persuaded by Cosmides justification of her account. They remark that as good deontic thinking is connected with successful behaviour in the sense of getting what we prefer, on evolutionary grounds it is expected that people will be equiped with a good deontic thinking ability. Given the complexity of natural selection for even simple physical attributes (e.g. Futuyma, 1979), psychologists would do well to refrain from generally uninformed, most likely spurious and unnecessary speculation.

From the perspective of the human-factors consultant operating in the commercial world, Leiser describes the sort of obstacles encountered in the attempt to sell and utilize the notion of mental models, particularly with reference to interface design and evaluation. Two sets of problems are described for current mental models accounts. The first concerns difficulties associated with the identification of mental models, and the second concerns certain aspects of human–computer interaction (HCI) which generally are not accommodated by HCI accounts.

In the context of theory development, Rutherford and Wilson (this volume) concluded that it is more important to specify in detailed process terms a hypothesized mental model and subsequently, assess its validity, than it is to provide a detailed account of the rationale that enables these stages. In contrast, Leiser claims that for commercial work, one of the major difficulties with the mental model notion is the lack of a general purpose, valid and reliable method for identifying mental models.

However, he also argues that due to the response strategies employed by users, attempts to determine mental models by overt (or explicit) methods will fail to identify important inconsistencies between system and user conception. Moreover, Leiser claims that it is not possible to devise means of determining such inconsistencies without having some initial idea as to what they might be. Leiser's final criticism on this topic concerns the limits of the mental model notion as a design tool. As mental models are identified by inference from empirical phenomena, it is argued that primarily they provide post hoc rather than a priori accounts. Consequently, the mental model notion is useful for providing some insight into users' performance on existing systems, but they provide little assistance at the design stage.

The set of difficulties described by Leiser illustrate the problem of applying and the doubts over the utility of the mental model notion in commercial settings that often are voiced by practitioners. However, the mental model notion is a theoretical construct, the main purpose of which is to provide an account of phenomena. It is not conceived as a tool to use in systems design (see Wilson and Rutherford, 1989, for further discussion of this issue). Nevertheless, it may contribute to system design, but the way in which it does so lies in the hands of those applying the theoretical construct.

The parallel with behaviourist learning theory drawn by Leiser can be used to illustrate this point. While there is no doubt that this theory of learning inspired many application techniques, still they had to be derived and developed from the theoretical base; they did not appear just as a result of the expression of learning theory. Similarly, many approaches and methods of eliciting mental model information have been reported in the literature (see Rutherford and Wilson, this volume). However, as was the case with the animal experiments which constituted much of the original learning theory literature, these methods are likely to require development for specific applied investigations.

Therefore, it is the reponsibility of those members of the applied research community who feel that the mental model notion has applied utility to equip themselves with appropriate application tools. Perhaps false expectations have been encouraged by the seemingly obvious validity of the idea and the apparent ease of deriving mental models from artificially simplified test systems (Wilson and Rutherford, 1989). As suggested by Leiser, it may be that the techniques developed to identify mental models will be of most utility and, as occurred with behaviourist learning theory, that these techniques will continue to be of use, even when their original theoretical base has been superseded.

Having said this, it is revealing to ask if the difficulties listed by Leiser in applying mental models are different to any significant extent to those of applying any other such notion. For example, in many other areas of research it is necessary to employ covert methods of investigation to ensure valid results. Research in social psychology quickly springs to mind, but such methods are needed in studies of cognition, such as with unintentional learning and aspects of language use and comprehension.

In psychology generally, many phenomena are counter-intuitive and so, they are unlikely to be self-evident. Often a great deal of research precedes accounts which later may seem to be "common-sense". Subsequently, analyses can be directed by expectations and indeed, classical experimentation relies on such a sequence of events (Rutherford and Wilson, this volume). Expectations are built on knowledge gained from past experience. Therefore, in principle, there is no difference between the situation described by Leiser where the practitioner needs to have some idea of what inconsistencies might exist before he can examine them and that encountered in academic research.

Leiser's final criticism on this topic, which is that the mental model notion provides little assistance at the design stage has a counterpart in task analysis: before a system is constructed, it is not possible to carry out a task analysis. At this design point a task synthesis is carried out. In other words, the best guess as to what the new system will be like is used to investigate how it may be used. Indeed, there is more than a coincidental parallel between task analysis/synthesis and mental models. The task analysis/synthesis can be thought of as a tool to reveal the users' possible mental model (e.g. Katzeff, 1990; Sanderson, Verhage and Flud, 1989; and see Shepherd, 1989).

The second set of problems described by Leiser concerns aspects of HCI that current mental model accounts do not accommodate. The effects of different types of alarms, different screen colours and patterns of behaviour imported from social interaction are listed as examples. Of these, Leiser concentrates on the latter, which he terms presence.

A variety of examples of presence are provided to illustrate the claim that HCI varies along a continuum of presence. However, as well as providing examples of HCI that might be located at points along the presence continuum, Leiser mentions instances where HCI appears to exhibit zero effect of presence also. Clearly, such phenomena are concordant with the notion of a continuum, but at such an early stage of theoretical account, the possibility that such phenomena are the result of different processes should not be discarded.

Another problematic theoretical issue is Leiser's use of the word belief. This term is not defined, but it would seem to refer to a level of conscious cognition that is provided by mental model processes. However, on this point Leiser may well respond that such issues fall within the academic psychologists' and not the consultant psychologists' realm of responsibility.

A need for theoretical clarification is to be expected when an attempt is made to marry previously disparate accounts. Nevertheless, if academic theories are to have actual impact in the real world, then such marriages must succeed. Given the impact that the HCI phenomena which Leiser terms presence might have on the operation of computer systems, a good understanding of the underlying processes is essential.

The apparent need to involve social factors in accounts of deontic logic and presence reveals that considerable theoretical development of the mental model notion is required. Nevertheless, despite the need for such theoretical development, amongst information processing based characterizations, the mental models framework appears to be the most likely source of adequate theoretical accounts.

References

Cheng, P.W. and Holyoak, K.J. (1985). Pragmatic reasoning schemas. *Cognitive Psychology 17*, 391–416.

Cosmides, L. (1989). The logic of social exchange: has natural selection shaped how humans reason? Studies with the Wason selection task. *Cognition 31*, 187–276.

Futuyama, D.J. (1979).   *Evolutionary Biology.* Sunderland, Ma.: Sinauer
    Associates.

Katzeff, C. (1990).   System demands on mental models for a full text database.
    International Journal of Man–Machine Studies 32, 483–509.

Sanderson, P.M., Verhage, A.G. and Flud, R.B. (1989).   State-space and verbal
    protocol methods for studying the human operator in process control.
    Ergonomics 32, 1343–1372.

Shepherd, A. (1989).   Analysis and training in information technology tasks. In
    Diaper, D. (ed.) *Task–Analysis For Human–Computer Interaction.*
    Chichester: Ellis Horwood.

Wilson, J.R. and Rutherford, A. (1989).   Mental models: theory and application in
    human factors. *Human Factors 31,* 617–634.

Chapter 20

Future Directions in Mental Models Research

Yvonne Rogers and Andrew Rutherford

20.1 Introduction

The collection of chapters in this book has shown clearly that there is no agreed definition of what is a mental model. Indeed, such is the confusion and ambiguity that a growing, albeit implicit, stigma is being associated with the term (even the name of the book was changed from the title of the workshop for "publishing reasons"). While Brewer (1987, p.192) proclaimed that "there is real trouble with the term mental model, O'Malley and Draper begin their chapter with the polemic sentence, "talking about mental models can be dangerous". Although the use of such statements may be more for rhetorical effect, they do highlight the problem that has resulted from an intuitively appealing, but under specified construct being embraced by a number of different researchers. While individual accounts are precise, the overall effect of diverse explications is that the concept has come to lack coherence.

Part of the problem stems from the rather unfortunate use of the identical title, *Mental Models*, by Gentner and Stevens (1983) and Johnson-Laird (1983) for their respective books, which were published in the same year. Although related, the chapters in the two volumes refer to theoretical conceptions with significant differences. To distinguish between the two, Brewer (1987) suggests that the models described in the collection presented by Gentner and Stevens, which are concerned primarily with models of causality in physical domains, should be termed *causal mental models*. On the other hand, the mental models described by Johnson-Laird can be viewed more generally, having "a content and form that fits them to

MODELS IN THE MIND:
Theory, perspective and applications. ISBN 0–12–592970–6

their purpose, whether it be to explain, or predict, or to control" (Johnson-Laird, 1983, p.410).

Several of the contributions in this volume have redefined the concept of a mental model by introducing new terms to refer to specific types of representation in given contexts. Examples include distributed representations (O'Malley and Draper) and multi-record representations (Duff). In doing so, they have moved away from both Johnson-Laird's (1983) original thesis and the models presented in the Gentner and Stevens collection. However, others have continued to develop their analyses closely within Johnson-Laird's theoretical framework (e.g. Byrne; Manktelow and Over; Payne). Alternatively, Anderson, Tolmie, Howe, Mayes and MacKenzie have taken the eclectic middle ground by combining opposing generative mental model theories to explain the dissociation of knowledge that occurs between the ability to predict and explain physical phenomena.

Nevertheless, while the chapters in this volume point to a lack of explicit commonality in the use of the mental model concept, it is interesting to note that implicitly, still there is a common thread behind the various research pursuits. In our discussions of the chapters, the editors agreed that the disparate manifestations of the original concept continue to allude to the importance of the dynamics of mental representations and more specifically, to the notion of the "runnability" of mental models. Central to the notion of running a mental model is the on-line operation of a mental simulation of some aspect of the real world. For example, if asked what would happen when you threw a banana and an apple you might run a mental simulation in which the throwing of each piece of fruit is imagined and their respective trajectories determined.

The importance of mental models' runnability is that it provides the means by which inferences can be made when having to decide, predict or interact in various domains. In the context of reasoning, the construction and inspection of mental models allows alternatives to be evaluated, providing the basis from which a conclusion can be drawn. When making predictions about physical domains, mental simulations enable inferences about future states of a system or object to be derived. With people, computers or other cognitive artefacts, running a mental model facilitates interaction.

20.2   The context of mental model accounts

Given the amount of mental models research, it might be expected that there would be clear advantages to this theoretical conceptualization. Yet accounts of mental model processes are described in such differing terms of abstraction and at such a variety of levels of explanation that apart from the notion of mental model processes enabling mental simulations, it is difficult to identify further common features that might provide this advantage. Moreover, not all researchers would support the view that mental simulation is a psychological phenomenon that requires special account. In particular, Rips (1986) has questioned the psychological validity of this whole approach. Referring to work by Forbus (1983) and de Kleer and Brown (1983), Rips claims that the extensive and complex branching of possible states involved in such simulations makes processing demands that are not realistic in psychological terms. Although Kuipers and Chiu (1987) have addressed this particular issue, the associated point made by Rips and supported empirically by Gentner (cited by Rips, 1986) ,that generally people do not engage in full scale simulations, stands. Nevertheless, because normally people do not embark upon complete simulations does not mean that they never employ such simulation in reasoning, and certainly it does not mean that people reason by employing some propositional calculus, as Rips has argued. Indeed, the difficulty that the vast majority of people experience when they try to employ such logical calculuses to reason must undermine seriously the plausibility of this sort of account. Moreover, the empirical work of such as Kuipers and Kassirer (1984) supports the view that people do use a form of qualitative simulation in their reasoning. Consequently, it becomes an empirical issue to determine the circumstances which elicit mental simulation and its degree, or alternative reasoning methods.

The question of what theoretical advantages mental model accounts provide over other theoretical perspectives has been raised in terms of the distinction between mental models and background knowledge (e.g. Rouse and Morris, 1986; Wilson and Rutherford, 1989; Rutherford and Wilson, 1991). Frequently, the exact nature of this distinction is hindered by the polysemy of many of the terms employed. Often representation is discussed without regard to the algorithms that constitute and extract information (Palmer, 1978), while one person's algorithm is another's process or another's routine, or even sub-routine (e.g. Marr, 1982 cf. Palmer, 1978). Although the mental model notion developed in the context of knowledge schemata that described the organization and use of background knowledge, the exact relationship between the two theoretical constructs has exercised the thoughts of several writers. Rumelhart (1984) describes a mental model as the total set of schemata instantiated at the time, while Johnson-Laird (1983) suggests that schemata provide the procedures from which mental models are constructed. Manktelow and Jones (1987) also provide an account of mental models in which they are described as arising from schemata. Brewer (1987) regards mental models as creations of the moment and although the same mental model may be reconstructed numerous times, it is schemata that are considered to be stored and activated. Bainbridge (1988, p.82) alludes to this distinction too, when she states that for ergonomists Johnson-Laird's terminology is confusing, as he uses the term mental model "to designate the temporary data structure built up during understanding, rather than the background knowledge it refers to".

Norman and Bobrow (1979) developed a similar notion to mental models directly from schema theory. They characterized the interpretation of external experiences in terms of schemata, which they saw as capable of being formed into composites called descriptions. This is similar to Rumelhart's assessment. However, in contrast to Brewer's distinction, Norman and Bobrow suggest that the description will be stored, or at least the ability to reconstruct it will be stored. Nevertheless, despite such theoretical deliberations, Johnson-Laird (1983) claims that formal distinctions or relations between mental models and schemata cannot be made, as both theoretical constructs remain to be defined sufficiently.

Given the theoretical relationship between schemata and mental models, it should be evident that the mental model notion is redundant if it lacks computational ability. As background knowledge, in terms of schemata, is taken to have a computational capability, it is the dynamic computational ability of a mental model, beyond that presumed of background knowledge, that provides the notion with its theoretical utility.

20.3   The nature of mental model accounts

It has been said that across mental model accounts much of the theoretical inconsistency is due to their descriptions employing many terms of abstraction and various levels of explanation. Given this state of affairs, questions about the development of theoretical descriptions of mental models are bound to be asked. Nevertheless, while only further research can supply definite answers to questions such as whether a single and appropriate form of mental model description might be found, it is possible at present to consider some of the issues of difficulty and to indicate a direction in which research might proceed.

Philosophy, theology and literature, as well as psychology, have attempted to describe thought and action. These efforts have provided a huge variety of accounts, with almost as many modes of expression. Indeed, in so far as any description of a phenomenon is an abstraction of the reality, there appears to be an unlimited number of forms of descriptive abstraction available.

Given such a situation, it is possible to conceive of the different modes of expression occupying an account space. Such a space would be occupied by both parallel and intersecting descriptive abstractions. With such a conception, one sub-set of descriptions can be regarded as employing abstractions that may be reduced from one to the other, to provide increasingly detailed accounts of phenomena. The reducibility of such descriptions is dependent on veridical relations between parallel levels of descriptive abstraction. The accounts of atoms and molecules and their relations in physics, chemistry and physiology are examples of such levels of explanation.

Commonly, it is agreed that the preferred level of an account of a phenomenon depends on the purpose to which the account is to be put. For example, as the oxygen carrying capability of haemoglobin is determined by the shape of the molecule, accounts of this phenomenon are pitched best at this level. Although ultimately, this phenomenon is related to atomic physics, for most purposes this level of account is unnecessary. Nevertheless, while the purpose of an account sets its preferred level, the degree of understanding of a phenomenon is defined by the number of veridical parallel levels in terms of which the phenomenon can be described. But given the number of descriptive abstractions available, how is an appropriate veridical route through the parallel levels to be determined?

Within this conceptual system, it is useful to consider another dimension on which an account may vary. A vitally important aspect of any descriptive abstraction is the extent to which it details a mechanism (i.e. a process) that can give rise to the phenomenon under study (Allport, 1980; Johnson-Laird, 1983; Winograd, 1977). Marr (1982) has identified three abstracted descriptions of a process, which may or may not be related in a veridical manner. However, given the preceding conception, it is likely that many more than three abstracted descriptions of a process are available (cf. Rumelhart and McClelland, 1985). Nevertheless, despite the number of descriptive abstractions of processes available, focusing on this form of account should not only provide some coherence between descriptions, but also it may facilitate the identification of a veridical route between various process oriented descriptive abstractions.

For mental models research where the numerous mental model descriptions can engender bewilderment and confusion, it is important to distinguish between the notions of descriptive abstractions and levels of explanation for theoretical clarity, even if it is to appreciate only that there may be legitimate accounts that have little utility. The need for a clear appreciation of such issues is illustrated by the syntax versus semantics debate considered by Byrne and Stenning in this volume, the relationship between the mental model accounts provided by Johnson-Laird and associates, and those presented in the Gentner and Stevens (1983) collection, as well as the issues raised by consideration of the social and cultural mediation of representations discussed in Section 20.5.

20.4 The phenomenological experience of implementation

Often the notion of running a mental model is illustrated by people's response to the request to count the number of rooms in their house. Spontaneously, most people conjure an image of their house and imagine walking through the various rooms counting the number of windows. Novel mental simulations may be constructed also in response to verbal invitations to reason about an imaginary situation. For example, the reasoning process that takes place when asked to comprehend the validity of the statement "if people had wings they would fly" may involve imagining the scenario.

Although several researchers acknowledge the importance of this type of phenomenological experience for reasoning or language understanding (e.g. Waltz, 1981) the tendency in mental models research has been to focus on the unconscious structures and processes underlying the use of mental models. While it is taken for granted that there is much we can be aware of, the fascination has been in explicating the numerous cognitive processes that are unavailable to conscious inspection. In particular, the main interest has been to understand how it is possible to talk, reason, predict, understand and solve problems without being conscious of the processes that enable us to perform such feats. Another reason for the research bias may be due to the seemingly intractable nature of conscious experience (Searle, 1990). In particular, since mental models have been considered only as transient, fleeting representations in consciousness, it is difficult to see how one could provide a systematic account that characterizes the phenomenological experience.

It is not surprising that most theoretical accounts of running mental models have focused on formalizing the underlying processes that make a mental simulation possible (e.g. Collins and Gentner, 1987; de Kleer, 1977; Hayes, 1985). Within this framework, the phenomenological experience is viewed often as the elaboration of the primary unconscious processes, serving no functional role. However, in casting the role of phenomenological experience as a by-product – or even an epiphenomenon – we may be throwing the baby out with the bath water. While it might appear to be secondary or of no consequence, it does not mean it is unworthy of study. In contrast, we may discover even that it plays a more important role in cognition than generally assumed. Certainly, there have been calls to this effect. For example, Shallice (1972) has argued always that consciousness is responsible largely for determining what goals are set and which actions are taken. More recently, Johnson-Laird (1988) has put forward a framework of intentions and self-reflection in which he sees their function as being instrumental in our reasoning and ability to explain events.

To appreciate more the possible functional role of consciousness, it is important to ask what causes some activities to engage reflection and conscious decision-making while others do not. Specifically, the question is what mechanism is involved in constructing mental models and how does it determine which parts of the model(s) are to be inspected at a conscious or unconscious level of awareness? To explain how the mechanism of consciousness might work, Johnson-Laird (1983, 1988) has developed a theory of parallel computation. A central tenet of the theory is to assume that many cognitive tasks are performed most efficiently via the running of parallel algorithms. However, parallel processing requires that information be coordinated and passed between the various processors. In order that the flow of information is able to run smoothly, the system needs to have immense flexibility, resistance to degradation and to be able to respond rapidly when breakdowns occur. In turn, this means that the system needs a high-level monitor to ensure process coordination. The theory proposes that there is a hierarchy of parallel processors, with the highest level containing the operating system. It is this operating system which is equated with consciousness and which provides the phenomenological experience of awareness. Primarily, the operating system is autonomous, setting goals for the lower level processors, although it is responsive to demands from lower level processors. As well as explaining how information may flow in a bottom-up and top-down manner, this model also describes how processors at different levels may interact with each other.

While providing a powerful description of the flow of information between processors, really the theory does not explain why certain processes are brought into awareness while others are not. In particular, what is needed is a more detailed account of the changes in awareness in terms of the interplay between the nonconscious processes that generate the conscious information to be processed and the way the outcome of conscious thinking is attended to by nonconscious cognitive processes (e.g. Mandler, 1982). However, to get any leverage on this problem initially may require the adoption of a lower level of theoretical commitment than Johnson-Laird's parallel processing model.

One approach might be to examine how everyday tasks involving some form of reasoning are mediated by external and internal representations (e.g. Kirsh, 1991). By analysing the different sets of conditions that trigger and interrupt consciousness and comparing these with activities that are determined situationally, it may be possible to elucidate the possible functional role of consciousness.

Many of the mundane decisions we make during our everyday lives are achieved automatically. In these situations, it is not necessary for us to be aware of our actions or to think consciously of the options available to us before acting. For example, the decision at what point to cross the street, whether to select a chocolate biscuit in preference to a plain one, or which article to read first in a newspaper are largely unconscious choices. Also, in our interactions with each other, it is rare for us to stop the flow of a conversation to run a mental model consciously in order to interpret the intentions of the other person(s). The same can be said about our interaction with artefacts. It is not common for us to control the behaviour of the artefact by running a mental simulation consciously during our interaction with it. Indeed, in many event-dependent conditions, it may be counter-productive to be conscious of what you are doing. For example, if consciously we think about how to drive a car while actually driving, interference with the normally smooth coordinated activity can result.

On the other hand, there are many choice situations where we are conscious of the decision we are taking and its possible consequence. The circumstance which is most likely to trigger the change between automatic and conscious processing in our everyday activities is when we are confronted with an unexpected choice that requires evaluation or understanding. Consider the example of navigating whilst driving. When we arrive at a roundabout we look for the sign that tells us which exit to take. If the information provided matches our expectation, no conscious decision-making is required. However, if we are confronted with two signs, e.g. one saying M4 east and the other M4 west, we are placed in a situation where a rapid decision has to be made. If we are uncertain of which choice to take, it may require us to construct a mental model of where we are at that point in time and where it is that we intend to go. On top of this we will need to map on the east/west axis. This might take the form of a mental simulation such as overlaying a mental analog compass or utilizing a propositional mnemonic, such as "Never Eat Shredded Wheat" to identify in clockwise order the (N)orth, (E)ast, (S)outh and (W)est points of the compass.

In many of these choice situations, the consciousness mechanism of the cognitive apparatus is activated when two or more (previously unconscious) mental contents are brought into direct juxtaposition (e.g. Mandler, 1982; Gregory, 1986). Also, an awareness of the situation may emerge when there is a discrepancy between our prediction and the outcome of an event (cf. "breakdowns", Winograd and Flores, 1986). Furthermore, subjective experience may be central to situations which require some form of calculation. For example, the decision whether to buy a large packet of washing powder or a small one depends on juxtaposing a number of interrelated context-bound considerations in order to determine what should be the best buy (Lave, 1988).

Therefore, the role of consciousness in everyday tasks provides a means of keeping track of the relevant consequences of actions and ignoring the stream of irrelevant inferences in real-time. Furthermore, the extent to which the cognitive processes of evaluating, comparing, choosing, calculating and diagnosing operate on the conscious content of a mental model depends very much on the structures that "can" enter the conscious state (Mandler, 1982). Importantly, what determines which structures can enter consciousness will depend largely on the situational, social and cultural relevance of the choice that has to be made. For example, one may choose to start a 100 metre hurdle race with the left or right foot based on knowledge of what will be most advantageous, taking into account various factors of distance and timing. Likewise, after reading a new notice on a door that informs us that leaving it open is a fire risk, we may become aware of the normally automatic choice that confronts us every time we go through a door; whether to close it or not. The content of the notice may cause us to infer the likelihood of a fire and the consequences of not closing the door. Subsequently, we may consider the choice of closing the door within the social context, e.g. who put the notice there in the first place, why was this form of communication used, who else is going to pay attention and so on. Hence, normally what would be a situationally determined action of little consequence can become one that is transferred to a conscious state where the consequences become highly relevant.

20.5   The mediation of representations: social and cultural aspects

Mental models research has focused largely on modelling the mental processes that occur inside the head of an individual in a given problem-solving situation. In doing so, little attention has been paid to the way in which individuals interact with external representations or each other when immersed in a cognitive activity. By assuming that an activity is based on individual problem-solving, the need to address the possibility of it being culturally and socially constituted in ways requiring theoretical treatment has been avoided (Lave, 1988). However, increasingly it is recognized that the use of talk, pencil and paper, diagrams, drawings, text and other types of external displays are fundamental to many problem-solving tasks (e.g. Larkin, 1989; Reisberg, 1987). Even when mental tasks are carried out by individuals in isolation, Wertsch (1991) argues that inherently they are social in many respects and almost always, they are carried out with the aid of tools such as computers, calculators or language. Clearly, there is a need to redress the conceptualization and analysis of a problem-solving activity within the context in which it occurs. Moreover, given the growing concern to develop accounts of cognition that are more "situated" in the context in which they occur (e.g. Newman, Griffin and Cole, 1989; Norman, 1990; Suchman, 1987), it seems that further developments in mental models research would benefit by examining the role played by social, cultural and external factors in mediating the development and use of mental models.

20.5.1 Alternative frameworks

To shift the unit of analysis from the individual to the cognitive activity in situ will require a reassessment of the premises which underlie existing theoretical frameworks of mental representations. It is very likely that many of the assumptions underlying the function of cognitive processes in guiding human performance will be found to be inappropriate. For example, O'Malley and Draper (this volume) suggest that functional and structural theories of mental models are too narrow in their scope to explain how users interact with systems in the environment. Newman, Griffin and Cole (1989) also have found it necessary to reject many of the standard assumptions in their account of how children learn in the classroom setting. Primarily, they consider the notion that there are well-specified "static" internal representations underlying an individual's behaviour to be inadequate. Lave (1988) in her critique of current cognitive theorizing also has discussed many of its weaknesses in accounting for "activity-in-setting". Alternatively, she proposes that in order for the study of cognition to move into the larger social and cultural world, a theory of what motivates people to undertake to solve a problem is required.

In conjunction with challenging general assumptions about mental representations, a situated perspective on the mediation of mental models needs to reconsider what is the most appropriate kind of theoretical framework and level of analytic description, and it needs to ask whether it should apply existing constructs or develop new ones. It even has to determine what are the interesting and relevant questions to ask. In establishing a new agenda, it is useful to look at what alternative methods of investigation are being developed to account for the social, cultural and/or situated nature of action. In general, these can be categorized with respect to their commitment to a cognitive or a socially constituted account of the phenomenon, with pluralist commitments in between.

At the cognitive end of the continuum are "revisionist" approaches which accommodate the context of an activity within the traditional cognitive framework. Core concepts, originating from artificial intelligence and cognitive psychology theorizing, are supplemented with other components. For example, within the field of human–computer (interaction HCI), Barnard (Barnard, 1991; Barnard and Harrison, 1989) proposes that the more "qualitative" aspects of cognition in user–system interaction can be modelled by incorporating an interaction model with their existing system model and cognitive model of the user.

At the social end of the continuum are "sceptical" approaches which reject the cognitive framework and instead propose a radically different frame of reference and a new set of analytic tools. Such a perspective is exemplified in the work of Potter and Wetherell (1987) on discourse and social psychology. They argue for analysis and explanation that is concerned with the way language is used in human activity, as opposed to one that posits human behaviour as a product of mental representations. They propose that people go through life "faced with an ever changing kaleidoscope of situations" and "so will need to draw upon very different repertoires to suit the needs at hand" (p.156). Hence, the assumption is that because human behaviour is variable always, a social psychological theory should be concerned with "interpretive repertoires", i.e. the various accounts people use in interpreting events and problems, rather than an explanation that focuses on invariant mental or social representations.

In the middle are the "eclectic" approaches, which seek to integrate a diversity of theoretical perspectives and constructs from a broad background embracing anthropology, artificial intelligence, philosophy, psychology and sociology. An underlying theme is to explicate structures and processes which are not attributed either to the outside or inside world, but are inextricably connected with each other. For example, Wertsch (1991) has proposed a socio-cultural approach to mind which is intended to provide an account of human mental processes that recognizes the essential relationship between these processes and their cultural, historical and institutional setting. Agre (1988) and Hutchins (1991) also discuss the importance of shifting the unit of analysis from positing representations in the individual to one that traverses across the boundaries of individuals. Moreover, the nature of the relationship is assumed to be complex; the loci of representations is assumed to be distributed dynamically across minds, bodies, activities and artefacts.

A primary objective of the eclectic stance is to avoid the narrow focus of the traditional scientific approach where opposing theories are constantly at battle with each other. However, as consideration in the philosophy of science reveals that such an adversarial approach is the result of the way in which people conduct what should be rational procedures, without changing the make-up of people, it is difficult to see how this can be avoided (Newton-Smith, 1981). Nevertheless, one way of bridging disagreements, is to call upon "third party" theoretical accounts. For example, Shore (1991) has attempted to overcome the impasse between subjective and objective accounts of meaning within cognitive anthropology by proposing that the relationship between cognitive processes and public cultural knowledge can be explained by recourse to their reciprocal grounding in sensory experience. To link the two views of meaning, he draws from Werner and Kaplan's (1963) phenomenologically-based theory of how people comprehend symbols.

In many ways, the revisionist approach has set itself the easier task, since its interpretation of situated context is constrained heavily by the principles and processes of existing models of cognition. The change in direction is largely empirical in nature; determining what are the most appropriate ways to model the "qualitative" aspects of the domain. Its interpretation of the empirical data remains very much within the confines of the prevailing cognitive theory. An approach that characterizes the situated "part" of an activity only as an add-on to existing cognitive theory is likely to fail to give proper significance to the role of social factors in human performance. While seeking to accommodate the more qualitative situational factors within a cognitive account of human performance, really this approach has not addressed the role of the social and cultural contexts in which the interactive activity takes place. Cooper (1991) also notes that such a pursuit can work only if a drastically impoverished interpretation of context is adopted.

In contrast, the sceptical view takes the position that cognitive representations are irrelevant to an analysis of interactive activities and in particular, language use. Although in most cases it is largely agnostic on the status of cognitive processes, it suggests that explicating mental events and processes is not a sufficient condition for understanding what is going on during the course of an interactive discourse. Simply, the relationship between language use and mental representations is regarded as a non-issue (Potter and Wetherell, 1987). From the sceptical perspective, the interesting problem is to describe the various resources that are used in constituting meaning. In this respect, the perspective is uncompromising; the proposition that the social and cognitive dimensions could be accommodated or integrated is considered untenable. Such theoretical orthodoxy also can be seen in Suchman's (1987) black and white opposition to the traditional AI view of planning, that conceives of action as being organized through the construction and execution of internal plans (Agre, 1990). In contrast, she proposes a notion of "situated action", where plans are not taken to be responsible for the control of action, but are considered to be only one of many resources.

Radical shifts in perspective may be necessary to expose the problematic claims of well-established theoretical positions. In doing so, they lay the groundwork for a widely differing conception of the phenomenon. An important shift has been to change the focus of attention away from individual user action to human (work) activity at large. The theoretical foundations on which this shift is based is human activity theory. Here, individuals' actions are considered to be bound inextricably within the larger structures of relationships and societies. Based on this premiss, the alternative assumption is that in order to understand the way in which artefacts are used and designed, work activities need to be analysed such that HCI is viewed as being only one part of the web of activity. The ways of doing work (i.e. its praxis), the organization of work activities (i.e. the division of labour) and the sharing of work through artefacts are other aspects of work that require to be explained.

Nevertheless, radical shifts in theoretical perspective can have the negative effect of inhibiting a dialogue between opposing views. Ultimately, despite the rhetoric of the extreme social and the extreme cognitive positions, a full account of the appreciation of meaning will need to encompass not only how meaning is constituted socially, but also how meaning is constituted within the person. Moreover, a good bet would seem to be that these aspects of meaning will interact.

The problem of combining social, cognitive and cultural accounts is exacerbated by not having a clearly established framework. However, as yet there is little in the way of explicit criteria to guide the selection of the most appropriate theory available from the rich diversity in the social, cultural and political traditions to facilitate a productive synthesis. A further problem is deciding how to reformulate the disparate parts into a new framework and set of descriptions. Importantly, there is the question of how theory is to be used within the new framework. Is it appropriate to follow the scientific method where hypotheses are derived from the theory and empirically tested or should such adherence to rigour be replaced by an approach typified in the social sciences where theory is used as a source with which to conceptualize the phenomena and to inform the analysis?

Of course, the treatment of theory in reformulating a phenomenon will depend largely on the background and philosophical predilection of the researcher. A common approach is to assess an alternative theory by juxtaposing it with a critical analysis of the cognitive theory. For example, several researchers dissatisfied with the cognitive view of users in HCI have developed critiques that discuss the limitations of these accounts by contrasting them with the contribution that can be gained from Soviet and European psychology and philosophy, drawing from the works of Heidegger, Vygotsky, Wittgenstein and more recently Leont'ev (e.g. Bødker, 1991; Ehn, 1988; Whiteside and Wixon, 1988; Winograd and Flores, 1986). A common theme has been to lift well-established ideas from the socio-historical literature, such as "readiness-to-hand", "breakdowns" and "language games" and elaborate them with respect to the design and use of computer artefacts. It is claimed that by building on these constructs valuable insight can be gained of the way artefacts are used in practice and understood by people. Also, Wertsch (1991) claims that drawing from Vygotsky's ideas provides a better point of entry into understanding the human mind and the environment.

While much leverage can be gained from examining a phenomenon through others' philosophical writings, there are a number of pitfalls. The process of abstracting theoretical constructs from their original context into a different one, especially an applied domain, often can lead one to oversimplify the implications (see Bannon and Bødker, 1991). Also, there is the problem of misinterpretation, especially when an attempt is made to bridge theories taken from differing historical and philosophical contexts. Lacking a sufficient depth of knowledge or training in another discipline can result in overlooking or failing to recognize that certain constructs are not commensurable, even though they appear to share common themes. For example, Sharrock and Anderson (1987) point out how the apparent similarity of frameworks from different disciplines in reality can be far from the truth. In their examination of the disputes between linguistics and conversation analysis over the practice of discourse analysis, they point how many of the disagreements are highly specific in nature. Consequently, the assumption that both disciplines have a common framework obscures the fact that each discipline has its own set of problems and issues.

20.5.2   Empirical studies of socially distributed cognition

As well as considering the development of a new theoretical framework to accommodate or contest cognitive, social and cultural accounts, there is an urgent need to go out into the field and observe how activities, involving groups of people working together, unfold in the exigencies of everyday life. The beginnings of such an endeavour can be seen in an ongoing anthropological project looking at cognition in the workplace and the design of facilities (see Suchman and Trigg, 1991). As part of the project Goodwin and Goodwin (in press) have been investigating how airport personnel "look" at planes in their working activities. Based on extensive videotaping of the work in setting, they report a number of observations of how baggage workers learn to "see" planes as task relevant objects. They point out how an array of technological artefacts, including video monitors, various documents and a wall-mounted clock, provide different kinds of structural information for the workers to "see" the planes. To be able to know what to do and make inferences about each plane's status requires the baggage handler to compare mentally the different representations. Goodwin and Goodwin propose that what is happening in this situation is that the baggage handler brings together multiple perspectives of the different representations resulting in an "assembled product". The way an individual learns to perform the mental ensembling and juggling is seen to be a function of the socially organized aspect of culture that is instantiated and maintained by the practice exhibited in the community in that setting. While alluding to the complex cognitive processes that are involved during the apprenticeship of "seeing", there is no real attempt to analyse the cognitive processes by which external representations are internalized and combined in memory. Alternatively, explanations of the phenomena are further developed in theoretical accounts derived from the sociology of science on representational practices (e.g. Latour, 1987) and human activity theory. This is a pity, since clearly there is a need to explain the activity of juxtaposing different representations as a cognitive process as well as one that is socially and culturally constituted. Furthermore, it could provide insight into the way reasoning and inferencing are mediated in a socially distributed setting where technological artefacts and other forms of representations are an integral part.

In contrast to Goodwin and Goodwin's (in press) primarily sociological and anthropological-driven framework, Hutchins (1990; 1991) has chosen to adopt a computational perspective as his point of entry to analyse the group work activity. His work involves studying socially distributed "cognitive systems" (functional groups as opposed to individual minds) in the fields of aviation and navigation. The theoretical emphasis of his approach has been to extend from the cognitive base, but also to show the connection between cultural and social structures. The overall goal is to account for how the distributed structures, which make up the cognitive system, are coordinated by analyzing the various contributions of the environment in which the work activity takes place, the representational media (e.g. instruments, displays, manuals, navigation charts), the interactions of individuals interacting with each other and their interactional use of artefacts.

The activities of navigating a ship and flying a plane are viewed as computations which take place via the coordination of structured representational media that are manifested in the use of an assortment of tools and instruments. Specifically, Hutchins proposes that a computational activity is "the propagation of representational state across media", where the media includes internal representations (e.g. memories of the individuals) as well as external representations. For example, the singular activity of taking a bearing on a ship involves coordinating a combination of events and media that are temporally and spatially bounded: the name of the landmark and the memory of the description of the desired landmark need to be coordinated. In turn this needs to be coordinated with an external sighting of the landmark itself and the instrument used to line up the landmark with a particular setting.

In presenting a computational account of navigation Hutchins (1991) proposes a set of principle constraints, a set of structures that represent them, properties of the representations, cognitive requirements of performance and an implementation of the basic computations. Somewhat ironically, Hutchins has capitalized on the computational metaphor, to explicate the structures and properties of the "cognitive system". In doing so, the status of mental representations is as one of many types of representational media, which is "internal" to the cognitive system (cf. Rumelhart, 1989).

The idea of distributed representations is used also to refer to the variability of knowledge across individuals. Similar to the idea of distributed computing (e.g. Chandrasekaran, 1981), socially distributed representations refers to the fact that individuals working together on a collaborative task are likely to possess different kinds of knowledge and so will engage in interactions that will allow them to pool the various resources to accomplish their tasks (Cicourel, 1990; Hutchins, 1990). This is particularly pertinent in domains where groups of individuals are required to work collectively to solve a problem (e.g. medical diagnosis), to construct a complicated object (e.g. designing and engineering a building) or to control a system (e.g. navigating a large ship). Different individuals need to cooperate to perform the task because no one has sufficient knowledge to do the task alone. Accordingly, it is not possible to predict the properties of a group of people working together based on the knowledge of properties of the individuals in that group. Of particular interest are the processes which allow individuals to use each other as resources and the properties (e.g. intersubjectivity, redundancy) which enable such coordinated activity. A further challenge is to develop a means of choreographing the flow of activity through individuals and technology.

20.5.3 Mental models and combined accounts of situated activity

Theoretical attempts to address situated human activity and problem-solving by integrating cognitive, social and cultural accounts are in their infancy. A primary concern of this approach has been to explicate human activity rather than to explicate the mind. As a result, there has been a shift away from mentalistic constructs to alternative constructs such as shared knowledge, collective remembering, inter-subjectivity, redundant knowledge, distributed resources and representational state that attempt to span internal and external representations. It is proposed that the construct of a mental model as exemplified in Johnson-Laird's work or Gentner and Stevens' collection could be elaborated to provide an account of the extent to which individuals share and construct similar mental models when interacting together at work or in other settings. Also, it would be interesting to develop an account that describes how mental models are constructed and manipulated commonly across a range of internal and external representations (cf. Hutchins, 1990; Middleton and Edwards, 1990).

Nevertheless, the appreciation of the role of the setting in which cognition takes place does not mean that individual cognition becomes less of an issue. It is equally important to understand the way in which individual cognitions may diverge from the group cognition. Moreover, although the most appropriate form of account abstraction will vary depending on its purpose, a complete account of phenomena such as meaning will require the operation of cognitive processes and the social constitution and any interaction, to be described. To this end, extending the construct of mental models should have value (cf. Leiser, and Manktelow and Over, this volume).

20.6 Applying mental models

Within HCI, a major thrust of mental models research has been to explicate the transformation of external representations into internal representations. In particular, the series of studies on learning devices and mental models (e.g. Bibby, this volume; Duff, this volume, Halasz and Moran, 1983; Kieras and Bovair, 1984) has led to the claim that a mental model (or device model) is something that can be acquired through exposure to external representations. This has been interpreted to mean that a mental model is something that can be given through a special set of instructions (e.g. Green, 1990) or a manual (e.g. Rupietta, 1990). The process by which this giving occurs has been characterized as internalization (see Bibby, this volume). The resulting mental representation is assumed to be equivalent computationally to the external representation.

The obvious practical implication for HCI design is that manuals and instructions should be designed to facilitate the development of an appropriate mental model, as empirical research indicates that enhanced performance and reduced errors will result. The same rationale has been applied to user interface design. A general principle is to make the system transparent so that it helps the user to "grow" a productive mental model of relevant aspects of the system (Brown, 1986, p.465).

The problem that confronts the designer is to figure out exactly what types of external representation should be made salient in order that the most appropriate mental model is internalized. Although there has been much discussion about the potential benefits and disadvantages of providing interface and instructional metaphors as suitable models (e.g. Booth, 1989; Carroll, Mack and Kellogg, 1988), all the guidelines resulting have tended to be rather abstract and ill-defined. In particular, they have focused on characterizing what mental models ought and ought not to do, rather than on how they could be manifested at the user interface. For example, generally it is agreed that mental models should provide an overall understanding of the workings of the system as well as helping users understand the interrelationships between structure, function and use.

Users' mental models of systems also have been noted for being incomplete, unstable, limited, easily confusable, unscientific and parsimonious (Norman, 1983). Here, the practical implication is that systems and instructional material should be designed to enable users to develop more coherent and consistent models. However, as commented by Leiser (this volume), in order to modify users' mental models, first it is necessary to know what are their internal inconsistencies. Currently, the problem appears to be the paucity of applicable conceptual tools and methods available to the designer that would elicit this information. Furthermore, the indirect characterization of the construct as utilized in theoretical research places an enormous burden on the designer's inferencing skills. To be able to determine what is the most appropriate user model is challenge enough, but then to have to work out a way of incorporating it within the design process, and subsequently to know how to evaluate it is asking a lot of the commercial consultant. As discussed in chapter 19, one way of overcoming this dilemma is for the applied research community to develop further the methods used in theoretical research to identify mental models. By customizing the basic research methods for specific applied problems, it can provide the designer with a better handle on the mental model notion than a set of normative prescriptions.

Human–machine systems (HMS) research has taken a slightly different perspective from HCI in dealing with the "ghost in the machine" scenario, insofar as it has attempted to explain the development of mental models that are geared more specifically towards practical ends. In particular, a main goal has been to model what properties an operator is likely to learn about a system and how they are going to use that knowledge when interacting with the system. A further goal has been to identify the discrepancies between the users' mental models of the system and the real system operation. By characterizing the matches and mismatches of knowledge, it has been possible to make deductions about the kinds of external representations that are needed to support operator performance.

The approach taken by Bainbridge (this volume) is to focus on detailing the various types of knowledge that are used in the cognitive skill of operating a process plant. From her analysis of the general mechanisms, a number of practical implications for job aids, training and display design are outlined. However, the level of her practical deducing is very general. For example, one recommendation is that "display formats be compatible with the type of knowledge represented". In defense of this approach Bainbridge stresses that there does not need to be a one-to-one mapping between the level of detail of the model and the specificity of the recommendations given.

A more closely coupled connection between theorizing and deducing practical implications is illustrated in Moray's (1988) work on operators' mental models. In particular, he has attempted to make concrete the process of translation between inference and specification by developing two overlapping theories that are mental model-based: (1) a theory of the cognitive processes and (2), a theory of design. The cognitive theory of mental models is based on the notion that mental models develop as homomorphs through inductive learning (cf. Holland, Holyoak, Nisbett and Thagard, 1987). The theory predicts that after lengthy exposure to the process plant, operators will eventually develop a sufficiently "complete model" for them to cope with all the situations that are likely to arise. At this point inductive learning ceases. The problem with having such a well developed model is that it becomes inappropriate for dealing with abnormal situations which have not been encountered before. Instead of exploring the system inductively for alternative solutions to deal with the novel problem, as would have happened in the learning stage, the operators tend to get trapped in a "cognitive lock-up", in which only rigid thinking is evident. The practical implication of this analysis is that information aids are needed to prevent the crystallization of mental models. The recommendation is that intelligent aids should be developed to act as guides to lead the user through different paths of the mental model, which otherwise would be inaccessible. The second theory, called the Lattice Theory of Intelligent Aiding, predicts how this would happen. However, Moray's analysis lacks a means of deducing the form that the aids should take and an account of how they might be implemented.

Hence, in both HCI and HMS design, the application of the mental model construct falls short of having practical utility. However, its value lies in its ability to explicate the underlying mental processes of user interaction with systems and in predicting potential performance deficits. In this respect, basic knowledge may have more to gain from applied mental models research than actual practice. Given the limited theoretical understanding of complex human action, such an endeavour can only be seen as favourable. However, it does not solve the designers' dilemma of how to make use of the construct for practical purposes.

It must be stressed that the difficulty of bridging theoretical treatments with applied concerns is by no means unique to mental models. Within HCI generally, there has been very little evidence of any significant "deductive" bridging taking place. Although there have been numerous attempts to download psychological theory into accessible design products (e.g. Gardiner and Christie, 1987) their utility has been regarded with scepticism (e.g. Carroll, Kellogg and Rosson, 1991). One of the main reasons for this state of affairs is the immature status of the basic theoretical claims; the majority can be generalized barely beyond the specific empirical settings in which they were determined (Barnard, 1991). Another problem is the large difference between scientific pursuits and the actual process of design. Many of the assumptions about what practical tools and methods are needed for design have gone unexamined. Furthermore, there has been little attempt to appreciate fully the process of design.

However, this is not to say that the "technology transfer" problem has gone unnoticed in HCI. Currently, a re-analysis of the relationship between theory and design in HCI is under way (Carroll, Kellogg and Rosson, 1991). As part of the new agenda, Barnard (1991) has proposed that theories will need to have wider and more significant scope and that research programmes will need to be directed towards theoretical concerns that are relevant to applied domains. Carroll et al (1991) also have committed themselves to the development of conceptual frameworks and analytical tools that are immediately applicable to HCI design. Their approach argues both for a widening of the scientific base from which to inform the analysis and a need to consider primarily the objects that are of direct practical importance to design. New methods which focus on the articulation of the design process are beginning to emerge also (e.g. Carroll and Kellogg, 1989; MacLean, Young and Moran, 1989; Norman, 1988).

The shift in ground from modelling users as cognitive constructs to analysing the way artefacts are designed and are used by people in their environments is intended to enhance the development of an applied psychology that supports the design of usable systems. Within this framework, the role of theoretical constructs, developed originally in basic research, will become largely secondary. Rather than using them as the basis for building design tools they will be viewed more as informative resources in which to articulate the design process. The recognition that basic theoretical constructs cannot be applied unidirectionally to a practical problem of design is a critical appreciation. In particular, the consequences for applied mental models research in HCI is that it need not concern itself with providing prescriptive advice. The challenge for "academic" mental models research is for it to extend beyond the existing theoretical base to include other concerns such as distributed representations, socio-cultural aspects and consciousness. At the same time, it should continue to develop basic theories of the cognitive mechanisms that give rise to the phenomena in question.

References

Agre, P.E. (1990). Review of L.A.Suchman's "Plans and Situated Actions". *Artificial Intelligence 43*, 369–384.

Agre, P.E. (1988). The dynamic structure of everyday life. MIT Technical Report No. AI-TR 1085.

Allport, D.A. (1980). Patterns and actions: cognitive mechanisms are content specific. In Claxton, G. (ed.) *Cognitive Psychology, New Directions*. London: Routledge.

Bainbridge, L. (1988). Types of representation. In Goodstein, L.P., Anderson, H.B. and Olsen, H.E. (eds) *Tasks, Errors And Mental Models*. London: Taylor and Francis.

Bannon, L.J. and Bødker, S. (1991). Beyond the interface: encountering artefacts in use. In Carroll J.M. (ed.) *Designing Interaction: Psychological Theory at the Human–Computer Interface*. New York: CUP.

Barnard, P. (1991). Bridging between basic theories and the artefacts of human-computer interaction. In Carroll, J.M. (ed.)*Designing Interaction: Psychology at the Human-Computer Interface*. New York: CUP.

Barnard, P. and Harrison, M. (1989). Integrating cognitive and system models in human computer interaction. In Sutcliffe, A. and Macaulay, L. (eds), *People and Computers V*. Cambridge: CUP.

Bødker, S. (1991). *Through the Interface: A Human Activity Approach to User Interface Design*. Hillsdale, NJ. LEA.

Booth, P. (1989). *An Introduction to Human–Computer Interaction*. Hove, Sussex: LEA.

Brown, J.S. (1986). From cognitive to social ergonomics and beyond. In Norman, D.A. and Draper, S.W. (eds) *User Centred System Design*. Hillsdale, NJ: LEA.

Brewer, W.F. (1987). Schemas versus mental models in human memory. In Morris, P. (ed.) *Modelling Cognition.* Chichester: Wiley.

Carroll, J.M. and Kellogg, W.A. (1989). Artefacts as theory-nexus: hermeneutics meets theory-based design. In Bice, K. and Lewis, C.H. (eds) *Proceedings of CHI '89 - Human Factors in Computing Systems.* New York: ACM.

Carroll, J.M., Kellogg, W.A. and Rosson, M.B. (1991). The task artefact cycle. In Carroll, J.M. (ed.) *Designing Interaction: Psychology at the Human– Computer Interface.* New York: CUP.

Carroll, J.M., Mack, R.L. and Kellogg, W.A. (1988). Interface metaphors and user interface design. In Helander, M. (ed.) *Handbook of Human-Computer Interaction.* Amsterdam: Elsevier (North-Holland).

Chandrasekaran, B. (1981). Natural and social system metaphors for distributed problem solving: introduction to the issue. *IEEE Transactions on Systems, Man, and Cybernetics SMC-11,* 1, 1–5.

Cicourel, A.V. (1990). The integration of distributed knowledge in collaborative medical diagnosis. In Galegher, J., Kraut, R.E. and Edigo, C. (eds) *Intellectual Teamwork: Social and Technological Foundations of Cooperative Work.* Hillsdale, NJ: LEA.

Collins, A. and Gentner, D. (1987). How people construct mental models. In Holland, D. and Quinn, N. (eds) *Cultural Models in Language and Thought.* Cambridge: CUP.

Cooper, G. (1991). Context and its representation. *Interacting With Computers 3,* 243–253..

de Kleer, J. (1977). Multiple representations of knowledge in a mechanics problem solver. In *Proceedings of the Fifth Conference on Artificial Intelligence.* Cambridge, Ma.: MIT.

de Kleer, J. and Brown, J.S. (1983). Assumptions and ambiguities in mechanistic mental models. In Gentner, D. and Stevens, A.L. (eds.), *Mental Models.* Hillsdale, NJ: LEA.

Ehn, P. (1988). *Work-Oriented Design of Computer Artefacts.* Falkoping, Sweden: Arbetslivscentrum/Almqvist and Wiksell International.

Forbus, K.D. (1983). Qualitative reasoning about space and motion. In Gentner, D. and Stevens, A.L. (eds) *Mental Models.* Hillsdale, NJ: LEA.

Gardiner, M. and Christie, B. (1987). (eds) *Applying Cognitive Psychology to User Interface Design.* Chichester: Wiley.

Gentner, D and Stevens, A.L. (eds) (1983). *Mental Models.* Hillsdale, NJ: LEA.

Goodwin, C. and Goodwin, M.J. (in press). Formulating planes:seeing as a situated activity. In Middleton, D. and Engeström, Y. (eds) *Cognition and Communication at Work*. London: Sage.

Green, T.R.G. (1990). Limited theories as a framework for human–computer interaction. In Ackermann, D. and Tauber, M.J.(eds), *Mental Models and Human Computer Interaction 1*. Amsterdam: Elsevier (North-Holland).

Gregory, R.L. (1986). Is consciousness sensational inference? In Gregory, R.L. (ed.) *Odd Perceptions*. London: Methuen.

Halasz, F.G. and Moran, T.P. (1983). Mental models and problem solving in using a calculator. In Janda, A. (ed.) *Human Factors in Computing Systems: Proceedings of CHI '83 Conference*. New York: ACM.

Hayes, P. (1985). Ontology for liquids. In Hobbes, J. and Moore, R. (eds) *Formal Theories of the Common Sense World*. Norwood, NJ: Ablex.

Holland, J., Holyoak, K. Nisbett, R. and Thagard, P. (1986). *Induction*. Cambridge, Ma.: MIT Press.

Hutchins, E. (1990). The technology of team navigation. In Galegher, J., Kraut, R.E. and Edigo, C. (eds) *Intellectual Teamwork: Social and Technological Foundations of Cooperative Work*. Hillsdale, NJ: LEA.

Hutchins, E. (1991). *Individual and Socially Distributed Cognition*. Course 234 Notes, Department of Cognitive Science, University of California, San Diego.

Johnson-Laird, P.N. (1983). *Mental Models*. Cambridge: CUP.

Johnson-Laird, P.N. (1988). *The Computer and the Mind*. Cambridge, Ma.: Harvard University Press.

Kieras, D.E. and Bovair, S. (1984). The role of a mental model in learning to operate a device. *Cognitive Science* 8, 255–273.

Kirsh, D. (1991). Today the earwig, tomorrow man? *Artificial Intelligence* 47, 161-184.

Kuipers, B.J. and Chiu, C. (1987). Taming intractable branching in qualitative simulation. *Proceedings of the 10th International Joint Conference on Artificial Intelligence (IJCAI-87)*. Los Altos, Ca.: Morgan Kaufmann.

Kuipers, B.J. and Kassirer, J.P. (1984). Causal reasoning in medicine: analysis of a protocol. *Cognitive Science 8*, 363–385.

Larkin, J. (1989). Display-based problem solving. In Klahr, D. and Kotovsky, K. (eds) *Complex Information Processing: The Impact of Herbert A. Simon*. Hillsdale, NJ.: LEA.

Latour, B. (1987). *Science in Action: How to Follow Scientists and Engineers Through Society*. Cambridge, Ma.: Harvard University Press.

Lave, J. (1988). *Cognition in Practice.* Cambridge: CUP.

MacLean, A., Young, R.M. and Moran, T.P. (1989). Design rationale: the argument behind the artefact. In Bice, K. and Lewis, C.H. (eds) *Proceedings of CHI '89 - Human Factors in Computing Systems.* New York: ACM.

Mandler, G. (1982). *Mind and Emotion.* Malabar: Krieger.

Manktelow, K. and Jones, J. (1987). Principles from the psychology of thinking and mental models. In Gardiner, M. and Christie, B. (eds) *Applying Cognitive Psychology To User Interface Design.* Chichester: Wiley.

Marr, D. (1982). *Vision* San Francisco: Freeman.

Middleton, D. and Edwards, D. (eds) (1990), *Collective Remembering.* London: Sage.

Moray, N. (1988). Intelligent aids, mental models, and the theory of machines. In Hollnagel, E., Mancini, G. and Woods,D.D. (eds) *Cognitive Engineering in Complex Dynamic Worlds.* London: Academic Press.

Newman, D., Griffin, P. and Cole, M. (1989). *The Construction Zone: Working for Cognitive Change in School.* Cambridge: CUP.

Newton-Smith, W. (1981). *The Rationality of Science.* London: Routledge.

Norman, D.A. (1983). Some observations on mental models. In Gentner, D. and Stevens, A.L. (eds) *Mental Models.* Hillsdale, NJ: LEA.

Norman, D.A. (1988). *The Psychology of Everyday Things.* New York: Basic Books.

Norman, D.A. (1990). Four (more) issues for cognitive science. Technical Report No. 9001. Department of Cognitive Science, University of California, San Diego.

Norman, D.A. and Bobrow, D.G. (1979). Descriptions: an intermediate stage in memory retrieval. *Cognitive Psychology 11,* 107–123.

Potter, J. and Wetherell, M. (1987). *Discourse and Social Psychology: Beyond Attitudes and Behaviour.* London: Sage.

Reisberg, D. (1987). External representations and the advantages of externalizing one's thoughts. In *Proceedings of the Ninth Annual Conference of the Cognitive Science Society.* Hillsdale, NJ: LEA.

Rips, L. (1986). Mental Muddles. In Brand, M. and Harnish, R.M.(eds), *The Representation of Knowledge And Belief.* Tuscon: University of Arizona Press.

Rouse, W.B. and Morris, N.M. (1986). On looking into the blackbox: prospects and limits in the search for mental models. *Psychological Bulletin 100,* 349–363.

Rumelhart, D.E. (1984). Understanding understanding. In Flood, J. (ed.) *Understanding Reading Comprehension.* Newark: International Reading Association.

Rumelhart, D.E. and McClelland, J.L. (1985). Levels indeed! A response to Broadbent. *Journal of Experimental Psychology: General 114,* 193–197.

Rumelhart, D.E. (1989). Toward a microstructural account of human reasoning. In Vosniadou, S. and Ortony, A. (eds), *Similarity and Analogical Reasoning.* Cambridge: CUP.

Rupietta, W. (1990). Mental models and the design of user manuals. In Ackermann, D. and Tauber, M.J. (eds) *Mental Models and Human-Computer Interaction 1.* Amsterdam: Elsevier (North-Holland).

Rutherford, A. and Wilson, J.R. (1991). Models of mental models: an ergonomist – psychologist dialogue. In Tauber, M.J. and Ackermann, D. (eds) *Mental Models And Human-Computer Interaction 2.* Amsterdam: Elsevier (North-Holland).

Searle, J.R. (1990). Consciousness, explanatory inversion and cognitive science. *Behavioural and Brain Sciences 13,* 585–642.

Shallice, T. (1972). Dual functions of consciousness. *Psychological Review 79,* 585–642.

Sharrock, W. and Anderson, B. (1987). Epilogue: the definition of alternatives: some sources of confusion in interdisciplinary discussion. In Button, G. and Lee, J. (eds) *Talk and Social Organization, Multilingual Matters.* Clevedon and Philadelphia.

Shore, B. (1991). Meaning construction and cultural cognition. *American Anthropologist 93,* 9–26.

Suchman, L.A. (1987). *Plans and Situated Actions.* Cambridge: CUP.

Suchman, L.A. and Trigg, R.H. (1991). Understanding practice: video as a medium for reflection and design. In Greenbaum, J. and Kyng, M. (eds) *Design at Work.* Hillsdale, NJ: LEA.

Waltz, D.L. (1981). Toward a detailed model of processing for language describing the physical world. In *Proceedings of the Seventh International Joint Conference on Artificial Intelligence (IJCAI-81).* Vancouver: University of British Columbia.

Werner, H. and Kaplan, B. (1963). *Symbol Formation.* New York: Wiley.

Wertsch, J.V. (1991). *Voices of the Mind.* Cambridge, Ma.: Harvard University Press.

Whiteside, J. and Wixon, D. (1988). Contextualism as a world view for the reformation of meetings. In Tatar, D. (ed.) *Proceedings of the Conference on Computer Supported Cooperative Work (CSCW '88)*. New York: ACM Press.

Wilson J.R. and Rutherford, A. (1989). Mental models: theory and application in human factors. *Human Factors 31*, 617–634.

Winograd, T. (1977). On some contested suppositions of generative linguistics about the scientific study of language. *Cognition 5*, 151–179.

Winograd, T. and Flores, F. (1986). *Understanding Computers and Cognition*. Norwood, NJ: Ablex.

Subject Index

Author Index

MY FATHER'S GEISHA

JAMES GORDON BENNETT

MY FATHER'S GEISHA

Delacorte Press

Published by
Delacorte Press
Bantam Doubleday Dell Publishing Group, Inc.
666 Fifth Avenue
New York, New York 10103

Portions of this novel first appeared, in different form, in the
following periodicals: "Dependents" in *The Virginia Quarterly
Review* and in *New Stories from the South: The Best of 1987;* "The
Sorrell Sisters" in *The Yale Review* (under the title "The Searle
Sisters"); "In the Grass" in *The Antioch Review;* "Good Hearts"
in *St. Andrews Review;* and "Pacific Theater" in *The Virginia
Quarterly Review* and in *New Stories from the South: The Best of
1989.*

Library of Congress Cataloging in Publication Data

Bennett, James Gordon, 1947–
    My father's geisha / James Gordon Bennett.
        p.   cm.
    ISBN 0-385-30097-2
    I. Title.
    PS3552.E54635M9   1990
    813'.54—dc20   89-77141
                                                            CIP

Manufactured in the United States of America
Published simultaneously in Canada

June 1990

10 9 8 7 6 5 4 3 2 1

BVG

To my father
To the memory of my mother
And to my sisters, Gail and Eileen

I would like to thank Amanda Urban for the call and Lisa Bankoff, my agent, for staying on the line. It's been my great good luck to have Jane Rosenman as my editor.

CHAPTERS

The Army is a wonderful atmosphere in which to bring up children.

—NANCY SHEA,
The Army Wife

Fifteen minutes ago they had been a family.

—F. SCOTT FITZGERALD,
Tender Is the Night

DEPENDENTS

"Get real," Cora says when I ask her how long she thinks Daddy will stay in the BOQ. "Just lighten up, will you?" and she folds the page over on her movie magazine.

One of my father's MPs is substitute bus driver today. Waves of heat are already rippling above the macadam so he keeps the door open, which Cora says is against military regulations. Then as soon as we're past the guard hut, he switches on his portable radio. "Another Article Fifteen for you," my sister whispers.

It's a half hour from the Proving Ground to Yuma Grammar. Right across the river is California, where the times change ("You can say that again," Cora likes to say), but on the long ride into the city there's nothing much to see except the desert and the Mexican border. And so mostly the enlisted kids do their homework. Except Jeffrey Orr, who Cora claims is narcoleptic. The time he fell into the aisle and knocked himself unconscious, our regular driver, Corporal Greenspun, had to race back to the dispensary, and we were an hour late for school. Now everyone tries to get Jeffrey to take an aisle seat.

The only other officers' kids are the Sorrell sisters, who no one sits next to. Cora says it's because Colonel Sorrell is CO. Still, I believe that Leslie and Claudine are in love with me, even though we never sit next to each other on the bus.

When we pass the giant saguaro with all the bullet holes in it, I ask Cora what a "philander" is.

1

"Philanderer, knucklehead. Give me a break, for Chrissake."

Cora will be salutatorian of her eighth-grade class ("Only because Sheila Haggar gets credit for crap like Home Ec") and is an expert on all celebrity crossword puzzles. "Your sister is precocious," my mother will say to me. "She is also given to moods. *Nota benhay.*" When I tell Cora this, she makes her favorite snorting sound through her nose. "What mother means is *nota bene.*"

My sister is preparing for our newspaper's annual Oscar Awards Night Contest. Last year she tied for runner-up ("Big deal, a crummy *Yuma Gazette* T-shirt"). This year she will win ("Because I'm *sick* of finishing second"). The grand prize is again a week for two at the luxurious Riviera Hotel in downtown Las Vegas, air fare included, only one entry per family permitted. Cora jots notes to herself in the margins of her magazines. Whenever an Oscar nominee is mentioned, she underlines it in red ink. "It's all political," she'll say, uncapping her pen. "You have to know who's in and who's out. Or whether the vote's going to get split. Or whether they want to give it to a musical two years in a row. In other words, too complicated to explain to you."

My sister doesn't care to play ridiculous children's games, and so when I see my first road runner of the morning, I don't bother to shout "Beep-beep" before anyone else on the bus. Even though Beth Sibula and I are tied in points.

My mother says that things will work out and that I am not to take the cares of the world on my young shoulders. Cora says that I should hang loose or I'm going to have a peptic ulcer before I can shave. "Besides," she'll say, "it's not the first time Daddy's been in the doghouse." But this time is different. This time my father is a philanderer.

The public school where I am in the sixth grade is not, according to Cora, academically sound. The best teachers come from the post and leave when their husbands are transferred. Many of my classmates are mestizos who live in adobes and go to school barefoot even in the winter. They have black, shiny hair and brown teeth, and always smile when they try to speak English. They are friendly and seem happy but will never, my sister says, graduate.

When I get to homeroom, Miss Clark is wearing her red Chinese dress. The one with the slit up the side and the same one my father saw her in at PTA. Afterward he joked with my mother that he regretted more than ever having gone to parochial school. My sister nodded at me and said that I could relax. Daddy wouldn't be missing any more parent-teacher meetings.

Cora says that my homeroom teacher is a tease and that she's been egging on some hick rancher for months. Whenever I see her in the cafeteria, she is always eating alone. Miss Clark thinks I will make an excellent college student someday. In the meantime she wants me to try to get outside and mix with the other boys and girls a little more. But during recess I prefer to sit on the swings and talk to her, because like me, she chooses to keep to herself.

This afternoon, when I point this out to her, she tilts the swing back and smiles. Her hands are raised overhead to grip the chains, and her bare knees locked to brace her feet in the sand. Under her arms a thin crescent darkens her Oriental dress. She squints in the bright sunlight, making her seem when she talks to me to be concentrating fiercely. And I can pretend to be her rancher. Cora, who misses nothing, is the first to suspect this ("Just watch she doesn't string you along like her lonesome cowboy").

"Well, young man," Miss Clark says finally, bending her knees to allow the swing to carry her forward, "then we must both come out of our shells."

When she says "young man," my chest prickles the same way it does whenever the bus hits a road runner.

Saturday, my father arrives to pick up my mother. Somebody big is coming through, and there will be a color guard reception at the officers' club. As provost marshal, my father is required to wear his dress uniform even when the guest is a civilian.

"Must be hot stuff," Cora says, tapping the ribbons over his pocket. "Pop's all dolled up."

I no longer ask my father how he earned his decorations. He would only tell me once again what some pedicab driver in Korea charged him for his Silver Star. And if he hadn't run out of them five minutes before, it could have been the Medal of Honor. When I was a boy, my mother frowned upon his joking with me this way. I would repeat the tales at school and they would come back to her through the parents of my classmates. That my father's master parachute wings were won at the Mount Tom carnival in Chicopee, for example. Or that the scars on his knees only *look* like shrapnel wounds. He had, in fact, accidentally knelt on a red ant hill while on a picnic with "your mother."

My father hasn't been by in three days, and the hothouse tomatoes he set out on the windowsill are now ripe.

"Look at that baby," he says, palming the biggest one admiringly. "Cora, *le sel.*"

My sister hands him the shaker, wagging her head. "You get that on you, mister, your ass is grass."

But my father expertly slices the large tomato in half and jabs the saltshaker at it repeatedly. "I get one seed on me," he says, thrusting his square chin forward, "I take it out on your hide."

The juice only dribbles a little down his chin and he slurps it up with his tongue.

"Our role model," Cora says to me.

Although my sister tries not to show it, she is excited to have my father back. She spent the morning adding to the movie-star collage on her ceiling and tells him that it's ready for inspection. But before he can get up from the table, my mother is standing in the kitchen door.

"Hello, Major."

I barely recognize her voice. It seems deeper, almost hoarse. And it is the first time I've ever heard her call my father by his rank.

"Come for your tomato?"

Even Cora laughs at this.

My father scrapes his chair back. "I guess we'd better march," he says, clearing his throat. He seems as startled by my mother's presence as I am. Something more than her voice has changed.

"You can check out the room when you come back," my sister says, and hands him his braided service cap. "Assuming you *do* come back."

When my father glances sheepishly at my mother, she only rolls her eyes. "Your daughter, Provost."

As soon as the car backs out onto Truscott Circle, Cora is pounding me on the shoulder.

"Could you believe that getup? Un-be-*liev*-able!" She smacks her forehead with her palm. "Where did I see it? Give me a second." She closes her eyes dramatically. "It's coming. *Un momento.* I see it. I got it." She grabs my wrist and drags me into the living room. "Sit." And she pushes me onto the couch. "Remain seated."

I watch her race back down the hall.

"Mom looks as good as a spit shine," my sister calls out to me from her room. "That Kraut won't know what hit her."

Cora claims that the other woman is some German hausfrau, the wife of one of my father's young lieutenants. ("Dad's a xenophile—one attracted to foreigners, nine across. What can you do?")

My sister wanders back, flipping through one of her magazines. "If it's not in here," she says without looking up, "then it's . . ." But she's found it. "There," and she thrusts the picture triumphantly before me. "Who's *that* remind you of?"

I study the black-and-white photograph of a woman standing beside a large canopied bed. She's wearing only a slip and has one arm over her head, gripping the wooden post.

"Jesus," Cora says, snapping the magazine out of my hands. "It's Liz. Doesn't *Butterfield 8* even ring a bell?"

But all we get at the post theater are John Wayne and Wile E. Coyote cartoons.

"Mom's vamping him," Cora says, more to herself than to me. "Obvious to everyone, of course, except a certain idiot sibling."

But the contest entry form has to be postmarked by midnight, and she retreats to her room with her red ink pen.

In the carport I unzip my father's golf bag and scoop out a handful of balls. He keeps two sand wedges, and I take the older, scratched one.

There's an abandoned parade field just up the block, and I wear my nylon baseball cap. It's probably close to a hundred degrees out. They test experimental equipment at the Proving Ground. Like the cap my father brought home. Somebody from Quartermaster said it was the original prototype and that it cost a couple million dollars to develop. When I told my father that my Little League cap was more comfortable, he said I was what made America strong and that I didn't have to worry about ever being drafted.

Even on the parade field you have to keep your eyes open. My father's first sergeant once killed a sidewinder in his three-year-old's sandbox, and every other dog you see has a limp. "Why don't they test something nuclear?" Cora likes to say. "Meanwhile we could all go up to Vegas for a couple weeks, government expense. Come back when all the snakes are dead. I wouldn't have to win any stupid contest."

I try to keep my elbow stiff on the backswing. There's enough room to hit a driver, but it's too hot to do much walking. Every other week my father lets me tag along with his foursome. I'll hold the flag or replace divots. He didn't mention anything about this weekend, though. So I guess it's off. When he goes fishing, he'll bring me along, and I'll be the only kid. Even though some of his buddies have sons my own age. Still, I didn't ask him about Sunday. He doesn't have to think about me all the time.

The ball makes a little puff of dust where it lands and you can't take your eyes off the spot or you'll lose it. But when I see Leslie walking across the parade field toward me, I forget about the ball. Her younger brother trails behind her, tossing a play parachute into the air. She suddenly stops and points at the ground.

"Got it," she calls out to me.

I wave the club and pick up the other ball. I don't want to risk sculling it. While they wait for me, her little brother wraps the handkerchief tightly about the rock and hurls it toward the road. It doesn't open.

Leslie stands with her hands on her hips like a runner. She's taller than me but still has a flat chest. We both watch her brother stretch his arm out behind him like a javelin thrower. He makes a grunting sound, heaving the rock with all his might. The handkerchief comes down again without opening.

"I guess everybody's over at the reception," Leslie says, taking the club from me.

I don't ask her where Claudine is. If her sister isn't at home reading a book, then she's at the library looking for a new one.

Leslie nods at the ground and I drop one of the balls at her feet. In the distance her brother stops to watch her take several practice swings. She bends both elbows the way girls do but I don't say anything.

"Your mom and dad go together?" she asks finally.

Cora says that it's always going to be news when "the goddamn provost marshal's living in the BOQ."

"Yes."

She swats at the ball but it only skitters off to the right.

"You probably think track's pretty stupid for a girl, don't you?"

I watch her squat down and scoop some sand into a small mound. The fine blond hair on her arm shines like gold.

"Well," she says, "I can't help it if I'm good at it."

Looking up at me, she holds her hand out and I set the second ball in her palm.

"I should tell you what my mother said about your father." She balances the ball on top of the mound. "It's rich."

Her brother yells something to her, but she ignores him.

"She said your father's the only man around here who knows how to wear a pith helmet."

This time she hits the ball solidly, and it sails high over her brother's head.

After dinner Cora and I talk my mother into letting us see *The Comancheros* at the post theater. Even though the Proving Ground is several hundred miles square, you can walk to everything in ten minutes.

"Mom's a wreck," my sister says as soon as we leave the house. "That stupid Kraut was at the reception."

It's already dark enough out to see a few stars. And in another hour or so you'll be able to hear the coyotes. They like to wander down from the hills for any scraps they can dig out of the mess hall cans.

"Dad introduced them," Cora is saying. "So now they're supposed to go over for drinks. Mom's ready to shoot him."

I find the Big Dipper. "The lieutenant?"

My sister glances past me at the canal across the road. It's stagnant and thick with algae, and her lip appears to curl up at its smell. "Daddy, moron."

There is a long line at the theater, and Cora spots a baby-sitter we used to have up near the ticket window.

"Every man for himself," she says, and is gone.

Ten minutes later Sergeant Shuman sticks his head out of the double glass doors to the theater.

"Sorry, folks. All sold out."

They'll have a second, special showing at eleven if we want to buy our tickets now.

I don't much feel like a movie anyway so I'm not real disappointed. There's a *National Geographic* special on at eight about the Arctic. Or I could just read.

I take the long way home, past the Sorrells' house. Leslie reminded me that as dependents we could use the driving range at night. For fifty cents split a large bucket of practice balls. Because she is athletic, she'd probably learn to keep her elbows stiff.

All the streetlights flicker on ahead of me like new bright stars. It's dark enough to see satellites.

But then suddenly I am sitting in the road, the pavement still hot from the heat of the day. To stand I have to grip the stop sign before me. And as I pull myself up I understand that it's what I walked into.

At home my mother puts me to bed, wrapping several crushed ice cubes in a facecloth.

"Miss Clark says you're preoccupied," she says, pressing the facecloth to my burning forehead. "That you daydream in class."

We both listen to the coyotes howling outside. Usually, for something like this, my mother will say, "Like father like son." But tonight she doesn't.

Some time later I am awakened briefly by the sound of voices in the kitchen. The hushed tone makes me cock my ear. And then it is Cora, I think, who I hear. Or perhaps my mother. In the dark it's hard sometimes to tell them apart.

I was dreaming of the Arctic and of playing golf with Leslie in the snow. It was as flat and bare as the Proving Ground, and each ball we hit hung in the air like a miniature moon. "Don't even bother to look," Leslie had said, dressed in her track shorts and sneakers. "You're not going to find anything."

I slide up against the headboard, shielding my eyes from the overhead light.

"Honey, you want to get up?"

It's my mother. And then Cora is standing in the doorway, both of them still dressed.

"Too bad you're not on the ballot," my sister says to me. "This is Oscar-winning stuff."

My mother stares at the sheet covering my legs. "That's enough, young lady." But then just as abruptly her voice is gentle and coaxing. "Put your clothes on, sweetheart. I need you for something."

As soon as she leaves, Cora crosses her arms as if to mimic my mother's stance.

"Don't let an MP near her," she says. "Her breath could kill a steer."

My mother waits for me in the car, the engine already idling.

"You feel all right?" she asks, reaching over to touch the Band-Aid on my forehead. There is quite a welt. But the stop sign probably kept me from wandering into the canal and drowning.

Cora comes out of the carport to shout, "Headlights," but my mother ignores her, shoving the gear shift into reverse. I know where we are going. My father took the staff car. Now my mother will retrieve him from the duplex over on Stillwell Avenue. Cora pointed out the flat-roofed house to me from the school bus. "Mata Hari's place," she said, and then fogged the window to trace a skull and bones. Even though Cora is older, my mother brings me instead because I am the male.

"You don't want the wrong impression here," she begins, gazing straight ahead. It is the kind of blank look she gets ironing my father's khaki uniforms. "Your sister can get a little carried away. Right now she's upset with your father. And she's probably said some things to you."

I crack my window. Not even the cooler air at night keeps the canals from smelling like rancid perfume. You can hear the frogs croaking as if even they can't stand the stench.

"He just wants his men to like him," my mother is saying. "Only, sometimes the social drinking gets out of hand." She glances over at me as if to be certain that I've not fallen back asleep. "We both know when to let Cora go in one ear and out the other."

My mother's voice grows sullen as we move out of the senior-grade housing and into the low, flat duplexes of the junior officers. I recognize the tone. It is the same one Cora uses whenever she believes things have gone beyond her brother's feeble limits.

"You may have your father's coloring," my mother says as if I just contradicted her, "but you've damn well got my eyes."

She concentrates on the straight road ahead but occasionally jerks the steering wheel sharply to keep from crossing the center line.

"I know what you're thinking," she says without looking over at me. "But I'm not."

The year before, her license was suspended when she accidentally drove the Buick into the canal. It was late, and she'd taken the turn off MacArthur Boulevard in third instead of second. The judge advocate told her she was lucky she hadn't drowned, and then put her on probation for six months. "Mom got off light," Cora told me afterward, "mostly because Dad has the goods on guess-whose sixteen-year-old?" The judge's daughter had been caught laminating fake IDs for the PX.

My father's familiar green staff car is parked in the double driveway of the duplex, and on seeing it my mother pulls up too close to the curb, squealing the tires. She leaves the engine on, looking first into the rearview mirror to wet down her eyebrows, and then at me.

"Your head must be pounding," she says, and hooks her warm

hand around my neck to draw me toward her. "I won't be a minute, sweetie. Then we can all go home."

There is rum on her breath. Cora fixed her piña coladas in the blender.

"I hate him," I say, but my voice catches, garbling my words.

"What?" My mother grabs my wrist when I try to open the door. "Sweetheart, you just sit and listen to the radio. I won't be a minute." And then, as if she'd finally been able to decipher what I said, smooths the damp hair back from my forehead. "Your father's the bravest soldier in the army, honey. This doesn't mean anything next to that."

Cora likes to say that my mother is your basic just-taking-orders kind of housewife. But even my sister knows better than to break The Rule. We are never to bad-mouth our father in her presence. Never.

I slump down in the front seat and watch my mother, one shoulder lower than the other, walk up the yellow patch of lawn as if trying to get to the front of a moving bus. Her toes point, like my sister's, slightly out. Cora says that the lieutenant's wife is built like a tank and that Daddy is bored with being provost marshal and wants to get back into Artillery.

When at last the screen door is pushed open several inches, my mother steps back out of the way as if to accept the invitation to come in. Instead, she waits until my father joins her on the porch, wearing civilian clothes and holding a glass in his hand. I turn off the radio but their voices are too low to hear. In a minute my father disappears back inside the house, and the lieutenant and his wife replace him, framed in the light of the door. The lieutenant's wife is nearly as tall as her husband. And I think of Miss Clark standing in line at the cafeteria, the heads of her students barely to her shoulders. They are both smiling, talking to my mother as if still trying to win her inside. But she doesn't uncross her arms until my father reappears, this time wearing his leather aviator jacket even though it is too hot for it.

At the driveway he turns to wave good-night to the couple, who have come out onto the porch holding hands. My mother does not turn or wave or say another word to my father. She walks instead ahead of him past the staff car and around the lieutenant's MG.

As soon as she is back in the driver's seat, my mother pats me twice on the knee and tells me never to marry a WAC. Then she tries to turn the key in the ignition but the engine is already on. When the gears grind, she snaps her hand back as if from a snake.

"I know what you're thinking," she says to me.

My father ambles up alongside the car, stooping so that his chin rests on my open window. "Hey, buddy," and he taps his forehead with one finger. "You been back-talking the old lady?"

My mother looks coolly at him. "Step away if you don't want any toes flattened."

My father's tanned face shines in the dark. He grins happily, his straight, even teeth those of a movie star.

"Sure you don't want to come in?" he says to my mother. "They're right nice people."

"Don't patronize me," she answers sharply. "That's your son sitting there."

My father reaches in to grip my shoulder. "Then maybe I ought to invite him in. What do you say, soldier? You want to show your mother how to be sociable?"

He squeezes my arm as if to gain my attention but I haven't taken my eyes off him. I've never seen my father smile that way before. My heart is racing even faster than with Leslie.

"Don't you ask him that," my mother says. "Don't you ask him anything."

Over my father's shoulder I can see the lieutenant and his wife still waiting on the porch. They shift their weight from one foot to the other in the cool night air. But they can't close the door on us.

"No," my father says resignedly, and takes a single duck step back from the car. "We don't want a momma's boy."

Before I can even turn to see her, my mother has flung her door open and is shouting over the hood.

"What did you say, mister? What the hell did you say?"

I twist in the seat as she flashes by the rear window. But by the time I unlock my own door, my father is grasping both her arms, dancing away from her furious kicks.

"You bastard!" she is screaming. "You lousy bastard!"

The lieutenant trots down the driveway but stops respectfully at the mailbox.

"Sir?"

His wife stays on the porch, one hand at her mouth.

"Sir?" he repeats, but then looks away helplessly.

My ears still ring from the stop sign and I cover them with my hands. As if in pantomime my mother attempts to wrench free until my father trips over the embedded sprinkler head and they both drop to their knees in the scorched grass.

"Don't you come home," my mother says, her face only inches from my father's. "You don't live there anymore, mister."

"Fine," he says, wishing only to calm her. "Fine. Let's just call it a night."

But he doesn't follow her across the lawn.

When she staggers around the car, my mother glares at me menacingly.

"And the kids are mine," she shouts, closing her eyes as if to steady herself. "Mine."

Back again in the front seat, she rests her forehead on the steering wheel.

"I could drive," I say, even though at home I've never gone farther than the curb.

She lifts her head tiredly. "I'll get us there, sweetheart."

And she does, but not without first backing into the lieutenant's mailbox, crushing the little red metal flag.

At the house my mother pours herself the rest of the piña colada mix from the blender and goes to bed, locking the door after her. It is what she does whenever my father is left to sleep alone on the couch.

Cora tiptoes down the hall to peek into my room.

"Any stabbings?"

I pretend to be asleep.

"Army life," my sister says, easing the door shut behind her. She kneels on the throw rug beside my bed. "The civilian population doesn't know the half of it."

Over her head I can just make out the different model airplanes suspended by fishing wire from the ceiling. Several of the real ones my father has jumped from on maneuvers. Once, when I asked him how it felt to fall all that way before his chute opened, he said he'd be able to explain it better when I was a little older and maybe had a sweetheart like Miss Clark.

"Don't take it too hard," Cora advises me, one elbow on the mattress. "They'll kiss and make up. Mom's not going to let him rot in the BOQ." When my sister stands up, she tries to touch the damp pillowcase without me noticing. "Listen, you're just an army brat. You don't know the whole story yet."

At the door she whispers that if she wins the contest, she'll think about taking me along. "Who knows, Vegas might be good for you. Give you a shot at the big picture."

However, Cora doesn't win the Second Annual Oscar Awards Night Competition. An unemployed typesetter who once worked at the newspaper does. "Mostly they was just guesses," he tells the reporter from the *Yuma Gazette*. "I never even seen the pictures." My sister's letter to the editor, in which she demands an entire revamping of the contest rules, still hasn't been published.

The following week, right after I watch Leslie sprain her ankle in the hundred-yard dash, Miss Clark breaks her engagement and leaves before the school year is even over. She was fired by the principal, Cora claims, because he found her in the teachers' lounge smoking a joint. "Except, what really did it," my sister says, "was finding her in front of the floor fan in her half slip."

The day my father moves back in, Cora strings a banner outside the house that says, ALL HAIL THE CHIEF! then we pile in the car and go out for steaks. There's a popular restaurant in town where the maître d' cuts off your tie and hangs it from the ceiling with the thousand others already pinned up. In the parking lot my father puts on the paisley tie we gave him for Christmas. Only, my mother doesn't find it particularly funny.

Now that he's back, my father has started taking a lot of inspection tours. Weekenders to places like El Centro and the Gunnery Range across the border. At night you can hear my mother arguing bitterly with him. But this morning Cora sits beside me on the bus without having been told to. And for the first time she seems to consider things I ask her seriously. For instance, when I wonder what makes army families any different from the rest, she peels her thumbnail back so far, the skin bleeds. "Dad tries to pull off any more one-night stands," my sister says, scanning the desert as if for a road runner, "Mom'll show him what a civilian family looks like for a change. *Nota bene.*"

BRATS

To get out of serving on the Welcoming Committee, my father volunteers to go up with the Ranger class himself. Because of this my mother refuses to join the other officers' wives in the viewing stands, and only Cora and I sit in the broiling bleachers. But school is out and neither my sister nor I have anything better to do.

Down below, a bright red carpet stretches from the podium to where the guest of honor stands beside Colonel Sorrell, the post commander. When I wonder aloud who the guest might be, my sister looks up from her movie magazine (she carries them in her bike satchel), her tongue poking into her cheek.

"Probably some South American dictator. I can smell the after-shave lotion all the way up here."

A convoy of staff cars from El Centro and Luke Air Force Range are parked behind the bleachers, and I count the number with red flags attached to their bumpers.

"I can't wait for the day Dad gets his star," I make the mistake of confessing to my sister. "We'll have our own driver."

Cora is wearing her Lolita sunglasses but I can still see the contemptuous look in her eyes as she peers back at me. "And go where?" she says. "The Gunnery Range?"

The Special Services Band sits just outside the shade that shields the row of VIPs. Their starched khakis are black with sweat as we wait for the transports to come rumbling in from the airstrip.

Although my father joked about going up with a bunch of skinhead Rangers, he seemed pleased that Cora and I would be in the stands.

Only the South American dictator appears unfazed by the humidity. Through his interpreter he flirts with the young wife of one of the generals' aides.

"Look at that oily little bastard," Cora says, rolling her magazine into a baton. "He runs a country? He looks more like a Cuban dance instructor."

Lately, my sister's thyroid has been acting up and it's hard to tell whether it's that or just nerves that make her so jumpy.

"Okay," she says irritably. "Here's the sixty-four-thousand-dollar question." And she stops to gaze at the empty horizon for some sign of the first plane. But there are only clouds, great big billowing ones rolling in low from the east. The kind that will surprise you in the desert in late July. "What's Dad get out of all this?" she asked. "Fifty measly more bucks a month. I mean, did he ever stop to think why they call it hazard-duty pay? I'll tell you why. Because it's hazardous to your health is why."

This is what happens when my sister sits in the sun too long. She starts worrying like my mother.

"Dad's a soldier," I say. "It's his job."

But she isn't in the mood to debate. Not, at least, at the risk of heat prostration.

The band, meanwhile, plays another Sousa march, their arms wilting beneath the weight of their instruments.

The clouds have darkened by the time the loudspeakers crackle with static and an amplified voice directs our attention toward the jump tower. It's a moment, however, before the transports, too far off yet even to hear, loom out of the low-hanging rain clouds.

"They ought to call it off," Cora says anxiously. "Look at that sky. What if it starts lightning? They'll be fried before they hit the ground."

I count six planes and know that my father, being the ranking officer, will probably be in the lead one. On the wall in my room is a black-and-white photograph of him dangling his legs out of the open cargo door of a C-47. What makes it scary is that the plane is ten thousand feet off the ground and he isn't wearing a chute. Cora hates the picture. "You want to hero-worship," she'll say, "tack up Steve McQueen. Steve jumps out of Rolls-Royces. He gets his stand-in to do the moron stuff."

As the planes circle, I wonder what my mother is doing. Probably the wash. The machine will drown out the jet engines. If she isn't stuffing my father's uniforms into the dryer, she'll be sitting in front of the television with the volume turned up. Just after Christmas my father was supposed to join some of his junior officers for a fishing trip to the Gulf. But when the weekend forecast called for a small-crafts warning, my mother drew the line. If he went, he wasn't to expect either her or the kids to be there when he got back. After spending half the night listening to her slam dresser drawers, my father finally gave in. The next day two of the men (my father's adjutant and a second lieutenant) drowned when the rented cabin cruiser sank less than a mile from shore. It's something my mother never lets Cora forget whenever my sister accuses her of being overly protective. But my father still claims it was because they were the only ones who weren't Airborne Rangers.

"This is crazy," Cora says. Traces of heat lightning have begun to flicker in the distance and she's persuaded that the airdrop should be canceled.

Everyone in the stands is hunched forward, hands cupped at their forehead, eager not to miss the first budding of chutes.

"What the hell," Cora says. "As long as we impress the crap out of Cesar Romero."

At this the major's wife just below us twists about to tap Cora on her outstretched foot. "You're a little young for that kind of language, don't you think?"

Even before my sister lifts her sunglasses, I know what's coming. Cora doesn't like to be touched. Ever. By anyone.

"I was speaking to my son," she says, looking down at the woman as if at a piece of gum stuck to the bleachers.

Caught off guard, the major's wife tilts her head back, raising both hands to shade her eyes against the sky's intense light. Even if my sister isn't a child bride, there is always the chance she could be a general's brat. But then, like a great clap of thunder, the band starts up again just as the C-47's rip through the clouds, bodies tumbling out of their cargo doors like bowling pins. And the woman turns her back to us, the roots of her bleached hair glistening with sweat.

I know that Cora only wants to distract herself from the sky's filling up with parachutes. The lightning worries her but she refuses to admit any chickenness on her part. It isn't the kind of ammunition to hand over to her next of kin.

"Thank you, Jesus," she says when the bandleader at last sits down. My sister still can't relax, her hands tucked beneath her thighs as the chutes stream from the backs of the planes.

Like tuning forks the men dangle at the ends of invisible cords.

It isn't something I ever want to do myself. I don't take after my father.

Without sunglasses I'm squinting narrowly when someone down near the front in the bleachers, a woman, I think, starts causing a real commotion. I'm trying to figure out what it's all about when Cora suddenly jumps up beside me as if for a foul ball. And then everyone is standing, arms raised as if at a revival and even the guest of honor is waving his swagger stick at the clouds. But I'm seeing double from looking into the sun and have to turn away.

As the first few jumpers hit the parade ground, they roll over to absorb the stiff shock of the hardpan. Puffs of dust rise from their heels as the silk chutes collapse about them like deflated hot-air balloons.

A second chorus of shouting wells up in the bleachers. Rows that resisted rising are all on their feet now, and I cup one hand at my brow, trying to train my eyes in the direction the others insist we look.

Beside me Cora makes a whimpering sound. Nothing more than a muffled "Oh," her fist at her mouth, as if she's about to be sick.

Then, an instant before it's too late, I catch the two chutes out of the corner of my eye: twisted into a single braid, twin figures no bigger than a thumb spinning about each other, spiraling at the end of the same ghostly knot, heads bent, arms up, legs pointed.

Already people are fleeing from the bleachers, while only a few hold on to hope, screaming their instructions. Their reserves, they should pull their reserves, they shout. But then abruptly it's over: the dull thump, a soundless crumpling. Like puppets they buckle at the waist, the entangled shrouds descending about them.

Cora has turned away and I sit down beside her now.

In the distance a small brown truck with a red cross on it already bumps slowly across the parade ground, dust curling up behind it. There is no reason to hurry. The chutes hadn't opened enough to make a difference, and I watch the last few Rangers sway gracefully in the sky, their own chutes perfect white cones above them.

Cora hasn't taken her hand from her mouth. Like everyone else she follows the slow progress of the truck until it disappears into its own cloud of dust.

The bleachers creak and are quickly empty. Down through the stands the ground is littered with mimeographed handouts. The airdrop was to have been only the beginning of the program. There was the precision flying team to follow.

"I guess they'll call off the rest of it," I offer.

Cora is clutching her sunglasses in her lap. There's a red mark on the bridge of her nose. And then she begins nodding her head as if admitting something to herself.

"It could be Daddy."

I am staring at her. She has the perfect profile of my father. The same fair skin. The same dark, thick hair. I look back down at my hands. They've begun to shake and I pin them beneath my legs. It's why we came. We're army brats. Yet we'd never seen our father, a master parachutist, jump before.

"No," I say, and my sister is suddenly shaking her head in agreement.

"There were hundreds," she declares. It's her Big Sister voice. "There were dozens in each plane."

"Daddy would know what to do," I say. "The others were only learning. One of them made a mistake."

Cora can't hide her pained expression. I must look pathetic to her. "Dad's made a million jumps," she says. "He packs his own chute."

The generals have moved off with their guest of honor. They stand beside the staff cars, shaking hands, looking solemn. Even the translator no longer smiles as he passes on the dictator's condolences.

"Let's go," Cora says.

We walk our bikes across the grass behind the bleachers. The area has been carefully policed. Everything scrubbed and edged. Even the large drum barrels given a fresh coat of paint, TRASH restenciled in white.

"There were at least three hundred," I say. "Fifty to a plane."

My sister continues out ahead of me. "Let's not ride yet," she says.

Heat lightning flashes beyond the jump tower as we bump our bikes over the concrete speed guards. Cars pass us slowly, some of them with their headlights on as if part of a funeral procession.

"What time is it?" Cora says.

Her voice shakes and she clears her throat.

"Two-thirty," I say, even though she is wearing her own watch.

We stay in single file. Heat waves ripple above the concrete like gas fumes.

"Let's find some air conditioning," Cora says over her shoulder.

She doesn't want to go home yet. Mom would know we were upset about something and start asking questions.

Behind us cars are pulling over to the side. It is the Red Cross truck come up the access road from the parade field. The driver eases over the curb onto the street without bothering with the siren.

We stop to watch it pass. I try to see in the small meshed window but it's too dark. Cora starts walking again and doesn't say anything until she comes up with the idea of catching the last half of the matinee. *Dr. No* is at the post theater. We've already seen it twice but my sister has made up her mind. After another block she straddles her bike and pedals off.

The breeze feels good and I think about my father. He is forty-one years old and already led a rifle company through Inchon and only come away with some shrapnel in his knee and neck. Which he just makes fun of, shaking his leg whenever it looks like rain. God wouldn't let some recruit's guidelines get mixed up with my dad's. If that happened then there can't be any God. But I'm afraid to say this to Cora. "Think about Jeff Chandler," she'd say. "Or Jayne Mansfield, for that matter." If accidents can happen to movie stars, what chance do the rest of us have? So I just ride behind her and keep my mouth shut, standing up on the pedals every once in a while to pump a few times before coasting.

In the dark, empty theater we sit on the aisle because Cora is claustrophobic. Sean Connery has already discovered Ursula Andress searching for conchs on the beach, and as soon as Cora sits down she starts mouthing the dialogue word for word. Half a dozen movie magazine subscriptions come to the house every month, which my father argues only fills my sister's head with fairy tales. But since Cora has always been at the top of her class, my mother wants to know who's doing any better than his daughter in school? Anyway, it's still a sore point between them.

By the time it comes to the scene where James Bond escapes from the island, Cora looks ready to go. Seeing her profile lit up by the screen, I'm reminded why people find it hard to believe that we are brother and sister. Even my mother has to admit it. "Your sister's your father's daughter, all right," she'll say to me. "But the two of you look like you came from different orphanages."

The lights go up in the theater before all of the credits have finished, which is one of Cora's pet peeves.

"Hicks," she says as I trail up the aisle after her. "Hayseeds," and she sails a flattened popcorn box at the projection booth.

Outside, Cora lingers in front of one of the posters for coming attractions, and I can tell that she wants me to leave her alone for a minute. So I walk down to the picture of Paul Newman leaning on a pool cue. After a while Cora comes up beside me and we both study the poster together without saying anything. But what I'm really doing is staring at my sister's reflection in the dull glass.

"If that was Daddy," she says without turning to look at me, "I'm coming back and burning this place down. I'll pour gasoline everywhere. And I won't care if some spec-2 janitor's still inside either." The tears curl down to her chin but she ignores them. "You can come with me if you want, it doesn't matter. I'm just telling you what I'm going to do."

My sister can scare me when she wants to. As she's scaring me now. But we're both afraid to go home.

Cora lifts her front tire out of the empty bike rack. She's wearing her Dick Clark Caravan T-shirt. Last month my mother drove us up to Blythe to see a rock and roll concert. She thought it would be a good way to get Cora out of the house and for us to do something together as a family (my father was on maneuvers). But my sister isn't interested in Dick Clark or *American Bandstand*. While all around us kids were screaming at Fabian, Cora only looked over at my mother and me and yawned. These weren't real stars, she wanted us to understand. These were rock and roll stars. You only saw real stars in the movies.

We're less than five minutes from the house and as I pedal beside my sister, I keep trying to think of something else we can do. The lanes are just thirty-five cents a string until six, but Cora hates to bowl. The only thing athletic she'll even consider is swimming, but, of course, we don't have our suits. And as we cross Truscott Circle, I think of turning back and hiding out in the post library but already we're picking up speed, coasting down Gavin Hill, my heart racing. Cora is standing up, her hair whipping about her head, and just by keeping her bike out ahead of mine, I understand that in her own way she means to look after me. Whatever we are riding toward, she'll be first to arrive at. She only needed a little extra time at the theater to prepare herself. My sister is braver than me because I'm not strong enough to nudge my front tire out ahead of hers. She will be the one to stride up to the front door of our duplex and if there is already an MP there or Dad's CO or a priest or even Mom crying, she'll turn and put her arm around me. I'm her younger brother and that will be her duty.

At the top of Eisenhower Street we can see the house for the first time. There is no provost marshal's car out front or anything official-looking from the motor pool. But then they could already have come and gone. Dad had been picked up by a driver. So it doesn't mean anything that there is no staff car around. We were at the theater over an hour.

At the curb we walk our bikes up the driveway and quietly lean them against the side of the carport. After a moment Cora thinks better of it and pries her kickstand down. She isn't ready yet and so I pretend to check the air in my tires. The backside of her shorts is pressed with the outline of her bicycle seat. She seems to cock her ear toward the dining-room window but there is nothing to hear. And as my sister steps past me, I want to reach out and hold her. But I don't, of course, because she doesn't like to be touched.

A staff car suddenly pulls up in front of the house, and Cora moves back beside me, looping her arm over my shoulder. My sister is half a foot taller than me and three years older but it is the first time I can remember her ever giving me anything like a hug. And I nearly lose my balance. Staff cars have green tinted windows, so we can't really see anything as it sits idling with whoever is inside in no hurry to get out.

When at last the passenger door swings open, my sister lowers her arm and steps in front of me so that I can't see the car. Afraid to look past her, afraid to see what she's already seen, I concentrate instead on the delicate cracks in the concrete driveway. Like a road map they zigzag in every direction. And I think of how many times we've followed the blue then red lines in the road atlas to our next assignment. Always at night with my father driving, my mother on the lookout for a motel with its neon vacancy sign still blinking. Cora bored and flipping through her magazines with a flashlight. And me massaging my father's stiff shoulders, watching his drooping eyelids in the rearview mirror. I know perhaps better than even my mother how his dark hair smoothly dovetails to hide the thin white scar of shrapnel.

"Oh," my sister says, and as I look up she turns, her expression as blank as if she's only holding the phone out for me. Then she steps back beside me and together we watch the man walk up the driveway toward us, his crisp khakis bloused at the boot. But my eyes have watered and he's wearing dark aviator sunglasses so it isn't until he smiles that I catch my breath.

"Some show," my father says.

My sister only stares up at him until her whole body begins to shake and she turns quickly to walk back to the house alone.

When the screen door slams shut behind her, my father lifts his service cap off and brushes one hand through his damp hair.

"I called your mother," he says as if to apologize. "No one was back yet."

I reach out to take his cap from him. His name and address are printed inside. But it is just like him, I think, not to include his rank.

"Your sister gets carried away," he says. "It's those damn movies."

I curl my fingers under the lining of the headband. The thin leather feels cool and moist. I'm thinking how flushed Cora's cheeks had been, as if she'd just run several blocks in the heat. Her eyes were shining. She hadn't wanted us to see her cry.

"Nobody's fault," my father says finally.

And I can't tell if he means Cora and me not knowing or just the chutes not opening.

"You see enough of these things," he says, still sounding apologetic, "you're going to run into this."

He takes his sunglasses off. The knuckles of his left hand are scraped and bruised, but it isn't anything that was there this morning.

"The funny part is," he says, and already I know that he only wants to smooth things over. He's frightened us badly and now he wants it all forgotten, "—I never even went up. They couldn't get the damn thing off the ground."

It's a lie, of course. But I don't want him to feel any worse about it. So I don't say anything and instead just start making wishes to myself the way I sometimes do. Mostly they're old ones like my father never going overseas again without the rest of us. They're not things you can say out loud. For instance, like wanting him always to love my mother and my sister and me as much as we love him. But even I know that my father can't make any of those promises.

At least not without crossing his fingers. Except, walking up the driveway with him, clutching his service cap with both hands, I don't care. He's my father and he's here and that's all that matters. "Army families are all alike," Cora will explain to me later, decorating the margin of her celebrity crossword with tiny penciled parachutes. "Which is why they have to keep us moving."

THE SORRELL SISTERS

My father's transfer has caught us all by surprise. We've been stationed at the Proving Ground for nearly four years, our longest assignment in one place. Now suddenly we're called upon to live apart again. After nearly two weeks of indecision my mother has decided that the rest of us will move to Los Angeles until my father's tour is over.

"All we ever get is the dregs," Cora complains. "Why couldn't it be England or Europe? Why does it always have to be some godforsaken outpost?"

This is ridiculous, of course. Just another popular misconception Americans have about the Far East. But when I try to argue that Taiwan is different, my sister looks up from the mound of shredded newspaper on the floor. "See what happens when they get a library card too soon?" Cora has been miserable our whole time in the desert and so L.A. is my mother's concession to her. I write my sister's prickliness off as just another effect of her condition. Whenever her thyroid flares up it's best to give her a wide berth.

Because my mother refuses to fly, my father is forced to take a week off from his hectic schedule to help with the drive. He wants my mother to know that this puts a tremendous professional strain on him and that he expects quid pro quo. Cora, the only one to have gone to a Catholic school (half a year in Ottawa), translates this as being basically a threat. Since we won't have a moment to lose, my father wants to be able to leave the office and step into the station wagon with all of us ready to hit the road.

"It's his whole attitude," my sister grumbles, wading through the excelsior in the living room. "Like we're a bunch of privates or something."

My mother wraps her favorite bone china in newspaper. "Your father's got a lot of pressure on him right now," she says. "It's no picnic for him either."

"Everybody's got this idea it's a rain forest," I say. "Actually, the capital gets—"

"Give me a goddamn break," my sister says.

My mother runs her damp sponge down the strip of masking tape. "I don't want to hear any more," she says. "I want the two of you back to work on your rooms. Now."

On the stairs my sister elbows me in the side. "Think about it," she said. "Your first French kiss could have been with a Chink."

"All right," my mother calls up to us. "I mean it."

In my room I take down the Raquel Welch poster. I hung it over my bed because it irritates my sister but also because it reminds me of the Sorrell sisters. Not that Leslie or Claudine looks like a cavewoman from one million years B.C. They just have the same kind of high cheekbones and long legs as the movie star.

But even though it's the Sorrell sisters I'll miss, it's my parents I worry about. My father's assignment has caused a lot of friction between them. Lately, every conversation seems to end in a stony silence. Cora is predicting a permanent separation ("I've seen the movie"). I've tried to be a comfort to my mother ever since the orders came down. And more than once she's told me how much she relies on my good sense. So I feel badly whenever Cora manages to goad me enough that my mother has to step in.

I stand by the window and look out at the cactus in the backyard. It's July and at night you can hear the coyotes, who know the pickup schedule of the Corps of Engineers. Saturday mornings there will be the usual litter of overturned garbage cans up the street.

I unplug the rock tumbler and take out all the stones. They shine like marbles, and I set them on the windowsill, where you can see their sheen in the sunlight. I'll miss the desert. Where else can you trip over an entire petrified tree on the way to school? You never know what to expect out here. "Except skin cancer," Cora will say. "That and second-run movies." But nothing seems to entertain my bored sister anymore. She gave up a long time ago even trying to make new friends.

I wait by the window. Leslie sometimes takes the path behind the house because it's a shortcut to the golf course, where she likes to jog. I can't keep up with her for more than five minutes before the first dagger cuts into my side and I have to put on the brakes. "Eat more bran," she'll say, running backward, her blond hair glinting in the sun. "Get more sex," I call back after her but not quite loud enough to be heard. "Wait till her knockers come in," my best friend Mick likes to say. "It'll improve your stamina." After being held back a year for poor academic performance, Leslie started an intimate diary, parts of which she permits me to read. My favorite entry is where she pierced her own ears in the girls' locker room after a track meet. But what I like best about her is the way she leans against the chain link fence after a softball game and says, "See you, Teddy," whenever my mother pulls up in the station wagon. And in the car I'll glance back to see her waving after me, one knee cocked, her foot pressed against the fence. "You're too young to worry about girls," my mother will say, adjusting the rearview mirror. "Keep your mind on your books. There'll be plenty of time for them later."

Now, I think, flopping down on my mattress, there won't be any more time for Leslie. Not to mention Claudine. Dark, quiet, studious Claudine. "That one at least has some semblance of a brain in her head," Cora will admit. Claudine belongs to Choral Society, but I was told that my voice ("How should I put it, dear?") hasn't quite formed just yet. Perhaps I should come back next year. But next year, as it turns out, I'll be a thousand miles away and not even on an army post. Despite her quick mind Claudine wasn't chosen for Debate. "Mr. Andrews doesn't think I'm aggressive enough," she told me after tryouts. "And he's probably right. I'm not like my sister. I don't run after what I want." Later, when I thought about it, I decided that Claudine had been flirting with me. She has a roundabout way of saying things, but I determined that in the future I'd try to be more attentive, not allow certain things she says to go over my head. Even if she *is* nearly three inches taller.

When I come back down from my room, my mother is putting all the photo albums in pillowcases.

"I thought we'd bring a few along in the car with us for conversation," she says.

"We haven't driven that far together in a while," I say. "I mean, what's it going to be like, the four of us on the road again?"

"Hell," Cora says. She's come out into the hall upstairs. "Sheer, unmitigated hell."

"Have you two made up?" my mother says.

"What's to make up?" my sister says. "It's his fault."

She's changed into shorts. Only, there is something else different about her. It isn't until she follows me into the kitchen that I realize what. Her eyes are rimmed with pencil liner.

"What're you staring at?" she says.

"What do you think? You look like a raccoon."

She stands in front of the cabinet, squinting at her reflection in the glass. "I barely touched them."

"With what? I say. "A tarbrush?"

She sits down at the Formica table.

"You're the only one in this family I can get an honest answer out of," she says. "Everybody thinks I'd wilt and die."

I know what she is going to ask. For the ten thousandth time my sister wants to know if her eyes bug out. It's the reason she spends most mornings in front of the bathroom mirror experimenting with mascara, eye shadow, and even fake lashes. My mother has warned me that my sister is sensitive to criticism right now and that I'm to try to be generous about her condition. But anyone can see that, in fact, her eyes *do* bug out. And not just a little. Her overactive thyroid is to blame and there's no hiding from it.

"They're no different from the last time you asked," I say finally. "And the last time you asked, they weren't any different from the time before that."

"Not froglike or anything?"

As a matter of fact that is exactly how they look. But I know better than to be the only one in the family to be honest. Sooner or later my sister will have to face the truth. Meanwhile, my mother argues, our job is to be gentle with her. That is what families are for.

I pour myself a glass of milk and try to picture the Sorrell sisters' eyes. Leslie's, I am fairly certain, are hazel, but Claudine's are a mystery. She rarely seems to look directly at me.

"I asked you a question," Cora says.

She wants to know if any of my friends, Mick, for instance, has ever said anything.

"About what?"

"Jesus," and she gazes up at the kitchen ceiling. "About my eyes, idiot."

"We've got better things to talk about."

I know that the more belligerent I am with her, the more convincing I'll likely sound.

She scrapes her chair back from the table. "Pretty impressive mustache. Too bad it's only milk."

I wipe my arm across my mouth, tempted to say something spiteful. But then it would be just like my sister to get me mad enough to tell her the truth.

I promised to meet Mick after lunch, and as soon as he sees me crossing the ballfield he sends a high fly towering in my direction. I raise my glove to shade my eyes but lose the ball in the sun. After a long, scary silence it thumps in the dirt at my feet.

"That was close," Mick says as I come down the third baseline. "I mean, another foot or so . . ."

I sit down in the dugout.

"You need to stay closer to the ground," Mick says finally. "It's what makes it so hard to pick up the ball when you're running." But it isn't really his nature to give advice, and he can see how shaky I am from almost getting clobbered. After a while he narrows his eyes at me, his broad shoulders arched back, his head slightly turned against the sun. He looks like his father, a staff sergeant who raised him like a recruit. "Heard something," he says, the bristles of his crew cut stiff as a hairbrush. "Something interesting."

I feel the dark pocket of my glove where my mother's sewing-machine oil has stained the leather. "What?"

Mick smiles at me. "Sheila was on the upstairs phone this morning. My sister has a big mouth."

I know the feeling.

"They're all sleeping out at the Sorrells'," he says. "They're using my dad's old service tent."

It is like another ball just missing me. "Leslie and Claudine's?"

Mick laughs. "Sheila spent twenty minutes on the phone trying to figure out how to get the poles over there. Like it was some kind of prison break or something."

I walk out to the mound. It feels good to be standing in the sun. It's a dry heat without any humidity. The desert sky is always blue and when it rains it's over quickly. The weather is the one thing you can count on.

I look at my friend standing at home plate, rotating his shoulders with the bat under his arms. He is the best player on our team. The only time I've ever seen him strike out, the pitch was at least six inches high but the ump refused to reverse his call. Even after both the third base coach and our manager stormed home, faces red and hats waving. Only Mick returned to the dugout without protesting. It isn't something his father ever wants to see from him. You don't question authority in the military, you don't question it on the ballfield.

"A slumber party," Mick says, tapping his cleats with the end of his bat. "Could be interesting."

There is no problem sneaking out Friday night. I've done it before. My father flew in from an inspection tour this morning and spent most of the day arguing with my mother. Cora went to bed early after taking her medicine. The dosage has been upped again and it makes her drowsy.

On the back porch I stare at the dark shapes of the saguaro that poke up like hatracks on the horizon. The black sky glitters with constellations. I am still star-gazing when a pack of dogs skulk out of the desert and cross the road. But they are too scraggy looking and slump shouldered for dogs. And I know they are coyotes. Come down out of the hills the night before garbage pickup. There are warnings in the daily bulletin about rabies and so I keep upwind of them. After a while, behind me, I hear the clatter of aluminum cans in the street.

The tent is pitched in the open and brightly lit from within by a lantern. The girls' silhouettes flutter against the canvas like shadow puppets. I stand for a moment, trying to make out their voices. But they all seem to be talking at once, at least half a dozen of them, kneeling or sitting cross-legged on their sleeping bags. When, suddenly, something the size of a dog moves up beside me and I lurch backward.

"Just me," Mick whispers. And he smiles his familiar gap-toothed smile. "Can you believe this? A tent full of girls."

It's something to see, all right. But my breath has already been taken away, and I have to sit still a moment longer, hand over my heart as if for the Pledge of Allegiance. Every once in a while the cicadas shriek in waves like banshees. There is the stench of the canals, the scum on top like lily pads. In only a couple more days, none of this, I know, will be there for me anymore: not the stars, not the desert, not the Sorrell sisters.

"You okay?"

It's Mick leaning over me. I hyperventilated.

"You skip dinner or something?"

Over his shoulder a cactus flickers like a compass needle.

"I don't want to move," I say.

Mick nods. "You hurt yourself?"

But I only meant from the Proving Ground.

"It's like some kind of henhouse," Mick says at last. "They haven't shut up since I got here."

Colonel Sorrell must have been the one to put up the tent. The canvas is as taut as a drum, with mosquito netting draped over front and back. Every few minutes one of the girls lifts the lid on the ice chest and opens another soda.

"You wonder when they come up for air," Mick says.

We can't really make out what anyone is saying. Just a lot of squealing and giggling. But as we crawl closer, their voices become more distinct. Besides Leslie and Claudine, I recognize Penny Allen, Nancy Fisher, Ann Innis (whose father is post chaplain), and Mick's sister, Sheila. You can tell they don't have any plans to go to sleep. They're excited and all talking at once.

Mick and I lie facing the street. If Colonel Sorrell decides to check up on his daughters, that is the direction he'll come. But I doubt he is too worried. There's practically a female squad in the tent.

After a while they settle down enough that you can follow a conversation. That is when I begin to feel a little guilty. It is like listening in on somebody's party line.

Mick lies on his back looking up at the stars. He doesn't seem at all troubled. Just bored. He's heard his sister before.

I only listen to hear Leslie's voice. Claudine rarely says a word. She is reading *Women in Love* and every so often stops to share a passage she thinks the others might like.

After nearly an hour Mick has gotten a kink in his neck and wants to go. But then Claudine suddenly flaps her book shut. "Sometimes I think Lawrence understood women better than we understand ourselves," she says.

"Isn't he the one who's so queer?" Penny says.

The others laugh, a harsh, collective laugh of derision. They are tired and the tent is cramped and they'd rather be at home in their own beds, comfortable and asleep. You can hear it in their groggy, slightly hoarse voices. They are still best friends, of course. Only things have gone on too long. That is in their voices too. They are getting on each other's nerves. Especially Claudine, who is smarter than the rest of them and just a little prissy about it with her nose in whatever boring book.

"Queer as a three-dollar bill," Nancy adds.

"Maybe a little like your boyfriend," Sheila says.

Now even Mick sits up.

"I don't know who you're talking about," Claudine says. She's opened her book back up as if to ignore them.

"Does the name 'Teddy' ring a bell?" Ann says.

I glance over at Mick. He's drawing circles in the sand with a stick. At the mention of my name the others laugh that same cruel laugh. And I think that my heart has stopped. I can hear everything. Can picture Claudine's quick, sharp intake of breath.

"You don't think your teddy bear's a little queer?" Penny says.

"His family's the one that's queer," Ann says.

"What's wrong with Teddy?" Leslie says. She's held back, caught between her friends and her sister.

"Maybe you're the one should tell us," Sheila says. "You two hang around so much together."

Claudine smooths the page out in her book. "Just ignore them," she says.

Leslie waits for the others to stop laughing.

"They're moving," she says finally. "So what's the difference?"

"You're not going to miss him?" Penny says.

"Why should I?" Leslie says. "We're not steady. Anyway, who cares?"

"You're going to be able to sleep without your teddy bear?" Sheila says.

"I'll live."

Then Ann says something I can't hear and in a moment they're all giddy again and hurling pillows at Leslie and tumbling about on their sleeping bags.

Penny at last sits up, catching her breath. "You ask me, I think his sister's the queer one."

"Cora?" Claudine says.

"She hardly ever leaves the house," Ann says. "Who ever sees her?"

No one says anything.

"That's what I mean," Ann says. "She doesn't have any friends. She's like a hermit."

"I guess I'd stay inside, too, if my eyes looked like that," Nancy says. "She's got some kind of disease."

"I'll tell you why they're leaving," Penny says. "His parents are getting a divorce."

"Mom said that a long time ago," Leslie admits.

"Tell us something new," Ann says. "Everybody knows that."

"Except maybe Teddy," Nancy says.

"Even my dumb brother feels sorry for him," Sheila says. "He says he's the worst player on their team. All he does is daydream out in right field."

Mick suddenly stands up, signaling for me to follow him. *It's only girls talking*, his pained expression seems to say.

"My sister's a jerk," he says as soon as we are out of earshot. He bends over to pick up a rock. And for a moment I'm afraid he's going to throw it back at the tent. But he only flicks it into the canal. "She doesn't know what she's talking about. None of them do."

We keep walking. "They were just shooting the breeze," I say.

But he doesn't look at me again until we get to the road. Then we both stop.

"I guess I'll see you tomorrow," Mick says, dusting his hands off.

I can't think of anything else to say.

"Well, anyway," I say finally, and shrug my shoulders. "Thanks for coming."

In the distance the water tower stands like a giant golf ball on top of a tee. There are off-limits signs but the chain link fence has never kept anyone out. The tower's crazy alphabet of graffiti even includes my own spray-painted initials. But I don't know any Jane who's supposed to love me.

I'm sweating when I drop to the other side of the fence. My heels hit the concrete hard and I feel the same cool tingling up my spine as when Ann first said my name. The metal ladder is at least seven feet off the ground but with a running start, I catch the bottom rung and start up, rust coming off on my palms. There's no wind but I don't look down again until I duck under the railing and am sitting on the wide catwalk.

It's a clear night and I can see Cassiopeia directly over the girls' tent. They still haven't turned off the lantern. The canvas glows like a small white triangle in the desert. My own house I can barely make out. A black square just beneath Andromeda.

I got what I deserved for sneaking. Lately, it's become a habit. It's all I seem to do around my parents. So I had it coming. But how else am I supposed to find anything out? For once I know how my sister feels. No one, including her brother, ever tells her the truth. All she has to do is look in the mirror. She really *does* look like that. Her eyes bug out and her throat is as swollen as an inner tube. She isn't pretty anymore and never will be again. That's the truth but none of us will tell her.

I can stand up and gaze down through the iron mesh of the catwalk. It's what I get for snooping, all right. But so what if my father doesn't love my mother? So what if he doesn't love any of us? What is he supposed to do? Tell the world? Why should he have to be the first to tell anyone anything in our family? No one else ever does. I close my eyes and lean over the railing. Maybe things will be different with him in another country. Maybe he'll get homesick with us in L.A. I bend my knees and teeter-totter on the metal bar, knowing that if I tip forward too much or even just open my eyes for a moment, I'll tumble over, and so I keep them closed, which seems the only way to keep my balance.

VOICES
I
LOVED

Cora squints at the oncoming headlights, brushing the tears from her cheeks roughly. She isn't used to crying in front of me.

"If you really think you can keep this from them," she says bitterly, "then it wasn't your tongue that needed stitching."

I'm still numb from the Novocain and too tired to write anything down. One of the nurses found a small chalkboard for me in the all-night gift shop.

"No week in a national park's going to turn them into newly-weds," my sister says, accelerating up the entrance ramp. "They'll be back at each other's throat before they pull into the driveway."

There is only one reason she hasn't already called the lodge. And that's because just yesterday I came in on her smoking pot in her bedroom.

But she starts nodding at the rearview mirror as if to convince herself that she hasn't been compromised in any way.

"If I want to tell Mom you bit off half your tongue, I'll tell her. Got it? They left me in charge, mister. Which makes you the minor and me the major."

However, I know that whenever my sister is bluffing she talks faster, and she's been going nonstop since we left the emergency room.

"I mean, what am I supposed to say when she tells me to hand you the phone?"

I keep the blackboard in my lap. She isn't really asking my advice.

"And just guess who's going to get strung up alive for this?" She flashes her brights at the van in front of us. "Move over, moron." The driver drifts out of the passing lane and Cora darts past him. "I'll be grounded so long, I'll forget how to drive."

My sister is hyper, and not just from worrying about what she's going to tell our parents. She's still shook up from the accident. I was out late sitting in the tree house when the plyboard suddenly opened beneath me and I seemed to fall forever, arms jackknifed overhead, until something seared my chin, snapping my mouth shut thickly.

I woke up with Cora aiming a flashlight at me in the ligustrum.

"Oh, Jesus," I heard her say. She couldn't keep the beam from jumping. "Oh, Jesus, Teddy."

My Disneyland T-shirt looked like a butcher's apron, splinters sticking from my chin like a goatee. But it was the little red leech stuck to my forehead that dropped the flashlight at my sister's feet. She rushed back into the house to empty a tray of ice cubes into the blender. When I opened my eyes again she was packing the severed tip of my tongue in a sandwich bag of crushed ice. It glowed like a goldfish in the moonlight. I could hear the station wagon idling in the driveway but after testing my weight, Cora decided instead to back the car right up to the side of the house. She hadn't called for help, either an ambulance or the neighbors. We aren't a family to ask favors.

It's after midnight when we get back from the hospital, and my sister has only her mute brother to talk to. Sitting down on the edge of my mattress, she picks up the postcard from my bed table. It's a picture of a car driving through the hollowed-out trunk of an enormous redwood. Beneath Mom's *Miss you* my father has printed the names of the three largest sequoias: Generals Sherman, Grant, and Lee.

"I guess they'll stop off in Tahoe," Cora says. "Must be nice without the brats."

My father has been in Taiwan over a year now and this is his first hardship leave: three weeks with the family.

Later, Cora comes back in and sets a TV tray down before me. It's an unaccustomed role: serving her invalid brother. She's heated up some of the soup Mom put in the freezer for us.

But I've lost any sense of taste, and the coordination of swallowing has become tricky. There's no feeling until the soup is halfway down my throat.

"That character they brought in to do the stitching," Cora says, and yawns deeply enough that her eyes glisten. "An absolute ringer for John Carradine. Not to mention looking half-tanked the whole time."

I study my feet at the end of the bed. They're sticking up under the sheet like a headstone.

My sister kicks off her leather sandals, her white socks grass-stained from when she ran out into the yard. "I mean, it's not like you'd be an orphan or anything. They'd still be your parents, for God's sake."

I take up the chalk and rub my pajama sleeve across the clouded blackboard. But my tears begin to roll down my cheeks.

"You need anything," Cora says, backing out of the room, "just whistle."

The next night my mother calls collect from the Lodgepole Visitors' Center.

"Practically in the clouds up here," she says after I carefully raise the other phone in the upstairs hall. "Your father's in seventh heaven. How's your brother doing?"

"Who cares?" Cora says with remarkable casualness. "He doesn't listen to a word I say anyway. Now he's got laryngitis to prove it."

"What're you talking about?" my mother says, and already I can tell that she regrets the trip. "It's the middle of July. Put him on."

"That's the thing," my sister says. "He can't really talk. His voice is shot. It'll probably be a couple days."

"He's lost his voice?"

"He never listens. I told him to stay out of that idiot tree at night. So, that's what he gets."

"Your weather's been good," my mother says. "I check it in the papers. What're you telling me? It's been sunny all week. Lows in the seventies."

"It has," my sister says, and I can't help admiring how confidently she lies. "He went out after his shower with his hair wet. Anyway, it's his own dumb fault. At least I'll have a little peace and quiet for a change. There's that."

"Put Teddy on," my mother says sternly.

When Cora tries to object, my mother stops her. "Get your brother on this phone. Now."

I wait for my sister to call me before pretending to pick up the extension.

"He's on," Cora says from the kitchen.

"Hello, sweetheart?" my mother says. "You really can't manage to say anything?"

I have to cover the receiver while I fight back a torrent of tears. My mother's voice has reminded me of the hopelessness of ever believing that she and my father will return to us any happier than they left.

"Probably not real smart to strain it," Cora offers.

My mother seems to consider this for a moment. "I don't like it," she says finally. "I don't like it one bit. And if I find out there's some kind of shenanigans going on . . . Just suffice it to say you'll wish there hadn't been."

She's going to hand the phone to my father now but first she wants Cora to know that she's calling Mrs. Grosset from across the street as soon as they hang up. And if she gets any kind of a different report, then she's calling back. "Pronto."

"Teddy, honey," she says sweetly, "you listen to your sister now and I'll call again when we can talk."

Then she passes the receiver to my father, mumbling something to him in an unfriendly voice.

"How you guys doing?" He sounds cheerful and rested. But then, my father rarely sounds any other way. "I take it we're a little under the weather."

Cora is still smarting from her conversation with my mother and only grumbles in response. Undeterred, my father happily goes on to describe one of the terrific trinkets they're working on over in Taiwan: walkie-talkies with TV capabilities. Platoon leaders or even tank commanders will be able to view each other in the field.

But I want to ask him how it's going with Mom. Whether the trip is helping them see things a little more eye to eye. But, of course, I can't.

"Well, listen," he says at last. "This is costing your vacationing parents, so let me hand this back to your mother."

I haven't been able to tell what kind of mood either of them is in. My father's hearty phone voice never seems to change, and my mother is too upset.

"There's nothing else you want to tell me, then?" my mother says to Cora.

My sister trusts only one defense. "What's the dif?" she says curtly. "You're not going to believe a word I say in the first place."

But there are all sorts of things I want to say. Only, ours isn't the kind of family you say them in. It wouldn't have made any difference if my entire tongue were missing. I know that nothing that really matters ever gets said between us anyway.

Five minutes after my mother hangs up, Mr. Grosset is on our doorstep. His wife has sent him over in her stead.

"*Bonanza?*" Cora says.

He nods. Mr. Grosset never seems to leave the house without a tie and jacket on, even though he's been retired for years. "She can't stand to miss a minute of that ridiculous thing."

Cora shakes her head. "You know why Ben Cartwright's sons have three different mothers? Because the old man's been widowed three times. If I were the next Mrs. Cartwright, I'd get the sheriff to look into that real quick."

I know that my sister won't have any problem with our elderly neighbor. Lately they've become fast friends. All because, two weeks ago, Mrs. Grosset mentioned to my mother that she and her husband once knew the same person everyone is reading about in the papers these days: Dr. Carl Coppolino.

"So, you keeping up with the trial?" Cora says.

It's the same question she asks each time she catches him hobbling down his driveway for the paper.

"I guess it's who I'd want for my lawyer," he says.

F. Lee Bailey is defending the doctor, who's accused of murdering his lover's husband. But the part my sister likes best is that the victim was a retired army colonel. The medical examiner performed an autopsy after the body was in Arlington for three years. Now the headlines are saying that the colonel was strangled.

"I guess it's true what they say about old soldiers," Cora says. "Apparently they don't fade away either."

Mr. Grosset smooths his white hair back with both hands. "It's all very suspicious, isn't it?"

Cora turns her palm up. "Anyway, I give you my dumb, in every sense of the word, brother."

I stay on the couch and Mr. Grosset gazes nearsightedly in my direction. The table lamp is off and Cora has dabbed some of her makeup on my chin.

"Well, he looks all of a piece to me," he says. "Your mother will be happy to hear it."

"From someone other than her impeachable daughter," Cora says.

Mr. Grosset pats her on the shoulder, something I know that my sister dislikes.

"Sylvia and I should travel," Mr. Grosset says to make conversation. "Only, to be truthful, I've never been a big fan of such things as water spewing up from the ground."

"Makes two of us," Cora says. "Give me Vegas any day."

"But I suppose when they're four of you involved, you're in for certain compromises."

"Right," my sister says. "Like leaving two of them behind."

Mr. Grosset makes his way over to me and I stand up. All I have to do, Cora has coached me, is keep my chin down and my mouth shut.

"Losing something like your voice," he says, "it puts things in perspective." And he squeezes the back of my neck like a doting uncle. "That's what happens when you get to be my age. You start losing all your senses, but everything's in perspective."

Although he means to be funny, everything he says always has a certain edge to it for me. My mother told us how their only child, a boy, died of some exotic disease when he was an infant. Dr. Coppolino had been the anesthesiologist.

"I'll pass the word on to your mother," Mr. Grosset says finally. "No adult supervision required."

"It's a test," Cora says, smiling at him even though I know that it's meant for me. "They want to see how we handle a broken home."

I push my tongue against the back of my front teeth. The tip still feels more like an earlobe: dull and slightly detached. And I wish that my sister's cruel teasing felt the same way. That somehow the Novocain could have deadened my feelings as well. But everything she says about us as a family seems as sharp and stinging as the needle had going into my tongue.

The next day, just to get out of the house, Cora drives us over to the diner near the Varsity Cinema. I've been up most of the night with a fever, flipping around in bed trying to fall asleep. Twice, Cora came in and held a damp facecloth to my forehead. She never said anything but I could tell that she was worried. The intern who looked like the movie star had told us that everything depended on how the muscles healed. "Whether he has a slur," Cora said, her own voice trailing off. The doctor then pointed his penlight into my mouth. "An impediment, yes, possibly," he said, turning my jaw to admire his handiwork. "Too soon to say." Sitting on the examining table, I held the magnifying mirror up to my face for the first time. The ugly black stitches zigzagged across my tongue like the tracks of my miniature railroad. When I opened my eyes again two nurses were peering down at me. "You passed out," one of them said as an orderly swept shards of glass into a dustpan. "My brother's prone to hyperventilate," I heard my sister say from somewhere else in the room. "You don't want to hand him any more mirrors."

There are only half a dozen wobbly stools in the diner and we sit at the end of the horseshoe counter. The only other customer is asking the waitress if she remembers all the tips he's left her this month.

"Didn't they do *The Killers* here?" Cora says, tucking the menu back behind the napkin dispenser.

I look at her blankly.

"*Film noir?*" She rolls her eyes. "Forget it. What're you having?"

I point to the small pen-and-ink drawing of a milkshake.

"Right," she says. "Something liquid."

The waitress comes down to us and swipes the counter with a dishtowel. "How you folks doing tonight?" She makes a face at Cora as if to say she gets characters like that all the time.

After taking our order the waitress rips the page from her pad and sticks it to the ventilator hood above the grill. The cook folds his newspaper in half and glances up at it without ever turning his back from us. Meanwhile, the man who's been heckling the waitress bites into his hot dog, lifting his chin to keep the sauerkraut from dripping. He alternates from watching the waitress's legs to gazing over at us without much interest. The grill hisses like a steam iron each time the cook presses the spatula down on Cora's hamburger. I tuck my knees in and spin one complete rotation on the stool. When I put my elbows back up on the counter, the man is staring at me.

"What's the matter, buddy?" and he wipes his chin with his sleeve. "Cat got your tongue?"

He takes another large bite out of his hot dog and works his jaw vigorously without closing his mouth.

Cora finishes cleaning her fork off with her napkin and smiles at me. "So show the man what the cat did to your tongue," she says, dipping her spoon into her water glass.

The waitress stops filling the saltshakers she's lined up on the counter and looks over at us. Even the cook turns and I see the rest of the faded blue arrow tattooed to his forearm.

After thinking about it for a minute I rotate a quarter turn and watch the man lower his hot dog as I slowly slip the tip of my tongue between my pursed lips. His eyes cross slightly as he leans

forward on the aluminum stool, his own lips parting until he blinks
and snaps his head back.

"Christ!" And he glares at Cora. "What the hell!"

My sister wraps the paper napkin about her spoon. "Cat got his
tongue."

The man pushes his plate away from him and looks about as if to
find the manager. But there's only the cook jiggling the cage of fries
in the hot grease.

Afterward, we cross the street to study the coming-attractions
poster outside the theater.

It's an old Art Deco place that only shows classic movies. Tonight
it's something called *Daisy Kenyon* with Joan Crawford. The poster
shows her in a low-cut dress with a neck pendant. "I don't belong to
any man" is emblazoned across the top in red letters. The dress
reminds me of the one my mother packed for the trip, the one Cora
joked about being so practical for the road. But my mother didn't
plan to spend much of her time sweating in the woods. So she'd
folded the cocktail dress on top of a pair of slacks and white cotton
socks. "Be prepared's Mom's motto," Cora had said. My mother only
winked at me. "Remember that," she said.

Neither one of us wants to go back to the house.

"It's dollar night," my sister says to me. "What else have you got
to lose?"

There are only two other couples in the deserted theater, but I
have trouble paying any attention to the black-and-white movie. It
isn't until Cora gets up to visit the ladies' room that I realize my leg
has fallen asleep. My sister comes back with a box of popcorn and a
Hershey bar for me.

"Thought it was something you could manage," she says without
taking her eyes off the screen. "My God, look at those shoulders."
Cora unfolds the top of the popcorn box. "You got to admire that in
a woman."

When Dana Andrews gets into his car and drives off angrily, I
can't help thinking about my parents. They were driving hundreds
of miles away to see if they could come back together. But Cora had

warned me not to get my hopes up. "Those two can't see the forest for the trees. Hitting the road's not going to get them anywhere except a damn park." Still, I wanted to believe that a change of heart was at least possible. That in perhaps forgetting about us they might think about themselves for a change.

As we come out of the theater the diner is lit up brightly across the street. There's no one at the counter, and the cook is scraping the spatula across the empty grill.

It's after eleven and Cora is worried that Mom might have tried to call.

"Maybe I ought to give them a quick ring," she says. "In case they've been trying the house."

It's started to drizzle, a fine mist that you can only see looking up at the streetlights.

"I can't wait not to have to answer to anyone," Cora says, hunting through her pocketbook for the number.

There's a pay phone on the corner and she turns her collar up. "Why don't you take a hike," she says. "You don't want to listen to Mom bugging me about her teddy bear."

In another six months, maybe a year, I'll be as tall as my sister. But rising only slightly on my toes I can already look her in the eye. Even if I don't have anything to look her in the eye about.

I wait beneath the awning of a jewelry store and stare at the diamond rings behind the protective metal gates. The more expensive ones have been taken in, leaving gaps in the velvet trays.

On the ride home Cora is quiet and I imagine at first that she is only thinking about the movie's unhappy ending. When she rolls her window down, her hair whips about her head crazily, and I keep my lips pursed, afraid that the breeze might catch my tongue the wrong way. Earlier, I made the mistake of sucking on some salted popcorn.

"Probably I ought to say something before you get carried away," Cora says finally.

I look over at my sister, who glances up at the rearview mirror as if I were sitting in the backseat.

"Apparently it's raining there too," she says. "Cats and dogs."

She is stretching the words out, which makes me think that for once she isn't bluffing. But I hate the familiar, Big Sister tone.

"They're coming back early," she says. "Tomorrow, as a matter of fact. They're both miserable. Mom's legs are supposedly killing her. Anyway, it's just not working out."

Her hair keeps flying into her mouth, and I stop listening when she starts in on why it's better that they go their separate ways. That with joint custody we'd get twice the benefits and only half the grief.

I turn on the radio. My sister is famous for being theatrical, for making a big production out of nothing. Next, she'll probably do her Katharine Hepburn routine and tell me she's going to have her tubes tied and never own anything that she has to feed or paint. I've heard it all before.

But back home she instead switches on all the patio lights and only stares out the kitchen window at the tree house. It's a shambles. The whole floor caved in under me.

"Getting a little old for stunts like that, don't you think?" When she turns around, her eyes are shining. Then she presses the back of her arm against her mouth and takes a deep breath, her whole body shaking. "So he goes and tears half his goddamn . . ." She leans back against the sink, her face contorted and angry. "Jesus, Teddy!" And she bows her head as if everything is hopeless: Mom, Dad, her brother.

I consider putting my arm around my sister's shoulder but, of course, don't. Instead, I open the cabinet drawer and pretend to look for something, pushing the utensils about noisily. I know that I'm not fooling anyone but then we aren't supposed to cry in front of each other either. And for once I wonder where all our family's unspoken rules come from. There seems to be one for every occasion and yet what good has any of them ever done us? But then it isn't the kind of question to ask and so I pick up the chalk and quickly scribble *Good night* across the board.

Upstairs, I hold the magnifying mirror under the desk lamp and try to curl my tongue. Even if things work out, there will still be a deep scar, one to hide whenever I smile. I'd climbed into the tree house to think about what it would be like not to live under the same roof with my parents anymore. Instead, I thought of the first time we were on our way across country to a new assignment. This was ten years ago and everyone was happy. My father because he'd just been promoted. My mother because my father was happy. My sister because she'd be starting a new school. And me because we'd stopped the car for a picnic. It was a small public park with shaded tables and a sparkling stream that ran through a thick stand of pines. Still too early for lunch we had the place to ourselves as I flapped around in the ice cold water in my underwear. It was so clean and clear that I could see minnows flash past at my feet like tiny tongues. But what I remember most was kneeling on the smooth stones with the water tickling my neck and suddenly looking up to see my mother and father and older sister together on the redwood bench, smiling happily, but without ever taking their eyes off me for a second. And so when the bough beneath the tree house broke and my arms shot out like a baby's, my hands clutching at whatever might break my fall in the dark, it was just as I'd felt on the phone, closing my eyes, listening to voices I loved, now too far away ever to hear me the same again.

OUT
of the
PICTURE

"I got some bad news for you, kiddo." Cora stands on the ottoman, using the same tack holes from last time to pin the sheet up. We're still in L.A. Still in the same stucco bungalow we've been renting and none of the furniture is ours. "Not even Hollywood families are forever."

I plug the projector into the extension cord. I know that my sister is just mad that we're not going to Panama. My father has been transferred to the Canal Zone, and my mother still won't budge. She's afraid the assignment won't be permanent and doesn't want us changing schools every fifteen minutes.

My father has sent another box of slides with his letter. The old ones I keep wrapped in tinfoil in my dresser so the sunlight won't fade them.

"You going to get her up or what?" Cora says.

My mother sleeps during the day and stays awake most of the night. She worries about all the crime stories in the supermarket tabloids, the ones Cora buys for the horoscope. But I don't know which stars my sister believes in more: the ones in the sky or the ones over in Bel Air.

"Come on, get Mom."

She wants to see the house my father has found. In his letter he talked about maybe hiring a cook and a maid. This was for my mother's benefit. For my sister's benefit he joked about how

53

Americans live like movie stars with the exchange rate the way it is. He didn't have to say anything for my benefit.

At the end of the hall I ease my mother's bedroom door open.

"Mom?"

Even though it's the middle of July she sleeps under a mound of blankets.

"Everything's set up for the slides," I whisper.

From habit she keeps to one side of the double bed. "What time is it, honey?"

"Almost six."

She sleeps in her bathrobe, which Cora argues is the first sign of a depressive. But I just think she misses my father.

"Did you get something to eat?" she asks.

"I fixed us a salad."

Cora claims my mother is a dead ringer for Tammy Grimes, whoever that is. The streak of silver in her hair looks like something she had done at the beauty parlor. "I got that when you were a baby," she'll say to me. "You fell out of the high chair and broke your collarbone." Other times it will be Cora's fault. "Your sister was five. I'd just punished her for something. And when I wasn't looking she took my sewing scissors and trimmed the living room drapes. Cut them two feet off the floor all the way across." That sounded like my sister, all right.

My mother pushes the covers back and curls her toes. "My legs are numb. They must not be getting any circulation."

Like Cora, my mother is sloppy and I have to pick up after both of them. There are empty glasses and saltine wrappers everywhere.

"I'm going to tell you now," she says, draping over her shoulders the cotton shawl my father sent from Portobelo. "I don't want a repeat of last time. I don't want you getting yourself worked up all over again. Do you hear me?"

I hear her.

"I'll pull the plug on that machine the minute I see it. I'm not kidding. And I'll tell your father no more slides."

In the kitchen I fix cheese and crackers and carry the tray into the living room.

"Any chance we get to see these this calendar year?" Cora says. She flings her movie magazine across the coffee table.

The square of light is too low on the sheet and I slide the magazine under the front leg of the projector. My mother and sister stare expectantly straight ahead, their faces pale as Kabuki dancers' in the reflected light.

Drawing the loader back, I feed the projector the first slide.

"Focus," Cora says.

My mother reaches past her for the cheese. "Just hold your horses. Your brother's doing fine."

I cup the lens and turn it until my father's favorite subject comes in more sharply. It's a sunny day and the great concrete locks are bleached white. "How's that?"

"Boring," my sister says. "Boring, boring, boring."

It's the Gatun Locks. You can see the lake, the second biggest artificial lake in the world.

"How many times do we have to tell him?" Cora says. "No more goddamn canal."

"Watch the language, young lady," my mother says.

"You talk about home movies," my sister says bitterly.

"You might as well settle back and relax," my mother says. "It won't be the last one."

And it isn't. Most of the slides are of ships inching through the locks. Or of water rushing out of one of the giant gates.

My mother isn't much interested in any of this, either, but sits patiently for the one or two slides that will include my father. He'll have to hand his camera over to someone else, of course. Which he hates to do.

When at last my father appears in a slide, he is deeply suntanned. There are a couple of Americans with him, standing slightly back, clearly happy to be in his company. And for a moment I am so proud of him that I have to look away. But I know better than to change the slide too soon. There would be an instant howl of protest from Cora. So with my mother and sister I gaze at my father's face that is bigger than life on the wrinkled sheet.

"Can you believe that tan?" Cora says finally. "He must be living outdoors."

My mother's voice is barely loud enough to hear over the hum of the projector. "He'll get too much," she says. "He doesn't know how to do anything in moderation."

One of the younger men beside him, I suddenly notice, is holding a beer bottle.

"It must be some kind of outing," Cora decides. "An office party or something."

There are two women in the picture, both in the background. They look Panamanian.

"Your father's always been one of the boys," my mother says. "It's just the way he is."

"What's wrong with that?" I say.

My mother turns on the couch. "Nothing, sweetheart." She's squinting into the light, surprised by my tone. "I wasn't criticizing your father."

"Where are they?" Cora says. "I don't recognize any of this."

There is another slide of the canal before a second one of my father kneeling on a large straw mat, an ice chest at his feet.

"What's that?" Cora says. She gets up for a closer inspection and the slide ripples across her back like a tattoo. "Some kind of dock?"

When she touches the sheet the picture sways and we wait for it to settle.

"Those are rods," I say. "By the tree there. You can see the reels."

"Leave it to your father to find a fishing hole," my mother says.

"I wish just once he'd give us a few clues," Cora says. "He never says a word about anything. Like we're supposed to be cryptographers or something."

"What's there to tell?" I say. "You can see what they're doing."

My sister glares at me.

"Okay, honey," my mother says, and I set another slide in.

But it's only the locks again without my father.

"I didn't know they had country like that," my mother says. She's still thinking about the last slide. "It just shows you how you can get the wrong picture."

The branch library nearest us has a whole shelf on the Panama Canal. One Saturday I read how there were still headhunters in parts of the Darien jungle. But I didn't say anything to my mother. She wouldn't have been able to sleep even in the middle of the afternoon.

"Let's go," Cora says.

My father stands in front of a plain clapboard house, the fronds of a banana tree drooping over its red tile roof. It's a small house. The carport doesn't even look big enough for an American car.

"You're telling me there's going to be a live-in maid?" Cora says. "Where's she going to live-in?"

The grass in the front yard is yellow, and my father is holding his hand up to block the sun.

"Let's see what else we've got," my mother says at last. She glances over her shoulder to check how many slides are left. It's against the rules to preview any of them before the projector gets set up.

"Two more," I say, and pull the loader back.

Cora groans at the picture of the traffic circle in downtown Panama City. Hundreds of colorful taxis swirl around a statue of some Indian holding a tomahawk and a peace pipe.

"Let's go, let's go," my sister says irritably.

My father isn't in the last slide but at least it's another one of the house. This time taken from the street.

"I don't see any window units," my mother says. "You think there's air conditioning?"

"He's got a damn flash," Cora says. "I mean, what the hell's the place look like inside?"

"They probably have overhead fans," my mother says without taking her eyes off the slide. "But I can't handle the humidity the way your father can."

My sister gets up to turn on the light. "He thinks he's being funny," she says. "I've come to that conclusion. All that jackass *National Geographic* crap."

"All right," my mother says.

"It's like he has no conception of us whatsoever," Cora says. "Two pictures of the house and the rest of that idiot canal."

"What do you care?" I say. "You don't even want to go."

"So what if I don't?" my sister says. "That doesn't mean I wouldn't come home on vacation. If there were something to come home to."

"You ought to know your father by now," my mother says. "He'd sleep in a tent if I didn't watch him."

"Well, it looks like a neat house," I say. "It looks real private." I say this because I know how much my mother likes her privacy.

"You're right, honey. Your father didn't mention anything about neighbors, did he?"

"So what's new?" Cora says. "Daddy never mentions anything about anything to us."

But my sister is only angry because no one will say whether she can board in the States next year. If we stay here my mother will want her to commute. If we join my father, then she'll have to do her senior year in the Canal Zone. Only, no one seems to know what we're doing as a family.

"Who's fixing something to drink?" my mother says, lifting her feet onto the ottoman. "My gams are killing me."

I'm in the kitchen emptying ice cubes into the blender when Cora pushes open the swinging door and waits for it to settle shut behind her.

"So what do you think?" she whispers.

My sister is suspicious about something but I don't even try to guess.

"About what?"

She studies the picture of the four of us that's stuck to the icebox with little fruit magnets. "About Mom and Dad, blockhead. You think she'll just call it all off now?"

"Call what off?"

My sister rolls her eyes. "What do I have to do, paint a picture? What'd you think all the boys were doing down by the river? Fishing?"

Last May my father flew up for a week's leave. The day before we saw him off at the airport, my parents had another fight. Because it was late, they closed their bedroom door after them. But you could still hear my mother shouting about junkets and the children and finally about lawyers and custody. "It's only Mom letting off a little steam," my sister said when I got up from our long session at the Ouija board. "Relax. You're not going to be an orphan." And, in fact, the next morning my mother seemed to have forgotten all about it, even though her face looked puffy and swollen.

"Who do you think took the picture?" Cora says. "The Tooth Fairy?"

Sometimes I don't even know what wavelength my sister is on. My father believes that Hollywood's to blame and that she lost it at the movies.

The Coke cracks the cubes in the glass and fizzes noisily.

"Anybody could have taken it," I say, and then make the mistake of taking a sip of my mother's drink. It burns the tip of my tongue along the ragged scar. "Maybe he just used the self-timer."

My sister places the tiny banana magnet so that it looks like it's coming out of my ear in the picture. Then she seems to change her mind about what she's going to say and instead just nods. "The self-timer," she says, still bobbing her head at me. "Now, why didn't I think of that?"

When I carry my mother's drink in to her she's studying the framed picture of my father that's always been her favorite. It was taken the summer she was pregnant with Cora. "And your sister was a pain even then," she likes to joke with me. "Unlike her brother, who never gives me a minute of trouble."

My mother sits on the couch, and Cora and I watch her sip at her Coke like an invalid.

"So," she says. "What's to watch tonight?"

As usual, my sister has already gone over the listings in the *TV Guide*. "Nothing," she says. "*The Rains of Ranchipur* and some western with Nick Adams. They're not even worth turning on."

"Let's take a ride, then," my mother offers. "I feel like rubbernecking anyway."

Lately, it's all we seem to do together at night: drive through Beverly Hills or Brentwood with the windows rolled down while

Cora reminds us who lives where. She's taken the celebrity bus tour of homes a million times.

My mother walks back through the house, turning all the lights on. She leaves the TV and radio going and lifts the phone off the hook.

I sit in the backseat of the station wagon. Even though it isn't a new car, the army would still pay to have it sent down. If we went down. They would have paid to have it sent over to Taiwan too. Now all our stuff is in storage waiting for my mother to make up her mind. But she's afraid of Panama turning out to be just another short-term assignment.

As we cross Wilshire Boulevard into Westwood, Cora points out Jimmy Stewart's place. And my mother eases up on the gas pedal for us to take in the enormous, hacienda-like mansion with its terra-cotta roof and elegant palms.

"It's a wonderful life," my sister says dreamily.

This is when I miss my father most. The last time he was home on leave, Cora bugged him to drive us up into the Hills. Afterward, we stopped at a Baskin-Robbins off Rodeo Drive and while my sister recalled the size of some movie director's helicopter pad, my father dug into his chocolate-chip sundae. "Mmmmm, mmmm," he said, winking at me across the marble-top table and then licking his spoon appreciatively. "Not even Paul Newman's going to get ice cream any better than that. What do you say, Teddy?" I didn't, of course, have to say anything. He feels the same as I do about Cora's movie stars.

We don't go over to Coldwater Canyon tonight even though my sister wants to see how far Zsa Zsa Gabor has gotten rebuilding her house that burned down in the last brushfire. My mother's legs are bothering her too much. I carry a little tin of aspirin in my pocket for her and reach over the seat with one.

"You're a godsend," she says, her eyelids hooded the way they get whenever she isn't feeling well.

It's after ten by the time we pull into the driveway. But before anyone gets out, my mother flicks the brights on and revs the engine a couple of times to be certain there are no prowlers.

"Wouldn't one of Cora's horoscopes have warned us?" I say.

My sister doesn't even bother to turn around.

When my mother's at last satisfied that no one is waiting for us in the hedge, I lead the way up the flagstone steps to the porch. It's all ridiculous, of course, but my heart is still pounding as my mother quickly double-locks the door behind us.

In the living room Cora flops down on the couch. "If we lived someplace like Holmby Hills," she says, "we'd have our own private police department. Not to mention escort service."

"Maybe you'll marry a general when you grow up," I say. "Then you can take the celebrity tour of homes in his staff car."

"We'll see who gets the last laugh," my sister says.

The Ouija board has told her that she'll marry someone with a European accent. "Like the count in *The Sun Also Rises*." She means the movie, not the book. "Gregory Ratoff played him. You can have your Jake Barneses. They never have two sous to rub together."

Later, after we've gone back through all the old slides that include my father, my mother gets up without saying anything and wanders into the kitchen for a drink.

"You can't tell me she's that thirsty," Cora whispers, trimming her thumbnail with her teeth. "She's just anxious, that's all."

"And I guess her legs don't really hurt her either," I say.

My sister inspects her nail before looking back up at me. "Is this where I get to explain the obvious to you?"

Cora thinks that it's all just psychosomatic with my mother. That her physical ailments and her fear of flying are only symptoms. The real problem is with Daddy.

My mother suddenly backs out of the kitchen with a paper napkin wrapped around her glass. "I guess I'll lie down if there's nothing on TV," she says. "My tootsies are giving me a real hard time of it tonight." She raises her chin at me. "I want to talk to you a minute before you go to bed, honey."

I change into my pajamas first and when I pass Cora's room again she's sitting cross-legged on her bed, eyes closed and fingers resting lightly on the planchette.

"I don't know what I'm going to do with your sister," my mother says as soon as I close the door behind me. She's propped the pillows up against the headboard. "You can see how hyper she's getting."

Lately, whenever my sister's thyroid acts up, she refuses to take her pills. She complains that they swell her face up so that she looks like Orson Welles. It's only one of the reasons she keeps to herself so much.

"You can't talk to her," my mother says. "She won't even try to get out and make friends. It's not as if we're only going to be here for the weekend. She's had plenty of opportunity."

My mother is right, of course. Cora does nothing but sit around the house like she's serving a sentence. Her empty room even looks like a prison cell, the walls covered with pinups of movie stars.

My mother sets her newspaper down. "I know what's got you so quiet lately," she says. "You're worried your father and I are having a hard time of it right now. And we are. I'm not going to lie to you. But I want you to promise me something."

I know what she's going to say. "That I'll stop worrying."

"That's right," she says patiently. "That's all I'm going to ask you. Let your father and me handle it."

Cora is holding up slides to the light when I come back down the hall.

"Where'd you get those?" I say.

She hunts through the pile she's dumped out on the card table. "They're communal property. You don't own them." She gets up to turn off the overhead light. "Anyway, I wanted to show you something. So just start the projector and don't have a conniption."

"Start it yourself. I've seen them."

My sister straddles the extension cord. "You're missing an education," she says. But she doesn't know how to work the machine and jams the first slide so that only part of it appears on the sheet. "That's what you're getting," she says, jiggling the loader. "Half the picture."

I push her hand away. "You'll scratch them doing that." It's the slide of my father standing with some people outside a basilica.

"Good," Cora says. "Now, pay attention."

She's picked out three others.

"This one here," she says, the back of her head blotting out my father's face. "Try to remember her." She points at a young Panamanian woman standing on the steps of the run-down church. "Even if they all do look alike."

In the second picture my father is leaning on a rail in front of an animal cage. He mentioned the Colón Zoo in a postcard.

"So?" I say. There's no one else in the frame, only the striped tapir turned away from the camera.

"You don't notice anything?" Cora says. Her eyes shine in the light from the projector. This is what happens when she doesn't take her medication.

I pick up the last slide but she stops me.

"The bench, knucklehead." And she pats the sheet with the back of her hand. "What're you, blind?"

Beside the concrete walkway is an iron bench with a woman's jacket folded over it. When the picture stops waving, Cora narrows her eyes at me.

"Now go back to the first one."

I don't have to. It's the same jacket.

"Okay," my sister says. "Go ahead."

The last one is of the outing. Only, this time I concentrate on the dark-haired woman and not on my father.

My mother suddenly steps out into the hall. "I thought you were watching TV," she says.

Cora yawns. She's always been good at not looking caught. "We wanted another peek at the house."

My mother's a little nearsighted and I wonder how much, if anything, she can see.

"I'm going to bed," I say.

"Good," my mother says. "You'll get a headache looking at those things too much."

Later, it's after midnight and I haven't been able to fall asleep when Cora pokes her head into my room.

"And not a creature was stirring." She has two pieces of cheese and holds one out for me. "Want some?"

"Dad has all kinds of people working with him," I say. "But you have to make a big production out of everything."

"Been thinking about it, have we?"

Her eyes bulge from the pressure of her thyroid. She's supposed to take one pill in the morning and two at night.

"You can stay here, for all I care," I say. "There'll be that much more room for the rest of us."

"In that house you'll need it." She's close enough that I can smell the cheddar on her breath. "Anyway, kiddo, I thought I'd give you a little sneak preview. So the time comes, it's not a real shockeroo. But you don't want to see it, you don't want to see it."

I turn my head away from her on the pillow. "You want to do me a favor, shut the door."

Afterward, when I can't sleep, I start thinking about how different things would be in Panama. Living so close to Hollywood, you can't help seeing a movie star every once in a while. Last week, for instance, in Hamburger Hamlet I sat in a booth across from Lee Marvin. He wasn't eating anything. Just drinking coffee and reading the paper. I didn't tell Cora. I never tell her when I see someone. Not even the time I passed Debbie Reynolds in a crosswalk. If I say anything to my sister I'll never hear the end of it. But I was tempted to lean over the booth and ask Lee Marvin a few questions about his family. Whether, for example, he finds it hard on his kids for him to have to travel so much. Only, I wasn't sure if he even had a family, so I didn't ask. Anyway, he has a right to his privacy.

Sitting up in bed, I fumble in the dark for the alarm. But, in fact, it's the phone making all the noise. And then Cora is pounding on my door.

"Wake up," she shouts. "It's Daddy."

In the hall my mother and sister press against each other, their ears joined Siamese twin–like to the receiver. They smile blankly at me as if drugged by the voice at the other end of the line.

It's only the second time my father has called in over a month but already I can see that they've forgiven him. It's two in the morning and Cora is a little giddy. Only my mother is wide awake. It's the middle of the afternoon for her.

When at last it's my turn to take the phone, it seems forever before my father's voice carries the thousand miles to America. "Your mother tells me you're a big help to her," he says. "That's good news, son. You got to look after the girls."

My mother and sister loiter nearby, ears pricked to overhear the wonderful sound of my father's voice. But all I can think to ask him is about the time he went to the zoo and whether he had fun.

"Nothing like the time we're going to have," he says.

And then with Cora frowning at me I ask who he went with and whether that person had a good time too. It seems forever before he answers and not just because there's such a distance between us. It's even longer than that.

"Wait till you get a load of the frogs down here," my father says. "They're this bright yellow. Millions of them sitting on water lilies. Over in El Valle."

I think at first that we just have a bad connection. He isn't answering anything I ask him. Then finally he tells me to put Mom back on. And that I'm to take Cora with a grain of salt.

"You know how she gets," he says. "What do you say? Man to man."

But I don't have anything to say and only hand the phone back to my mother while my sister glares at me.

All the air-conditioning vents are closed in the hall, and I lean back against the bathroom door, trying to remember the dream I was having just before the phone rang. Research and Development had come up with a new kind of cable that was going to earn my father his first star. "It'll carry as much information as a forty-inch-thick copper wire," he explained to us happily. Then he reached over and plucked a strand of hair from my mother's head. "No thicker than this." We all stared at the silver strand stretched like wire between his fingers. Instead of electricity the cable would carry pulses of light. "And that's where the promotion comes in."

In the kitchen I stand in front of the sink and let the water run. Then I try to remember my father ever calling me "son" before. It had sounded like something in a foreign language.

After a while I hear my mother tell Cora to sit with her brother for a few minutes. When my sister wanders into the living room, I pretend to be reading one of her magazines.

"You're such an idiot," she says, curling her legs up under her on the rug. "See if I ever tell you anything again."

I look back down at the magazine but my eyes water and the tears start to pat on the page.

"Jesus," Cora says. "Do you believe *everything* I tell you? I mean, when I told you Charles Laughton was probably a woman, did you believe that too? Don't you know when I'm only thinking out loud?"

But I'm not really listening to her anymore. I'm trying to overhear my mother on the phone. Only, she isn't saying much. At least not enough for me to figure anything out.

Cora isn't fooling anyone either. All the time she's jabbering at me she keeps one ear open. My sister still believes she can get away with anything. But I've been onto her a lot longer than she thinks.

My mother at last joins us in the living room and tries to look cheery. Except I can tell that it isn't her legs that are troubling her.

"Who wants to take a spin around the block?" she says. "You two look more awake than I am." And she smiles anxiously at Cora, who stops whistling and slaps the *TV Guide* shut. My mother wants to get her out of the house. "What do you say? We can drive by that boarding school."

Cora sits up front in the car and pops her gum, her feet pressed against the glove compartment. It's hard to tell how much it's my sister and how much it's the medicine to blame (my father talked her into taking her pills again).

My mother drives cautiously up the narrow, winding roads of Coldwater Canyon. She glances back at me in the rearview mirror and wonders if it's too much air. Should she roll up the window a bit? The way she asks it makes Cora turn around to look at me. But my sister doesn't stop rattling off which celebrity homes have burned to the ground recently.

"Every year it's the same thing," she says, and then waves her hand out the window at some producer's place. "He did *Spartacus*.

It's just whichever way the wind's blowing. Everybody's out by their swimming pools holding a hose, waiting to see if they're—"

My mother takes one hand from the steering wheel and pats my sister on the arm.

"Why don't we just enjoy the scenery for a few minutes?" she says.

Cora stops drumming her fingers on the roof and peers back over her shoulder at me. "Christ," she says. "Mr. Sensitive."

We're up pretty high now and you can see the city, its lights sparkling like a runway below us.

But then suddenly the station wagon jerks like a bumper car.

"Something's wrong, Teddy," my mother says. "It's not doing anything. I've got my foot all the way down on the accelerator."

"We're going backward," Cora says, her eyes wide. "We're going the other way."

"My foot's on the floor," my mother pleads.

I reach over her shoulder to help steer us onto the side of the road.

"Set the emergency brake," I say as soon as we come to a stop.

"Oh, Lord," my mother says. She lowers her forehead to the steering wheel. "I thought it was me. I thought I wasn't feeling anything in my legs."

But we're just out of gas. The needle is in the red.

"I thought he's supposed to be the man of the house now," my sister says, hiking her thumb back at me. "So how come he doesn't take care of the damn car?"

"All right," my mother says. "I don't want to hear any of it. Just lock your doors and keep the windows up."

Everyone is quiet for a moment, even Cora, and you can hear the cicadas outside hissing in the dry brush. Then my sister remembers reading how they found some starlet's body near here.

"Right off Mulholland," she says. "It couldn't be more than a half mile over—"

"Honest to God, Cora," my mother snaps, twisting her hands on the steering wheel. "Will you just be quiet this once? I swear to God."

I lean against the door and after a while try to think about

Panama. One other thing I remember about the Darien jungle was how the children in the tribes there never cried. The person who wrote the book thought it was because the Indians didn't really seem to get attached to anyone, not even to members of their own family. After every place the author had been in that country, he still thought it was the strangest thing he'd ever seen.

Up ahead a house on piers juts out from the side of the mountain. The windows must be twenty feet high and I wonder if it's ever had to be rebuilt. It's so big, it could belong to anyone, and I try to imagine myself standing in the living room gazing down at my mother and sister in their stalled car beside the road. I'm older, as old as my father, and rich enough that I'd never have to worry about a brushfire burning everything to the ground. If I wanted to I'd just build it all back up the next year. Or if I changed my mind I could move to someplace like Panama and stay there as long as I wanted, but it wouldn't really matter since no one would be waiting for me back in the States.

PARIS
of the
ORIENT

My father returned from Vietnam in no mood to hear about his second cousin twice removed. But Cora has finally tracked down the former child actor who was once under contract with MGM. Only, my father will have nothing to do with her proposed family reunion and spends most of his first week home up in the attic packing for our next assignment. We are off to Ft. Polk—everyone, that is, except Cora, who will start back to college the end of the month.

"I mean, when's he going to come down to earth?" my exasperated sister says as my father's footsteps thump overhead.

"Try to remember where your father's been," my mother reminds her. After Panama my father volunteered for Vietnam. "Just give him a little time."

But both Cora and I have seen *The Green Berets* and for once I have to agree with my sister. Whatever my father is suffering from, it isn't shell shock.

By Friday, Cora decides on a different tack. She's studying film at UCLA, isn't she? Then who better to get to know than a relative practically born in the business?

"The man's a producer," she tries out at breakfast. "Think of the people he must know. What do you think? Lucy Arnaz made it on raw talent alone?"

But my father isn't about to impose on a complete stranger.

"We played with each other a couple times when were were kids.

Way before his mother took him out to Hollywood. I wouldn't recognize the man today if he walked through that damn door." And he points with his fork. "So your answer is no. I'm not having us barge in on anybody I don't know from Adam."

Just the day before, my sister's thyroid erupted again. Now she touches her swollen throat and I know she's going to pull out all the stops. As a family we must seem relentless to my father. My mother bitterly resents his spending so many years overseas. Nor is she any happier about having to leave Cora behind while the rest of us set off for some outpost in the Deep South. After being passed over for promotion for the first time in his career, my father volunteered for combat. Yet even I feel cheated by his listlessness. Who else, after all, is he supposed to get excited about seeing than his own family?

Later, having emptied the attic, my father descends to the greater challenge of the basement. But when he starts carting up Cora's mammoth collection of movie magazines, my sister rushes down from her room breathless and infuriated.

"They're going with me," she insists. "I'm taking them to school."

My father toes one of the bulging boxes. "Used to be they had you read books in college."

My sister, who never cries, is very nearly in tears. "You come back here like you're Sam Goldwyn or something," she says, her shoulders trembling. "Well, you're not. You're not even a star."

My father appears dumbstruck.

"That's enough of that kind of talk," my mother says.

But Cora's hyperthyroid eyes are popping. "Maybe I should just go out and rip up all his ridiculous tomato plants," she says. "See how he likes it."

My father slides the box into the corner, then looks up. "That'll do," he says.

And Cora knows from his tone that it will. For a moment I have to read lips to follow anything. The blood is pounding in my ears. My father hasn't been back ten minutes and already everybody is at each other's throat.

That night, in bed, I listen to him try to get my mother to keep her voice down. But except for when she hisses the word *geisha* so that it sounds like a threat, not much is new. When, at last, their light goes out, I put my hand on my chest and feel my heart pumping crazily. This is when I like to think about gurus. About how they can make their pulse slow down by falling into a certain trance. But it's impossible for me to imagine ever being able to think like a swami. Especially with my family.

The following morning my father is out in the yard digging up his tomato plants. Whenever he's home on leave, it's all he seems to tend to. Somehow a few have managed to endure his long absences. Now he wants me to see if a couple of the hardier ones might survive a week in a U-Haul.

"Kind of a rough night," I say, watching him aerate the soil with a trowel.

He looks up at me blankly. "You mean your sister?"

It turns out that Cora had been sick.

"You saw her throw up?" I say skeptically.

My father crawls on his hands and knees to the next plant. Fingering its weak stem, he decides it's too fragile for the move and passes it up. I can see how his hair is thinning on top. He's getting older, something more noticeable to me after not seeing him for so long.

"She doesn't take her pills," he says, flicking the dirt from his fingers, "and then she wonders why she gets nauseous."

I sit on the edge of the stone patio as he considers whether the leaf rot looks fatal. Something is definitely different about my father. He's become preoccupied, abstracted, like a boarder eager to move on. And it strikes me that whatever this house is for the rest of us, it's never been home for him.

"So what's it like over there?" I ask, stretching my legs out on the warm stones. "I mean, when they're not shooting at each other."

My father wipes his hands on his khaki pants and leans back on one elbow. I can see from his sunny expression that just the thought of the place relaxes him.

"Remarkably practical people. Humble. Straightforward. Not a sneaky bone in their body. Things you just don't see much of back here."

"Pearl Harbor wasn't sneaky?" I'm jealous of my father's affection. I want it all for myself, not squandered on foreigners.

"Wrong country," he says.

"You mean if you've seen one you haven't seen them all?"

He's heard this sort of thing from Cora but seems surprised to hear it from me.

"If they're such paragons," I say, "how come they can't even live together? I mean, they're not even one country?"

When he stands up, the joints of his ankles crack.

"Got me there," my father says, peeling his damp T-shirt over his head.

His chest is pale, the tanned line of his arms like a paper-doll cutout. And I feel a sudden rush of remorse. He has enough trouble with Cora and my mother without having to put up with my carping.

"You need some help with the basement?" I offer.

He twists his T-shirt over one of the tied-up tomato plants, the sweat coiling out.

"It's a miracle the junk down there hasn't spontaneously combusted by now," he says. "Sometime when you were all asleep."

"Mom's up half the night whenever you're away."

My father gazes at the chain link fence that separates the yard from our neighbor's.

"Your mother wouldn't go to the pound with me. If she'd put a damn dog out here the way I tried to get her to, she might get to bed at a decent hour."

"You know Mom," I say.

My father wraps the damp shirt around his neck. "That's the problem."

"What do you think?" Cora says, peering over my shoulder at the bathroom mirror. "Are they puffy?

It's the second time she's asked me in the last hour. My sister is anxious about meeting my father's cousin.

"Trust me," I say, drawing the razor across my smooth jaw. Several new whiskers have sprouted on my chin, and to show off, I've left the door open. "They're as ugly as they've always been. Nothing's changed."

She continues to study herself in the mirror. "I can't get an honest answer out of anyone in this family. Mom lies through her teeth, and Daddy pretends not to know what I'm even talking about. But I can see for myself. I look like Peter Lorre. I'm not blind."

I bend over and splash water in my face. "You keep looking long enough," I say, "you're going to see whatever you want to see."

"I look like a goddamn bat," and she presses down gingerly on one eyelid. "It's not fair," she says, catching me staring at her the wrong way. "I had eyes like Liz."

When my sister isn't driving me crazy, I manage to feel sorry for her. It *does* seem unfair. People always said she had beautiful eyes. Something they don't say anymore.

My mother stops me in the hall. "Look at this," she says, lifting my chin. I stuck a piece of toilet paper to a nick. "You have no business with a razor in your hand. Now, I don't want to see you carving up your face again."

Downstairs, my father is already dressed, rereading the thick letter from one of his former Vietnamese counterparts. He spent most of the afternoon grousing, until my mother put her foot down.

"So what's your pen pal got to say?" I ask.

Before he can fold the letter back up, I see his name printed across the top in a childlike scrawl.

"Worrying about the kids mostly."

"I thought they were supposed to honor their parents so much."

My father pulls the car keys from his pocket. "They're all watching American TV now. The youngest one wants her eyes less slanty."

Cora, who inherited her radar ears from my mother, suddenly saunters in from the kitchen. "She can have mine," she says. "My compliments."

"*Gunsmoke*'s a big hit," my father says. "Somehow they pick up the satellite feed from France."

Cora laughs. "I can just see it," she says. "Festus ordering a shot of rotgut. *'Donnez-moi un Dubonnet.'*"

When my mother comes down, I can tell that she expects my father to say something about her outfit. She's spent almost as much time as Cora getting ready. But my father only sulks out the door to the carport.

"Like an hour out of his life is such a big deal," my sister says.

"I wouldn't press your luck with your father right now," my mother says. "I really wouldn't."

"Give me a break," Cora says. "It's his own damn cousin, for cryin' out loud."

"Second cousin," I say, scratching the tissue paper from my chin. "Twice removed."

They both look over at me as if one of the house plants just talked.

"Does he really have to go?" my sister says. "I mean, what if it calls for adult conversation?"

"I'm warning you two," my mother says. "Your father's not in the best frame of mind for this."

In fact, we're barely out of the driveway before he glances murderously into the rearview mirror.

"His mother knew my mother," he says. "That was the extent of—"

"Why don't we just enjoy the scenery," my mother says. "It's a lovely sunset."

And it is: a great big orange volleyball sinking into the ocean beyond Santa Monica. As we rise into the tortuous Hollywood Hills, the thick palm and banana trees hide many of the houses set back from the narrow streets. Heeding my mother's advice, Cora dispenses with her usual travelogue.

But as we come up Mulholland Drive less than a block from the address, my sister lurches forward, pointing like a gundog.

"Look!"

I turn to see someone shooting baskets in a driveway.

"Didn't you recognize him?" Cora says, beaming excitedly. "*My Three Sons*? Tim Considine?"

She'd spun around in her seat as we passed, shaking her head in disbelief. But none of us really got a good look.

At the corner my mother nods at a disappointingly plain, ranch-style house that could fit into any middle-class suburb.

"That's it there," she says, having already scouted out the neighborhood with Cora.

My father pulls over, the hubcaps scraping against the curb. He turns off the engine and glares at the rearview mirror.

"One drink and we're out of here."

Cora has flipped open her compact and is squinting at herself. "Daddy, I don't see why—"

"Sixty minutes," he says. "End of discussion."

We follow him up the brick walkway to the porch while my sister explains to the rest of us why the really powerful people in show business prefer to live inconspicuously.

"They don't want a lot of hoopla in their everyday lives. They get enough of that in—"

"I'm going to knock on the door," my father says. "Are we ready to calm down here?"

My mother smiles at my sister. "I know you're excited, sweetheart. But let's just see if we can take it a little slower."

Cora is on her tiptoes, craning to see if Tim Considine is still in the driveway when the door eases open and a tall Oriental woman peers out at us. It's obvious that she has no idea who we are.

"Is Mr. Kelly in?" my father says.

Cora steps forward. "He's expecting us. I talked to him on the phone. A couple times."

The woman closes her eyes, shaking her head. "Of course. Of course." There's not a trace of an accent. "I'm so sorry. Jimmy's so forgetful. He's over on the tennis courts. Come in. Come in." And she bumps the door open with her hip. "He shouts a dozen things at me before he flies out of the house. He just went to hit a few balls. He should be back any minute."

She's too casually dressed for a domestic (white shorts and a halter top), and I can see my mother already sizing her up. As she sizes up every younger woman in my father's company. But coincidentally Susie is from Sasebo, Japan. A city my father once refueled in.

While our hostess fixes gin and tonics, Cora points out the signed pictures of celebrities on the piano. But neither my mother nor I can take our eyes off the life-size, full-frontal nude oil painting over the fireplace.

"Jimmy's second wife," Susie says when she catches us gaping. She sets the tray of drinks down on the glass coffee table. "A very talented off-Broadway actress."

"And you're Mrs. Kelly?" my mother says.

Susie glances in my general direction. "His houseguest," she says cheerfully. "Jimmy and I met in Tokyo. He was working with the Ice Capades. And there I was."

"In the show?" Cora says.

Susie wipes the bottom of her glass across her bare forearm. "Strange as it seems."

"Then you're a professional skater?" my father says.

"Oh, a few years back. I actually learned in Rockefeller Center, believe it or not."

I can tell from my mother's expression that she doesn't.

"I wasn't as good as most of the girls," she says. "But then most of the girls couldn't speak Japanese."

"It must have helped," my father says. His mood has improved considerably.

"I wound up a kind of union representative. Which was good because I broke my leg two days into the show. And Jimmy just sort of took me under his wing."

My father and I can't help glancing at her shapely legs. They're tanned and long and show no sign of any injury.

Later, after several uneasy lulls in the conversation, a small, wiry, remarkably freckled man bounds in the front door with a tennis racket at his hip.

"Fuck," he says, wrapping his arm around my father's shoulder. "I'm late." Then, seeing me, he covers his eyes comically.

My mother swirls her gin and tonic with her finger. "He's heard worse."

When everyone turns expectantly toward me, I nod in agreement. "Mostly from my sister."

Jimmy spears his tennis racket in the brass umbrella stand and bursts out laughing. "So this is my pen pal," he says, winking at Cora. "Jesus, Susie, look at this knockout."

And even I have to admit that my sister looks good. But then over the years she's probably picked up more beauty tips from the stars than anyone alive. Cora spent most of the day trying to conceal the effects of her condition. A high collar and scarf cover up her throat, but there's no way to hide her eyes.

"Lovely," Susie says. She's retreated politely from the conversation, standing back, content to agree with whatever Jimmy asks. This is perhaps just the sort of humility my father was talking about. And the reason he suddenly seems so much at home.

Jimmy sits down next to Cora on the leather couch and pats her knee. My sister doesn't like to be touched but she is also a very good actress.

"Absolutely incredible, her take on this town," he says. He's still sweating from the tennis and runs his fingers through his damp hair. "It's like I'm talking to some talent agent fifty years in the business. I say to Susie she's a fucking . . . she's like this Hollywood almanac. Am I right, honey?"

Susie nods at the rest of us. "It's exactly what he said."

My mother guzzles her gin and tonic as if she's been the one out on the courts. I can see that she'd be happy to keep our visit to the quick drink my father insisted on. But Jimmy has already whisked him out to the pool to reminisce about their lost childhood in upstate New York.

Susie, again thrust into the role of hostess, can only ply my mother with more gin and tonics, and my sister and me with one of Jimmy's early scrapbooks.

"I see you're neighbors with Tim Considine," Cora volunteers when my mother makes no effort to be sociable.

Susie bends another plastic tray of ice cubes over the pitcher. "Jimmy's right," she says. "You really *don't* miss anything." And with no one else seeming to pay any attention to her, she smiles at me. "Tim pretty much likes to keep to himself."

I know even before she looks up from the album how my sister is going to take this.

"You don't have to worry," Cora says, smoothing out a clipping of Jimmy in some Broadway musical. "I'm not interested in autographs."

Susie shakes her head. "Oh, I didn't mean—"

But my father suddenly steps back in from the patio.

"I ought to put this guy on the payroll," Jimmy says to my mother.

Cora's ears prick up.

"Jimmy's thinking about doing something on Ho Chi Minh City," Susie says.

My mother holds her palm up like a traffic cop. "Well, he ought to know that neck of the woods by now."

"Look at this," Cora says. She turns the thick album for the rest of us to see. There's a photograph of Jimmy as a teenager sitting next to Liz Taylor when she was in *National Velvet*.

"A publicity still," Jimmy says dismissively. "Everyone under contract had their picture taken with her. The poor kid. There was enough envy coming from the rest of the studio brats to light Warners."

"But you knew her?" Cora says.

"We were supposed to be one big happy family," Jimmy says. "We weren't. We were a bunch of—little egos. It's boring, really." He looks over at Susie. "We got swimsuits for this crowd? I need a dip. I've been sweating like a pig." He stands beside my father as if to compare physiques. "Mine'll be a little loose on you. That's not a married man's gut. You working out?"

My father avoids my mother's eyes. "Just clean living."

After outfitting my sister, Susie finds a pair of large boxer trunks for me.

"My son wears these when he visits," she says, and then smiles when she holds them up. "You're built like your father."

Outside, I pad barefoot across the redwood deck, a towel wrapped around my waist. My father is standing in the shallow end of the pool.

"It was the Paris of the Orient," Jimmy is saying to him. "What we've done to that city's criminal."

My father listens solemnly, arms crossed at his chest. It's hard to tell if Jimmy is trying to start an argument with him. My father is the least political man I know.

My mother sits on one of the chaise lounges, her feet up and her shoes off. She's still in her clothes.

"I didn't know you liked gin and tonics that much," I say to her.

"What do you think, sweetheart? Your mother needs to lose a little weight?" She wasn't able to fit into any of the swimsuits. "Your sister says it's what keeps daddies down on the farm."

She gazes past me, and I turn to see Cora and then Susie come out through the sliding glass door. As my sister walks toward us, she rolls her eyes. Susie has on a spectacularly revealing bikini (from Ice Capades?). It's a solid caramel color and I have to squint. She'd stepped over to the ladder, and with her back to us I thought at first that she wasn't wearing anything.

Cora sets her towel down. "That ought to shake up the troops."

She means, of course, to goad my suspicious mother. It doesn't help that Susie is both attractive and Oriental. While my father fought one war overseas, my mother was waging another at home. His absence has not made her heart grow any fonder. Only xenophobic.

"It doesn't surprise me," she says under her breath. "In the least."

My father scoops water over his shoulders to try to appear indifferent. He knows that my jealous mother is watching his every move.

"Let's go," Jimmy shouts, waving to the rest of us. "Everybody in the pool."

My suit hangs too low on me, and Cora grins when I stand up. She has on a simple maillot that fits her better than her own. I can tell that she thinks it's flattering.

Diving into the deep end, I have to grab my trunks as I come up.

Cora walks around the pool and sits down in front of me, dipping her toes in the water.

"Quite a bod the girl's got," she whispers. Susie is sitting cross-legged on the wooden deck trying to pin her hair up. "Bet she keeps the old boy's skates sharp."

"Why don't you get off Mom's case," I say. "She doesn't need you telling her she's fat."

My sister only shrugs her shoulders. "Hey, just some daughterly advice."

More than once during the next hour I try to catch my father's eye. I'm not interested in poring over any more Hollywood scrapbooks with Cora. Or in listening to Jimmy's complaints about Vietnamese bureaucrats. ("Everything has to be done behind someone's back. It's a way of life over there.") I don't care about Vietnam. All I want is for the war to be over between my mother and father.

As it gets darker, Susie lights the kerosene torches around the pool, and the water shines in brilliant strips of turquoise.

"Actually," my sister says, watching Susie stretch back out on her towel, "she's not all that bad. If you can look past the exhibitionism. As I know you can."

"I think Mom's looped," I say. "That's about five gin and tonics."

Cora yawns. "On the other hand, Jimmy's a jerk."

For some reason my father's cousin hasn't lived up to her expectations. I'm not sure why, exactly. Other than that my sister has a habit of always building things up in her head.

Susie has brought out the box of cigars Jimmy asked her for, and when she leans over the edge of the pool with the lighter, the top of her swimsuit droops open.

"Now, *that's* a smoke," Cora whispers.

Jimmy raises one of the cigars for my mother to see. "Cuban," he calls out. "All the way from Hong Kong."

From the other end of the deck my mother lifts her glass as if in a toast. "Better watch your friend there. He's not used to them."

My father grins sheepishly.

"No problem," Jimmy says, encouraged that my mother seems to be warming to him. "We know CPR here."

Susie only occasionally tiptoes up to my mother with a bowl of macadamia nuts (declined) or the fortune cookies from Jimmy's own homemade recipe.

I smile at my sister, pleased to know something she doesn't. "Guess who has a kid as old as you?" I say.

Cora flips her wet hair straight back. "Let me guess. Is he bigger than a bread box?" She speaks out of the corner of her mouth like a cabdriver. My father and Jimmy aren't that far away. "Does he have great big shoulders too?"

"What's so funny?"

My sister holds on to the side of the pool and flutter-kicks her legs a few times. "My, what big shorts you have on." And she laughs. "You really are priceless."

I don't want to listen to whose swimsuit she thinks it actually is. It would only be some crackpot idea she's come up with. "Let *me* guess," I say, looking out at Susie, who's standing between my father and Jimmy in the water. "Tim Considine's really *her* third son."

I don't know whether it's the chlorine or her medicine that makes my sister's eyes glisten. But for a second I think that this is what a crazy person looks like.

"Very good," she says. "And just when I was about to give up on my little brother."

I pull myself out of the pool, tugging my swimsuit back up on my hips. "And I guess the letters Dad gets aren't really from who he says they're from, right?"

She only tilts her head as if there's water in her ear.

"Everything has to be some kind of Hollywood plot with you," I say. "You live in a dreamworld."

My mother smiles dimly at me as I come over to her.

"My boy's getting so big," she says. "He's not my baby anymore."

I sit down on the other folding chair. "Tell that to Cora."

When she reaches for the towel to wrap around my shoulders, the empty pitcher shatters on the deck.

"Nobody move," Susie says. She's already up, prying her sandals on. "I'm an old hand at this."

My mother doesn't seem at all embarrassed and so I know that she's drunk. While our hostess bends nimbly at the waist, poking the broom under the chaise lounge, my mother keeps her bare feet up.

I look over Susie's backside at my sister, who puckers her lips and blows a kiss back at me.

"Time to go," my mother says, and stands up, her arms out like a tightrope walker's.

Jimmy objects only halfheartedly, and my father comes up the pool steps slowly, looking a little peaked from the cigar.

I follow my mother into the house and wait outside the bathroom with my ear to the door. "I'm going down the hall to take off my suit now," I say.

After a while I hear her clear her throat. "Fine, honey," she says weakly. "You do that."

Jimmy has drawn my father into the den to show him a few last mementos from his Far East travels. Cora, meanwhile, changes quickly and wanders out the front door to avoid Susie, who's wrapping up the leftover fortune cookies for us.

I hang my suit on the shower rod and then open the medicine cabinet above the sink. Except for a razor and a can of shaving cream, it's empty. I examine my chin in the mirror and don't know what to be more depressed about: snooping or taking my sister seriously.

Cora has opened the back of the station wagon when the rest of us emerge from the house together. She lowers the tailgate with a curious half-mocking expression. She's been up to something but I don't know what. We all shake hands and promise to get together again, which only my father probably thinks is possible.

Susie, wearing a man's terry cloth robe, waves bravely at us. The robe, I notice, is several sizes too big. Jimmy stands beside her puffing away on a new cigar.

"Mr. and Mrs. Sonja Henie at home," Cora says, rolling her window back up. She seems a little out of breath, as if she's just run around the block.

My father isn't a smoker, and as he steers the station wagon down through the steep hills, the back of his neck grows damp and clammy, until my mother, doubled over beside him from all the twisting and turning, raps the dashboard with her knuckles to stop the car.

"You all right?" my father asks her.

"Just pull over."

It's pitch dark out as the tires crunch on the gravel shoulder of the road. My father sets the brake and comes around the front of the car to unlock my mother's door.

"You need to be sick?" he says, ducking in, his grim face only inches from hers.

I watch them hobble together down the shallow embankment, where my mother drops to her knees like a penitent in the singed grass.

"Pathetic," Cora says, glaring out her window at them.

We listen to my mother heaving her gin and tonics in the ditch.

"Why don't you cut them a little slack," I say angrily. "They're having a hard time of it right now. Can't you see that?"

The whites of my sister's eyes flash in the dark, and for a moment I half expect her to lunge at me in the backseat.

"*They're* having a hard time of it! *They're* having a hard time of it!" She unravels the silk scarf from her throat. "And who do you think caused this?"

She's convinced herself that her condition was brought on by stress.

I look out at my father, slumped beside my mother as if joining her in prayer. "Probably them."

Stunned by my concession, my sister can only nod, mumbling under her breath, "That's right."

I don't want to argue and instead hold out the bag of fortune cookies, which seems to calm her down.

"Mom ought to get a boyfriend," she says finally. "That'd settle his hash."

I open my own door. "Somebody's liable to come around that curve too fast to stop."

My sister slides across the seat after me. "Hold on a minute. I got a little souvenir for you."

I start walking backward up the hill as she reaches in to pull something out of the rear of the station wagon.

"Amuse yourself," Cora shouts, and then flings a basketball that bounces once on the macadam before rolling off the side of the road.

I come back and pick it up.

"There it was, just sitting in the driveway," my sister says. "And Tim nowhere to be found for an autograph."

I can hear my mother still retching in the dark. "You're crazy," I say, tucking the basketball under my arm. "You're all crazy."

A van strains up the hill, the driver flicking his brights on when he sees us. But it's traffic coming the other way that worries me. I turn and trot far enough up the road, where I can at least flag anyone down in time.

Sitting on one of the guard-rail stumps, I try to catch my breath. Below me the city sparkles like the stars used to in the desert.

I press my fingertips to my neck and feel my pulse still throbbing wildly. From the crumbled cookie in my pants pocket I pull the small tape out and try to read my fortune in the moonlight. My sister is right. There's nothing inscrutable about my future the way I'm going. I'm headed for an ulcer before I have a driver's license. Only, what else am I supposed to do? Let some semi plow into the station wagon? I'm almost bitter enough to look the other way. To let them suffer whatever fate comes barreling around the bend. But of course I don't. In a few more minutes my mother will be able to crawl back into the car and we'll all be on our way again.

I set the basketball down and try to remember which of the three sons was Tim Considine. I never really watched the show that much in reruns. Mostly because every week one of the boys would get into trouble that was pretty trivial when the biggest trouble of all no one ever seemed to mention. What bothered me so much was how they kept pretending to be one big happy family. But how could they be, really? They didn't even have both parents. And how was anything supposed to be funny after that?

THE HOMEFRONT

"And the puffiness?" my mother asks. She stands beside Cora's hospital bed, anxiously twisting the corner of the starched sheet.

"That's something that's hard to predict," the captain says.

What was less difficult to predict was that my sister would fall in love with her bachelor physician.

"But it should start to go down?" my mother says.

Cora sits up in the elevated bed. She is sensitive about her protruding eyes. She doesn't want them talked about in front of her leading man.

"There'll be a pencil-thin incision," the doctor says, drawing an imaginary line across my sister's neck, "which should heal nicely. With a little sun it'll hardly be noticeable."

I can see Cora smile at the thought of basking on the beach at Grand Isle with her favorite army physician. But I notice that the captain avoids saying anything about what a little sun will do for her eyes.

"And the swollenness?" my mother persists, gently tracing Cora's brow with her finger.

My sister ducks away from my mother's hand. "If it doesn't bother me, why does it bother you so much?"

But my mother only wants her daughter's best feature, her large, lovely eyes, back to normal.

"Let's just see how it goes," my father says. He's as eager as Cora for her to be able to get back to school in the fall. She has been a difficult patient. But by having it done here at Ft. Polk during the summer, the army will pay for everything. A civilian hospital on the West Coast would have cost a fortune.

"Undoubtedly best," the captain says, relieved not to come between his commanding officer's wife and petulant daughter. "I think we're all going to be happy with the results."

My mother nods confidently. "She'll thank me later."

"Thank you for what?" Cora says. She shifts against the stacked pillows at her back. "What're you, assisting in the operation?"

One of the classic symptoms of my sister's condition is a general edginess, a hypersensitivity. With Cora, of course, it's hard to know when it's her thyroid and when it's just her prickly personality.

Still, it isn't a simple procedure even for an accomplished surgeon. But I know better than to ask upsetting questions in front of my sister the day before her operation.

"You're my daughter," my mother says. "I want to know what's being done for you. That's my responsibility."

A nurse sticks her head in the door and smiles at the captain. "Call on seven, doctor. You can take it in the hall."

He steps around my mother to squeeze Cora's shoulder affectionately. "Can't wait to get my hands on this young lady's throat," and he winks at my father, who lowers his *Army Times*.

"Thanks for everything, Doc."

My sister winces. I wave good-bye. And my mother eyes the attractive nurse suspiciously.

"Who's hungry?" my father says as soon as the door swings shut. "How about some takeout?"

Cora has already had a salad prepared by the dietician.

"Nothing for me," my mother says.

But the point is to get her out of the room for a while. Cora is ready to pounce on the next word my mother utters.

"You keep the patient entertained," my father says, steering my mother past me and into the hall. "We'll bring you something."

As soon as they are gone, Cora presses her fists to her temple. "That woman drives me absolutely bananas."

"She's just nervous," I offer, unzipping my backpack. "You know how she is about hospitals."

"I don't care about how she is," my sister says bitterly. "*I'm* the patient. *Me.* Can't she get that through her thick skull?"

Cora blames my mother for putting her here. She's persuaded that her goiter is the result of unreasonable pressures put upon her. I don't know exactly what pressures she believes my mother has exerted, but I decide against asking. As my sister's thyroid has enlarged these past few months, so has her general hostility toward my mother. The tension between them has driven my father on repeated out-of-state inspections.

I reach into my backpack. This girl I've been seeing, Patricia, will be seventeen on Saturday and I found an antique perfume bottle in the thrift shop run by the Officers' Wives Auxiliary. The silver top had to be replated, which wound up costing more than the bottle had originally, but it came out beautifully and I want to show it off to Cora.

Lifting the lid from the box, I set the bottle down on the bed stand. "What do you think?"

My sister looks curiously at me for a moment and then picks it up, examining its markings and the sunburst design in the crystal. "I probably won't die, you know? I mean, people survive this all the time."

"What?"

She is suddenly blinking rapidly. "It's not that big a deal."

But I don't know what she's talking about.

"I've got the best surgeon in the army," she says.

I start to reach down for the perfume bottle but catch myself.

"It was a very sweet thing to do," my sister says, and sets it in her lap. "And very uncharacteristic."

I nod gloomily.

"You had the top redone," she says. "That must have cost you."

I run the tip of my tongue along the back of my teeth. The ridge is like a miniature mountain range and I bite down until it stings.

"They did a nice job," Cora concedes, squinting appraisingly at the Art Nouveau design. "But for future reference, you don't want to alter an antique. It takes away from its value." She places the perfume bottle back down on the nightstand and checks the *TV Guide*. "*On the Beach* is on at eight," she says. "Tony Perkins with an Australian accent. Great casting."

But I'm trying to think of what else I can come up with for a present by Saturday.

". . . a captain," Cora is saying, aiming the remote control at the television. "The man's a god. And single. How is it humanly possible?"

I consider stealing the bottle back and letting her think that someone has taken it.

Of course I'm glad that my sister has such faith in her doctor, but even she has to doubt that the effects of her condition are completely reversible. I want to say something about my tongue being pretty much back to normal but think better of it. It still looks a little mangled, but at least I can keep my mouth shut. Which this time, at least, I manage to do.

My parents come back with Chinese, and Cora watches sullenly as we eat. She isn't allowed anything until morning.

Afterward, she falls asleep while my mother and I sit through the rest of the movie. My father has gone down to the lobby to finish a letter to one of his Vietnamese buddies.

"I don't want to watch the ending if it's going to be sad," my mother whispers. "You think it's going to be sad, honey?"

I look over at her. The entire human race has been obliterated by a nuclear war. And now Tony Perkins and his wife are about to kill themselves after just having put their baby out of its misery.

"It doesn't look real promising, Mom."

"Let's turn it off, then."

But I know that she won't let me.

"Why does Hollywood have to be so negative?" my mother says, keeping her voice down. "When I was growing up you could still go to the movies and be entertained. Now it's all gloom and doom."

"Maybe because there's a lot of it around," I say.

We watch Perkins swallow the last cyanide pill.

"I don't see why he has to do that," she says.

"What's the alternative?" I say. "He's going to be breathing radioactive dust here any minute."

"You always have a choice," my mother insists. "Don't let anyone tell you different."

It's the kind of conversation I could only have with my mother. I've tried to persuade her, as long as she's here, to have a few tests run on her legs, which continue to give her trouble, but all she wants to worry about right now, she says, is Cora. And so we both watch the young naval lieutenant lie down beside his dead wife and close his eyes. The first time I saw the movie with Cora I had to struggle to keep from blubbering. My sister had seemed unmoved. "Perkins just doesn't do it for me," she said as the lights came on in the post theater. But the truth is my sister takes after my stoic father.

My mother wipes her nose with one of the paper napkins from the Nankin Inn.

"I don't know what the point is," she says, shaking her head at the television as the credits roll against the ocean's backdrop. "Why do they show stuff like that? Just to upset people? Aren't there enough terrible things going on that they don't have to make movies about them?"

"It's supposed to make you think," I say.

My mother stands up, wincing from the pain in her leg muscles. "I want to be entertained. I don't want to have to think. I have enough to think about already."

"Well," I say, "it's a pretty important subject. I mean, look what can happen."

"I already know what can happen. It doesn't take a genius to figure that out."

"Maybe it's a good idea to remind ourselves."

"That's why we elect a president." She pulls the blanket up over my sister's shoulder. "So *he* can remind himself."

I laugh mockingly. Not for anything she's said but because I suddenly want to blame her for Cora's condition too.

"You'd rather pass the buck," I say, "instead of facing the truth and trying to do something about it."

When she turns around, her brow is creased as if she's trying hard to figure out what I'm talking about.

"I'm just one person," she says, and lowers her voice when my sister stirs. "Who cares what your mother thinks? What difference is that going to make?"

"You elected the president, didn't you?"

She smiles sadly at me. "I didn't vote, sweetheart. Your father was out of the country. I never got down to the firehouse to register."

In her sleep my sister's eyes look like poached eggs. I'm nervous about the operation. I've read too much about what can go wrong.

"That's typical," I say, and my mother waves her hand for me to keep my voice down. "I mean, aren't we supposed to be citizens of this country? Okay, we're a family. You're my mother. She's my sister. And Dad's down in the lobby. But we're Americans too. That's what a democracy's about. Only, nobody in this family even takes the time to vote."

My mother stops nodding.

"You're right, sweetheart." She suddenly looks tired and defeated. As if my civics lesson has summed up all her failings. "I don't do my share. I'm too caught up in our own little world to think about the bigger one the way I should. That's why I'm sending you and your sister to college. So you can make up for your uneducated mother."

It's useless to argue.

"I guess I'll get a ride from Dad," I say. "I can still make the last half of class." I've started taking karate lessons.

"He's probably fallen asleep." My mother spreads the sheet over the couch and tucks it under the cushions. "He likes the chairs down there."

I swing my backpack over my shoulder, glancing at the perfume bottle on my sister's bedstand.

"I don't think your father slept well last night either," my mother says.

With the television off there's only the light from the small bed lamp. My mother changes into her pajamas in the bathroom. She'll spend the night on the narrow couch to be with Cora.

"Your sister's going to be fine," she says when I apologize for arguing with her. "That's all that matters."

And when I look at Cora in the raised hospital bed, her throat swollen and her closed eyes twitching, I think that my mother is right. What *does* it matter if the world blows up tomorrow? As long as my sister is going to be fine.

"I want you to be careful with all that punching stuff," my mother says. "I don't need two of you in the hospital."

I find my father slumped over in one of the plastic chairs in the empty waiting room.

"Dad?"

He opens one eye.

"Mom's gone to bed," I say. "You think you could drop me off at class?"

He exhales heavily. "Your mother's going to put her legs out of commission on that damn couch."

He doesn't see the point of her spending the night again. Cora's medication will keep her out until morning.

"But that's your mother," he says, patting his pocket for the keys. "You want to drive?"

In the car we keep the windows open, which makes it difficult to hear each other.

"Your sister's going to do great," my father says, raising his voice. "I'm not worried about her. It's your mother should be seeing someone."

I nod. "It's like pulling teeth."

My father doesn't look over at me. We've had this conversation before. "This is true."

The dojo is on the second floor of one of the old war barracks that's been converted into a teen center for dependents.

My father slides over into the driver's seat when I get out.

"I guess I'll call if I can't get a lift," I say.

He readjusts the rearview mirror. All he seems to do is chauffeur the rest of us. He is as eager for me to get my own license as my mother is reluctant.

After three months of classes two nights a week, I am still only a white belt. Our instructor, a staff sergeant with tattoos of dragons on his forearms, doesn't believe in early promotion.

I quickly change into my *ghi*, taking my place in the back row. Beneath the thick cotton uniform sweat starts to trickle down from under my arms, even though I've missed the strenuous warm-up.

The rest of the hour we are paired off for arm and leg pounding, a painful exercise of beating on each other's limbs to harden our bodies. I've taken to wearing long-sleeve shirts even in the dead of summer to conceal the bruises. The first welt my mother spotted would have ended any more arm and leg pounding. Not to mention the sergeant's having to explain his regimen to the MPs. If Patricia hadn't been paired off with me that first night, I doubt I would have come back for more.

After class I meet her on the street. She has her own car, a convertible she bought from her stepfather, a warrant officer who my father describes as a "head case."

"We'll stop by my place," she says. "I want to get out of this stuff."

She has on a T-shirt beneath her *ghi*. It's soaked to the skin.

The only time I've brought her by the house, she wasn't wearing a bra and I never heard the end of it. "Kind of thing to cause a stampede," Cora said to me later. "If you're a steer." My mother had simply remarked that she hoped her only son could do better than that. "Got to believe," my sister said.

"I guess this operation's got everybody spooked," Patricia says. The top is down on the convertible and she climbs into the driver's seat without opening the door. "Whatever you do, don't get my old lady started on surgery. She's had one of everything taken out."

When she stops at the gas station right outside the gates, I walk over to the pay phone and call my father.

"I'll leave the door unlocked" is all he says when I tell him I don't need a ride.

Patricia had pulled up to a self-service pump but the attendant has come out anyway. He's stocky and appears to be something of a body builder.

"Hey, lady," he is saying when I walk back. "I'm just telling you how I see it."

"Right," Patricia says.

The attendant grins at me. "Your sister?"

"Your mother," Patricia says. She leaves the exact change on top of the pump.

"Okay," the attendant says. He shifts his weight evenly as if to jerk a pair of weights over his head. "Give me your best shot."

Patricia ducks her shoulder when I nudge her toward the car.

"Can you believe this character?" she says.

I walk around to the passenger side. "Let's just go," I say.

She tugs once at the stiff green belt at her waist but then opens her door and gets in.

As we pull away from the station the attendant is still standing with his legs apart as if bracing himself. Patricia gives him the finger.

We drive back through the gates of the post, and the guard doesn't even step out of his hut as we pass. Ft. Polk is an ugly post and my mother can't wait for us to be transferred, even though we've only been here a year.

With her hair blowing back I notice a scar on Patricia's forehead.

"Compliments of my stepfather," she says when I ask her about it. "For mouthing off."

We pass post headquarters, where my father works. He recently ordered the building whitewashed and it appears to glow in the dark.

"Whereas you get along with your old man," Patricia says.

There is an edge to her voice and I don't say anything.

The parade field was mown this afternoon and I can still smell the diesel fumes from the tractors.

"Your family was a trip, all right," she says. "Talk about negative vibes."

I stare at the hole in the dashboard where her radio has been taken out.

"You don't talk much about your parents," I say.

"Parent," she corrects me. "I don't count the warrant officer."

The enlisted housing on the post is run down. My father has tried to get the Corps of Engineers involved but everything moves slower in the South. Even the army.

Patricia's stepfather has complained of having to share a duplex with an enlisted family, but there is a housing shortage. My father tells me that they are actually lucky to get something on the base.

Mrs. Sherman is hard of hearing. And fond of television. The result is that Patricia insists that whenever she is home her mother wear earphones to listen to the TV. Otherwise she blasts it loud enough to hear from the street.

"Teddy and I will be in my room," Patricia shouts at her mother, who smiles back as if she's not quite taken it all in.

"Your father's bowling," she says. "I'm watching Perry."

Patricia nods at me. "Perry Mason. They're bringing back the original cast for a two-hour special."

The house smells of kitty litter, even though I've never seen any cats.

At the end of the hall Patricia grabs a towel out of the closet.

"You can snoop around while I take a quick one," she says. "I can't stand the smell of myself."

I follow her into her room.

"We really are different," she says, rummaging through her dresser. "You can't wait to get home and I can't wait to get out."

The bed is unmade and clothes are strewn about the floor. Two large stereo speakers are suspended from the ceiling with nylon fishing tackle. Her stepfather claims she'll get a better sound.

"Five minutes max," Patricia says, and closes the door after her.

After a while I can hear the shower through the thin walls and I imagine Patricia standing beneath the spray. She doesn't need the martial arts to keep in shape. As soon as she graduates she wants to work in a health club a thousand miles from here.

The shower has been off for a while when she leans back into the room, wearing only a towel.

"Damn," she says. "I wanted to catch you at something."

I'm sitting on the bed, reading the liner notes on one of her country-and-western albums.

"How do you like the mattress?" she says.

I press down on it. "Feels like a diving board."

"Hard's good for the spine." She shakes her head at the sound of the TV. "Christ," and pads back down the carpeted hall to shout at her mother to put her earphones on.

When she was eight Patricia tried to kill her stepfather. But the paper-doll scissors were too blunt and barely pierced his uniform. Recently, she thought of trying it again. "Only, with something sharper."

She comes back and kicks the door shut behind her. "That's all she does with her time. Watch that idiot tube." She bends over to brush her wet hair straight down. When she snaps her head back, her face is flushed. "I smell better than you do."

"Much better."

She sits down next to me on the bed and the towel splits open halfway up her thigh. "So what's the secret of your folks' success? They live together, right?"

It's Ivory soap and it smells wonderful.

"Dad hits the road every chance he gets."

"That's the thing. Give each other some breathing room." There are still pearls of water on her bare shoulders. "You can have your family," she says, and leans back on her elbows.

"Do I have any choice?"

"Well," she says, "you probably feel different. But I'll tell you what. If they can just keep an eye out for you. Till maybe you're five or something, then okay. So you don't drown or electrocute yourself. After that I'd say you're better off on your own."

"Six on?"

She nods without smiling. "What about your sister? She blames your mother, right?"

"My mother. Me. My father."

"That's what I mean. You're just asking for it, you stick around too long."

She studies me critically for a moment as if daring me to glance down at the towel.

I stand up and touch one of the speakers, which sends it spinning.

"It's one of the reasons I'm going to school in the fall," I say.

She raises, then lowers, her leg, her foot still pink from the hot shower. "College," she says. It's the same flat tone she used with the service station attendant. "Tell me something," she says finally, her eyes glaring like a sparring partner's. "You think I'm a little dumb, too, don't you? Like your mother and sister."

I'm shaking my head. "That's not true."

"It's like all of you thought you were so much better than what you were looking at. That was a real trip, let me tell you."

I think suddenly of telling her about the perfume bottle. But the whole thing seems ludicrous now.

"I'll take you home," she says, rotating her foot in small circles. It's one of the warm-up exercises in class. "Why don't you see if the old lady's figured out who did it yet. She's good at that."

In fact, Mrs. Sherman has changed channels. "I didn't like Perry so old," she says, the earphones resting atop her head.

I'm sitting on the vinyl sofa, trying to pay attention. But it's as if a trapdoor has opened under me and now I'm in the living room. Patricia is right, of course. It was exactly as she described it. Cora and my mother were condescending and aloof, and instead of telling them both off in front of her, I only tried to gloss it all over afterward.

On the ride home Patricia doesn't say anything until we turn into the officers' housing.

"The other side of the tracks," she says as if talking to herself.

At the house she leaves the engine idling and only nods when I tell her I'll see her in class.

"To tell you the truth," she says bluntly, "I don't think it's your sport."

Then I watch her back the convertible out onto the street and squeal the tires without waving to me.

It's a warm, clear night and I sit down on the porch and think about everything I said to her after she came back from the shower wearing only a towel. It's too late now to say anything, of course. But what I should have said was that they'd been that way because she'd made them every bit as uncomfortable as they tried to make her. It had been a great, braless entrance. For once someone had given them a dose of their own medicine. So what if she wasn't Grace Kelly. Who made us the royal family?

The following morning my father and I drive to the post hospital, and beside my exhausted mother, watch Cora, sedated and eyes rolling, get wheeled on a gurney into the operating room. After nearly an hour the captain strolls out to the lobby still wearing his green surgical garb to report that everything went pretty much as anticipated. The only surprise being the relative size of the goiter. It had been a good deal larger than he expected. In fact, one of the larger benign tumors he's ever removed. But happily none of it had any effect on the actual width of the cut. In six months the thin incision would fade from sight and not even her family would likely notice it.

But then the good doctor has the wrong family. Nothing, I'm convinced, ever quite escapes the critical net of my sister. And should something miraculously manage to winnow past her, there is always my mother trawling close behind. Only, today I can't hold anything against either of them. Babbling incoherently under the powerful anesthetic, her eyes big as fists, Cora has to be kept from tumbling off the narrow cot in the recovery room. And so each of us takes shifts watching over her. We could all go home for a nap and come back in a few hours when, as the captain assured us, the patient would be more rational. However, as my mother tried to explain between her tears, no one, not even someone who had operated on her (and she'd seized his hand, raising it reverently to her lips as if he were Prince Rainier himself), not even as wonderful a surgeon as he was could ever really know what was going on inside a child like its own family.

IN
the
GRASS

"My brother, the real estate mogul," Cora says. She steps over the freshly painted molding I've set out to dry on newspapers. "No wonder HUD's giving them away."

In the kitchen she shakes her head at all the cabinet doors stacked against the wall.

"Jesus, and look where he keeps the Cheerios. Under the sink with the Clorox."

Cora will finish up at UCLA this summer and so her visit home has to be short. We are living in Baton Rouge now, where my father heads the ROTC program, the largest in the South. Cora is staying on campus with my parents in the Commandant's House, an enormous antebellum home where Zachary Taylor supposedly once slept.

Upstairs, I follow my sister down the narrow, unlighted hall ("This the rite of passage?") to the bedroom.

"A hammock," she says. "And get a load of the victory garden." She kneels over the rows of starter pots by the space heater. "What in God's name are you growing?"

"I thought I'd try some radishes. There's full sun this side."

"Radishes," she says. "Of course. What was I thinking?" But she's dusting her hands off again. "All right, I'll give you this much. You're out of the house. You don't have to listen to those two

99

anymore. But, Christ, Teddy. This the best you could come up with?"

"The closing costs were less than they'd be paying to keep me in the dorm."

"All Mom talks about," my sister says, "is how her college boy's going to blow the formative years. Over here banging away at some white elephant instead of hitting the books."

I ask her how she thinks Mom's getting along now that the nest is more or less empty.

"Fretting, mostly. Over the prodigal son. And having seen what the prodigal's gotten himself into, I can't blame her." Cora smiles, squinting at me. "So where's *la femme,* kiddo? I've *cherchez*'d everywhere."

"You might try the public library," the student worker at the reference desk suggests.

I tell her I already have and when she shrugs her shoulders, I notice how her breasts rise with the gesture. Then she asks me what kind of carpentry project I'm into and I start in about the house.

"Sounds like an obsession," Janice says to me later. It's her lunch hour and we've walked over to the student union.

I mention how after a couple semesters of college I wanted to do something with my hands. How I thought renovating an old house over the summer would be exciting. Then I go into how I've already spent next year's tuition to cover some hidden expenses.

"How'd that go over with the folks?" she says.

"My mother wanted to know what was wrong with getting an education first. She said I had the rest of my life to get excited."

Janice nods sympathetically. "Sounds like a mom to me. All she wants is the best for her boy. Am I right?"

I admit that she is.

"Well," she says, "if it's any consolation, I don't think you're the first guy ever disappointed his mother."

"Probably not."

"There you are," she says brightly. "Got to be true to your school."

*   *   *

To keep from thinking about the termites, I spend the rest of the afternoon ripping off wallpaper in the den. Beneath the tacked-up cheesecloth are pressed the droppings of countless cockroaches. Each time I tear another strip from the ceiling, the tiny black pellets rain down upon me. The hardwood floor looks like a sea of caviar. Afterward, when I've finished vacuuming, I stand under the shower for nearly twenty minutes lathering my hair until my scalp aches.

"Enough to do Europe for the summer," Cora said before driving over to the mall, "and he blows it on the enchanted cottage."

The following morning I rent a power sander to strip the oak floor of several layers of yellowed varnish. But the coarse bands of sandpaper are difficult to pry onto the belt and cut deep gashes into the wood.

"You need a pro for that sort of work," my sister says on the way over to the med school's library. "You know. Someone with a calling in life."

My hands have developed thick calluses from smoothing the joint compound on the Sheetrock. Wearing only shorts, I tie a handkerchief over my nose to help keep from breathing the grainy particles that cloud the air. And still my nostrils become so clogged that in bed I cough up wads of thick white dust. My hair is continually tinted a soft silver gray.

"Very distinguished," Cora says when she gets back from campus. She stands by the door as I sit atop the stepladder sanding the strip of Sheetrock over the fireplace. "You look like one of the stiffs they dug out of Vesuvius."

But when the air grows as thick as a pool hall's, she waves her hand in front of her face.

"This supposed to be the home you never had? An army brat's idea of permanence? Because considering what you shot the wad on, I find that ironic."

I have dinner with my mother and sister. Even without central air conditioning the Commandant's House is as cool and damp as a cellar. The walls are packed with Spanish moss gathered by slaves a hundred and fifty years ago. Ancient, motor-powered fans turn slowly overhead from the high ceilings.

Cora complains that after L.A. it's like living in a time warp.

"I feel like ordering a hoop dress," she says. "I wouldn't last fifteen minutes here. It'd be like Chinese water torture."

"Oh, I don't know," my mother says. "You're here awhile, you get used to it."

"What about Dad?" Cora says. "He used to it?"

My father is working late. He's in the middle of a recruiting drive.

"Your father's never been able to sit still for very long," my mother says. "It's just his nature."

"Whereas his son can't wait to sink in his roots," Cora says. "No pun intended."

"What's wrong with settling down?" I say. "We've already seen the world."

"You mean *Dad*'s seen the world," my sister says, scraping her chair back from the table in the cavernous dining room. "We haven't seen, pardon my French, *merde*."

"That's not true," my mother says. "You've been all across this country."

"Mom," Cora says, "I hate to break this to you, but this country ain't the world."

My sister believes that we missed out on Europe and half a dozen other overseas assignments only because my mother wouldn't fly.

"Well, I guess it's what you do with where you are," I offer.

Cora smiles at my grim-faced mother. "Almost makes you wonder what the little renovator's been up to over there."

"I've always had this physical thing about books," Janice says, raising both arms over her head in the hammock.

My sister has taken in the afternoon matinee at the University Theater. No doubt because I mentioned that a friend ("So *that*'s what the little renovator's been up to") might be stopping by.

"I just like being around them," Janice is saying. "Physically."

Last year, she'd quit her part-time job at the branch library downtown because of the way they manhandled their collection. "I couldn't stand it anymore. Everything from cutting holes in the dust jackets to crushing spines in these huge sorting bins. Books have personalities for me. Anyway, it was criminal, so I quit. Of course, it didn't help that my immediate supervisor also happened to be a lech."

I tell her it's one of the things I like best about the renovating. It's the first summer I haven't had a boss.

"It's great," she says, and swings both feet out of the hammock. "I could move right in."

I'm sawing off dead branches from the cedars when Janice rides her bike up onto the front lawn.

"Got the stickers," she says, and disappears into the house.

When I come in for a glass of water, I find her sitting cross-legged on the floor, surrounded by stacks of books which she's carted down from upstairs.

"You're getting a modified Dewey decimal," she says, and licks one of the gummed labels. "You can go right to what you want now. It'll save you all kinds of time."

I watch her affix several more call numbers before she untucks her blouse from her jeans.

"God, it's hot in here," and she fluffs her short sleeves. "Anyway, I wanted to ask you about your sister. Why we haven't crossed paths. I'm just sort of curious."

I look down at my father's pruning shears. "I don't know," I say finally. "I guess unconsciously I try to keep anyone I like from meeting a blood relative."

Janice nods thoughtfully.

"More likely it's because I don't want to have to hear what they think," I say. "Even though I don't especially care what they think anymore."

"Your sister?"

"My sister. My mother. They're like Scylla and Charybdis."

Janice looks at me. "In other words you don't want the hassle of bringing anyone home because they're so critical."

"Right."

"It'd be like putting someone through the gauntlet?"

"Exactly."

She seems to consider this. "That explain this place?"

"Could be."

"Interesting."

"Pathetic's probably closer to it."

"Oh, I don't know," she says. "Nothing wrong with aiming to please."

"It's *who* I aim to please is the problem," I say. "That's what I'm working on."

"That and an old house."

"That and an old house," I say. "Works in progress."

The following morning my mother's legs are bothering her too much to drive down to New Orleans and so she says good-bye to Cora at the house. My father is off at some ROTC convention in Atlanta. As I wedge Cora's suitcase into the trunk of the VW, she looks back up at the enormous house the university offers rent free to the commandant of cadets. In the shade of the columned front porch my mother waves to us from her rocker.

"All that's missing is a couple of mint juleps," my sister says. "And the commandant, of course."

On the ride down to the airport Cora wears her sunglasses and seems not to notice the spectacular scenery of the bayous. When I point out egrets nesting in the cypress like Christmas ornaments, she barely seems to turn her head. We wind up listening to the radio.

At the airport I pull into short-term parking just as a plane thunders overhead. Cora leans forward, craning to see the jet through the cracked windshield of the VW.

"What do you think it is with Mom?" I say. "Why she'll never get on one?"

My sister makes her patented snorting sound. "Because opposites attract and Dad jumps out of them. Next question."

When she gets like this there's no use in trying to make intelligent conversation. I'm her younger brother. End of discussion. Still, it rankles. How often do I get to see her anymore and yet we haven't managed two intelligent words to each other the entire week. I want to blame Janice's presence but, of course, it's nothing new.

"Traveling light," I say, lifting her suitcase from the trunk.

"The only way to go, kiddo. No commitments."

"What about grad school?" I say. "You're committed to that, aren't you?"

She ignores the question as if the answer is obvious.

"So what's your little friend like?" she says. "Out there pulling crab grass together. It was enough to bring tears to my eyes."

Several times she'd seen Janice's bike and driven by without stopping.

I follow her across the parking lot. In the bright sunlight the concrete is like a white lake. Cora wears mirrored sunglasses that I can see my own reflection in.

"Janice?" I say. "I guess you'd have to say she's very honest. Very straightforward. Someone who doesn't care all that much what other people think. It's too bad you didn't get to meet her."

Cora breezes past me through the automatic doors of the terminal. "I'll try to catch her at the pageant. What's her state?" She glances both ways before spotting her airline counter. "So anyway, what's Wonder Woman do for a living?"

Even though we are early, my sister hurries ahead of me, her carry-on bag thumping against her hip.

I'm lugging the suitcase and am half out of breath keeping up with her.

"To tell you the truth," I say, "I don't think it much matters to her *what* she does for a living. Janice has her own agenda."

Cora's sunglasses bob at the end of her nose as she turns to peer over the top of them at me.

"I have this theory about brothers," she says. "Very Margaret Meadish. Want to hear it?"

"Shoot."

"It's sort of tribal, actually." And she stops to glance up at the board to see that her flight is on time. "The whole thing is for them *not* to marry their sister. So they bend over backward to find her opposite."

"You should try to get your mind off the house," Janice says. She sets her book down. "Take a day off and just relax."

I am lying on the mattress watching a cockroach search for an opening between the exposed pine planks of the ceiling. "Your sister thought the house had a lot of possibilities," my mother said to me on the phone the other day. I could just imagine how that translated into Cora's words. "She only had a few reservations about the neighborhood." I asked if Dad was still awake. "His trip took it out of him," she said. "He was up till two last night watching some Japanese movie your sister recommended." I wondered how her legs were doing. "Your mother's just an old war bride," she said. "You're the only one ever worries about me anymore."

After a brief thundershower the sun comes back out and I try working in the yard, but Janice sees that I'm dawdling and suggests a bike ride instead.

"Maybe it'll help snap you out of it," she says.

I toss the hand trowel on top of the clump of unplanted monkey grass.

"Won't that dry up in the sun?" she says.

When I shrug my shoulders, she looks at me curiously.

We take University Avenue down past the faculty housing and onto the dirt path around the lake. As we approach the stretch of cypress knees along the bank, Janice jumps off her bike and lets it career into the deep weeds.

"Come on," she says excitedly, and I watch her run across the path, then cut in toward where the snakes sun themselves. After skidding to a stop I pry the kickstand down and walk back.

It's no more than five yards from the bike route to the water's edge, but every inch is thick with growth. Some of the weeds reach to my waist and I have to part them like curtains, when abruptly I come upon Janice. She is sitting on the damp scrub grass with her blouse untucked. Just behind her in the water the moccasins are entwined about the cypress limbs.

"Come on," she says. "Forget about the house." When she lies back I notice how white, almost translucent, her skin seems in the sunlight, and as the snakes begin to move ominously on the stumps, my heart is pumping so fast, it's hard to hear her beside me.

"Think about your books," Janice whispers. "Think about how they're all alphabetized now."

One of the thicker moccasins slides into the dark water, moving along the surface, its head up like a tiny periscope.

"How about I think about you?" I say.

She pries her sneakers off, stretching her legs out in the grass. "So what do you think?"

What I think is that she is nothing like us. She is not hypercritical. She does not read her horoscope as if it were a medical prescription. She does not own a Ouija board. She does not know why Liz left Eddie. She does not subscribe to *Lotto,* the international journal for lottery lovers. She is a registered voter. She lives on and cares about the future of this planet. All of which, of course, is exactly my sister's point. No one would ever mistake her for one of the family.

"You're so tense," Janice says. "You're tight as a harp."

But just then, right across the lake, I notice that a magnificent rainbow has arched out of the clouds to touch down on the Commandant's House, my parents' temporary home, as regal and permanent as I imagine someday my own place to be.

GOOD HEARTS

When she got bored with graduate school, Cora surprised us all by coming back East and marrying a doctor. What *didn't* surprise me is that he's apparently a lot older than her. How much older, my mother won't venture over the phone. "Anton's Romanian," she says the day I get her letter. "It's hard to say with foreigners." But when she refuses to hazard a guess, I know we aren't talking about any beach boy. "Anton's a very distinguished man," my mother adds. "He went to the Sorbonne. He's a heart specialist." Cora met him last summer when my father got her a job editing training films at the military labs where he is now director. The people there work with NASA dreaming up things like granola bars made from the space crew's own fecal matter. "Nutritional supplements," the scientists call them, but my sister tells me that they taste like what they are.

Two years ago my father was assigned to the army research facility outside Boston. They've only recently bought a house and so I have to ask for directions.

"It's a little off the beaten path," my father says. "Your mother picked it out. If the roof lasts the winter I'll be thrilled."

Of course, what I really want to hear about is my new brother-in-law, only my father's conspicuously avoiding the subject.

"Even the Century 21 gal tried to talk her out of it," he is saying. "Not a real healthy sign."

But these are long-distance rates and I know when my father is stonewalling.

"So," I say at last. "A real doctor in the house. Even if he *is* a little long in the tooth."

I can hear my mother kibitzing at his elbow.

"That's the least of it," he offers finally. "Believe me."

In the morning before leaving I drop off a late makeup paper and my overdue books. I've switched majors again and am auditing a few courses in landscape architecture. I leave a message on Janice's answering service asking if she'll take some notes for me in class today. Actually, it's just an excuse to talk to her when I get back. I decided against inviting her to come up with me. And that's caused some friction. But we've already been through Meet-the-Family once before and I don't see the point of putting us through it again.

With frigid air blowing through the VW's heater vents, I have to pull off the freeway every other Howard Johnson's to thaw my toes. Usually I wait for the men's room to clear before using one of the hand dryers. But sixty miles from my exit my feet are so cold, I don't care who sees me.

It's snowing and I've lost all tactile sense by the time I reach the Route 9 cutoff. The rambling, three-storied Victorian house is on one of the finger lakes near Framingham. I turn down the snowplowed dirt road and the signs of neglect are immediate. Still, the house sits atop high ground and there's a lovely panoramic view of the lake. As soon as the VW's engine clatters off, my mother appears on the wide, screened-in porch.

"Your father's getting his lottery tickets," she says, eyeing the car. "I thought you were going to get rid of that."

I follow my mother into the large foyer. Because of the oil prices they've closed off most of the downstairs. We cross through the chilly dining room to the parlor, where I quickly back up against the crackling fire.

"Your father's been buzz-sawing up a storm," my mother says. She eases down into the wing chair like an old person. "Two weeks ago you couldn't see the house from across the lake. He's cut a path out there like a meteor."

I tug my shoes off, my feet prickling agreeably with the warmth of the fire.

"How're your legs doing?" I ask. She'd winced lifting them up onto the footstool.

"I wish I could saw them off, honey."

But that's as much as I'll get her to say. She'll no more see anyone about them than join the Officers' Wives Auxiliary. My mother has never been interested in anyone's health but her family's.

"So when do Dr. Frankenstein and his bride get here?" I say.

The newlyweds have rented a bungalow across the lake.

"You know your sister," my mother says.

But I'd never go that far.

"Tell me the truth," I say, trying to draw her in. "How much do you know about this guy? I mean, Cora can't have known him that long."

My mother's eyes narrow but we both turn at the sound of my father in the hall, his jump boots thumping on the hardwood floor.

Reunions tend to be awkward in my family. We're not, as Janice likes to say, a particularly kissy-huggy household. My father is wearing his Eisenhower jacket, his earlobes red as a thermometer bulb. And when I reach out to shake his hand he hesitates as if trying to recall the meaning of the custom.

"Heard you got some tickets," I say.

He opens his wallet. "I played your birthday."

But when I look at the numbers I see that he's confused the date with Cora's.

"I'll get the hot water heater going," my mother says, shooting a last warning look at my father. "Your sister and Anton are supposed to be here at eight."

My father moves the screen aside to set another small log in the fire. It's obvious that he's had the clamps put on him.

"So tell me about Dr. Kildare," I say. "What's an M.D. doing in a research lab?"

My father seems to weigh his response for a moment. "Not there anymore."

The hot water pipes rattle overhead.

"He's not?"

My father rotates his head slowly. "Nope."

"There was a problem?"

He closes his eyes, nodding just as slowly. "Yep."

I listen to the shower running upstairs. "You're not allowed to volunteer anything but it's all right to answer yes or no?"

"Yes."

"This problem," I say. "Are we talking mental or physical?"

"Yes."

I look down at my feet. "Mental?"

He nods.

"So," I say, suddenly less enthusiastic about the game. "Cora's catch ain't such a catch."

My father doesn't stop nodding.

It's almost a relief when my mother knocks on the upstairs bathroom wall. The water is ready.

She's set out monogrammed towels and my father's shaving kit. "So, you and your girlfriend . . ." my mother says, adjusting the taps on the huge porcelain tub. "You're still seeing each other?"

"Touch and go," I say. "But I guess a little more touch right now than go."

"Well, maybe now you can concentrate on your books a little more," she admonishes me. "Stop flitting around from one subject to the next. You have a perfectly good mind."

I study my hair in the pitted, beveled mirror. It's starting to thin out at the temples.

"That's what comes from not listening to your mother," she says, peering over my shoulder. "You wouldn't be going through this now."

"What? A receding hairline?"

"You know what I'm talking about."

She sets new underwear out for me. The T-shirt still has the gray cardboard sheet in it.

"What about Anton?" I say. "Still got it all on top?"

"Your brother-in-law's a doctor. He doesn't need any hair."

Later, from the upstairs landing, I see a Yellow Cab pull up in front of the house. The shutters on the living-room window are open and I watch my sister lean over the seat to pay the driver.

Cora strides in ahead of Anton. They're both wearing fur coats.

"You look ten years older," my sister says as soon as she sees me. Her breath is visible in the cold foyer. "Anton." And she turns indifferently to her husband. "My sibling."

"Ah, yes," Anton says, trying to peel his kid glove off. His thick accent is only the second shock about him. The first is his age. He's at least as old as my father. But considerably shorter and more rotund. "You are Cora's younger brother."

"Even if he doesn't look it anymore," my sister says, and leads the rest of us back to the parlor.

"No car?" I say to Anton, who keeps his fur hat on.

He appears stumped by the question and looks to his wife.

"At the shop," Cora says, glaring at both of us.

In the parlor my father only glances over the top of his bifocals, then resumes reading the paper.

Anton straddles the arm of the wing chair. There's the mad-scientist look about him: stray strands of hair twist up from his bushy eyebrows.

"Cora say you want to draw landscape," he says genially. "There is money in this?"

"Not the way I do it."

"Mr. Modesty," Cora says. "As a matter of fact, my brother has very good taste. In art."

The allusion escapes my brother-in-law, of course. My sister refuses to ask me anything about Janice. The one time they met, they did not, to no one's surprise, hit it off.

Anton pulls down a small leather bag from the bookcase.

"It is time for the checkup," he says, and draws a stethoscope from the black satchel. "Everybody, raise the sleeve, please."

My mother suddenly appears at the door. "Good," she says. "Just enough time before dinner."

My brother-in-law has apparently gotten into the habit of checking everyone's blood pressure. He starts with my father, who keeps the paper folded in his lap.

"Everybody in this family has a good heart," my mother says as soon as Anton finishes with her.

I sit down on the couch beside my brother-in-law. His pinstripe suit is rumpled, his silk tie knotted haphazardly. After wrapping the Velcro about my arm, he pumps the rubber ball, concentrating intently. And for the first time I am persuaded that he is, in fact, a doctor.

The vein in my wrist throbs as Anton releases the valve on the armband. He nods silently with each count of pressure.

We all wait for the verdict until my brother-in-law at last looks up.

"Once more," he says too loudly, the stethoscope still in his ears.

My mother wipes her hands on her apron. "It doesn't mean anything," she assures me. "He'll just double-check when it's someone he hasn't done before."

Anton bows his head as if to hear better and I notice his bald spot, as perfect as a yarmulke. He lowers the stethoscope about his neck and hesitates as if still uncertain about his reading.

"Okay," my brother-in-law says without looking up. "Now we go to eat."

My mother is all smiles. "What did I tell you. Everybody in this family has a good heart."

The single radiator in the dining room is turned up as far as it will go, and the door into the kitchen is left propped open for the heat from the stove. Yet by dessert it's cool enough for a sweater.

"So why didn't you bring us some drawings?" Cora says. She's on a diet and picks at the chocolate icing Anton has left on his plate.

"You see one picture, you've seen them all."

My mother shakes her head. "How are businesspeople going to take you seriously if you don't take yourself seriously?"

She's embarrassed for me in front of her accomplished son-in-law. But I doubt that Anton has heard a word of it. He sits beside Cora sketching a Rube Goldberg–like contraption on his paper napkin. Every once in a while he blurts out something in Romanian to himself and then erases furiously. I'm sorry Janice can't be here to meet him. She's a psych major.

With the radiator clacking annoyingly all of us retreat to the parlor with our coffee cups. Except my father. There's a *National Geographic* special on, and he wanders upstairs to the television in the bedroom.

I turn the log over in the grate. "We need some wood."

"Your father will come down later," my mother says. She's been watching Anton uneasily. He's smoothed something out on the floor that looks like a blueprint. And then I can see that it's the same machine he sketched on his napkin, only in more detail.

"Where's the woodpile?" I ask my mother.

Anton lets the drawing curl back up. "I will help," he says.

"Just a small log," my mother concedes.

Once outside, my brother-in-law pulls his pack of Gauloises greedily from his coat. Cora won't let him smoke in the same room with her.

"I must speak to you about your habits," Anton says. His breath whistles in the cold.

But I'd suspected as much. He's kept quiet until my mother wasn't around.

"Your diet," my brother-in-law says solemnly. "No more red meat. No more salt. No more like what your momma make tonight. These are the habits you must break."

"No more pasta," I say. "Hurt me."

Anton inhales deeply. "This can be worse," he muses, and then crushes the empty cigarette pack as if it were my heart. "You can be dead."

We come back around the house, each of us cradling a small log in our arms. Shuffling in front of me in his dark fur coat and hat, my burly brother-in-law looks like a washed-up circus bear. I don't understand my sister. Why she would give up graduate school to marry a man twenty years older than her. A man who barely speaks her language, in every sense of the word. A man she already holds in contempt. But then who did I expect? Louis Pasteur? My sister isn't exactly Madame Curie.

It's after one and I'm reading in the parlor when my father comes down in his robe to check on the fire.

"Still a little wound up from the trip," I say.

He lifts the other log up with the pincers.

"Point of information," I say, but he keeps his back to me. "Why'd Anton blanch when I asked about their car?"

It's the least of my questions, but I don't want to scare him off. My father nestles the log onto the grate.

"It's a touchy subject," he says. "Your brother-in-law's not supposed to drive."

I know that with all the medication Cora has to take no insurance company would touch her, but no one has said anything about Anton. "Why not?"

My father holds his hands out to the fire and smiles over his shoulder at me. "Because the judge said he couldn't."

Just last month Anton had run a red light and slid into a snowbank.

"And they suspend your license for that?" I say.

My father yawns, closing his eyes and tilting his head back. "Not if you're wearing your clothes. That's where your brother-in-law went wrong."

By the time a squad car arrived on the scene, Anton had stuffed every stitch on his back into the glove compartment.

"Mercedes have a larger-than-average glove compartment," my father adds.

After meeting my parents Janice described my father as "laconic." He was the only one she managed to get along with.

"So what are we talking about here?" I say. "Just the tip of the snowbank or what?"

My father smiles crookedly. "Funny you should mention snowbanks. He emptied your sister's jewelry box into one just the other day."

I ask if Cora has him going to anyone, a psychiatrist.

"Your sister," my father says. "She and your mother make a great pair: See No Evil and Hear No Evil."

"So why don't you say something to him?"

He rubs his palm across his chapped lips. "We talking about the same guy? Look, you call some doctor's secretary, she tells you the patient has to come in on his own volition."

"Did you tell them Anton's an M.D.?"

"I told the first one that. She practically hung up on me. Head doctors don't like to see heart doctors with head problems. Something to do with insurance and lawsuits."

"What kind of sense does that make?"

My father shrugs his shoulders wearily. "It's been my experience."

Thursday afternoon Cora calls to ask if someone will pick up Anton. He's missed the last commuter bus in from Natick. Apparently he has started doing some kind of consulting work in Boston now that he's no longer at the labs. My father has just gotten home from work and puts his coat back on slowly.

"Take your son," my mother says, and holds the car keys out. "Let him pick some numbers."

The station wagon is still warm, and my father adjusts the rearview mirror, turning his jaw as if to shave. "They don't know the first thing about this character," he says.

The sharpness of his tone surprises me. But then, he's had a long day at the office.

"They know he's a doctor," I say. "I guess that's all they need to know."

We wait at a light, the engine chugging in the cold.

"He gives physicals for some insurance companies in the city," my father says. "I doubt he can even practice in this country."

I've decided to head back early. Midterms are coming up and I'm on probation.

In town, gray meter heads poke up through the plowed snow.

"Well, what do you know," my father says, cutting sharply into an empty lot.

At first, I imagine one of the chains has fallen off. But when we come to a complete stop, my father turns off the engine.

"Show time," he says, and sets the hand brake.

The hood ornament of the station wagon is pointed directly at a bus stop across the street. There's a single empty bench with a see-through weather shield.

"By the hydrant," my father says, lifting his chin slightly.

I hunch forward. "What is it?" It looks like a tarpaulin.

"Your brother-in-law," my father says. "The doctor."

I jerk the door handle down but my father reaches across me.

"Relax," he says calmly. "He's all right."

"He's all right! It's ten degrees out there."

My father lets go of my arm. "What do you think, this is something new?"

But he can see that I'm upset.

"Okay, okay," he says, unlocking the door. "Take it easy."

I trot ahead of him across the street. It's Anton, all right. Flat out on his back, his coat open and his shirt unbuttoned to the waist. But he doesn't seem in any physical pain.

"Anton," I say, and kneel beside him. "Can you get up?"

His eyes are open, his barrel chest pink from the cold.

"Tell him his mother-in-law's got dinner on," my father says from the bench.

"Why don't you sit up," I try coaxing him. "You must be freezing."

But he only gazes serenely past me. It's impossible to be angry with him. It's my mother and Cora I blame.

My father comes back from the station wagon. "Let's try this," he says, holding his fist out. "It's worked before."

There are half a dozen paper clips in his palm and he sets one down on Anton's bare chest.

"Found them in the car," my father says when Anton flinches. "I thought they might be from the Reduction Machine."

I look at my father.

"Something your brother-in-law's been working on," he says. "For heart stress. Those were the blueprints in the parlor."

For the first time Anton appears to be paying attention.

"Trouble is," my father says, "there's no copyright on the damn thing."

Anton pushes up onto his elbows, the paper clips sliding off his chest. "'S.P.,'" he whispers.

I stare blankly at my father.

"Solar power," he explains. "Your brother-in-law's machine relies on the sun. That's what he's been doing out here, absorbing the rays." My father pretends to lower his voice so that Anton can't overhear. "I worry about somebody stealing the idea. Somebody from the labs, for instance."

Then he steers me over to the curb out of Anton's earshot. A squad car turns up the street and we both stiffen. But it passes.

"If I thought there was any chance he might hurt your sister," my father says, "it'd be different. But he's harmless. He clicks in and out every once in a while."

Anton suddenly scrambles to his feet, hops over the fire hydrant, and looks both ways before crossing to the parking lot.

"Let's wait till he's settled in the car," my father says. "You don't want to set him off again."

In town we stop at the drugstore for lottery tickets.

"Let me pick up a few things for dinner," my father says, glancing up at me in the rearview mirror. He wants me to stay with Anton. My brother-in-law sits rigidly in the front seat, twisting a paper clip around his wedding finger.

To break the ice I offer that he might try the Reduction Machine on me. With my blood pressure up so high I seem the perfect candidate for a test run. But when I ask Anton what he thinks of the idea, he only leans one elbow on the dashboard and starts writing an equation across the fogged-up windshield.

"Good advice," I say, and sit back in the seat.

My father returns from the deli with a loaf of pumpernickel, some hard rolls, and a cheesecake.

"I talked to your mother," he says, and hesitates a moment before flicking the defroster on to clear the windshield. "We're supposed to pick Cora up for dinner."

We take a different route back around the lakes. As we pass under an old stone overpass, I ask when Anton is likely to snap out of it. My father smiles wryly in the mirror.

"Soon as he sees your sister."

When we pull up in front of the bungalow, I notice the Mercedes parked in the driveway. The entire grill is mashed in. The car had to have been towed. When my father beeps the horn twice, Anton turns about in the front seat.

"So you have come along for the ride," my brother-in-law says, grinning happily.

I nod. "How you doing?"

Cora inches up the walkway cautiously, her coat pulled back so she can see her feet. "I hate the snow," she is saying. "I hate, hate, hate it." Anton meets her halfway and she seizes his arm. "What'd you sit on?" she says. "Your coat's all wet."

Anton brushes his backside. "Maybe it happens on the bench."

My sister raises an eyebrow at him but doesn't pursue it. When she slides into the backseat next to me, I decide not to ask her anything about the car. And neither does my father.

At the house my mother comes to the door, her face flushed from standing in front of the stove all afternoon. I can tell that her legs are sore. She has that look.

"How'd you get so wet?" she says, and carries Anton's coat into the downstairs bathroom. "It's sopping."

But Anton is as puzzled as my mother.

At dinner Cora talks about how they plan to move into the city soon. Some new apartments are going up near the river.

"Most of them are already presold," she says. "Especially the ones with any kind of view of the water."

Anton's brow furrows. "This place," he interrupts. "Where is this place you are talking about?"

My sister wets her napkin to dab affectionately at his spaghetti-splattered chin. "You remember, honey. I showed you the ad in the *Globe* Sunday."

Anton's bushy eyebrows twitch anxiously.

"What you buy is essentially just the frame," Cora continues, undeterred by her husband's memory lapse. "You bring in your own floor plan. Which is the only way to do it, as far as I'm concerned."

It's after midnight when I drive them back in the station wagon. We all sit in the front seat listening to the tire chains crunch on the packed snow.

I might not see them again and so I come in for a drink. The furnished bungalow is musty smelling and cramped.

"I'm a city girl," Cora says, flopping down on the mildewed sofa. "It's all right for Mom and Dad. But, I mean, we're talking major cultural blight out here."

Anton wheels in a tea caddy on which he's set out cheese and crackers.

"So Mom tells me you're thinking about landscape architecture?" Cora says, making a strained effort to be sociable.

There's no point in asking about her own studies. Why, suddenly, she's given up on her graduate program. Flightiness is obviously a family gene.

"For the time being anyway," I say.

Anton slumps in the La-Z-Boy recliner. He keeps his coat on, unbuttoned, one hand tucked under his arm. I'm too tired to try to include him in the conversation. We both simply listen to Cora and her ambitious interior designs ("The minute I laid eyes on this picture of Merle Oberon in her living room, I said to myself, 'Now, *that's* what I want it to look like'").

When, at last, I mention having to hit the hay, my sister offers no objection and we both push up from the flimsy couch at the same time, nearly tipping it backward.

"Well," Cora says, "guess I'll see you when I see you."

Anton escorts me to the door. When I turn around, my sister is already down the hall.

"Now we may talk," my brother-in-law whispers, squinting ferociously at me. He clamps my forearm like a drowning man. There are other drawings he wants me to see. But because Cora makes him keep them outside, his mildewed blueprints have become "greenprints."

In the cluttered garage Anton flicks on a light bulb to unlock a metal filing cabinet. The printed tabs are all in Romanian and he lifts out several water-spotted manila envelopes.

Then, reaching up, he unhooks an aluminum chaise lounge from the pegboard. "For you," he says, and retrieves a second lounge chair for himself.

My father warned me about letting my brother-in-law pull me off to the side. It didn't take much to uncork the genie from his bottle.

Anton bumps open the door, rattling the awkward chair after him. "Here it is not safe," he says. "Come."

I watch him poke his pointed Italian leather shoe into the crusted snow as if testing his bath. Satisfied that it isn't too deep, he high-steps it halfway down the backyard before I can stop him.

"Anton! For cryin' out loud."

Like a raccoon caught in a car's headlights my brother-in-law gazes back up at me. "This way," he says, his voice husky in the cold.

I pull the lawn chair after me, my pulse throbbing in my throat. It doesn't surprise me that my sister doesn't hear us. Her pills knock her out two minutes after she takes them.

"Wait!" I shout when Anton tries to unfold the rusted chaise lounge. "Just hold it there."

Unable finally to pry it open, he hurls the chair onto the ice, where it skitters twenty feet from shore. But when he steps out onto the ice himself, my heart freezes. I've not seen any kids skating since I got here.

"Christ, Anton!"

He ignores me, inching each foot forward like a tightrope walker. I've no idea how deep the water is. Or how abruptly the shelf falls off.

"This is crazy," I call out to him.

He manages to open the chaise lounge and now eases himself onto it. I stand on the bank trying to coax him back in.

"You'll sink like a rock," I shout, hands cupped into a megaphone. "They won't chip you out till the spring."

He angles the chair so that his back is to me.

"They'll send someone over from the labs," I yell. "He'll get the frozen blueprints and forget about you."

Anton only hikes his thumb up at the moon. It's full and he has his shirt open again, basking in the chaise lounge as if on the deck of an ocean liner.

I haul the garden hose back down from the garage, lassoing the nozzle end out to him.

"Catch hold," I plead, but instead he wriggles up from the folding chair and wraps the hose once about his thick waist. It's a brief tug of war. Even with both heels dug in the snow I'm no match for him. Tumbling out onto the ice, I try to keep my legs from scissoring when Anton snaps his end and I go down heavily.

Some time later when I open my eyes, the hose is tangled about my ankles and I wait for the ice to crack like a fault.

"This lake is not so deep." It's Anton. He's leaning over me, his large head blocking out the moon. "Maybe ten feet here is all. This is nothing."

My ears are thumping and I touch the knot at the back of my head. My left shoe, I notice, is off, the sock stuffed inside. And I understand that I've been unconscious.

"You are sleepy for a little while," my brother-in-law is saying. He runs a car key up my bare foot and nods when my toes curl over. "You see, it is only a bump. There is no problem."

I'm sitting in the chaise lounge in the middle of the lake, the bungalow lost in the distance. Beside me, in the other folding chair, Anton explains how all of this is "made-man," a vast project of the WPA during the thirties. The lakes are artificial, not really real. I believe him but am careful not to shift my weight in the chair. We are, I estimate, roughly the length of a football field from land.

My brother-in-law's fur coat covers my legs. He studies his blueprints, his hair still damp from dragging me across the ice. I neglect to ask how this was managed but suspect that the garden hose, coiled nearby, must have figured into the enterprise. My heel marks recede like train tracks into the dark.

Although the trees obscure my parents' house, I can see vaguely where the pier juts into the water. It's a toss-up as to whose side of the lake we're closer to. But when I think of where I am, I experience a sputtering sensation in my chest, like a propeller backfiring. My brother-in-law, meanwhile, speaks sotto voce of the security measures he's had to take to protect his invention. Even here, he whispers, he must be careful which way the wind is blowing.

In fact, the chill air is breathless. And yet every imagined sound, no matter how harmless, causes my heart to stutter-step. Closing my eyes, I think again about last night. I'd stretched the upstairs phone into my bedroom to call Janice. I wanted to ask her if there was any assignment. But then someone whose voice I didn't recognize answered after the first ring. "Janice?" he asked pleasantly. "Sure, Janice is here. Hold on a second." While I waited I could hear faint laughter above the stereo. Then Janice came on. "So what's up?" she asked finally. But I hadn't planned on this (I'd forgotten her mentioning she was going to have some people over) and could think of only Anton's report on my high blood pressure. "Well, there you are," she said coolly. "Must run in the family, honey. Everything else seems to." I glanced at my watch, trying to recall in my confusion if they were an hour later or an hour earlier. "I guess I better let you go," I offered at last, the receiver warm against my ear. Janice held the phone away a moment to hush her playful friend. She came back, her voice tinged with bitterness. "That's probably not a bad idea, Teddy."

Although it would be foolish to admit it to Anton, I can't deny the eerie beauty of our perspective. It's as if our lawn chairs have descended on the vast, pocked crater of another planet. Too cold for life, everything is tinted blue by a single, orbiting moon. Peering over the arm of the chaise lounge, I imagine sighting down one leg of a space probe's landing pod. And try to envision what it would be like to discover a new world. But somebody over at the labs said in the paper the other day that if we're ever going to make it to another galaxy, someone is going to have to have his heart freeze-dried. Or at least slowed down to where it's more or less in suspended animation like a goldfish frozen in a pond. It's hard to fathom how it would feel to have your heart gradually thaw back into life. Still, for all the scientists know, you could wake up without a shred of memory of even your own family, so that from that moment on everything and everyone would be absolutely new.

THE KING
and QUEEN
of REX

Out of the blue Cora phones me from a suite in the Maison La Mont. It's a bad sign. The expensive hotel is the only five-star establishment in New Orleans and I know that she can't afford it. Still, after a year without a word, I'm eager to see her. There is no explanation for the long hiatus other than that my sister is my sister.

And so I don't ask about Anton. Not even *he* could drive her this far South. Only my mother's illness could do that.

As soon as I hang up, I call Janice at the day-care center. After selling the HUD house for a loss, we moved down closer to the city. Then the economy went sour and neither of us has had much luck finding work. Janice tried a couple of different bookstores in the Quarter but recently has been filling in for someone on maternity leave over at the Little Folks Day Care Center.

"So how's Cora sound?" she asks. "Still crazy after all these years?"

That's exactly how she sounded and it depresses me to admit it.

"You think it's safe to go alone, then?" Janice says. She is only half joking. My father has been relaying to us some of Anton's most recent antics.

"I got the impression she wants to keep him under wraps," I say.

Janice laughs, already a little beat from her morning with a classful of three-year-olds. "Sort of like you'll do with me, right?"

"That's not true," I say, even though it is. "You can come if you want. We could take in a parade after."

It's Mardi Gras week and the coldest on record.

"No," she says, yawning into the receiver. "You go ahead. Talk to your sister. Say hi to the doctor for me if he's around."

"You could drop by after work," I say, knowing that she won't. "We can compare notes afterward."

But one of her colleagues needs to use the phone.

"Teddy, I've got to get back to the kids. I'll see you when I see you."

"I'm not staying out late with them," I say. "I'll probably get back before you do."

"Whatever."

"You're sure you don't want to come?"

She is silent for a moment. "Honey, when you don't mean it, don't say it," and she hangs up.

The VW sits in the driveway, its back tires flat. We can't afford the premiums. I hail a cab and the driver gives me the once-over in the rearview mirror.

"Took the king of Bacchus up there the other day," he says. "Jesus, what's his name? Does all the telethons. You can't turn on the tube and not see him."

But Janice hates TV.

"They get 'em all," he assures me. "Everybody who's anybody."

When we pull into the hotel's sweeping horseshoe drive, a porter is at my door before the taxi even rolls to a stop.

I tip the cabbie almost as much as the fare but he only smiles crookedly. He knows a fish out of water when he sees one.

Still, this is the Maison La Mont. And neither the concierge nor the bellman can be friendlier, trained as they are to offer the benefit of the doubt.

At the desk the clerk rings up Cora's room, and I wait in the warm lobby, watching as one Mercedes after the next glides under the portico to receive the same imperial reception. When, at last, the burnished doors to the elevator sweep open, and my sister, wrapped in her full-length fur coat (an early extravagance from Anton, the suitor) steps out, my knees very nearly buckle.

"I know," she admits. "I've put on a few pounds."

But this doesn't tell half the story. My sister is twice the size I remember her. Even her eyes are slits, pushed shut by her Eskimo-fat cheeks.

"Not a word about the hair," she cautions me. "I'm leaving it. I'm not going to live a lie."

I want to say that it's as good a place as any for us to start but I'm speechless. I would not have recognized my own sister on the street. It's not enough to say that she's let herself go. She has become unmoored.

"Let's take a little constitutional," she says. "Work up an appetite. The hotel puts out a fabulous buffet."

An ancient doorman rises from his bench and like royalty my insouciant sister passes her subject without a nod.

Outside, she turns up her collar as if the wind were a personal affront. There has never been a Mardi Gras with temperatures below zero. Still, the crowds are here. Just fewer exhibitionists among them.

To break the ice Cora remarks on the unseasonable cold. It monopolizes the news. The city has opened its gymnasiums to the homeless. Derelicts hover about every warm grate. We step around them even this far from the Warehouse District.

"The weather?" I say contemptuously, as if that is the best she can come up with after our own long chill.

My sister stops before a particularly pathetic soul who teeters on his knees beside a steaming grate. He is swathed, mummy-like, in soiled rags. The unwrapped big toe of one foot is black from either dirt or gangrene or both. It is doubtful he knows the difference anymore. Hunched over, he gazes into the depths of the sewer as if to coax some sturgeon from an ice hole.

Cora stuffs several bills into his empty pork-and-beans can.

"God bless you," the man rasps, his head rotating up at us like a mechanical toy's.

My sister smiles beneficently. She is Mother Teresa and I don't know whether to cry or to wring her neck. I don't give a damn about the weather. I want to know what in hell has been going on with her. But, of course, I don't ask. Around my sister I have always been the sorcerer's apprentice. And I am reminded that nothing is revealed except by indirection. I must keep my ears pricked to what *isn't* said.

"Your brother-in-law's at some symposium," she volunteers.

"In New Orleans?"

She winks at me. "What'd you think? I came unescorted?"

But this is the problem with my sister. I never know when she is lying merely to have the last word.

Cora stops before the window of an exclusive art gallery near the waterfront. A converted loft, it is the kind of establishment to sniff its nose at anyone who can't afford the works on display. In other words, no place for the impoverished like me.

"Let's browse," my sister says, and rings the bell above the brass mail slot.

We are ushered in by a slight man whose plucked eyebrows seem permanently arched. "Madame? Monsieur?"

But when he reaches for my sister's coat, Cora hesitates as if to consider whether the showroom is worth her time. Her glance takes in the magnificently varnished floors and high-tech spiral staircase. She nods finally an appraiser's approval, surrendering her coat with a remarkably nimble twirl.

I have to stand back to take her in. Yet there is no getting around it (in every sense of the word), she dresses elegantly even for her size.

"Cappuccino?" the gallery owner asks, cupping one hand beneath his pointed chin.

"*Deux, s'il vous plaît.*"

I am fairly certain that exhausts my sister's French. But at this point if she started speaking in tongues I wouldn't be surprised.

Our friend's black leather pants swish irritatingly as he retreats.

"So, how's Anton doing?" I ask, tired suddenly of all the pretenses. "We going to get together this visit?"

Cora has stepped over to the first of a series of gouaches in which muscular blacks cut cane in a brake.

"He's supposed to meet one of his cousins at this conference. A lawyer or something from Prague. Anton never tells me much about his family."

"Then you two must have a lot to talk about."

My sister offers me one of her patented smirks. It's as close as she'll come to a compliment.

The owner rattles a tea caddy back across the hardwood floor.

After a quick tour of the gallery Cora and I, empty porcelain cups in hand, stand before a bronze, steroid-muscled nude in the center of the room.

"Probably out of my price range," I say.

My sister glances at me as if at some lint on the sleeve of her fur. "What isn't?"

My mother has told her that I've dropped out of school for the time being. No doubt they both blame Janice. And I run my ravaged tongue across the back of my teeth, silently counting to ten.

Afterward, at the beveled glass door, the gallery owner shakes hands with me like a man who knew all along he was wasting a cup of cappuccino.

Outside, the first breath of cold air is like acid in my nostrils.

Cora is already reaching into her coat for another wad of bills. Ahead of us half a dozen derelicts, like war wounded, lie propped up against a marble office building.

Back at the hotel we cross the deserted dining room to a corner table.

"The buffet today," Cora says to the waiter without bothering to take the menu. "The guava is fresh?"

The man assures us that it has just fallen off the tree.

"*Deux* buffet, then," my sister says, and he backs away like something out of a Swiss cuckoo clock.

I follow Cora to the magnificent array of fruits and vegetables set out on an elaborately carved oak table.

"*Deux* buffet," I say. "Is he still painting?"

My sister ignores me, intent as she is in stacking her chilled plate with guava that, as a matter of fact, *does* look wonderfully fresh.

At the table she snaps her starched napkin at her side like a matador, her plate a shameless cornucopia.

Behind us the constant rush of a waterfall is like Muzak. It is there, of course, to fill in for any gaps in the conversation. But for my sister and me that would require something on the order of Victoria Falls. My mother is seriously ill and absolutely nothing is permitted to be said on the subject. So profound would the breach in family etiquette be. "People deal with things like this differently," Janice has said of my mother's deteriorating condition. "Your sister's always been a dreamer. So she's going to dream it away. Why should that surprise you?"

"I'm curious," Cora says, and just from the tone of the question I know what is coming. She wonders if I have any plans beyond my current dead-end ones.

When I push the *crème brulée* aside, the waiter sweeps down upon it. The La Chute Room has been empty for hours and he is eager for a respite.

"Everything is satisfactory?" he asks my sister.

She gazes at him icily, having sniffed the faint scent of petulance in his voice. "For the moment."

The waiter forces his best five-star smile. "Certainly."

I can't take my eyes off my sister. We can't be related. Our spines are made of entirely different DNA.

"None," I say as soon as the waiter has backed off. "Nothing but dead ends on the horizon."

"Then the family's to abandon all hope?" she says.

"Now *I'm* curious," I say. "Which family we talking about?"

Cora pats the corner of her mouth with her cloth napkin. "You only get one per life, kiddo."

I suddenly want to seize the tablecloth and rip it out from under all the crystal and china and tear off my tie and leap into the goddamn waterfall screaming what a lie it all is. We aren't rich. Never have been, never will be. This is a hand-to-mouth guy sitting here. And that one there, my big, and I mean *really* big sister, can afford it even less.

"Tell me something," I say at last. "That family include Mom?"

But my sister's withering gaze fixes instead upon our hapless waiter.

She calls him over. "We'll be having coffee. And some of your pastries. Whatever's out." She turns back to me. "Speaking of Mom. She's right, you know. That's always been your problem. You don't take yourself seriously enough. You never have."

I dip the end of my napkin in the ice water, pressing it to my forehead. My face is on fire.

"Look," I say. "You want to go on believing we're the Chosen Family, terrific. Go ahead. I just think we're all getting a little long in the tooth for that charade." I stop and look up at the chandelier, trying to calm down. I'm afraid I'll say something about my brother-in-law. How I know all about the bankruptcy and his frequent-flyer trips to Bellevue.

It seems to be the day for tea caddies. The waiter draws one up to our table laden with pastries.

"That's fine," Cora says when he lingers. "You can leave it." She reaches for one of the eclairs and passes it under her nose as if it were a fine cigar. "It's the reason I think your friend never clicked with Mom."

I'd forgotten this favorite tack of hers: using my absent mother as mouthpiece.

"I take it we're talking about Janice here?"

There is, I suspect, a clinical term for it. Perhaps Yahwehism. But over the years my sister has never spoken a single one of my girlfriends' names.

"Mom just thought you needed someone with a little more ambition in her bones. Someone to spur you on."

That was the Christmas I surprised everyone by bringing Janice over to the house. Cora was home for the holiday break and we all drove down to Gramercy to see the bonfires on the levee. It's an old tradition, the bonfires. No one seems to know exactly what they commemorate. But every season great log pyramids are doused with fuel and ignited along the Mississippi as far down as New Orleans.

"Your sister's critical of everybody but herself," Janice remarked after an hour of strained conversation in the station wagon. We were strolling alone along the levee, the fires like oil rigs in the distance.

"Whereas you think I'm just the opposite. Easy on the world but hard on us."

Farther up the levee my father was trying to time his camera to catch the embers as they gushed from one of the crumbling logs. Cora and my mother, bored with the festival, had crossed the street to the firehouse. Folding tables were set up and several marshals busily ladled out homemade gumbo.

"My moral compass," I said. Janice's skin seemed to glow from the light of the fires.

"It's why they don't have any friends," she said. "You know it's true. Who wants to put up with that kind of scrutiny? Heck if I'm sticking around." She did a Jackie Gleason–like imitation, fingers pointing from her forehead. "I mean, feets don't fail me now."

Afterward, we'd both given up any hope of either my mother or sister ever warming to her. And that night, in bed back at Janice's apartment, we tried to make light of the terrible tension all day.

"I forget," Janice said, the electric blanket clicking as it heated up. "Which one's Scylla and which one's Charybdis?"

I turned onto my side. "Didn't Scylla have all the teeth and bark like a dog?"

She laughed.

"I guess that would be my sister," I said.

But then, everything was funnier in the dark.

Cora raises the éclair as if to receive communion, her eyes half closed.

"No ambition," I repeat dumbly.

She finishes chewing and nods. "It's as if you don't aspire."

"Mom's sentiments?"

"She just wonders what you're waiting for."

I look over at our waiter by the maître d's podium. "Probably the same thing he's waiting for: the check." I wind my watch. I have a desperate urge to catch Janice before she leaves work. "I have to get back."

My sister considers her eyes in her compact, then gazes across at me with contempt. "To what?"

I'm tempted to wipe the smirk off her face with one of the cherry jubilees. Instead, I take out my wallet.

"Let me pay for this."

My sister's expression doesn't change. "With what?"

I want to lash out at her. Tell her that at least I live in the real world. The one where mothers die and screwball surgeons with the shakes aren't allowed to practice. In other words, the world she's been trying to imagine away.

"They don't take cash," she says as our waiter whisks over to assist with her chair. "It goes on the room."

I wait in the lobby as Cora jots down something on hotel stationery and leaves it at the desk for the manager.

"A little slap on the wrist for our friend," she says.

Which, of course, is exactly what she'd like to give me, only across the face. Anything to snap her brother out of his lethargy.

"Come up for a minute," she says. "I want to show you something."

Janice is off at five but I can catch the bus on Decatur and be over there in twenty minutes. There is no reason for the rush, of course. I will see her at home. But I can't stop thinking about our conversation. It's as if I abandoned her for my sister.

On the seventh floor Cora slides her room card into the lock, the tumblers clicking until the door opens like a bank vault.

"You're in a hurry," she says, throwing open one of the expansive closets. The racks are empty except for a spectacularly sequined cape and matching mask. She grins as if she's hand-stitched them both herself.

I'm looking around, trying to find some sign of my brother-in-law's presence. But everything has been made up.

Cora backs me out into the hall. "Well," she says coldly, "it's been real."

Only, now I don't want to let her go. I worry that it will be another year of silence. And that next time, instead of a suite, she'll be in a holding cell, or worse, a padded one.

"How about I drop by for a drink a little later?" I say.

It's more of a sigh than a yes as she nods sadly at her unambitious brother.

Janice sits slumped over on the bench across from the day care when I step off the bus. Like my father, she is one of those rare people capable of nodding off in the most public of places.

I sit down beside her and she even wakes like my father: head back, eyes flickering open.

"What?" She leans past me, shivering and still a little dazed. "Where's your sister?"

"Orbiting Pluto."

I put my arm around her. She's wearing the coat she found at a neighbor's garage sale. And I suddenly feel sorry for myself. Some provider.

"So what happened?" she says, tucking her hands between her knees. "What're you doing here?"

At the end of the block I can see the bus, diesel fumes billowing, turn onto Esplanade and head up our way.

"Cora's like strychnine," I say. "You have to take her in small doses."

Janice fishes out her bus pass. I've stopped raising the question of marriage. She says if the time is ever right again, we'll know it. But her coolness on the subject is still unnerving.

The empty bus rattles down upon us and I'm tempted to stand up my sister.

"Remind me to tell you what one of the kids said today," Janice says, raising her voice.

"Tell me now."

The bus squeals to a stop directly before her.

"He asked me if I'd be his mommy." She steps back as the bus rocks from its heavy idling and the door hisses open. "He thought it'd be nice to have one at home and one at school."

"Bright kid."

She bounds up the steps, holding out her pass for the driver. Then with one arm hooked around the pole, she hunches over to look back at me. "Guess who he reminded me of?" she shouts.

But the driver doesn't wait for my answer.

It's dark by the time I get back to the hotel. When Cora doesn't answer her phone I wait for over an hour in the lobby. This, of course, is her way of getting back at me, having surmised the reason I had to rush off. "If there's one thing I like about your sister," Janice will say, "it's that she honestly doesn't believe anyone's good enough for her brother. At least not in this world."

I leave a note at the desk and walk back down Esplanade. There's an early parade on Poydras and I cross over to Canal Street to watch it unwind toward the Quarter.

But it's too cold to be outdoors and so I find a small bar on Julia Street where the Mardi Gras special is two hurricanes for the price of one. I don't believe for a minute that Anton is around anymore. But then I never got the impression that my brother-in-law was more than a blip on Cora's emotional cardiogram. It's not that my sister is heartless. Only that she marches to a different beat. She is running away from her marriage for the same reason she is running away from her mother's illness. It is not her idea of a double feature.

Happy Hour is over and I lower both feet from the stool. Already I regret the second hurricane. It is a potent concoction. I decide against giving Janice a call. She will want to come pick me up.

Outside, it takes me longer than usual to button up my coat. The uneven brick streets of the Quarter are murder on drunks and so I keep my head down to watch my step. All the way up the boulevard men in rags warm themselves beside smoldering trash barrels. Occasionally something soaked in gasoline will explode, sending whoever is standing too close to the barrel reeling back from the flames.

At the hotel, for some reason, my heart begins to race when I ask the concierge to ring my sister's room again. It is as if I already know what he is about to tell me.

"Madame has checked out."

I glance down at the ledger as if to correct his mistake. But I have to step back to keep my balance. When I look up again, the concierge is studying me critically.

"When you say she's gone," I manage finally, bracing my hip against the high counter, "do you mean she's square with you people?"

The man tilts his head slightly and I'm thinking how unpleasant the French can be.

"I mean," I say, "did she pay her goddamn bill?"

An elderly couple have come up behind me. And I know that I am causing a delay and even creating a little scene and that in a moment the doorman will be over here.

"Fine," I say, both hands up. "Terrific. No problem."

Only, now the doorman *is* moving toward me. Then someone in a uniform asks if I might keep my voice down.

"Hey, I'm out of here," I tell him.

But just to be certain, two bouncers dressed as bellhops seize me by the elbows and without so much as a word we move discreetly toward a door. It isn't a door I've noticed before. And on the other side, as it turns out, is an alley.

Neither of my young escorts bears me the least ill will. Indeed, they both wish me a hearty *"Bonne chance."*

Nevertheless, I am standing in the cold. Apparently right outside the hotel's kitchen. There is the scent of nouvelle cuisine in the air.

It's a clear night and after a while I look up to find the North Star. However, it's the distant sound of a parade that gives me my bearings.

At an all-night liquor store off St. Peter's I buy a jumbo bottle of Dixie. It's the one place in America where the cops won't hassle you about an open container.

The floats are backed up half a mile on Canal. Bored Shriners sit waiting on their midget funny cars, sick from inhaling their own exhaust. Behind them the high school band from DeRidder perches on their helmets in the street. The cheerleaders, freezing in mesh stockings and skimpy skirts, pass the time flirting with gangs of males who shout obscene suggestions to them. They are separated by a barricade of brawny chaperones.

I am leaning against the window of a pawnshop when a thunderclap of cheering makes me look up. A mammoth papier-mâché float shimmies through a sea of waving arms, bumping down Canal like some Gargantua in a low-budget film. The crowd is showered with gold doubloons. Great gobs of plastic necklaces are slung overhead as I'm swept forward, helpless against the frightening undertow of bodies. Suddenly on my knees at the curb, I gaze up to catch in a kind of tunnel vision the most fabulous krewe of all, the burly king and queen of Rex, waving stiffly to their supplicants: a masked brother-in-law and sister bright as twin stars in their sequined robes.

MY FATHER'S GEISHA

The sudden revelation of my father's adultery has been unsettling to my sister and me. That the woman is Oriental and apparently has known my father for years hasn't helped.

"The man is kicking sixty," Cora argues long distance. "Who does he think he's kidding?"

Darlene, her roommate, picks up the extension downstairs. "Hi, Teddy."

"For instance, that she's just a houseguest," my sister is saying. "That's been my personal favorite. I mean, let's get with the program."

My father has retired and is still living in the old house on the lake. Up until last month, we thought, alone.

"The last time he was overseas," Cora says, "Mom joked about how he'd probably wind up running off with some Chink in a pedicab. Well, she wasn't so far off."

My mother passed away last year. She had let her health go for so long that when she came down with a simple cold it quickly escalated into pneumonia. Two weeks later she lapsed into a diabetic coma. But now my sister is convinced that the real cause was a broken heart—my mother having found out about my father's geisha.

Just for the sake of argument I offer that maybe the woman *is* his houseguest. From both receivers there comes an audible sucking in of breath.

"Are you serious?" Darlene says.

It's a moment before Cora seems to gather herself. "Oh, he's serious, all right. Seriously out of it, per usual."

As soon as I hang up, I find Janice downstairs.

"I guess we should have seen it coming," she says, closing her book. She's been waiting for me to get off the phone so we can go to bed.

"Seen what coming?" I say.

She looks at me and then rests her hand on my shoulder.

"You don't really want your father to live the rest of his life alone, do you? What would that prove?"

"How about that he'd been faithful?"

She doesn't say anything to this and I follow her back upstairs. We undress and I set the alarm.

"Just don't let Cora get you all worked up," Janice says. "You'll be exhausted in the morning."

Later, after at last falling asleep, I dream of making love to identical Taiwanese twins, but in the morning make no mention of it to Janice. She's already busily recording her own dreams in the loose-leaf binder she keeps on her night table. Recently, because things haven't been going well between us, she's especially meticulous about her entries.

After finally finishing up my degree through the extension college, I've taken a temporary position with the city's Department of Beautification. It's an election year in New Orleans and so mostly the mayor has us beautifying the more conspicuous civic landmarks. That means clipping a lot of topiary hedges and supervising two blacks, a couple of DWIs, and a Filipino. I gave up Day One trying to enforce any kind of discipline. It's enough that I get them to mow the embankments and stay inside the truck to smoke their dope.

Monday, after plugging pine seedlings all morning, we break for lunch and I spend the hour thinking about my father. After two wars he can trigger an airport security alarm from the grenade shrapnel left in one kneecap. Still, it's impossible to get a war story out of him. For twenty years my mother couldn't wheedle him into wearing his Silver Star with the oak leaf cluster. Not even on his dress uniform.

Yet sitting in the sun today, watching my charges share a joint in the back of a battered government pickup, I have to wonder how much of my father's stiff upper lip comes from a bad conscience. Had some of those metal filings lodged in his heart as well?

The following Sunday Cora calls up with the latest dispatch from the front. The day before, she'd driven in from the city to claim a few of Mom's things before the "bitch starts selling the silver."

"Turns out it was his Saturday to host the boys for poker," my sister begins.

She hadn't warned him she was coming, and I try to imagine the look on my father's face. But ever since Cora's fiery separation from Anton, he's learned to expect the unexpected.

I ask her what he'd said.

"He said he was entertaining. Did I want to come back in an hour or so?" She stops to clear her throat. Her voice is gravelly, no doubt from staying up all night with the blow-by-blow account for Darlene. "Not to worry, I told him. I knew my way around."

My sister's new business, "Save-Your-Party," films special occasions like children's birthdays and bar mitzvahs. They always come out looking a little staged to me but her customers never seem to complain. Probably because she shoots everything through a gauze-covered lens.

"So there she was in stretch pants," Cora is saying. "Ms. Rose herself. Serving little watercress sandwiches to the high rollers."

That's when she decided to make a scene.

"So I made one. I said a few things. And not in Japanese. I could see the boys wanted to take a rain check. But Ms. Butterfly just sat on the couch looking inscrutable."

Cora suddenly holds the phone away. Darlene has come in. She waits for her to pick up the other line.

"Has she gotten to the dresser part?" Darlene asks.

"I was coming to it," Cora says.

"I love this part," Darlene says.

"So, anyway, I got a trash-can liner from the kitchen. One of those big green numbers. Meanwhile, the boys are trying to settle back down to their game. But really they're just holding their cards, waiting to see what the colonel's crazy daughter's going to pull next."

"Did she tell you her nickname?" Darlene interrupts.

"Yoko," I say.

"Isn't that priceless?"

"I told them if they were *real* gamblers, they'd stick around," Cora says. "But by then even the old man was having trouble with his poker face."

Darlene urges her to get to the dresser part.

"I emptied it out in the hall," Cora says. "She had her crap in every drawer. It ticked me off."

"The boys got an eyeful," Darlene adds happily.

"You wouldn't have believed it," Cora says. "It was Frederick's of Tokyo. Talk about the Yellow Peril."

"I thought she was Vietnamese," I interrupt.

"What's the difference," Cora says.

She describes how the others started trickling out, offering their condolences to my father. But I'm having trouble concentrating anymore. It's impossible to picture my father under such circumstances. To see him standing alone in the living room, contrite and embarrassed as his friends fled the house.

Monday morning I call in sick. My allergy is acting up and we're scheduled to lay in ligustrum all along the riverfront.

"You're letting it get to you," Janice says. She hands me two antihistamines and a glass of water. "Try to look at the bright side. Your mother never knew about it. There's that."

But, as it turns out, there isn't even that. Sifting through her bag of memorabilia, Cora has come up with evidence too damning to wait for the evening rates.

"I found some letters," she begins soberly. "Love letters."

They'd tumbled out of the trash-can liner in a single neat stack bound by rubber bands.

"So take a stab at how long it's been going on," Cora says.

I carry the phone into the bathroom. Leaning close to the mirror over the sink, I stick my tongue out. It looks pasty, especially where it was sewn together.

"Houston to *Apollo*," my sister says at last.

I explain about my sinuses. "It's something in the air down here."

"I see." She's irritated that I don't seem to be taking any of this seriously enough. "That your own father's a philanderer. That doesn't mean anything to you?"

It does, of course. But what can any of us do?

"In other words, let him dance on Mom's grave." I can hear her tapping the capped front tooth I accidentally chipped with a shovel as a child. "This is doing real wonders for my work. I just finished cutting Sheldon Rubenstein's thirteenth birthday. It's supposed to be a festive occasion. It looks like a memorial service to Anne Frank."

Wednesday afternoon, I sit in the pickup truck watching Marcos (the nickname assigned him by his racist fellow workers) dig a posthole. We're at the Burden Lane turnoff to put up an exit sign. Somehow the mayor's name manages to be prominent in the phosphorescent lettering. Marcos's companions have all stepped out of the sun and into the dark shade of several pin oaks. They sit in a semicircle, their backs to the freeway, hands cupping a joint against the faint breeze. Through the love-bug-splattered windshield I consider the ragged line of pampas grass along the median. It's a shabby job of planting, but then, as Janice consoles me, it's a shabby crew did the planting.

On the seat next to me are the dozen or so letters which my father's houseguest once wrote to him using an APO address out of San Francisco. Cora bundled the lot up and sent them special overnight delivery. After arranging the envelopes in chronological order by their postmarks, I work my way through the mangled syntax and awful grammar of each hand-printed paragraph. For three years the spelling never improves. It's always "My deerest kernel." There are no indentations, scant punctuation, endless run-on sentences. And my mother is not once mentioned.

Several times, stumped by an indecipherable phrase, I call Marcos over and he holds the letter up to the sun and smiles ruefully, his fingernails rimmed with dirt.

"She say her man make her feel 'full.'" (It looks like "fool.")

When he says this it's everything for me to keep from choking him with the damp red bandana at his scrawny throat.

"She say he must come back to her if they to be 'truly'"—spelled "chewly"—"happy again."

No doubt I'm touchy but the man gets on my nerves. He seems not to care in the least that the crew ostracizes him. The others suspect he's an illegal alien and thus stealing work from their brothers. This is absurd, of course. He's the only one of the lot to cooperate and do what I ask. Unfortunately, Marcos takes my request to help with the letters as a social invitation. As soon as he finishes with the sign, he wanders back to the truck grinning.

"This happen," he says, squinting into the sun. "It's no matter. You will forget her. You can be sure."

I open the cab door and step out onto the running board.

"You got the wrong idea. They're to my father."

However, he's already nodding his head. "Well, this happen. But you forget her, no?"

I unfold my handkerchief to blow my nose. I'm building up an immunity to the antihistamines.

Marcos peers up at me. "It is nothing," he says with deep sympathy. "In the end she will mean nothing."

Back in the office I use the WATS line to dial my sister's apartment. But she's had her unlisted number changed again and the Boston operator won't give it out.

"I'm her brother," I tell the woman. "She *wants* me to have her number."

"I'm sorry, sir. There's nothing I can do."

Twenty minutes later I manage to get through to the Special

Northeast Regional Supervisor in charge of Restricted Access Calls.

"Afraid not," she says. "Company policy."

"I understand the policy," I plead, worn down finally by her irrefutable logic. "But who the hell is supposed to have her number if I don't? This is her brother, dammit."

"I'm sure it is. But we're just not allowed to take your word for it. After all, how do we know, proof positive, that you're not the one that made her go unlisted in the first place?"

"Because I'm not. It's my sister's ex-husband she doesn't want to hear from."

She's silent for a moment, the line crackling between us.

"And how do I know you're not he?"

"Because he's Romanian for one thing and has a thick accent for another." But I can't even convince myself anymore. "Just skip it, then," I say at last. "What's another broken family to South Central Bell?"

"I'm going to break a promise," Janice says dolefully. "But I don't think your mother would mind."

We're sitting up in bed.

"My mother wouldn't mind what?" I say, and lower the ice pack from my eye.

"It's just the way you've been moping around the house the last week, honey. I think you're taking your sister too seriously. You know how she is and yet you give credence to the craziest things she comes up with."

I press the heels of both hands against my eye sockets. They feel like sponges.

"So I think I should try to put the record a little straighter." She stops as if to allow me to object. When I don't she nods soberly. "Anyway, I'm not saying your mother and I were all that chummy. We weren't. But toward the end there she really didn't have anyone else to talk to. I mean, it wasn't exactly the kind of stuff she could unload on Cora."

Her hesitancy is alarming. And when she takes my hand, I know that she wants more than anything to protect me from the truth.

But more frightening still, I know she respects the truth too much to lie. It's only one of the things that make us so very different from each other.

"Don't get me wrong. I'm not saying your mother had some kind of last-second conversion. She didn't decide, after all, that she loved her son's live-in best."

Janice has taken a full-time position at the Little Folks Day Care Center. She has a natural way with children and I recognize her tone as the same one she employs at work with her little folks. Because she honors confidences, people unburden themselves with her. But my mother is another story.

"What I'm saying is that she was completely isolated from your father. She couldn't talk to him anymore. I don't think he even knew how sick she really was. Or didn't want to. I mean, she was practically crippled, wasn't she? Whenever you or Cora came up, they'd sort of put on a show for the kids' benefit. But that was all it was."

The ice pack is melting in my other hand and I set it down. "By 'kids' I take it you mean Cora and me?"

But I know that she wants only to soothe the telling. Janice is incapable of vindictiveness.

"I guess they just didn't want to hurt you."

"Well, they did a bang-up job of it. Now I can't even dial my father without going through some Oriental answering service."

Janice smiles sympathetically. "You want to talk to him, I'll call for you."

She's the sweet voice of reason and so I can't resist lashing out at her.

"You sound like some call-in psychologist. This is my mother and sister we're talking about. You remember, the ones that were so pleased to meet you?"

She takes up the ice pack and gently applies it to my swollen face. She does this, I know, because she's afraid my teary eyes embarrass me.

"All that's over with, Teddy. We're none of us the same."

* * *

The mayor has decided to make Veterans Boulevard the most beautiful thoroughfare in the state. He believes there's a vote in every azalea blossom we can get to bloom between now and November. To that end we dump several tons of fertilizer along either side of the street. Within the hour the temperature has risen into the nineties, making the manure particularly offensive to shovel. Everyone complains except Marcos, who simply wears his bandana over his mouth like a bandit but appears otherwise unaffected by the stench. His companions, meanwhile, continually threaten to bring suit through the Labor Relations Commission, whatever that is.

I pass the morning sketching some possible site designs: How to manage the drainage, the sprinklers, the lighting. The mayor's going all out. He wants fountains, brickwork, even a couple of cypress gazebos. None of my drawings will be used, of course. A local landscaping firm and major contributor to the mayor's reelection campaign will handle everything. Still, it keeps my mind off the allergy and my sister.

Cora hasn't called in weeks. She's disowned both my father and me. But Janice believes that her grudge will pass and that we'll all eventually kiss and make up. But I doubt it. We were never a kissing family.

At the stroke of noon the others drop their shovels and drive over to the Frosttop for root beers. To keep their morale up I promised earlier to let them take the truck. Marcos stays behind with me to look after the equipment. We sit in the shade of a Japanese magnolia and watch the downtown lunch traffic whisk up the boulevard to the mall. Marcos, whose real name, he tells me, is Francis, has recently separated from his wife. She ran off with some salesman of women's hairpieces. Apparently the best wigs come from the Orient, where the hair is thick, healthy, and abundant. His wife had been approached by the salesman to buy a cutting.

"He take Missie with it," Francis remarks pathetically. "She don't even write."

I offer him half of my tangerine, but instead, he slips what appears to be a small cigar from the breast pocket of his sweat-stained cotton shirt. It is, in fact, a very large joint.

"Colombia," my friend smiles, his sharp, crooked teeth as delicate as a child's. Bought, no doubt, from his companions at triple the street rate. I try to imagine what life must be like for him here in his adopted homeland. Having been cheated on and abandoned by his wife, he's daily cheated and abandoned by his fellow workers. Although it's foolish to risk a toke in broad daylight, I don't have the heart to turn him down. He's all politeness and generosity with the joint, passing it to me as if it doesn't represent half his week's earnings. But like the rest of us he's only a temporary who the city can afford to pay coolie wages.

The drug's effect is predictable, moving over me like a familiar cloud. After a fleeting garrulousness I become pompous, reflective, and finally sentimental. Francis listens without interruption. All families are alike, I advise him. They're as tenuous and imperma-nent as the smoke we are inhaling. Having lost his, he is more to be envied than pitied. Take my own family, for example. My mother's influence on us has been formative and perhaps, in the end, destructive. Her children hero-worship. But their idol turns out to be someone else and they're left with memories they can no longer trust. Francis follows none of this, of course, but smiles good-naturedly. And, in a minute, falls asleep. His companions are tardy. They take advantage of us both.

Lately, Janice quotes statistics on the frequency of divorce among couples our own age. The charts tell us, the odds are we'd come unraveled within five years. Except what could be worse, she implies, than to wind up in our declining years, married and miserable? How much better to light up the sky if only for a brief while than to peter out in perpetual orbit. My father's own case has been instructive. Who is his daughter (or even his son, for that matter) to say that he's not now happier? Can't I read between the lines of all those confiscated letters? Can't I see what's there that so irks my bitter sister? Do I really believe it a coincidence that those bound envelopes should find their way into the sack Cora hauled home? What I would fail to see is that there are no real accidents. And that my father's mistress, like all women, should never be underestimated. As I ponder this, even if hazily, a fierce possessiveness nearly overwhelms me. My mother is gone. My father a stranger. And my sister unlisted.

This morning, after I dropped Janice off at the day care, I was halfway to work before I noticed her glasses still in their case on the dashboard. She's recently gone back to wearing contacts but still can't quite make it through the whole day with them on. When I pulled into the horseshoe driveway of the Center, I saw her kneeling beside the day care's yellow van. She was consoling one of the children who had apparently already taken a dive on the concrete. The boy's pants were shredded at the knee but the wound turned out to be superficial. In a minute Janice had convinced him to rejoin his classmates and he hobbled off theatrically. All of this I watched through the pollen-dusted windshield until she turned, her quizzical smile that of my own Miss Clark a thousand years ago in a desert a thousand miles away.

The lunch traffic along North Boulevard has subsided and my companion snores peacefully beside me. I relight what's left of the joint, holding it to my pursed lips with a sharpened drafting pencil. There's just enough for a final, dizzying toke, which I draw into my lungs lustily. The shade has shifted so that my outstretched legs are no longer sheltered by the magnolia, and I move my knees up out of the sunlight. The pickup is nowhere in sight and there's nothing to do but wait. In the meantime, while my friend sleeps, I play around with my blueprints, penciling in all sorts of decorative extras at the taxpayers' expense. But, in the abstract, my plan for the boulevard's an imaginative one, I think, and even Janice agrees that it's a pity the mayor won't use it.

PACIFIC THEATER

I'm on the phone in my father's bedroom trying to keep my voice down. Janice thought it better I come up alone.

"Just try to relax, sweetheart," she says. "Talk to him for a change."

I pick up the brass Oriental calendar from my father's dresser. It's made from an artillery shell. "The man's been in combat half his life," I say. "Guess how many war stories he ever told me."

"What about that one where he parachuted into a dump?" Janice says.

"That was only jump school. And I practically had to hound him to death just to get it." It's a two-thousand-year calendar and I set the disk on my mother's birthday. "Anyway, I was twelve then. What chance am I supposed to have now?"

"Didn't he land on an old hospital bed or something?" she says.

"He got lockjaw from the rusty springs. He only told me that because he thought it was funny."

Janice laughs. "Your father would, wouldn't he?"

"And he hasn't changed one iota."

"Well, hound him, then."

I unwrap the phone cord from my finger. "Besides, it's depressing around here. She's turned the place into Pier One, for Christ sake."

Sing, the woman my father has been living with, is part Vietnamese, part Korean.

"Think of it as a learning experience," Janice says.

It's dark in the room, and I suddenly notice something curious about my father's bed. The mattress is moving.

"You're not going to believe what I'm looking at," I say, lifting up one corner of the quilt. "They've got a water bed. What next?"

What next, as it turns out, is a six-course meal of authentic Korean cuisine. Sing has spent the afternoon in the kitchen hunched over a steaming wok. Each vegetable comes wrapped in a thin sheet of dark green seaweed. Piled atop a hot plate on the table, strips of beef simmer in soy sauce while all around me metal dishes brim with exotic concoctions.

My father, meanwhile, acts as if the feast is only the most common daily fare for him. Nor does Sing give any indication of having slaved for hours for her guest's benefit. She only smiles shyly when I deign to compliment the moist lotus roots of her parboiled *poon* dip.

Still, there's no mistaking my father's pride in the shipshapeness of his redecorated quarters.

"I'd like to propose a toast," he says after lighting the candles.

Even in his sixties my father is still a handsome man. The racquetball no doubt helps, but more than this, he seems happier than I remember him ever being with us.

"To my bride."

It isn't the pickled egg that drops my jaw, and it's a minute before I hear any more of the toast. My heart is pounding in my ears.

"We decided not to live in sin any longer," my father is saying, still holding his glass out to Sing. "It's been long enough."

Now we're both staring at the ridiculously bashful woman seated between us.

"How long?" I manage to blurt out at last. "I mean, how long ago did you get married?"

When my father confesses that it's been nearly two years, I have trouble concentrating. Even though I should have seen it coming. They weren't exactly living as brother and sister. But it's hard not to feel a little provoked. Aren't *I* the one who drove a thousand miles to get here? Where's *my* toast? Only, it isn't sympathy I see in my father's face. Or even gratitude for his dutiful son. It's bliss. Second-time-around bliss that has nothing, absolutely nothing to do with me.

"Well," I offer weakly, and Sing bows her head at her new stepson. "All the best."

I know that he doesn't intend to be callous. It's just his way. And that my own thin skin could use a little thickening. Besides, it's typical. My father doesn't know the meaning of brood. I'm my mother's son.

For dessert there's a small glutinous rice cake that's filled with bean paste. A tradition at Oriental weddings, the happy groom remarks.

Afterward, when Sing refuses to let me help with the dishes, I drift dumbly down the hall to the phone.

"There you have it," I break the news to Janice. "Straight from Number One stepson."

"Honey, I've known for a while."

My ear feels like a suction cup on the receiver. "What?"

"Your father told me."

I want to take a hatpin to the water bed or at least kick over one of the Korean goddess lamps. "Well, look who's turning inscrutable on me."

"I didn't think you were ready yet."

She has the stereo on, which is unusual for her.

"What were you waiting for? Chinese New Year?"

"You should try to talk to her," she says coaxingly. "Really. Her English isn't all that bad."

"I don't have anything to say to the woman. And I've got even less to say to her husband."

"Teddy, if it's any consolation, I was surprised too. But you're his son. It's just going to take—"

"Time. Right?"

Her breath whistles in the phone. "Well," she says wearily, "maybe we ought to try this conversation again tomorrow."

We both listen to the stereo for a minute and then politely agree to call it a night.

In the hall Sing has hung up several framed scrolls commemorating my father's long military career. I study the picture of him in starched khakis and pith helmet presenting a silver bowl to some generalissimo. There's a pained expression on his face. It was about the same time my mother refused to bring the rest of us over. She wasn't interested in mosquito nets and water buffalos and military compounds surrounded by nine-foot walls.

As soon as Sing sees me, she pads into the kitchen for some *hung yun char* (almond tea) and *farr shung tong* (peanut brittle). She's been playing cards with my father. Along with ballroom dancing they take courses in bridge at the community college.

"A little colder than you're used to," my father says. He pretends to study his hand.

"Much colder."

It's the first time we've been alone together, and we're both eager for Sing to come back.

"What're you fixing now?" my father calls out to her.

But she only answers in Vietnamese.

"You don't watch the calories and they start to add up," he says, tapping the deck on the folding table.

"Like everything," I say.

He gives me a fishy look and yawns. "So what do you hear from your sister? She's been laying pretty low."

"Oh, we keep in touch. She brings me up to date."

I sit down on the rattan chair and watch him go through the cable stations with the remote control.

"The numbers come on at eight," he says. "The jackpot's up to twelve million."

Sing carries a tea tray in, and I can smell the almond.

"Your father," she says. "He always play the same numbers."

"You pick any six between zero and forty," he says. "We box them for a buck."

"Once your father get four," Sing says. She sets the peanut brittle out on my mother's china. "Closest he come."

"And what'd you get for that?" I ask her.

"Eighty bucks," my father says. "About a month's worth of tickets."

Sing wags her head. "Your father like to gamble all his money away. I tell him to buy present instead."

My father checks his watch. "It gets the adrenaline going."

I think of how Cora would have said something. But my sister doesn't have much to do with us anymore. In any event, I have my own little surprise for the newlyweds. I'm heading back tomorrow.

"Peter very lucky," Sing says. Her brother works in the city. "Only one missing two times already."

My father stoops in front of the set to adjust the picture. Someone in a tuxedo is explaining how tonight's numbers will be drawn.

"In morning," Sing says to me, "Peter come to see you. He very eager to meet your father's son."

"Well . . ."

We all stop to watch a Ping-Pong ball get sucked up through a clear plastic cylinder.

"Good start," my father says as the number is turned toward the camera.

"Not us," Sing says.

We wait out the other numbers.

"Peter and Esther have a six-year-old," my father says, turning the sound off. "You won't believe the kid's English. She's always correcting her parents."

Sing is smiling proudly. "Once she stay with your father and me. She not want to come home again."

"Where'd her parents go?" I ask.

"Nowhere," my father says. "They just wanted some time to themselves. Peter's an interesting character. He taught himself computers. Three years ago he's driving a taxi in the city. Now he's pulling down twice my retirement."

Like his sister, Peter was born in Saigon, where their father had been a successful manufacturer.

"The Vietnamese businessman's worse than your Japanese," my father says. "They're nonstop. They don't know when to quit."

I ask Sing what kind of business her father had been in, but we've been talking too fast for her.

"He was back and forth to Taiwan," my father says. "Before Uncle Ho took a bead on him."

Sing doesn't stop smiling, and so it's a minute before I realize what my father has just said.

"He was shot down?" I say.

My father cups his hands like a plane nosediving. "On his way to his shoe factory."

Sing cracks a piece of peanut brittle between her teeth and blushes. It's the first time I've seen her eat anything. She can't weigh a hundred pounds.

My father gets up to peer out the window at the gray sky. "Supposed to get some snow."

"You like more tea?" Sing asks me. "Very good for hair." She smiles at my father.

It's the mother's side determines, of course, but I don't say anything.

Sing stacks our plates. She hand-washes them in the kitchen despite the automatic dishwasher.

"What's on the tube tonight?" my father asks as soon as Sing comes back with the kettle. Whenever she's out of the room we struggle to make conversation.

"Your father like his TV," Sing says. "All the time he watching the news."

"I switch around," my father says. He holds up the remote control. "You can see how they twist the same story. It's whatever they want it to come out."

I think of how my sister would have caught my eye.

"At least with Cronkite," he says, "you feel the guy has a little more to him."

Sing has fixed a darker tea for herself. She studies the guide for something that might interest my father.

"Didn't Peter Jennings adopt a Vietnamese kid?" I say. "I thought I read that somewhere."

My father only stares at the commercial.

"It wouldn't surprise me in the least," he says.

I follow Sing back into the kitchen, and she smiles expectantly at me. "I thought I'd have some Coke," I say.

She rinses a clean glass from the shelf and dries it with a paper towel.

"Your father fall asleep now," she says, twisting the cap from the liter bottle. "Sometime he feel a little sore."

"He ought to quit that ridiculous racquetball," I say, but it's more for my benefit than hers.

She sets the bottle back on the counter. Nothing in the house is allowed long out of its place. "He take his medicine," she says, rubbing her hands together as if to point out where it hurts. "Only, his fingers not change."

"His fingers?" I say. "I don't understand."

"Your father not going to say," and she giggles as if at a promise not to tell. "He just go to sleep and wake up better."

Her broken English requires a fierce concentration and I focus cross-eyed on her lips.

In the living room my father sleeps with his chin on his chest. His hands, resting peacefully on his stomach, rise and fall with his faint breathing. And for the first time I see that his thumbs are gnarled and swollen.

I tiptoe back down the hall looking for Sing. I want to ask her about tomorrow. But she isn't in the kitchen or the dining room. I don't think to knock on my father's bedroom door but as soon as I push it open, Sing, bent over at the waist, looks upside down at me, her shiny black hair nearly touching the rug.

"Christ, I'm sorry."

She's holding my mother's sterling silver hairbrush.

"You use phone," she says, apologizing for me. "Other one wake up your father."

She tries to move past me but I block the door with my arm.

"It's your house now," I say. "I should knock."

With the brush behind her back she covers her mouth with her other hand. "Your father wake up in maybe half hour."

I nod. "I'll make a quick call, then." And I lower my arm. "I'm charging them to my own number."

But she only smiles, easing the door shut after her.

Janice, pulled from her shower, nevertheless listens patiently.

"I think it's all the serenity getting to me," I tell her. "He sits around like Gautama or something. I mean, it's the Inn of the Sixth Happiness up here."

"They get along," Janice says.

"And my folks didn't," I say. "Is that what you're saying?"

"You know better than me, Teddy. You were there."

"That's right. And now I'm here. Wherever the hell that is."

"Your father's not going to change, you know. He's an old soldier and old soldiers never die. That's what you tell me all the time, isn't it?"

"You're saying he's just going to fade away."

"Teddy, honey, you might as well dig a great big foxhole and jump in. Your father's your father. He was that way with your mother. He was that way with your sister. Why should he be any different with you?"

"What about Sing?"

"I don't know," she says. "Maybe it helps not to speak the same language."

In the morning a bright white glare illuminates my bedroom like a floodlight. It's been a while since I've seen snow, and raising the bamboo shades, I wipe my sleeve across the glass. Everything is either white or black. The property slopes down steeply to the frozen lake. My mother hated the claustrophia of wherry housing and insisted on a big backyard.

On my bedstand there's a covered cup of tea and two almond cookies. I dip my finger in and it's still warm.

Sing is in the kitchen making pancakes, which incredibly she flips with chopsticks.

"Your father outside," she says.

She turns her back to me to adjust the gas on the stove. Her straight black hair is streaked with gray. Although younger than my father, she's hardly a young woman. And then I wonder how long they must have known each other. There's always been a large Asian community in the area, and I just assumed that they met here. But then I've never really gotten the chronology straight. The few times my father ever wrote or called, Sing's biography was always nebulous.

"How many for you?" Sing asks. The warming plate is stacked high with pancakes.

"A couple's fine."

She pours a tall glass of orange juice. "Your father think you too skinny. I tell him because you don't have wife."

"What's he doing out there?"

Sing wipes the kitchen window with a dish towel and taps on the glass.

"He likes to shovel it," she says.

My father signals that he's almost done.

"It runs in the family," I say.

At the garage door I watch him hike the shovel briskly over his shoulder, his breath steaming in the cold air.

"Breakfast," I shout.

But there's only a small patch to go and he raises his gloved hand without looking up.

On the other side of the car, stacked against one wall of the stucco garage, are several boxes with TROPHIES printed in Magic Marker across them. I pry open the lid on the top one and pull out a brass plaque with my father's name on it. It's for some tournament last year in Las Vegas.

"Your father not let me bring them in house," Sing says when I ask her about the boxes.

"He was really in Nevada just to play racquetball?"

"Last time to Canada. Your father senior champion."

"You're kidding."

"Have to be sixty," she says proudly. "Golden Masters. Your father win all time."

In the dining room I sit at the table until I hear my father stamping his boots on the porch. I feel like telling him that I'd forgotten to mention the lottery I won last month. Ten million a year for the rest of my life. I'm thinking how he doesn't share anything with me. Doesn't tell his own son a damn thing. He never has. And never will. By the time he sits down at the table, his ears red tipped and his face beaming robustly, I'm frustrated enough to empty my pancakes in his lap.

"I thought I'd swing by and see Cora tomorrow," I say finally, setting my knife on the edge of my plate. "Then head on back."

My father stirs his coffee. Sing has given him a large soup spoon, which he grips awkwardly.

"Sorry to hear it," he says. "We had some things planned."

"Tomorrow?" Sing asks my father. "He go home?"

"Sounds like it," he says.

"Oh, no," Sing says to me sadly.

My father folds the corners of his paper napkin into an origami stork. "You're not exactly driving a snowplow."

"I'll take it easy," I say.

But we all turn at the sound of a car in the driveway. Sing stands up and quietly lifts her chair back under the table.

"Sound like Peter," she says.

"Sounds like a damn tank," my father says.

We don't bother with our coats. Although Peter appears at least as old as his sister, his wife, Esther, looks younger than me. Their daughter, Roberta, hugs Sing about the waist.

"You'll put that thing out of alignment," my father scolds his brother-in-law.

The car, a bright red Mercedes, is laden down with chains on all four tires.

"This deep," Peter says, patting his ankle to show how much snow has fallen on the freeway.

My father looks over at me. "There you go."

Esther and Sing collect bags from the trunk of the car and carry them into the kitchen. Roberta trails after them with a Snoopy doll balanced on her shoulder. Only Sing, the first to get her green card, has yet to adopt an American name.

At the door Peter peels off his galoshes. He's dressed up: a pinstripe suit and black wingtips. And I wonder how much of this is for me.

In the living room my father turns a football game on but keeps the volume low. He's obviously heard his brother-in-law's stories before. And Peter is a talker even though his English isn't much better than Sing's.

Although the women stay in the kitchen, Sing is her usual attentive self. Every five minutes she emerges to check our glasses or to carry out another snack tray. I never hear a peep from the child.

By halftime my father is out cold on the couch. And I discover that Peter (who, innocent of any intrigue, answers all my questions candidly) has known him even longer than Sing.

"So you two go back a ways together?" I say, but rephrase it when he only smiles blankly. "You've been friends for what? Since before Roberta was born?"

"Yes, yes," he says happily. "Your father my commanding officer. All through war."

But this is typical of my closemouthed father. He'd never said anything. Never mentioned exactly when he met my step-mother. Or that it hadn't, as a matter of fact, even been in this country.

"You were with his battalion, then?" But it all makes sense, of course. My father had volunteered a second combat tour despite my mother's long-distance tirades and suspicions.

It shouldn't exactly be a revelation to me this long afterward, of course. For once I might have listened to my sister.

"Yes, yes," Peter says solemnly. "Your father very great man."

There's no point in calling Janice. I know what she'd say. My mother has been dead and buried a long time.

My father hasn't budged at the end of the couch. He looks like a crafty barn owl with his chin tucked against his chest. And I'm reminded of how he always used to fall asleep while we watched *The Big Picture* together on Saturday afternoons. It wouldn't surprise me if he asked Peter out here on purpose. But as I stare at his painfully swollen hands I can't help wishing that they were mine and not his to suffer.

Peter, meanwhile, watches with a foreigner's fascination the parade of high school bands that march with military precision across the football field. Sing, clearly happy with the miraculous assembly of her new family in one place, comes in to set a bowl of pretzels down like an offering on the table before me.

Even though I try, it's impossible to hate her. To believe she's anything more than what she is: a Vietnamese immigrant by way of Saigon by way of some idiot war by way of Boston. Safe here in America with her arthritic, racquetball-playing retired colonel and his sullen son.

I borrow my father's boots from the hall closet and sneak out of the house through the garage. The snow is already crusty on top, and in the backyard I can see where my father must have put his tomato plants in this year. The row of sticks barely pokes through the drift of snow along the basement wall. No matter where we were stationed or how little soil my father had to work with, he always seemed to have tomatoes picked and ripening on the kitchen windowsill.

Down closer to the lake I find the apple tree Sing had told me about. It's a strange-looking hybrid: its branches gnarled from various graftings. I can't quite picture the thing in bloom, but in the summer, my stepmother assures me, it will produce several different kinds of apples. She's shown my father how to band the limbs together, and next season he wants to put in a whole orchard of them.

I've decided to hang around a day or two longer. Who knows? Maybe Roberta's my half-sister. It wouldn't surprise me in the least. Yet I noticed that the six numbers on my father's lottery ticket were our birthdays, my mother's included. I would have thought he'd forgotten all that. The way only great men can. But when I turn back toward the house, I look up to see everyone smiling down at me from the big picture window of the living room. Peter is waving, his diminutive wife next to him, while at their feet their daughter presses her small, flat face to the glass. And on either side of them, like happy temple dogs, stand Sing and her bridge partner. An all-American family, I think, and struggling back up the embankment, try to keep from slipping in my father's unlaced combat boots.